Rethinking Techno-Politics in the Digital Age:

Global Technology Relations and Security

Alp Cenk Arslan
https://orcid.org/0000-0002-5526-2089
Turkish National Police Academy, Turkey

Murat Tınas
https://orcid.org/0000-0001-5844-0808
Turkish National Police Academy, Turkey

IGI Global
Scientific Publishing
Publishing Tomorrow's Research Today

Vice President of Editorial	Melissa Wagner
Director of Acquisitions	Mikaela Felty
Director of Book Development	Jocelynn Hessler
Production Manager	Mike Brehm
Cover Design	Jose Rosado

Published in the United States of America by
IGI Global Scientific Publishing
701 East Chocolate Avenue
Hershey, PA, 17033, USA
Tel: 717-533-8845 | Fax: 717-533-7115
Website: https://www.igi-global.com E-mail: cust@igi-global.com

Library of Congress Cataloging-in-Publication Data

Names: Arslan, Alp Cenk, 1992- editor | Tınas, Murat editor
Title: Rethinking techno-politics in the digital age :
global technology relations and security / edited by Alp Cenk Arslan, Murat Tınas.
Description: Hershey, PA : IGI Global Scientific Publishing, 2026. | Includes bibliographical references and index. | Summary: "This book aims to offer a comprehensive exploration of the shifting interplay between technology and political authority, focusing on digital governance, security, and global dimensions"-- Provided by publisher.
Identifiers: LCCN 2025021011 (print) | LCCN 2025021012 (ebook) | ISBN 9798337324593 hardcover | ISBN 9798337324609 paperback | ISBN 9798337324616 ebook
Subjects: LCSH: Public administration--Technological innovations | Internet in public administration
Classification: LCC JF1525.A8 R473 2026 (print) | LCC JF1525.A8 (ebook)
LC record available at https://lccn.loc.gov/2025021011
LC ebook record available at https://lccn.loc.gov/2025021012
British Cataloguing in Publication Data
A Cataloguing in Publication record for this book is available from the British Library.

Table of Contents

Detailed Table of Contents

This chapter introduces techno-politics as a conceptual lens through which technology is understood not merely as a tool (techne) but as a world-creating force (poiesis). Drawing from thinkers such as Schmitt, Winner, Jasanoff, Latour, and Ellul, it shows how digital infrastructures restructure sovereignty, blur public-private boundaries, and generate new political orders. The rise of Big Tech as quasi-sovereign actors and the emergence of hybrid governance regimes illustrate how power now flows through code, platforms, and algorithms. Moving beyond regulation, the chapter proposes a poietic approach that treats technology as an ontological force, calling for governance models attuned to its generative capacities and civic responsibilities. By treating technology as an ontological force, the chapter advocates for security governance that addresses both generative potentials and emergent risks.

The primary driver for how technological developments are currently scrutinized and regulated is not due to an examination of risks, as one might expect, but from large American tech firms (Big Tech) fortifying their influence with the state. Given this primary motive, technologies like AI have their associated policy approaches framed to benefit tech firms through fundamentally shaping underlying ethical values. This chapter will investigate how the deepening integration between technology corporations and state institutions systematically privileges operational values like security and efficiency over social impact values such as fairness, detailed accountability, and sustainability as the tech industry merges with the state, due to its attempt to preserve and bolster itself by forming a cooperative association.

AI has rapidly transformed societies, economies, and governance, but it has also exposed critical challenges in global AI regulation. This chapter examines the contrasting governance models of the European Union, the United States, and China—each reflecting distinct values and strategic interests. These differences have led to fragmented global AI governance, creating compliance burdens, stifling innovation, and risking human rights. To address this, the chapter proposes a hybrid governance model combining national sovereignty with global interoperability. This model is built on three tiers: universal norms, national and regional frameworks, and sector-specific adaptations. It balances data, technological, and normative sovereignty, providing a scalable solution for ethical AI governance. The chapter concludes by assessing the model's feasibility, emphasizing the need for international cooperation to ensure responsible, adaptable, and coherent AI regulation worldwide.

In an era where data rivals oil as a source of power, who truly governs: states or corporations? This question drives the exploration of techno-politics, a field examining how technological advancements reshape political authority and governance. This paper investigates the state-company struggle through three interconnected dimensions: the tension between states and corporations, the rivalry among states exemplified by China and the USA, and the competition between companies. Together, these dynamics signal a profound shift toward digital states, where power hinges on control over digital infrastructure and data.

This article explores the interconnections between Kondratieff's Long Wave Theory, Schumpeter's concept of creative destruction, and the collapse of neoliberal informationalism, framing these within the context of Europe's emerging techno-political landscape. The piece argues that the current technological crisis, fueled by the monopolistic expansion of the Magnificent 7 and the rise of techno-imperialism, presents an opportunity for Europe to assert its digital sovereignty. Drawing on historical precedents, Europe's regulatory response, which is embodied in the

This volume rethinks techno-politics by examining how digital technologies reshape authority, security, identity, and governance. Challenging the notion of technology as neutral, it shows how systems like AI, OSINT, and algorithmic governance act as political agents embedded in legal, infrastructural, and ideological frameworks. Through theoretical insights and empirical cases, the chapters explore digital sovereignty, anticipatory security, epistemic inequality, and techno-geopolitical fragmentation. The volume argues that technologies not only reflect political will but actively produce new regimes of power and legitimacy. The concluding chapter offers a forward-looking roadmap, emphasizing inclusive, ethical, and participatory models of digital governance. It proposes a human-centered approach to reclaim techno-politics from extractive and opaque systems, envisioning just and accountable digital futures. By linking structural analysis with normative inquiry, the book contributes to both critical theory and practical strategies for navigating the digital political condition.

Preface

Technological advancements permeate every facet of human existence. The symbiosis of technology and politics, "Techno-Politics", has emerged as a pivotal domain of inquiry. *Rethinking Techno-Politics in the Digital Age: Global Technology Relations and Security* delves into the multilayered ways in which digital innovations reshape political authority, governance structures, and global power dynamics. At its core, Techno-Politics represents the symbiotic relationship between the realm of technology and political processes, where algorithms, data flows, and cyber infrastructures not only facilitate but also challenge traditional notions of sovereignty, security, and societal organization.

The volume begins by establishing the theoretical foundations of Techno-Politics, exploring how technology has evolved from a mere enabler of political action to a constitutive element of power itself. We examine algorithmic governance, where data-driven decision-making influences everything from public policy to electoral outcomes, often blurring the lines between efficiency and ethical accountability. Key themes include digital sovereignty, which grapples with the control of cross-border data flows in an increasingly interconnected world, and the ethical dilemmas posed by innovations that prioritize speed and scalability over human rights and equity.

A significant portion of the book addresses cybersecurity, portraying it not just as a technical challenge but as a political arena fraught with threats, strategies, and resilience-building efforts. We dissect the weaponization of technology through cyber warfare and misinformation campaigns, highlighting how states and non-state actors exploit digital vulnerabilities to undermine stability. Surveillance practices are scrutinized in the context of privacy and civil liberties, revealing the tensions between state security imperatives and individual freedoms in the digital state.

Artificial intelligence (AI) features prominently, particularly its role in risk management and governance. *Rethinking Techno-Politics in the Digital Age: Global Technology Relations and Security* explores how AI systems can enhance predictive analytics for crisis response while also introducing biases that exacerbate inequalities. Critical infrastructure protection is another focal point, emphasizing the vulnerabilities of connected systems in sectors like energy, transportation, and finance. On the global stage, Techno-Geopolitics is analyzed through the lens of competition and power shifts, including the rise of techno-diplomacy, alliances, and emerging norms that govern international digital relations.

Furthermore, *Rethinking Techno-Politics in the Digital Age: Global Technology Relations and Security* confronts pressing social issues such as the digital divide, which perpetuates socio-economic inequalities, and technology's potential in addressing climate and environmental challenges. We discuss regulatory frameworks for emerging technologies, advocating for global regimes that balance innovation with oversight. Through interdisciplinary lenses, drawing from political science, international relations, computer science, law, and beyond, this collection offers both theoretical refinements and practical case studies. By integrating diverse perspectives from academics and practitioners, the book not only maps the current landscape of Techno-Politics but also proposes pathways toward inclusive, accountable, and sustainable political systems in the digital age.

This exploration underscores the dual nature of technology: as a force for empowerment and progress, yet also as a vector for control and division. The chapters collectively illuminate the complex tensions between innovation and regulation, providing readers with analytical tools to navigate the evolving techno-political terrain.

Techno-Politics is not an abstract academic pursuit but a lived reality that defines the contours of global affairs. As nations grapple with the fallout from events like the Russia-Ukraine conflict, where cyber-attacks have become as critical as conventional warfare, and the ongoing U.S.-China tech rivalry, the interplay between technology and political authority has never been more salient. Digital platforms now mediate political discourse, as seen in the role of social media during the Arab Spring uprisings or the 2020 U.S. elections, where misinformation amplified polarization and eroded trust in institutions. *Rethinking Techno-Politics in the Digital Age: Global Technology Relations and Security* positions itself at the heart of these dynamics, offering insights into how states harness or contend with technological shifts to maintain or contest power.

The topic fits squarely within the broader geopolitical landscape, where digital sovereignty has become a battleground. For instance, the European Union's General Data Protection Regulation (GDPR) exemplifies efforts to reclaim control over personal data amid U.S.-dominated tech giants like Google and Meta, while China's "Great Firewall" illustrates a model of state-centric digital governance that prioritizes security over openness. Globally, the rise of AI-driven surveillance in smart cities, from Singapore's efficient urban management to more contentious applications in Xinjiang, highlights the ethical tightrope walked by governments. Techno-Politics also intersects with economic inequalities, as the digital divide widens gaps between developed and developing nations; sub-Saharan Africa, for example, struggles with limited internet access, hindering participation in the global digital economy and exacerbating vulnerabilities to cyber threats.

In the realm of security, the topic addresses urgent contemporary challenges like ransomware attacks on critical infrastructure, such as the 2021 Colonial Pipeline hack in the U.S., which disrupted fuel supplies and exposed systemic fragilities. The weaponization of technology extends to hybrid warfare, where state-sponsored hackers and disinformation campaigns, as evidenced by Russia's alleged interference in Western elections, blur the lines between peace and conflict. Moreover, amid climate crises, technology's role in environmental governance, through satellite monitoring of deforestation or AI-optimized renewable energy grids, offers hope, yet raises questions about equitable access and corporate influence, as seen in debates over green tech patents held by wealthy nations.

Rethinking Techno-Politics in the Digital Age: Global Technology Relations and Security's exploration of Techno-Politics also resonates with ongoing global dialogues on regulation and norms. Initiatives like the UN's efforts to establish cyber norms or the OECD's AI principles reflect a push toward international cooperation, yet they contend with fragmented alliances, such as the U.S.-led "Clean Network" versus China's Digital Silk Road. In socio-political movements, technology empowers grassroots activism, from #MeToo to climate strikes organized via apps, but it also enables backlash through deepfakes and online harassment. As we stand on the precipice of quantum computing and 6G networks, which could revolutionize data security and connectivity, Techno-Politics provides the analytical framework to understand these innovations' political ramifications.

By situating itself amid these real-world contexts, the book bridges the gap between theory and practice, contributing to a discourse that demands adaptive governance. It challenges the notion of technology as apolitical, instead revealing how it reinforces or disrupts hierarchies of power, from gender biases in algorithms to colonial legacies in global data flows. In a world where pandemics like COVID-19 accelerated digital transformations, enabling remote governance but also amplifying surveillance, the topic's relevance in fostering resilient, ethical systems is indispensable for navigating an uncertain future.

Rethinking Techno-Politics in the Digital Age: Global Technology Relations and Security is intended for a wide-ranging readership eager to engage with the nuances of Techno-Politics, encompassing those who shape, study, and navigate the digital-political interface. Primarily, it appeals to academics and researchers in political science, international relations, computer science, law, and allied fields such as sociology and ethics. These scholars, the volume offers a rich array of theoretical advancements and empirical evidence, from refined models of algorithmic governance to case studies on cyber diplomacy, enabling them to build upon existing literature and pursue innovative research agendas.

Graduate students, particularly those pursuing advanced degrees in interdisciplinary programs like Science and Technology Studies (STS), Science, Technology, and Society, or Cybersecurity Policy, will find the volume an essential resource for deepening their analytical skills. Its blend of conceptual frameworks and practical examples provides a solid foundation for theses, seminars, and coursework, encouraging critical reflection on how technology intersects with power structures in diverse contexts.

Beyond academia, *Rethinking Techno-Politics in the Digital Age: Global Technology Relations and Security* targets policymakers and government officials involved in digital strategy, national security, and international negotiations. For these readers, the discussions on regulatory regimes, ethical guidelines for AI, and strategies for mitigating cyber threats offer pragmatic tools to inform decision-making. In an age where policies must evolve rapidly, such as crafting responses to AI ethics or negotiating data-sharing agreements, the volume's insights can guide the development of inclusive frameworks that prioritize sustainability and equity.

Practitioners in the technology sector, including cybersecurity experts, data scientists, and tech entrepreneurs, represent another key audience. They will appreciate the volume's focus on real-world applications, such as resilience-building for critical infrastructure or addressing the digital divide in product design. Ethical considerations woven throughout the chapters will aid in aligning technological innovations with societal needs, fostering responsible practices that mitigate risks like privacy breaches or biased algorithms.

Additionally, professionals in non-governmental organizations (NGOs) and think tanks working on digital rights, environmental tech, or global development will benefit from the volume's emphasis on inequalities and inclusive approaches. For journalists and public intellectuals covering tech-politics beats, the accessible yet rigorous analysis provides fodder for informed commentary on current events.

This volume's target audience spans from theoretical thinkers to hands-on implementers, united by a shared interest in understanding and influencing the political dimensions of technology. By catering to this diverse group, the volume aims to spark cross-sectoral conversations that drive meaningful change in our digital world.

CHAPTER OVERVIEW

The chapters in *Rethinking Techno-Politics in the Digital Age: Global Technology Relations and Security* collectively delve into diverse facets of techno-politics, each offering significant contributions to the field by illuminating the intricate interplay between technology, governance, and societal transformation in the digital age. From analyzing the geopolitical ramifications of AI regulatory races and the socio-economic fallout of internet shutdowns to exploring the evolution of virtual identities through curated online aesthetics, these submissions provide critical insights into power structures, ethical dilemmas, and innovative strategies. By addressing pressing issues such as digital sovereignty, algorithmic influence, and human-centric policy frameworks, the chapters foster a deeper understanding of how technopolitical dynamics shape global inequalities, cultural norms, and future trajectories, equipping researchers, policymakers, and practitioners with essential tools to navigate this rapidly evolving landscape.

In "A Conceptual Introduction to Techno-Politics in the Digital Age: From Techne to Poiesis" by Alp Cenk Arslan, the chapter lays the foundational theoretical groundwork for understanding techno-politics as a transformative force in contemporary governance. Drawing on ancient Greek philosophy, it distinguishes between techne, the instrumental craft of technology, and poiesis, its generative capacity to create new political realities, illustrating how digital innovations have shifted from mere tools to ontological shapers of power structures. Through a canonical review of thinkers like Carl Schmitt, Langdon Winner, Sheila Jasanoff, Bruno Latour, and Jacques Ellul, Arslan elucidates technology's non-neutrality, its entanglement with social orders, and its role in redistributing agency and sovereignty. The analysis extends to empirical realities, portraying Big Tech giants such as Google, Apple, Meta, Amazon, and Microsoft as quasi-sovereign entities with market capitalizations exceeding national GDPs and user bases rivaling global populations, thereby blurring state-corporate boundaries in areas like content moderation, data governance, and cybersecurity. Examining hybrid governance models, including regulatory frameworks like the EU's Digital Markets Act and corporate initiatives such as Microsoft's Digital Geneva Convention, the chapter highlights negotiated power dynamics amid tensions like antitrust battles and tech diplomacy. Concluding with a poietic framework, it advocates for governance that embraces technology's creative potential while fostering pluralistic, accountable systems. This chapter is pivotal to the book, as it not only defines techno-politics but also integrates philosophical depth with current events, providing an interdisciplinary lens that informs subsequent explorations of digital sovereignty, ethical dilemmas, and global inequalities, ultimately guiding readers toward sustainable approaches in an era where technology co-produces political worlds.

In "The Quiet Displacement of Social Values in AI Policy" by Matthew A. Murphy and Jonathan M. Stein, the chapter investigates how the deepening integration between Big Tech and U.S. state institutions systematically prioritizes operational values like security, efficiency, and competitive advantage over social impact values such as fairness, accountability, and sustainability, driven by tech firms' self-preservation motives and their fusion with government functions. Analyzing historical corporate theories and contemporary examples, like Trump's 2025 inauguration attended by tech CEOs, the revocation of Biden's EO 14,110, and initiatives such as Project Maven and Stargate, the authors demonstrate how this value displacement manifests in policy shifts, creating accountability gaps and embedding corporate ideologies in AI systems. Comparing the U.S. model with China's state-directed approach and the EU's values-first framework, the chapter highlights alternative governance paths while critiquing how AI's "arms race" framing marginalizes social considerations, as seen in cases like Workday's discriminatory hiring algorithms and global resource exploitation for data centers. Proposing solutions including regulatory markets, independent public research, participatory mechanisms, and clearer liability standards, the authors advocate recognizing corporations as moral agents to rebalance values. This chapter is crucial to the book, as it exposes the techno-political mechanisms undermining ethical AI development, linking corporate-state convergence to broader inequalities and offering actionable reforms that advance the volume's exploration of algorithmic governance, ethical dilemmas, and sustainable digital systems in an era of geopolitical competition.

In ""(Em)Power Games" A Therapeutic Techno-Political Approach to the Global Artificial Intelligence Race" by Warren Alan Bowles explores the dual-edged impact of artificial intelligence (AI) in the global race for dominance, framing it as a "coin" where one side represents AI's potential to reshape geopolitics, alliances, and power structures, exemplified by disruptions like OpenAI's ChatGPT and China's Deepseek AI, which triggered market upheavals and intensified competition, while the other highlights ethical risks, inequalities, and harms to human flourishing amid unchecked innovation. Analyzing key regulatory frameworks, including the OECD's principles for trustworthy AI (emphasizing inclusivity, human rights, transparency, robustness, and accountability), the EU AI Act's risk-based prohibitions and requirements for high-risk systems, the U.S. Trump administration's deregulation push for market-driven leadership, and China's state-backed strategy via its Next Generation AI Development Plan, Bowles critiques the competitive "arms race" dynamics that prioritize economic and national superiority over people. Proposing a "therapeutic techno-politics" approach, integrating centralized (top-down) and distributed (bottom-up) models to empower stakeholders, foster multi-stakeholder collaboration, and depoliticize human uniqueness, the author advocates for human-centric governance that balances innovation with fundamental rights, ensuring AI benefits all humanity through shared knowledge, ethical safeguards, and equitable transitions, ultimately transforming the race into a collective win for global well-being.

The chapter "Smart Cities and Control: Reconsidering Techno-Politics and Individual Agency in China and the UK" by Ufuk Ayhan offers a comparative analysis of the techno-political dynamics shaping smart city development in China and the United Kingdom. It argues that digital infrastructures, far from being neutral tools, embed political ideologies that influence governance and reshape citizen subjectivities. While China's Social Credit System represents a centralized, overt model of behavioral control rooted in state-defined moral hierarchies, the UK's smart city strategies operate through subtler mechanisms such as corporate surveillance, behavioral nudging, and opaque algorithmic decision-making. Drawing on techno-political theory, the chapter demonstrates how both models inscribe visions of the ideal citizen, whether as obedient subjects or responsible consumers, and explores how individuals navigate, resist, or negotiate these systems in everyday life. It calls for reimagining smart cities around transparency, democratic accountability, and social justice.

In the chapter by Atdhe Lila "AI, Digital Sovereignty, and Global Governance - Towards a Hybrid Regulatory Model", the author analyzes the divergent regulatory approaches of the EU's rights-focused AI Act, the U.S.'s innovation-driven decentralized model, and China's state-centric ideological alignment, highlighting how these reflect unique values and priorities while contributing to fragmentation in cross-border data flows, compliance challenges, and inconsistencies in human rights protections. Exploring digital sovereignty's dimensions, data, technological, and normative, the chapter critiques its contradictions with globalization, such as regulatory fragmentation and risks of a "splinternet," and assesses whether full sovereignty is realistic or desirable amid global interdependencies. Proposing a three-tier hybrid model, universal norms via multilateral platforms like OECD and UNESCO, national/regional adaptations for local contexts, and sector-specific rules for domains like healthcare and defense, the framework aims to balance sovereignty with interoperability through mutual recognition, certifications, and capacity-building for developing countries. Addressing implementation via institutions like GPAI and G7, alongside barriers like geopolitical rivalries and enforcement gaps, the chapter advocates for dynamic mechanisms to foster ethical, inclusive AI. This chapter is vital to the book, as it synthesizes comparative governance analyses with a pragmatic hybrid solution to fragmentation, advancing discussions on regulation, sovereignty, and ethical innovation in techno-politics, while providing a roadmap for sustainable, cooperative global systems.

In "Digital States: The New Frontier in the Techno-Political Power Struggle" by Büşra Begçecanlı, the chapter probes the reconfiguration of power in the data-driven era, framing techno-politics as the interplay of technology and authority through three dimensions: state-corporate tensions via technolibertarianism (e.g., Musk and Thiel's influence on U.S. policy), interstate rivalries like the U.S.-China AI and chip wars (e.g., DeepSeek's R-1 challenging OpenAI), and inter-corporate battles (e.g., NVIDIA vs. Huawei in semiconductors). Drawing on 2025 events such as Silicon Valley's Trump alliance, China's AI summit rallying private tech, and EU regulations curbing U.S. dominance, the analysis illustrates how these struggles erode traditional sovereignty, birthing digital states where governance stems from data control and platforms. Highlighting case studies like TSMC's geopolitical role, U.S.-Gulf AI deals, and Russia's BRICS synergy with China, the chapter reveals how corporate-state convergence, amplified by the Jevons Paradox, influences policy, innovation, and global hierarchies. This contribution is central to the book, as it synthesizes multi-level power dynamics in techno-politics, exposing the shift to digital statehood and its implications for democracy, equity, and governance, thereby advancing the volume's exploration of corporate influence, geopolitical competition, and sustainable frameworks in an algorithmically mediated world.

The chapter, "Europe's Technological Sovereignty & American Techno-political Influence: Clash of Digitalization", by Enes Kılıç explores the evolving landscape of technopolitics, where technology intersects with policy and geopolitics, arguing that Europe's regulatory approach, exemplified by laws like the GDPR, AI Act, Digital Markets Act, and Digital Services Act, represents not a lag in innovation but a proactive strategy to forge a new Global Techno-Politics (GTP) paradigm emphasizing digital sovereignty, ethical governance, and societal benefits over unchecked corporate dominance. Drawing on Kondratieff's long wave theory and Schumpeter's creative destruction, it traces the shift from Keynesian Fordism to neoliberal informationalism, portraying the latter's collapse amid crises like data exploitation, polarization, and monopolies by U.S. Big Tech (GAFAMX), which promote deregulation under techno-nationalist guises to maintain hegemony against China while pressuring Europe. Contrasting this with Europe's humanized innovation model, including initiatives like EuroStack for autonomous digital infrastructure, the chapter reframes regulation as an enabler of sustainable growth, addressing counterarguments about compliance burdens on startups by highlighting structural factors and historical lessons from the Industrial Revolution to advocate for flexible, outcome-based rules that balance innovation with democratic values, ultimately positioning Europe as a pioneer in a post-neoliberal techno-political era amid global tensions.

In "Perception Management through Implicit Learning in Digital Media", Zeki Can Saroğlu examines how digital media platforms have transformed the architecture of influence by embedding perception management into the everyday flow of algorithmically curated content. Rooted in the transition from top-down, vertical models of mass communication to horizontal communication systems characteristic of the network society, this new paradigm shifts influence from overt messaging to subtle, cumulative exposures. Through psychological mechanisms such as implicit learning, the mere exposure effect, filter bubbles, and micro-targeting, platforms do not just deliver information, they shape cognition, preferences, and behaviors without users' conscious awareness. In horizontal systems where users are both content consumers and producers, influence is decentralized but not neutral; algorithmic infrastructures amplify familiar, emotionally resonant content that aligns with engagement goals, often reinforcing homogeneity and suppressing dissenting perspectives. Saroğlu argues that this ambient environment conditions belief and behavior through repetition, emotional tone, and personalized delivery, ultimately normalizing ideologies, aesthetic standards, and consumer desires. To counteract this, he calls for a rethinking of media literacy, one that includes awareness of algorithmic design and exposure diversity, and for regulatory frameworks that prioritize transparency, autonomy, and cognitive agency in the digital public sphere.

"The Rise of Internet-Curated Aesthetics: A New Form of Virtual Identity in the Age of Digital Media" by Zeynep Melike Saroğlu examines the emergence of internet-curated aesthetics, such as cottagecore, balletcore, tradwife, and mobwife, on platforms like Instagram, TikTok, and Pinterest, positioning them as fluid, visually driven modes of virtual identity formation that prioritize individual expression, consumerism, and algorithmic appeal over the ideological resistance and collective defiance characteristic of historical subcultures like punk, goth, hip-hop, and grunge. Tracing the symbolic role of clothing from pre-industrial markers of social class and status to postmodern tools of self-presentation, the author contrasts subcultures' bricolage-style resistance against mainstream norms, rooted in shared socio-political struggles and authenticity, with the depoliticized, commodified nature of internet aesthetics, which foster homogeneity, performative conformity, and escapism through "vibes" and curated lifestyles, often lacking critical discourse or transformative potential. Drawing on theorists like Hebdige, Han, and Giulu & Berghman, Saroğlu argues that this shift reflects a digital panopticon where visibility trumps depth, leading to the erosion of oppositional youth culture, the mainstreaming of once-rebellious styles, and a broader depoliticization of identity in an era dominated by positivity, exhibition value, and algorithmic control, ultimately rendering internet aesthetics inauthentic simulations that reinforce rather than challenge societal structures.

Finally, the concluding chapter "Conclusion: Reclaiming Techno-Politics from Structural Insight to Normative Futures", by Murat Tınas and Alp Cenk Arslan, synthesizes the volume's exploration of techno-politics in the digital age, reframing technology not as neutral tools but as active agents shaping sovereignty, governance, security, and power dynamics. Drawing on theoretical foundations from Winner, Feenberg, and others, it revisits techno-politics through lenses of techne and poiesis, examining digital sovereignty's hybrid forms, algorithmic governance's reordering of authority, anticipatory security paradigms in predictive policing and surveillance, digital inequalities amplifying biases in identity and representation, and techno-geopolitical contests over norms and infrastructure. The chapter outlines a roadmap for policymakers and researchers, advocating multi-stakeholder models, ethical foresight, and inclusive innovation to foster human-centered techno-politics grounded in justice, care, and democratic accountability, ultimately calling for normative reimagination to counter deterministic trends and build equitable digital futures.

In synthesizing the diverse threads of Techno-Politics explored throughout this volume, it becomes evident that *Rethinking Techno-Politics in the Digital Age: Global Technology Relations and Security* stands as a transformative contribution to the burgeoning field of technology and political studies. By weaving together theoretical rigor with empirical depth, it not only refines existing scholarship but also charts new territories for understanding the intricate dance between digital innovation and political authority. At a time when the digital realm increasingly dictates the rhythms of global power, this collection addresses a critical gap in the literature: the need for an interdisciplinary framework that transcends siloed approaches. Traditional political science often overlooks the technical intricacies of algorithms and data infrastructures, while computer science frequently neglects the power dynamics and ethical implications of deployment. Here, we bridge these divides, offering a holistic lens that integrates insights from international relations, law, ethics, and beyond. This interdisciplinary synthesis empowers scholars to move beyond descriptive analyses toward prescriptive models that anticipate the political ramifications of emerging technologies.

The volume's impact is particularly pronounced in its advancement of theoretical frameworks for Techno-Politics. By delineating the concept as a core paradigm, linking technology not merely as a tool but as a constitutive force in political ontology, it challenges and expands upon foundational works in the field, such as those by scholars like Manuel Castells on network society or Shoshana Zuboff on surveillance capitalism. We introduce innovative analytical tools, including hybrid models for assessing algorithmic bias in governance and matrices for evaluating digital sovereignty in geopolitical contests. These tools are not abstract; they are grounded in concrete case studies, from the GDPR's implementation in Europe to China's Belt and Road Initiative's digital extensions, providing testable hypotheses for future research. In doing so, the volume refines scholarship by highlighting underexplored areas, such as the intersection of AI with environmental governance, where technologies like blockchain for carbon tracking could democratize climate action but risk entrenching corporate monopolies. This refinement fosters a more nuanced discourse, encouraging academics to interrogate the power asymmetries embedded in code and connectivity, ultimately elevating Techno-Politics from a niche subfield to a central pillar in political theory.

On the practical front, the volume's contributions extend to guiding policymakers and practitioners toward sustainable digital ecosystems. In an era marked by escalating cyber threats and regulatory fragmentation, it equips decision-makers with actionable strategies for building resilience. For instance, chapters on cybersecurity and critical infrastructure protection offer blueprints for hybrid defense mechanisms that combine technical fortifications with diplomatic alliances, drawing lessons from real-world incidents like the SolarWinds hack and evolving ransomware ecosystems.

Similarly, discussions on techno-diplomacy propose frameworks for forging global norms, such as multilateral treaties on AI weaponization, which could mitigate risks akin to those seen in autonomous drone deployments. By emphasizing inclusivity, addressing the digital divide through case studies on equitable tech access in the Global South, the volume advocates for policies that prioritize marginalized voices, countering the techno-colonial tendencies that perpetuate inequalities. This practical orientation not only informs immediate policy responses but also inspires long-term visions for accountable governance, where innovation serves the public good rather than elite interests.

Moreover, *Rethinking Techno-Politics in the Digital Age: Global Technology Relations and Security* contributes to the subject matter by amplifying voices from diverse stakeholders, thereby democratizing the conversation on Techno-Politics. Bringing together academics and practitioners from varied geographical and disciplinary backgrounds, it counters the Western-centric bias prevalent in much of the existing literature. This inclusivity sparks cross-sectoral dialogues, potentially influencing international forums such as the United Nations' Internet Governance Forum or the G20's digital economy working groups. In contributing to these arenas, the book positions itself as a catalyst for change, urging a shift from reactive regulation to proactive stewardship of the digital commons.

The impact of this volume lies in its forward-looking ethos, positioning Techno-Politics as a vital lens for navigating an uncertain future. As we confront horizons shaped by quantum computing, metaverse governance, and bio-digital convergences, the book's insights provide a roadmap for ethical innovation. It underscores that technology's political embeddedness demands vigilant oversight to harness its emancipatory potential while curbing anti-humanistic drifts. By fostering a deeper appreciation of these tensions, this work not only enriches the academic field but also empowers societies to build digital systems that are equitable, secure, and resilient. In essence, it contributes to a paradigm where politics reclaims agency over technology, ensuring that the digital age advances human flourishing rather than fragmentation. Through this lens, *Rethinking Techno-Politics in the Digital Age: Global Technology Relations and Security* emerges not just as a scholarly endeavor but as a beacon for transformative action in our techno-political world.

Indeed, perhaps most importantly, we would like to express our sincere gratitude to all contributors who responded to the call for this volume. The authors come from diverse institutional affiliations, disciplinary backgrounds, and national contexts, enriching the book with a wide range of perspectives and insights. Their engagement reflects not only the intellectual depth of the topic, but also the value of this collective endeavor. We are also deeply grateful to the reviewers who contributed to this volume, not only with their academic expertise, but also by generously devoting their valuable time to the preparation process of the book. We believe that this volume represents more than a set of chapters. It is the beginning of an emerging network of scholars working at the intersection of technology, politics, and security. By bringing together researchers from different traditions who share a commitment to understanding the techno-political condition, *Rethinking Techno-Politics in the Digital Age: Global Technology Relations and Security* aims to foster future collaborations and dialogue across disciplinary and institutional boundaries.

Alp Cenk Arslan
Turkish National Police Academy, Turkey

Murat Tınas
Turkish National Police Academy, Turkey

Section 1
Philosophical and Normative Techno-Politics

Chapter 1

From Techne to Poiesis: A Conceptual Introduction to Techno-Politics and Security in the Digital Age

Alp Cenk Arslan
https://orcid.org/0000-0002-5526-2089
Turkish National Police Academy, Turkey

ABSTRACT

This chapter introduces techno-politics as a conceptual lens through which technology is understood not merely as a tool (techne) but as a world-creating force (poiesis). Drawing from thinkers such as Schmitt, Winner, Jasanoff, Latour, and Ellul, it shows how digital infrastructures restructure sovereignty, blur public-private boundaries, and generate new political orders. The rise of Big Tech as quasi-sovereign actors and the emergence of hybrid governance regimes illustrate how power now flows through code, platforms, and algorithms. Moving beyond regulation, the chapter proposes a poietic approach that treats technology as an ontological force, calling for governance models attuned to its generative capacities and civic responsibilities. By treating technology as an ontological force, the chapter advocates for security governance that addresses both generative potentials and emergent risks.

INTRODUCTION

The concept of techno-politics can be traced back to the philosophical distinction between techne and poiesis. In ancient Greek thought, techne referred to the practical knowledge or craft of making things, often associated with skills and techniques used to achieve specific goals. Poiesis, on the other hand, denoted a more generative and

DOI: 10.4018/979-8-3373-2459-3.ch001

transformative process, a form of creation that brings something into being beyond mere technical application. In the digital age, techno-politics has evolved from techne, the mere application of technological tools for governance, into a form of poiesis, wherein technology constructs new realities, shaping political, economic, and social orders. This transition signifies that technology is no longer just an instrument wielded by states and corporations but a force that generates its political dynamics, producing unprecedented power structures and governance models.

Techno-politics is a concept that defines the role of technology within political power and relationships. Various thinkers have examined this concept from different perspectives in past literature. In the early 20th century, Schmitt argued that technology has a "neutralizing" effect in modern society, transforming politics. According to Schmitt, every powerful political entity starts utilizing technology instrumentally; thus, technology ceases to be a neutral domain and instead becomes a new battleground for political struggle. In the 1920s, Schmitt introduced the notion of the "age of neutralizations," emphasizing that although technology initially appears neutral, it ultimately needs to be controlled by the sovereign political will (Schmitt, 2005; 2007a; 2007b). He criticized the liberal order for reducing politics to technical administration and highlighted the potential of technology to overshadow political decision-making. This battleground extends to security realms, where digital technologies enable both state surveillance and non-state cyber threats, transforming security from a state monopoly into a techno-political contest.

A significant figure in science and technology studies, Winner, in his 1980 essay "Do Artifacts Have Politics?" demonstrated that technological artifacts and systems are not neutral but inherently political. According to Winner, technical artifacts can embody social power relations or necessitate specific forms of governance through design choices. For example, the low bridges built by Robert Moses in New York restricted bus access, thereby excluding certain social and racial groups, essentially turning "bridge construction" into a form of social engineering (Winner, 1980). Through such examples, Winner argued that technology carries embedded politics, and large-scale technical systems (such as nuclear energy, and highway networks) can reinforce centralized or hierarchical societal structures. Winner posited that technology has its own politically significant reality and can shape social order.

As a pioneer of the co-production approach, which examines the mutual shaping of technology and society, Jasanoff argued that the boundaries between science, technology, and politics are constantly negotiated (Jasanoff, 2004). She emphasized that technological policies are not based solely on technical rationality but are also shaped by social values and institutions. For instance, Jasanoff explored how scientific expertise is mobilized in law and policymaking to produce "serviceable truths (Jasanoff, 1990)." She also introduced the concept of the socio-technical imaginary, analyzing how nations envision and shape the future through technology, such as space programs or biotechnology policies (Jasanoff & Kim, 2015). Her work underscores that the governance of technical knowledge is inherently social, and technology is deeply integrated into political decision-making processes.

These theoretical perspectives reveal that techno-politics is not a neutral domain but rather an arena where power struggles unfold. Gabrielle Hecht's definition further supports this view: techno-politics is "the strategic practice of designing or utilizing technology to achieve political objectives (Hecht, 1998; 2011)." This definition underscores that both the design and use of technology constitute political acts, and the resulting power structures exhibit hybrid characteristics that are both technical and political. In sum, the techno-politics literature provides a theoretical framework to explain the bidirectional relationship between technological systems and political power where technology shapes political decisions, and political forces shape technology. In this hybrid framework, security emerges as a core domain, with technologies like encryption and AI-driven threat detection shaping bidirectional power relations between states and private actors.

In the 20th and 21st centuries, the relationship between technology and the state has undergone a dramatic transformation (Zuboff, 2019). Big Tech companies, such as Google, Amazon, Facebook (Meta), Apple, and Microsoft, are at the center of this transformation. Initially emerging as innovative commercial ventures, these corporations have evolved into quasi-sovereign global actors, blurring the traditional boundaries between politics and commerce (Cohen, 2019; Culpepper & Thelen, 2020).

The fact that Facebook's user base exceeds the population of any single country and that platforms like Google and Amazon serve billions worldwide grants these companies unprecedented influence (Meta, 2023; Statista, 2023). For example, Facebook's monthly active user count approaches 3 billion, surpassing the population of the largest nations (Meta, 2023). Similarly, Google's search engine and Android operating system constitute the backbone of global digital communication, while Apple and Microsoft set technological standards (Cusumano et al., 2019; Statista, 2023). This scale has positioned these companies as transnational semi-sovereign entities. They have been likened to federations of semi-governments, given their vast user communities, economic power, and decision-making autonomy (Gillespie, 2018).

The market capitalization of Big Tech companies exceeds the GDP of many nations (Yahoo Finance, 2023; World Bank, 2023). As of 2023, Apple's valuation surpassed $2.5 trillion, outstripping the annual GDP of most countries (Yahoo Finance, 2023). Microsoft, Amazon, and Alphabet are also among the world's top-valued corporations (Yahoo Finance, 2023). This immense economic scale grants these companies significant leverage in their dealings with governments (Culpepper & Thelen, 2020). For instance, Google and Facebook not only dominate the technology sector but also control the digital advertising and media industries, establishing economic platform power (Vaidhyanathan, 2018). Their influence over taxation policies, competition laws, and regulatory decisions allows them to shape the political landscape in their favor (Khan, 2017; European Commission, 2016). Some governments even offer them preferential treatment due to their economic significance (European Commission, 2016).

Modern states and societies have become highly dependent on Big Tech for digital infrastructure and services. Public communication, financial systems, and everyday life rely heavily on these companies' internet services, cloud computing platforms, and software. For example, critical government institutions and countless private companies store their data on Amazon Web Services (AWS) or Microsoft Azure; millions of small businesses conduct sales through Google and Facebook's advertising infrastructure (Statista, 2023). Society's access to information is mediated largely by Google search results, communication through WhatsApp and Gmail, and socialization via Instagram and YouTube. As a result, these corporations have evolved into not only economic actors but also infrastructure providers and regulators of the public sphere. Their policies shape content moderation, misinformation control, and data privacy, effectively governing aspects of social life traditionally overseen by states.

Big Tech companies exert direct influence on politics through extensive lobbying efforts. In Washington and other capitals, they engage in substantial political advocacy. For instance, in 2018 alone, Alphabet (Google's parent company) spent $21.7 million on federal lobbying (Bloomberg, 2019). These figures exclude donations to think tanks and indirect influence campaigns. Additionally, Big Tech CEOs and executives frequently hold meetings with government officials, providing strategic advice on critical issues (Vaidhyanathan, 2018). The rise of "technology diplomacy" has led some countries, such as Denmark, to appoint "tech ambassadors" to Silicon Valley (Bjola & Zaiotti, 2021). These developments highlight the increasing role of technology giants not merely as stakeholders but as global political actors.

In areas such as security and infrastructure, the boundaries between governments and technology corporations have blurred. While governments seek to leverage Big Tech's data and communication infrastructure for national security purposes, corporations rely on government support and regulatory advantages. Social media platforms play crucial roles in election campaigns and public diplomacy, while governments use these platforms for crisis communication and disinformation control. However, this close relationship also generates tensions: while states attempt to assert digital sovereignty through regulations, global platforms strive to implement universal policies. Ultimately, a negotiated governance model emerges, where public and private sectors share regulatory responsibilities. Initiatives like Microsoft's Digital Geneva Convention (on cybersecurity) and the Global Internet Forum (a joint effort by YouTube, Twitter, Facebook, and Microsoft to counteract terrorist content) illustrate how private companies are stepping in to fill international policy gaps (Microsoft, 2017; GIFCT, 2023). These factors demonstrate that the relationship between technology and politics has shifted from a state-centered model to a new, intertwined structure. Today, private enterprises are not merely economic actors but also play significant roles in security and societal stability (Ağırdil, 2025a). This entanglement positions Big Tech as co-producers of security, where platforms like AWS host classified data and algorithms detect threats, shifting security from state-centric techne to a poietic hybrid of public-private world-building. These initiatives exemplify poiesis in security, as private actors generate new normative orders for cyber-threats that states must navigate.

This chapter proceeds in five parts. It begins by unpacking the philosophical roots of techno-politics through the concepts of techne and poiesis. It then surveys key theoretical contributions from selected scholars, tracing how technology became intertwined with politics over the 20th century. The third section explores how Big Tech corporations have emerged as quasi-sovereign actors in global affairs. Fourth, the chapter examines the hybrid governance models that now structure interactions between states and digital platforms. Finally, it concludes by proposing a *poietic* reading of techno-politics, arguing that technology today does not merely serve political goals but actively co-produces political realities.

FROM TECHNE TO POIESIS: PHILOSOPHICAL FOUNDATIONS OF TECHNO-POLITICS

The introductory section of this chapter argues that the digital age marks a decisive shift from an instrumental, state-centered view of technology (techne) toward a generative, reality-constituting understanding (poiesis). To develop that claim rigorously we must first reconstruct the classical distinction between techne and poiesis, trace how it re-appears (often implicitly) in modern philosophy of technology, and show how it grounds the contemporary conception of techno-politics as an ontological rather than merely managerial arena of power. Doing so clarifies why the "political" of techno-politics can no longer be cordoned off inside formal state institutions but is distributed across socio-technical assemblages that actively produce political orders.

In Aristotelian terms, techne (τέχνη) designates a form of epistēmē oriented to poiēsis—the making of something that could be otherwise (*Nicomachean Ethics* VI.4; Aristotle, 1984). Yet while every techne aims at producing an artefact, the Greeks nonetheless placed techne below both phronēsis (practical wisdom) and sophia (theoretical contemplation) (Aristotle, 1984). It is rule-guided, concerned with means, and valued for its utility; the good physician or ship-builder gains renown precisely in reference to their finished product rather than their inner disposition.

By contrast, poiesis (ποίησις) points to the act of bringing-forth (physis also "brings forth," but without human agency). In *The Republic* Plato distinguishes three beds: the Form (divine making), the carpenter's bed (poiesis), and the painter's imitation (Plato, 1935). The middle term exhibits a creative ontology absent from mere technique; it inaugurates the novel and stabilises it in the world (Roochnik, 1996). The craftsman uses techne, but the transformative moment that ushers the artefact into being is properly poietic.

Classical tragedy displays this tension dramatically. When Prometheus steals fire—the paradigmatic technical resource—he unleashes both productive power (techne) and the open-ended possibility of new worlds (poiesis), prompting Zeus's anxious re-assertion of sovereignty (Vernant, 1988). Already, then, the link between fabrication and political order was thematized as a contest for founding authority.

The scholastic and early modern periods gradually collapse poiesis into techne. Bacon's *Novum Organum* (1620) casts knowledge as power over nature (Bacon, 2000); Descartes famously seeks to make humans "masters and possessors of nature" (Descartes, 2006). Science and technique function as instruments for projecting human will rather than as occasions for co-creative disclosure. The Enlightenment reinforces that valuation through utilitarianism and political economy: technologies are neutral tools enabling productivity, prosperity, and state capacity (Feenberg, 1999). Seen in this light, the Industrial Revolution institutionalizes techne as the dominant paradigm, subordinating politics to the administration of technical systems, a tendency Carl Schmitt will later decry as the "age of neutralizations" (Schmitt, 2007a).

Yet the very scale of industrial technology re-opens the poietic question. Railroads compress space-time; electrical grids synchronize social rhythms; statistical bureaus convert populations into governable objects (Edwards, 2010). Technology no longer merely serves pre-given political ends; it shapes what those ends can plausibly be. This latent poiesis of technics becomes explicit in twentieth-century continental philosophy (Heidegger, 1977).

Martin Heidegger's 1953 lecture "Die Frage nach der Technik" reframes technology as a mode of revealing (*alētheuein*). Modern technicity is captured by the term *Gestell* (enframing): a posture that sets-upon the world as "standing reserve" (*Bestand*). While Heidegger sharply criticizes this reductive stance, he simultaneously insists that the essence of technology is not itself technological but ontological (Heidegger, 1977). He retrieves the Greek sense of poiesis as a bringing-forth that co-resonates with *physis*. Once enframing is recognized as only one historical modality of revealing, alternative poietic possibilities, such as the artist's or the craftsperson's relation to beings, can be cultivated. Heidegger thereby sets the stage for conceiving contemporary digital infrastructures as ontological projects that format the horizon of political action. In security contexts, this enframing manifests in global surveillance networks that treat populations as data reserves, revealing security not as a mere tool but as a poietic disclosure of threats and protections.

Hannah Arendt, in *The Human Condition* (1958), distinguishes labor, work, and action. Work, the domain of *homo faber*, fabricates durable objects and, with them, a common world (Arendt, 1998). Although Arendt is wary of an instrumental reason that annihilates the space of plurality required for political action, she recognizes that the built environment conditions what forms of politics are thinkable. The modern elevation of fabrication over speech thus threatens to transform politics into administration, a diagnosis echoing Schmitt's (Schmitt, 2007b), but Arendt adds the insight that every technical project implicitly proposes a shared world and thus a civic ordering (Arendt, 1998). Where Heidegger stresses ontological revealing, Arendt foregrounds the worldly durability and publicness generated by technological work. Both converge on the idea that technics is never merely neutral.

Gilbert Simondon offers perhaps the most directly applicable framework for digital techno-politics. Rejecting hylomorphism, he treats technical objects as ongoing processes of individuation that co-evolve with humans and milieus (Simondon, 2017). In *Du mode d'existence des objets techniques* (1958) Simondon coins "concretisation": as machines evolve they resolve internal tensions, becoming more integrated with their associated milieu (Simondon, 2017). Political power, in this light, does not simply wield finished artefacts; it intervenes in the very regimes of individuation (Hui, 2016). Code, protocols, and standards mediate continuous transductions between users, data, and institutions (Mackenzie, 2015). Simondon thus furnishes an ontogenetic account of why governance increasingly operates through technical parameters (such as algorithmic recommender systems) rather than legal decrees alone (Simondon, 2017). In security domains, such as cybersecurity protocols, political power modulates algorithmic individuation to preempt threats, co-evolving with digital milieus.

Bringing these thinkers together reveals a clear trajectory. In antiquity, *techne* is bounded by, and subordinate to, higher forms of reasoning; by early modernity it becomes the privileged site where reason realises mastery. However, once technical systems acquire the scale and complexity of electrical grids, mass media, or cloud platforms, they begin to generate the social conditions of their own necessity. Instrumentality shades into *poiesis*: technology not only fulfils ends but supplies the very categories—speed, efficiency, connectivity—through which ends are articulated.

The global spread of the internet supplies a paradigmatic case. Originally conceived as a resilient military-academic network (ARPANET), it quickly became an infrastructure of everyday life. Protocols such as TCP/IP encode design assumptions (end-to-end addressability, packet switching) that privilege certain forms of communication and commercialisation. These choices were not value-neutral; they instituted a bias toward decentralised innovation, but also toward data extractability. As winner's analysis anticipates, the "artefact" Internet embeds liberal-individualist imaginaries (open access) and cybernetic forms of control (surveillance, feedback loops). Thus, governance debates over net neutrality, platform moderation, or encryption are contests over a *poietic* field already partially sedimented in code.

In the present era of machine learning and ubiquitous datafication, the *poiesis* of technology achieves a new intensity. Algorithms such as large-language models not only mediate but actively synthesise text, images, and decisions, thereby scripting possibilities for collective thought. The opacity of training data and model weights means that the generative process is delegated to machinic ensembles whose internal logic resists public scrutiny. What was once a contest over *using* technologies becomes a struggle over *how realities are generated*, whether through recommender systems shaping public discourse or smart-city sensors delimiting urban citizenship.

Heidegger's danger, that enframing conceals alternative modes of revealing, resurfaces in concerns about AI "lock-in": once administrative and legal systems rely on statistical inferences, the threshold for re-opening political contestation rises sharply. Arendt's worry that fabrication will displace speech is mirrored in social media architectures that privilege virality over deliberation. Simondon's milieu-dependent individuation finds its counterpart in adaptive algorithms that continuously re-align user preferences with platform revenue models. Thus, the classical distinction between *techne* and *poiesis* is not an antiquarian curiosity; it is the conceptual key to grasping why algorithmic infrastructures function simultaneously as tools *and* as autonomous generators of social order.

Recognising the *poietic* dimension compels analysts to move beyond questions of "regulating technology" toward examining how political possibilities are encoded, afforded, or foreclosed by design. The politics of facial-recognition, for example, is not exhausted by debates over accuracy or privacy; it concerns which ontologies of identity—biometric, probabilistic, behavioural—become authoritative. Similarly, blockchain protocols instantiate libertarian imaginaries of trustlessness and self-sovereignty, challenging the statist monopoly over ledger-keeping. Each case exemplifies a co-production of technical form and political norm.

Moreover, the shift from instrumentality to creative ordering reconfigures sovereignty. When financial markets hinge on high-frequency trading algorithms, or when pandemic responses depend on genomic surveillance platforms, decision-making authority is distributed across human-machine hybrids. Schmitt's sovereign who decides on the exception has not disappeared but is now entangled in technoscientific procedures, APIs, risk models, sensor networks, that may trigger states of exception automatically (such as algorithmic credit freezes, real-time misinformation takedowns).

If technology today acts as *poiesis*, then techno-politics must account for creativity, emergence, and world-building, not merely for control and neutrality. The task is two-fold: first, to diagnose how contemporary infrastructures enact particular political imaginaries; second, to articulate counter-poietic interventions that reopen the field of possibilities. Critical design, open-source protocols, feminist and decolonial hacking practices, these are concrete efforts to redirect the generative power of technology toward pluralistic ends.

THE CANNON: TECHNOLOGY AS A POLITICAL FORCE

The previous section demonstrated that modern technology has travelled from the instrumental realm of *techne* into the generative domain of *poiesis*, thereby restructuring the conditions of political life. The thinkers examined in this section, Carl Schmitt, Langdon Winner, Sheila Jasanoff, Bruno Latour, and Jacques Ellul, supply the conceptual arsenal for understanding that transition in explicitly political terms. Though they differ in philosophical orientation and empirical focus, all insist that technology is never a neutral backdrop. It is an active participant in the constitution, contestation, and legitimation of power.

Carl Schmitt's scattered but influential remarks on technology appear chiefly in *The Age of Neutralizations and Depoliticizations* (1929) and *The Nomos of the Earth* (1950) (Schmitt, 2007a; Schmitt, 2003). For Schmitt, each era centres on a "decisive concept" that organises friend–enemy distinctions. In medieval Christendom, that concept was theology; in the Enlightenment, it was moral-humanitarian progress; in the industrial era, it becomes technical rationality (Schmitt, 2007).

Schmitt calls this shift the "neutralisation" of politics. Technical rationality purports to ground decisions on objective expertise, thereby evacuating the existential stakes that once demanded sovereign judgment. Yet Schmitt also argues that neutrality is itself a political position. The sovereign now hides behind the mantle of technical expertise, ruling by bureaucratic decree rather than explicit decision (Schmitt, 2007). Thus, technology does not dissolve sovereignty; it re-inscribes it within technocratic institutions whose authority rests on claims of rational efficiency rather than on public deliberation. This re-inscription is evident in digital security governance, where algorithmic tools for threat detection delegate sovereign exceptions to code, often without transparent accountability.

In the digital age, Schmitt's analysis anticipates the rise of algorithmic governance (Johns, 2017). Risk-scoring tools, predictive policing software, and high-frequency trading platforms appear "neutral," yet they encode value-laden thresholds that can only be set by a decision-maker who remains politically accountable, though frequently invisible. Schmitt therefore provides the first canonical warning that technics can become a covert locus of sovereign power, a theme elaborated by every author in this canon.

Fast-forward a half-century and Langdon Winner's seminal essay "Do Artifacts Have Politics?" (1980) offers a systematic framework for Schmitt's intuition. Winner makes two complementary claims. First, As Langdon Winner argues, technical arrangements often carry political consequences and may even be deliberately designed to serve specific power structures. His famous case is Robert Moses's low overpasses on Long Island, allegedly designed to prevent buses, and therefore poor Black riders, from accessing elite beaches. Second, entire sociotechnical systems require particular political relationships if they are to operate at all. Large-scale nuclear power, for example, demands hierarchical management because of its safety protocols, capital intensity, and secrecy (Winner, 1980).

Winner's contribution is to shift attention from overt policy debates to the material forms that silently organise power. Every bridge, protocol, or database is a crystallised negotiation among social groups; once built, its affordances and constraints discipline future action (Winner, 1980). In Winner's vocabulary, artefacts have inherently political properties. This argument dovetails with the poiesis trajectory: technologies do not merely serve external purposes; they instantiate durable orders that pre-structure political possibilities.

In our contemporary context, consider the data architectures of global cloud providers. By designating where data can be stored, replicated, or deleted, firms create de facto border regimes that complicate national claims to digital sovereignty (Amoore, 2020). Winner teaches us that these architectures are not only logistical choices but political acts, effectively redrawing jurisdictional maps.

Where Winner excavates politics embedded in artefacts, Sheila Jasanoff extends the analysis to the epistemic and normative visions that underwrite technological projects. Across works such as *States of Knowledge* (2004) and *Dreamscapes of Modernity* (2015), she develops the concept of socio-technical imaginaries: collectively held visions of desirable futures animated by technological advances (Jasanoff & Kim, 2015). These imaginaries legitimise specific institutional arrangements, guide investment, and delineate acceptable risks (Jasanoff, 2004).

Jasanoff's method is the co-productionist idiom: knowledge, technology, and social order evolve reciprocally (Jasanoff, 2004). This perspective destabilises the linear model whereby society "impacts" technology or vice-versa. Instead, nuclear energy regimes, genomics programs, or AI ethics boards are co-produced ensemble formations in which epistemic authority and political power are negotiated simultaneously.

Her framework is invaluable for decoding digital phenomena. Take the European Union's General Data Protection Regulation (GDPR). Rather than a purely legal instrument, GDPR embodies an imaginary of fundamental rights-centric digital modernity. Conversely, Silicon Valley's enthusiasm for "move fast and break things" expresses an entrepreneurial imaginary of frictionless innovation. Competing data regimes reflect divergent settlements over privacy, growth, and autonomy. Jasanoff's lens illuminates how such normative visions are sedimented in code, regulation, and organisational routines, thereby extending Winner's focus on artefacts to encompass culturally embedded futures.

Bruno Latour's Actor–Network Theory (ANT) radicalises the ontology of techno-politics. In classics like *Science in Action* (1987) and *Reassembling the Social* (2005), Latour instructs analysts to follow heterogeneous networks of "actants", humans, machines, inscriptions, microbes, without a priori privileging either side (Latour, 1987; Latour, 2005). This is known as the principle of generalized symmetry (Callon, 1986).

ANT treats power not as a property held by pre-constituted actors but as an effect of successful enrolment (Latour, 2005). A speed bump is persuasive because it recruits asphalt, traffic law, driver psychology, and municipal budgets into a stable association (Latour, 1999). Power, in Latour's phrase, is "that which, while not exercising itself, renders others compatible with itself" (Latour, 2005).

For techno-politics, ANT yields two insights. First, it dissolves the notion of a unidirectional causal arrow from technology to politics or vice-versa; instead, political order is a contingent achievement of networked alignments. Second, it widens the analytic field to include mundane devices as loci of governance. Consider the cookie protocol: a few lines of text stored on browsers align advertising markets, privacy norms, and user identities. Latour would insist that the cookie is as much a political delegate as any elected official, "spokesman" for an advertising assemblage.

Integrating ANT with the techne–poiesis narrative clarifies that the generativity of technology arises precisely from its capacity to forge new heterogeneous collectives, not merely from its material affordances. In security networks, elements like encryption keys or drone swarms enroll actants into alliances, redistributing agency in counter-terrorism or border control.

Long before ANT, Jacques Ellul sounded a prophetic alarm in *La Technique* (1954) and *The Technological Society* (1954, Eng. 1964). Ellul defines technique as the totality of methods rationally arrived at and having absolute efficiency in every field of human activity (Ellul, 1964). Over time, technique becomes autonomous, pursuing efficiency regardless of ethical or cultural considerations.

Ellul's pessimism stems from the feedback loop between technological complexity and social dependency (Ellul, 1964). As societies rely on technical systems, they must adopt additional techniques to manage unintended consequences, thereby accelerating systemic momentum. Democratic control erodes because political deliberation cannot keep pace with exponential technical change.

Although Ellul writes pre-digitally, his thesis resonates in debates over AI "alignment" or climate geoengineering (Feenberg, 1999). If technical systems evolve faster than governance frameworks, then the field of possible futures is effectively narrowed by path dependency. Ellul thus completes the canon by introducing the dimension of temporal acceleration; technology's political force lies not only in embedded hierarchies or imaginaries but in its relentless self-augmentation (Ellul, 1964).

Across Schmitt, Winner, Jasanoff, Latour, and Ellul, six common propositions emerge, constituting the canonical core of techno-political theory: 1) non-neutrality of technology (Zhao et al., 2004; Almazán Gómez et al., 2024), 2) material-discursive entanglement (Barad, 2007), 3) redistribution of agency, 4) transformation of sovereignty, 5) path dependency and lock-in (David, 1985; Arthur, 1989), 6) poiesis as world-making.

When we approach to each propositions, the descriptions are as follows: Non-Neutrality of Technology; All authors reject the liberal myth that technologies are neutral means toward exogenous ends. From Schmitt's hidden sovereignty to Ellul's autonomous technique, neutrality is exposed as a political alibi. Material-Discursive Entanglement; Winner foregrounds material artefacts, Jasanoff emphasises imaginaries, Latour follows hybrid networks; together they show that hardware, code, discourse, and institutions are inseparable strands in political ordering. Redistribution of Agency; Technology reconfigures who or what can act. Speed bumps slow cars; algorithms score credit; satellites redraw territorial surveillance. Agency becomes relational, distributed across sociotechnical constellations. Transformation of Sovereignty; Whether via Schmitt's technocratic decisionism or Big Tech's cloud hegemony, sovereignty migrates into infrastructural zones where authority is exercised algorithmically, contractually, or architecturally rather than solely through law. Path Dependency and Lock-In; Ellul's autonomy thesis and Winner's large-system argument highlight how initial design settlements entrench future options, making reversal politically costly. Poiesis as World-Making; All ultimately converge on the insight that technologies no longer merely implement decisions; they constitute the ontological scaffolding within which decisions acquire meaning, thereby validating the transition from *techne* to *poiesis* traced in Section 1.

Applying the canon to current phenomena elucidates the stakes of the digital age. Consider facial-recognition systems. According to Schmittian Lens: Who decides when to classify a face as suspect? The algorithm appears neutral, but the threshold embodies sovereign discretion—often delegated to private vendors. A Winnerian lens reveals how neural-network architectures depend on vast quantities of labeled data, thereby incentivizing surveillance infrastructures that reinforce centralized control. From a Jasanoffian perspective, competing sociotechnical imaginaries, such as public safety versus civil liberties, shape regulatory outcomes, with each imaginary scripting a distinct constitutional order. A Latourian interpretation draws attention to the heterogeneous assemblage of actants involved, including CCTV cameras, GPUs, legal classifications of identity, and the behavioral adaptations of citizens themselves. Finally, through an Ellulian lens, we see how, once such systems are deployed at scale, their operational efficiency drives further expansion, across airports, schools, and retail spaces, rendering their abolition politically unthinkable. Such multi-layered analysis demonstrates why piecemeal regulation is insufficient: the political force of technology is systemic, temporal, and ontological.

Juxtaposing the canon with the *techne–poiesis* divide clarifies each thinker's contribution: Schmitt diagnoses how technical neutrality masks decisional power, revealing *techne*'s hidden politicisation. Winner and Jasanoff expose *poietic* dimensions, artefacts and imaginaries that create new social realities. Latour offers the methodological bridge, tracing how *techne* and *poiesis* interweave through actor–networks. Ellul warns that when *poiesis* accelerates autonomously, political deliberation risks obsolescence. Together they supply the conceptual tools needed to interrogate Big Tech's quasi-sovereignty (Section 3) and the hybrid governance regimes analysed later in this chapter.

The canon attests that technology has always been political, but the digital epoch intensifies three canonical themes: scale, speed, and opacity. Cloud infrastructures span continents; machine-learning cycles iterate in weeks; algorithmic complexity obscures causal chains. Under these conditions, the classical problem of legitimate rule resurfaces in novel guises. Who governs the governors when the governors are code?

Addressing that question requires the conceptual clarity provided by Schmitt, Winner, Jasanoff, Latour, and Ellul, combined with the *poietic* sensibility outlined earlier. Only by recognising technology as an active world-builder, not a passive instrument, can scholars and policymakers craft responsive forms of digital sovereignty, democratic oversight, and pluralistic design.

THE RISE OF TECHNO-SOVEREIGNTIES: BIG TECH AS GLOBAL POLITICAL ACTORS

The canonical theorists converged on one insight: technology is an active political agent. That claim becomes empirically palpable when we turn from conceptual debate to the economic giants that now structure everyday life. Google (Alphabet), Apple, Meta Platforms, Amazon, and Microsoft, henceforth the "Big Five", command resources, rule-making capacities, and infrastructural depth that rival, and sometimes surpass, those of nation-states (Cohen, 2019). Their ascendance signals a new modality of sovereignty exercised not through territory but through technical systems that bind users, data, and capital into enclosed, privately governed spaces (Srnicek, 2017).

Sovereignty presupposes material power, and the Big Five possess it in unprecedented scale. Apple's market capitalisation reached US$3 trillion as of May 2025, while Microsoft stood at approximately US$3.3 trillion, making it one of the most valuable publicly traded firms on the planet (Statista, 2025b). Amazon and Alphabet anchor a second tier of trillion-dollar platforms, valued at roughly US$2.15 trillion and US$2 trillion respectively, while Meta Platforms sits at US$1.6 trillion (Statista, 2025b).

Traditional political economy treats firms of this magnitude as "too big to fail"; techno-political analysis reveals something deeper: sheer valuation grants the capacity to shape macro-economic conditions (Culpepper & Thelen, 2020). When Apple issues green bonds it sets de facto standards for corporate climate finance; when Microsoft purchases tens of gigawatts of renewable power for its data centres it shifts national energy portfolios. Market capitalisation therefore functions as territory translated into balance sheets: a liquid base from which companies project infrastructural power.

Valuation alone, however, does not constitute sovereignty; what matters is command over people. Here Big Tech's reach dwarfs most states. Facebook operates with billions monthly active users (MAUs), roughly a remarkable part of humanity (Meta, 2025). WhatsApp's billions of MAUs, Instagram's approximately 2 billions, and Google Search's significant share of the global queries market give these firms unfettered access to, and behavioural data on, populations larger than those administered by any political unit save China and India (Statista, 2025a).

Such user bases are not merely markets; they resemble polities. Like citizens, users are subject to binding rules (terms of service, community standards), taxed through data extraction or subscription fees, and disciplined by algorithmic sanction (de-platforming, demonetisation) (Gillespie, 2018). Meta's "Oversight Board" or Apple's App Review process operate as quasi-judicial bodies with real coercive capabilities. This governance structure exemplifies Winner's insight that artefacts embed politics: servers, APIs, and machine-learning pipelines crystallise normative judgments, but at planetary scale.

If the feudal order rested on land and industrial capitalism on factories, platform capitalism rests on digital enclosures. The Big Five own or control the core chokepoints of the contemporary information economy, mobile operating systems (iOS, Android), browsers (Chrome, Safari, Edge), app stores, identity layers, and cloud backbones. These "bottlenecks" function as tollgates through which smaller firms must pass, paying rents in revenue shares or advertising dollars.

Amazon Web Services (AWS) illustrates the dynamic. Holding roughly 30 per cent of the global cloud-infrastructure market in 2025, AWS is more than a hosting service; it is an essential utility (Richter, 2025). When governments migrate citizen data to AWS, sovereignty is partially outsourced to contract law and service-level agreements. Microsoft's Azure, with an estimated 20 per cent share, plays a parallel role (Richter, 2025). Such dominance is reinforced by economies of scope:

AWS revenues topped US$107 billion in 2024 and reached US$29.3 billion in Q1 2025 alone, beating both Microsoft and Google for cloud revenue (Amazon, 2025; Haranas, 2025).

In Winnerian terms, the architecture of hyperscale data centres mandates centralised control. Latency requirements, capital intensity, and proprietary tooling create high exit barriers, locking clients, and by extension states, into vendor ecosystems. The platform thus wields a private veto over digital industrial policy: a unilateral change in pricing or API access can cripple thousands of dependent businesses overnight.

Nation-states have not passively accepted this displacement of authority. The EU's Digital Markets Act (DMA), enforced from March 2024, classifies Apple, Meta, Google, Amazon, and Microsoft as "gatekeepers" and imposes strict anti-steering and interoperability obligations (European Commission, 2024). In April 2025 the European Commission formally found Apple and Meta in breach for restricting alternative payment systems within the App Store, opening the door to fines of up to 10 per cent of global turnover (European Commission, 2025).

Across the Atlantic, the U.S. Department of Justice secured a string of antitrust victories: a landmark 2024 ruling condemned Google's search-distribution contracts, while a follow-up case in 2025 seeks structural remedies in its advertising stack (U.S. Department of Justice, 2025). These actions underscore a Schmittian drama: public regulators attempt to reclaim the "decision on the exception" from private code.

Yet the complexity of platform ecosystems often blunts regulatory intent. Meta and Spotify, for instance, delayed implementation guidelines for the EU's forthcoming AI Act, arguing that ill-defined risk categories threaten open-source models and innovation (Reuters, 2024). By stalling, lobbying, or re-architecting services, platforms transform legal injunctions into protracted technical negotiations, effectively co-producing regulation in Jasanoff's sense.

Google processes billions of queries per day, mediating epistemic access for half the globe. Control over ranking algorithms shapes what counts as credible knowledge, influencing elections, health behaviours, and consumer choices. Apple's iOS and Google's Android jointly power of smartphones shipped in 2024. Through default settings, push notifications, and app-tracking transparency screens, OS vendors regulate the attention economy more heavily than broadcasting authorities once did.

WhatsApp's end-to-end-encrypted messaging has become indispensable in the Global South for everything from remittances to crisis response. A unilateral policy change, such as Meta's decision to share select metadata with parent servers, can therefore disrupt social coordination at national scale.

Instagram Reels and YouTube Shorts compete to define cultural taste, while Facebook's centrality to local commerce in the developing world turns "community-standards" violations into economic penalties. When content moderation errors de-platform journalists, the incident resembles state censorship, yet without constitutional safeguards or judicial appeal.

Generative AI supply chains hinge on proprietary foundation models (GPT-4o, Gemini Ultra, Llama 4) and scarce GPU clusters. Microsoft's exclusive provisioning of OpenAI models on Azure positions the company as a sovereign allocator of cognitive capacity, echoing Ellul's warning about autonomous technique accelerating beyond social oversight.

Sovereigns maintain embassies; platforms cultivate "government affairs" and strike treaties. Denmark, Japan, and the United Arab Emirates have appointed official "tech ambassadors" to Silicon Valley, acknowledging that negotiations with corporate entities are increasingly as consequential as traditional diplomacy (Bjola & Zaiotti, 2021). Conversely, Microsoft's Digital Geneva Convention proposal (2017) and Meta's partnerships with electoral commissions demonstrate corporate ambitions to write international norms (Microsoft, 2017; Meta, 2024). These hybrid arrangements instantiate Latour's actor-network thesis: states, firms, standards bodies, and NGOs become interdependent nodes in a polycentric diplomatic web. This framing treats security as a poietic domain, where technology generates new threat landscapes and defensive realities, requiring hybrid models attuned to algorithmic vulnerabilities.

Fiscal power constitutes a classic attribute of sovereignty. Amazon's marketplace fees and Apple's App Store commission function as private tariffs on digital commerce. Attempts to launch platform-native currencies, Meta's ill-fated Libra/Diem, Apple's Apple Pay Later, Amazon's AWS credits redeemable for services, illustrate ambitions to carve monetary jurisdictions beyond central-bank oversight (Gorton & Zhang, 2024). Regulatory pushback halted Libra, yet the episode revealed latent capacities. Meta could, in principle, mobilise a wider tax base than any nation-state.

During the COVID-19 pandemic, Apple and Google jointly engineered the Exposure Notification API adopted by more than 50 governments (Apple, 2020; Google, 2020). This private standard determined acceptable thresholds for proximity detection, data retention, and interoperability, decisions normally reserved for public health authorities. Similarly, Microsoft's takedown of state-linked cyber-espionage domains or Amazon's covert logs-sharing under U.S. national-security letters reveal a blurry frontier where corporate and governmental security apparatuses entwine (Microsoft, 2023). In Schmittian terms, the platforms often decide on the exception (malware, misinformation, terror content) before states legislate.

Ellul's prophecy of escalating technical interdependence is visible in the cost curves of "multicloud exits." For example, X reportedly cut cloud costs by 60% after migrating critical workloads back in-house (Ambasna-Jones, 2025); many Southeast Asian countries, such as Malaysia, Indonesia, and Vietnam, are developing sovereign cloud strategies and planning to establish local data centers within this framework (Kaur, 2025). Lock-in is not merely financial; it is epistemic. Proprietary machine-learning toolchains (SageMaker, Vertex AI) define workflow grammars that entrench developer habits, making alternative infrastructural imaginaries increasingly unthinkable.

Civil-society actors challenge platform dominance through antitrust coalitions, privacy litigation, or the promotion of decentralised architectures (Mastodon, ActivityPub, Solid) (Doctorow, 2021). Yet these efforts often collide with winner-take-all network effects. For every user who migrates off Instagram, another tens of thousands join for the social graph advantages. The logic mirrors Wallerstein's core–periphery: value flows to nodes controlling the most data and compute (Wallerstein, 2004).

Emergent strategies include data trusts, federated AI, and public cloud utilities. The EU's GAIA-X aims to create an interoperable European data space; India's Unified Payments Interface offers an example of state-run digital infrastructure that competes with private wallets (European Commission, 2023; Cornelli et al., 2024). These projects signal a nascent *techno-pluralism*: multiple sovereignties contending over compatible yet contested layers of the stack (Jasanoff & Kim, 2015).

Bringing theory to bear on the above realities clarifies the specificity of techno-sovereignty. From a Schmittian perspective, the sovereign decision now migrates into opaque algorithmic thresholds and content moderation policies. Winner's framework highlights how cloud regions, ranking algorithms, and App Store rules solidify long-term hierarchies. Jasanoff draws attention to how imaginaries such as "frictionless innovation" or "responsible AI" serve to legitimise corporate governance structures. In Latour's view, power emerges as an effect of actor-network enrolment, involving elements such as GPU supply chains, open-source communities, and algorithmic auditors. Finally, Ellul's perspective underscores how self-reinforcing loops of efficiency propel technological expansion at a pace that outstrips the ability of democratic oversight to respond.

Recognising Big Tech as techno-sovereigns neither abolishes nation-states nor renders regulation futile; instead it reframes politics as negotiation across overlapping jurisdictions. Content-moderation councils, data-transfer "adequacy" agreements, and joint cyber-defence task forces illustrate emergent hybrid governance forms. Section 4 analyses these negotiated regimes in detail, asking whether new checks and balances can tame infrastructural Leviathans without stifling the *poiesis* that drives digital innovation.

HYBRID GOVERNANCE: NEGOTIATED POWER BETWEEN STATES AND PLATFORMS

Section 3 showed that the Big Five platforms exercise functions once monopolized by the territorial state: taxation-like fees, rulemaking, security provision, even tentative monetary experiments. Yet the Westphalian state has not disappeared. Instead, jurisdictions now overlap. “Hybrid governance” names this messy negotiation, in which corporate technical systems and public legal systems co-produce binding norms (Jasanoff, 2004; Culpepper & Thelen, 2020).

The rise of major technology platforms has reshaped the traditional roles once held solely by governments, from setting rules to providing security and managing economic systems (Ağırdil, 2025b). Yet, the state, with its territorial roots, has not vanished. Instead, a complex overlap of authority has emerged, where corporate digital systems and public legal frameworks intertwine to create new norms. This intricate dance, often termed hybrid governance, captures the ongoing negotiation between global tech giants and national governments, where neither fully dominates, but both shape the rules that govern digital life.

At the heart of this negotiation lies a tension between the desire for digital sovereignty, where data, infrastructure, and technological standards reflect a society’s shared values, and the inherently global nature of digital platforms. Governments, particularly in regions like Europe, have championed this vision, pushing for regulations that require platforms to work seamlessly with other systems, evaluate potential harms, and operate transparently. These rules mark a significant shift from earlier, less demanding frameworks, signaling a broader ambition to align technology with public priorities rather than corporate agendas. Alongside these efforts, other initiatives focus on ensuring data can move freely within trusted boundaries and that advanced technologies meet safety standards, extending regional influence over global digital practices.

Sovereignty, however, is not just a matter of laws; it hinges on control over infrastructure. European initiatives have sought to unite cloud providers under shared standards, creating a secure environment where data remains within regional borders while meeting legal requirements. Major tech companies, in response, have pledged to store data locally and maintain services despite global challenges, reflecting a delicate balance. Governments offer access to their markets, while platforms agree to localize operations and allow oversight, though they carefully guard their autonomy. This exchange reveals a pragmatic reality: neither side can fully dictate terms, but both must compromise to operate in a shared digital world.

Technology firms are not mere followers of rules; they actively craft them. Some have proposed global agreements to protect digital infrastructure from state-led threats, framing cybersecurity as a universal concern and positioning themselves as leaders in setting international norms. Others have launched voluntary programs to shield users from online dangers, adopting the language of global cooperation to fill gaps where public regulations lag. These moves blur the line between private enterprise and diplomatic authority, creating a web of interdependence where governments, companies, and other groups collaborate to shape digital governance.

Another approach involves partnerships across various stakeholders. Groups formed by major platforms to address global security threats now include numerous companies and advisors from civil society and governments. These coalitions can swiftly coordinate actions, such as removing harmful content during crises, often outpacing traditional regulatory bodies. Yet, their closed-door decision-making raises questions about openness and accountability, as technical solutions can obscure deeper power struggles, echoing concerns that seemingly neutral systems hide significant authority.

To counter this corporate sway, governments have positioned themselves closer to the heart of tech ecosystems. Some nations pioneered this by appointing diplomats to engage directly with platform headquarters, establishing a presence in global tech hubs. This model has spread, with many countries and international bodies adopting similar roles to negotiate over content rules, market fairness, and technological safety. Unlike traditional diplomacy, where governments meet in capitals, these envoys visit corporate campuses, reflecting the platforms' growing influence. Larger powers have followed, opening offices or launching dialogues to guide companies through complex regulations or align on emerging technology standards, further entrenching this new form of engagement.

Content moderation is a key battleground for these negotiations. Some platforms have created independent boards to rule on controversial content decisions, aiming to lend legitimacy to their governance. These bodies influence company policies but face challenges when corporate leaders override their guidance, sparking debates about their independence. In parallel, public regulations in places like Europe require large platforms to offer users access to independent dispute resolution, with certified centers handling complaints and feeding broader oversight efforts. This dual system, private boards and public mechanisms, shows how the digital public sphere is being reshaped through a patchwork of corporate and regulatory processes, neither fully aligned nor entirely separate.

Data governance is another critical arena. Agreements between major powers have sought to enable cross-border data flows, but these remain fragile, prompting calls for localized data storage. Cloud providers have responded by offering region-specific solutions, ensuring data stays under local control. Efforts to standardize these commitments aim to make them lasting, beyond fleeting corporate promises. In contrast, some Global South nations have built public digital systems that integrate payments, identity, and commerce, governed by open standards. These models, adopted by other countries, demonstrate that sovereignty can be asserted by creating state-led infrastructure that rivals private platforms, offering an alternative path to digital control.

The deepest impact of hybrid governance emerges when public services rely on private technology. Healthcare systems in some countries store sensitive records on corporate clouds, financial authorities use platform analytics for enforcement, and local governments depend on tech firms for emergency communications. These arrangements promise efficiency but introduce risks: a shift in corporate policies or global restrictions could disrupt vital services. This reliance creates a new kind of civic order, where access to essential functions, healthcare, disaster response, even democratic participation, depends on corporate agreements rather than public guarantees, raising profound questions about the nature of governance in a platform-driven world.

This negotiated order reflects a broader shift in how power operates. Technology platforms and governments are locked in a continuous dialogue, each wielding distinct strengths, platforms with their speed and global reach, states with their legal authority. Smaller nations often find themselves adapting to rules set by larger players, while public voices risk being sidelined unless transparency is enforced. The result is a governance system that is neither purely public nor fully private but a hybrid, shaped by ongoing contests over authority, values, and control.

This hybrid governance confirms technology's evolution from a tool to a creative force, no longer just serving political aims but actively shaping the realities in which those aims are formed. Laws, diplomatic roles, and public services are now crafted within digital architectures, where code influences law and law seeks to guide code. Power is negotiated not only in traditional arenas but in the technical details of digital systems, from content policies to data storage decisions. The challenge lies in navigating this messy, contested space, ensuring that the generative potential of technology fosters diverse possibilities without undermining public accountability or democratic control.

Across these domains, five patterns recur: 1) Functional interdependence: States need platforms for surveillance, public messaging and AI capacity; platforms need states for legal shield and spectrum licences. 2) Normative cross-pollination: Private standards (hash-sharing, responsible-AI checklists) migrate into public regulation, while statutes (DSA, DMA) codify previously voluntary disclosures. 3) Infrastructural diplomacy: Diplomatic missions relocate to data centres and developer conferences, treating code commits as treaty drafts. 4) Procedural hybridity: Dispute-resolution bodies combine corporate funding with quasi-judicial procedure (Oversight Board, Appeals Center Europe). 5) Recursive legitimation: Each side invokes the other's authority: companies cite "alignment with EU values," regulators praise "industry collaboration on best practices." These patterns echo Jasanoff's co-production thesis: social order and technical order are built together.

Hybrid governance is not an even playing field. Platforms enjoy informational asymmetry (traffic logs, A/B-test results) and speed; regulators wield coercive force but move slowly, as illustrated by multi-year antitrust proceedings. Smaller states may lack both capacity and leverage, becoming "rule-takers" in a governance system drafted elsewhere. Civil-society voices risk marginalisation unless transparency requirements, like the DSA's mandatory researcher access to data, are enforced.

Hybrid governance confirms the earlier philosophical arc: technology has crossed from *techne* to *poiesis*. Regulatory texts, diplomatic titles and public-health dashboards are now *born* inside platform architectures; law *descends* into code and code *ascends* into law. Power is thus negotiated not only in parliaments or boardrooms but in pull-requests, trust-and-safety playbooks and latency-budget spreadsheets.

Section 5 will ask whether this negotiated order is sustainable and what a *poietic* approach to techno-politics might look like, one that embraces technology's generative capacity without surrendering democratic control. For now, the lesson is clear: neither "hands-off innovation" nor "state command-and-control" is feasible. The future lies in carefully engineered hybrids, messy, contested, but capable of steering a socio-technical planet.

TOWARD A POIETIC TECHNO-POLITICS: RETHINKING POWER AND CREATION

The preceding sections traced an arc from the classical *techne–poiesis* distinction through canonical theories of technological politics, the rise of corporate techno-sovereignties, and the tentative hybrid governance regimes that now straddle public and private authority. Taken together, those inquiries reveal an epochal shift: technology no longer merely *implements* political aims; it *constitutes* the ontological ground upon which political categories, citizen, property, security, even truth, are articulated.

To speak of ontological politics is to move beyond the managerial vocabulary of regulation or innovation policy. Ontological politics asks: *What kinds of worlds come into being through specific socio-technical assemblages, and who gains or loses the capacity to inhabit them?* Streaming platforms do not simply deliver entertainment; they compress cultural time into algorithmic simultaneity, dissolving local genres into global mood playlists. Cryptocurrency protocols do not just facilitate payment; they materialise libertarian imaginaries of trustlessness, challenging orthodox monetary sovereignty. Large-language models do not merely summarise text; they co-author epistemic reality by foregrounding some archives and eclipsing others.

Recognising these stakes obliges a poietic perspective. If *techne* emphasised mastery over means, *poiesis* foregrounds *bringing-forth*—a generative process that cannot be reduced to efficiency metrics. The task, then, is to theorise and design governance frameworks that engage technology at its creative core, rather than at the margins of after-the-fact compliance.

The leap from discriminative to generative AI rekindles ancient debates about *logos*. Models such as GPT-4o, Gemini Ultra and Llama 4 do not recognise patterns alone; they synthesise prose, images, and code that circulate as plausible *futures* in human discourse. Their parameters embed massive corpora of law, literature and online chatter—effectively "vectorising" cultural memory. Every prompt is a micro-constitutional act: a user specifies constraints, the model instantiates a possible world, and society absorbs or rejects the newly minted text.

From a poietic standpoint, three qualities matter: opacity, plasticity, and composability. 1) Opacity: Neural weights resist intuitive explanation, creating epistemic asymmetry between model owners and downstream publics. 2) Plasticity: Fine-tuning and retrieval-augmented generation render models mutable, allowing rapid adaptation to political agendas or cultural trends. 3) Composability: APIs permit routine knitting of cognitive functions into spreadsheets, court filings, and weapons systems, blending machine agency with institutional workflows.

A poietic techno-politics must therefore treat AI not as a siloed sector but as cognitive infrastructure, a substrate for thought itself, demanding governance models on par with constitutional design rather than product safety.

CRISPR-Cas9, mRNA platforms, and synthetic-biology foundries reposition cells as programmable media. Where early biotechnology re-purposed microbes for drug production, gene-editing tools now enable direct rewriting of germ-line inheritance. The ontological consequence is a blurring of the boundary between *given* and *made*: species integrity becomes a design parameter, and public health merges with molecular logistics.

Traditional bioethics, rooted in risk-benefit calculus and informed consent, cannot fully grasp this novelty. The challenge is not only whether a modification is safe but *what kind of being* it brings forth: de-extinct mammoths, heat-tolerant crops, or immuno-privileged "universal" organs. Each breakthrough drafts an implicit social contract on kinship, ecology, and scarcity. A poietic governance frame would embed community deliberation at the point of genomic design, treating biolabs as constituent assemblies of multispecies futures.

Quantum computing and quantum-secure communications disrupt two pillars of modernity: deterministic calculability and cryptographic secrecy. Shor's algorithm, when run on sufficiently large fault-tolerant qubits, could render RSA encryption obsolete, compelling a transition to quantum-resistant schemes. Entanglement-based networks present the possibility of "non-local" coordination, challenging spatial logics of jurisdiction.

Here, techno-poiesis manifests as probabilistic ontology: bits become qubits, embodying superposition until observation collapses states. Concepts such as "state secrets," "border," or "timestamp" take on new meanings in a world where information can be teleported or encrypted against future computers. Governance must anticipate temporal spill-overs, data stolen today decrypted tomorrow, and the strategic realignments that follow. To channel the creative force of frontier technologies toward democratically legitimate ends, a shift from compliance-centric policy to design-centric governance is imperative. Below are four interlocking principles.

Borrowing from Simondon, technical ensembles should remain *under-determined* enough to accommodate new moral insights and social movements. Open-source licences, modular architectures, and adversarial audits act as institutionalised "poietic pauses", moments when the artefact can be re-articulated rather than rigidly locked into path dependency.

If data and algorithms are constitutive of reality, ownership regimes must reflect plural ontologies. Data cooperatives, Indigenous data-sovereignty protocols, and genomic trusts exemplify collective property models that distribute both risk and authorship. Plural ownership ensures that creation is not monopolised by a corporate or geopolitical elite.

Jasanoff's co-production thesis suggests that publics and prototypes co-evolve. Therefore, deliberative fora, citizens' assemblies on AI, community labs in biotech, should be embedded *upstream* in research pipelines. Such structures treat world-making as a civic ritual, not a technical afterthought.

Ellul warned of technological acceleration outpacing human control. Temporal stewardship, sunset clauses in algorithmic deployment, moratoria on germ-line editing, staged release of quantum capabilities, permits iterative evaluation and intergenerational responsibility.

Elinor Ostrom's theory of polycentric governance gains new traction in a poietic context. Imagine a constellation model in which nation-states, cities, cloud providers, research institutes, and data trusts share sovereignty across functional domains. Each node wields partial authority, cyber norms, bio-risk oversight, model-weight escrow, yet remains subject to mutual monitoring.

If algorithms are de facto lawmakers, constitutional principles must become machine-readable. Research on "policy-as-code" embeds normative constraints directly in software, think GDPR compliance libraries or differential-privacy budgets enforced at runtime. A future Poietic Charter for AI could specify rights (to explanation, to contestation) and duties (fairness metrics, energy caps) in a reference ontology interpretable by both neural networks and human judges, enabling continuous constitutional dialogue at digital speed.

Blockchain projects like Regen Network and Toucan Protocol already tokenize carbon credits, treating ecological restoration as an on-chain asset class. A bolder vision recasts the state itself as an *ecological ledger*: citizenship accrues not solely through birth or boundary but through contributions to planetary commons, seagrass restoration, data stewardship, open-source climate models. Smart contracts allocate dividends or voting weight in proportion to regenerative activity, knitting environmental poiesis into political franchise.

To pre-empt quantum weaponisation, allied states and research consortia could establish quantum federations: treaty-backed enclaves that pool qubits, share error-correction breakthroughs, and co-certify post-quantum encryption suites. Such federations blur economic and security alliances, creating *entangled sovereignties* in both the physical and informational sense.

A poietic techno-politics must grapple with ethical horizons that extend beyond anthropocentric or presentist frames. Three vectors are salient: 1) Inter-species Justice: Synthetic-biology interventions can rescue coral reefs or endanger wild genomes. Ethics must therefore address stewardship obligations to non-human kin. 2) Deep-Time Accountability: Nuclear waste tombs and genomic edits endure for millennia. Deliberative mechanisms must represent future persons, perhaps via democratically selected "trustees of posterity." 3) Plural Cosmotechnics: Yuk Hui argues that every civilisation harbours its own cosmotechnics—unified views of cosmos and technics. A global poietic order must honour indigenous and non-Western design logics, resisting universalising templates that risk digital colonialism.

Up to now, this chapter has mapped the terrain: technology's ontological turn, the canon's political insights, corporate techno-sovereignties, and hybrid governance. The move toward poietic techno-politics translates diagnosis into praxis through three strategic shifts: 1) From Risk to Responsibility: Governance should move from minimising downside risk to cultivating affirmative responsibilities: to augment collective intelligence, to regenerate ecosystems, to democratise cognitive labour. 2) From Centralised Enforcement to Distributed Alignment: Compliance agencies alone cannot scale with AI or biotech. Dynamic alignment protocols, federated audits, zero-knowledge proofs of policy adherence, can decentralise enforcement while preserving privacy and innovation. 3) From Static Law to Iterative Constitutionalism: Recognising that artefacts evolve, legal frameworks must emulate agile sprints: pilot zones, reversible permissions, periodic recommissioning of models or bioplatforms.

In classical Greece, *poiesis* referred to the act by which poets, sculptors and builders brought something new into existence. Today, cloud engineers, genome editors, and quantum architects occupy that mantle, wielding instruments that sculpt not marble or verse, but the very substrates of cognition, life and reality. A poietic techno-politics does not seek to halt creation; it seeks to pluralise it, ensuring that the capacity to invent futures is widely shared, reflexively governed, and ecologically attuned.

Such a politics will be messy, iterative, and perpetually unfinished. Yet the alternative, relegating generative power to opaque corporate regimes or ossified bureaucracies, risks a future where innovation persists without imagination, and efficiency marches on without meaning. By embracing poiesis as both a conceptual lens and a design mandate, scholars, engineers, and citizens can collaborate on a new social contract: one that treats every line of code, every strand of DNA, and every qubit entanglement as an invitation to co-author the worlds we wish to inhabit.

This poietic approach holds particular significance for security in the digital age, where technology's generative capacity reshapes the boundaries of safety, sovereignty, and power. Digital infrastructures, such as cloud platforms and AI-driven surveillance systems, do not merely defend against threats but actively construct new security realities. For instance, algorithms embedded in facial-recognition systems or predictive policing tools generate probabilistic ontologies of risk, determining who or what is deemed a threat, often beyond transparent human oversight (Amoore, 2020). These systems, as Schmitt might argue, delegate sovereign decisions on the exception to code, creating new battlegrounds where security is co-produced by public and private actors. A poietic security governance must therefore prioritize transparency and civic deliberation to ensure that these emergent orders align with democratic values rather than entrenching opaque techno-sovereignties.

Moreover, the rapid evolution of cybersecurity threats, from quantum-enabled decryption to AI-driven disinformation, underscores the need for governance models that match technology's temporal acceleration. Drawing on Ellul's warnings, the unchecked momentum of security technologies risks outpacing political control, as seen in the proliferation of autonomous cyber-defense systems that react faster than human judgment allows. A poietic framework would integrate temporal stewardship, such as staged deployments of security algorithms or moratoria on high-risk applications, to foster iterative accountability. By treating security as a world-making process, techno-politics can balance the generative potential of digital defenses with the imperative to safeguard pluralistic and equitable futures.

ACKNOWLEDGMENT

This work utilized AI tools (ChatGPT and Grok) to enhance writing quality and clarity. All analytical content and interpretations remain the sole responsibility of the author.

REFERENCES

Ağırdil, O. (2025a). Almanya'nın Kamu Güvenliği Politikaları: Strateji Belgeleri Üzerinden Bir İnceleme. *Liberal Düşünce Dergisi*, (118), 199–230. DOI: 10.36484/liberal.1683028

Ağırdil, O. (2025b). Fransa'nın Kamu Güvenliği Politikaları: Strateji Belgeleri Üzerinden Bir İnceleme. *İletişim Ve Diplomasi* (14), 23-44. DOI: 10.54722/iletisimvediplomasi.1667005

Almazán Gómez, M. A., & Pradanos, L. I. (2024). The political ecology of technology: A non-neutrality approach. *Environmental Values*, *33*(1), 3–9. DOI: 10.1177/09632719231209745

Amazon. (2023). AWS annual report 2023. Retrieved from https://aws.amazon.com/about-aws/annual-reports/

Amazon. (2025). Amazon.com announces fourth quarter results. *Business Wire*. https://ir.aboutamazon.com/news-release/news-release-details/2025/Amazon-com-Announces-Fourth-Quarter-Results

Amoore, L. (2020). *Cloud ethics: Algorithms and the attributes of ourselves and others*. Duke University Press.

Apple. (2020). Exposure Notification API. Retrieved from https://www.apple.com/covid19/contacttracing/

Arendt, H. (1998). *The human condition* (2nd ed.). University of Chicago Press. (Original work published 1958) DOI: 10.7208/chicago/9780226924571.001.0001

Aristotle, . (1984). Nicomachean ethics. In Barnes, J. (Ed.), *The complete works of Aristotle* (Vol. 2, pp. 1729–1867). Princeton University Press. (Original work published 350 BCE)

Arthur, W. B. (1989). Competing technologies, increasing returns, and lock-in by historical events. *Economic Journal (London)*, *99*(394), 116–131. DOI: 10.2307/2234208

Bacon, F. (2000). *The new organon* (Jardine, L., & Silverthorne, M., Eds.). Cambridge University Press. (Original work published 1620) DOI: 10.1017/CBO9781139164030

Barad, K. (2007). *Meeting the universe halfway: Quantum physics and the entanglement of matter and meaning*. Duke University Press. DOI: 10.2307/j.ctv12101zq

Bjola, C., & Zaiotti, R. (2021). *Digital diplomacy and international organisations: Autonomy, legitimacy and contestation*. Routledge.

Bloomberg. (2019, January 22). Google set 2018 lobbying record as Washington techlash expands. Retrieved from https://www.bloomberg.com/news/articles/2019-01-22/google-set-2018-lobbying-record-as-washington-techlash-expands

Callon, M. (1986). Some elements of a sociology of translation: Domestication of the scallops and the fishermen of St. Brieuc Bay. In Law, J. (Ed.), *Power, action and belief: A new sociology of knowledge?* (pp. 196–233). Routledge & Kegan Paul.

Cohen, J. E. (2019). *Between truth and power: The legal constructions of informational capitalism*. Oxford University Press. DOI: 10.1093/oso/9780190246693.001.0001

Cornelli, G., Frost, J., Gambacorta, L., Sinha, S., & Townsend, R. M. (2024). The organisation of digital payments in India – lessons from the Unified Payments Interface (UPI). In *Faster digital payments: Global and regional perspectives* (BIS Paper No. 152, pp. 61–?). Bank for International Settlements. https://www.bis.org/publ/bppdf/bispap152_e_rh.pdf

Culpepper, P. D., & Thelen, K. (2020). Are we all Amazon primed? Consumers and the politics of platform power. *Comparative Political Studies*, *53*(2), 288–318. DOI: 10.1177/0010414019852687

Cusumano, M. A., Gawer, A., & Yoffie, D. B. (2019). *The business of platforms: Strategy in the age of digital competition, innovation, and power*. Harper Business.

David, P. A. (1985). Clio and the economics of QWERTY. *The American Economic Review*, *75*(2), 332–337.

Descartes, R. (2006). *A discourse on the method* (I. Maclean, Trans.). Oxford University Press. (Original work published 1637)

Doctorow, C. (2021). *How to destroy surveillance capitalism*. Medium Editions.

Edwards, P. N. (2010). *A vast machine: Computer models, climate data, and the politics of global warming*. MIT Press.

Ellul, J. (1964). *The technological society* (J. Wilkinson, Trans.). Knopf. (Original work published 1954)

European Commission. (2016). State aid: Ireland gave illegal tax benefits to Apple worth up to €13 billion [Press release]. Retrieved from https://ec.europa.eu/commission/presscorner/detail/en/IP_16_2923

European Commission. (2023). GAIA-X: A federated data infrastructure for Europe. Retrieved from https://www.gaia-x.eu/

European Commission. (2024). Digital Markets Act: Rules for gatekeepers. Retrieved from https://digital-markets-act.ec.europa.eu/

European Commission. (2025). Commission finds Apple and Meta in breach of the Digital Markets Act [Press release]. Retrieved from https://ec.europa.eu/commission/presscorner/detail/en/ip_25_1085

Feenberg, A. (1999). *Questioning technology*. Routledge.

GIFCT. (2023). Global Internet Forum to Counter Terrorism: About. Retrieved from https://gifct.org/about/

Gillespie, T. (2018). *Custodians of the internet: Platforms, content moderation, and the hidden decisions that shape social media*. Yale University Press.

Google. (2020). Exposure Notification API. Retrieved from https://developers.google.com/android/exposure-notifications

Gorton, G. B., & Zhang, J. Y. (2024). Protecting the sovereign's money monopoly. *Alabama Law Review*, *75*(4), 955–1007.

Haranas, M. (2025). Microsoft vs. AWS vs. Google Cloud earnings Q1 2025 face-off. *CRN*. https://www.crn.com/news/cloud/2025/microsoft-vs-aws-vs-google-cloud-earnings-q1-2025-face-off

Hecht, G. (1998). *The radiance of France: Nuclear power and national identity after World War II*. MIT Press.

Hecht, G. (Ed.). (2011). *Entangled geographies: Empire and technopolitics in the global Cold War*. MIT Press. DOI: 10.7551/mitpress/9780262515788.001.0001

Heidegger, M. (1977). *The question concerning technology and other essays* (W. Lovitt, Trans.). Harper & Row. (Original work published 1954)

Hui, Y. (2016). *On the existence of digital objects*. University of Minnesota Press. DOI: 10.5749/minnesota/9780816698905.001.0001

Jasanoff, S. (1990). *The fifth branch: Science advisers as policymakers*. Harvard University Press.

Jasanoff, S. (Ed.). (2004). *States of knowledge: The co-production of science and social order*. Routledge. DOI: 10.4324/9780203413845

Jasanoff, S., & Kim, S.-H. (Eds.). (2015). *Dreamscapes of modernity: Sociotechnical imaginaries and the fabrication of power*. University of Chicago Press. DOI: 10.7208/chicago/9780226276663.001.0001

Johns, F. (2017). Data, detection, and the politics of algorithmic governance. *Big Data & Society*, *4*(1), 1–13.

Kaur, G. (2025). Sovereign cloud set to grow in APAC amid security concerns. *Fierce Network*. https://www.fierce-network.com/broadband/sovereign-cloud-set-grow-apac-amid-security-concerns

Khan, L. M. (2017). Amazon's antitrust paradox. *The Yale Law Journal*, *126*(3), 710–805.

Latour, B. (1987). *Science in action: How to follow scientists and engineers through society*. Harvard University Press.

Latour, B. (1999). *Pandora's hope: Essays on the reality of science studies*. Harvard University Press.

Latour, B. (2005). *Reassembling the social: An introduction to actor-network-theory*. Oxford University Press. DOI: 10.1093/oso/9780199256044.001.0001

Mackenzie, A. (2015). The production of prediction: What does machine learning want? *European Journal of Cultural Studies*, *18*(4–5), 429–445. DOI: 10.1177/1367549415577384

Meta. (2023). Meta Q4 2022 earnings report. Retrieved from https://investor.fb.com/financials/

Meta. (2024). How Meta is preparing for the 2024 South African elections. *Meta*. https://about.fb.com/news/2024/04/how-meta-is-preparing-for-the-2024-south-african-elections/

Meta. (2025). Meta Q1 2025 earnings report. Retrieved from https://investor.fb.com/financials/

Microsoft. (2017). A Digital Geneva Convention to protect cyberspace. Retrieved from https://blogs.microsoft.com/on-the-issues/2017/02/14/need-digital-geneva-convention/

Microsoft. (2023). Microsoft Digital Defense Report 2023. Retrieved from https://www.microsoft.com/en-us/security/security-insider/microsoft-digital-defense-report-2023

Plato. (1935). *The republic* (P. Shorey, Trans.). In *Plato: Republic* (Loeb Classical Library). Harvard University Press. (Original work published ca. 375 BCE)

Reuters. (2024). Meta, Spotify CEOs take aim at European AI regulations. *Reuters*. https://www.reuters.com/technology/artificial-intelligence/meta-spotify-ceos-take-aim-european-ai-regulations-2024-08-23/

Richter, F. (2025). Amazon and Microsoft Stay Ahead in Global Cloud Market. *Statista*. https://www.statista.com/chart/18819/worldwide-market-share-of-leading-cloud-infrastructure-service-providers/

Roochnik, D. (1996). *Of art and wisdom: Plato's understanding of techne*. Penn State University Press.

Schmitt, C. (2003). *The nomos of the earth in the international law of the jus publicum Europaeum* (Ulmen, G. L., Trans.). Telos Press. (Original work published 1950)

Schmitt, C. (2005). *Political theology: Four chapters on the concept of sovereignty* (Schwab, G., Trans.). University of Chicago Press. (Original work published 1922) DOI: 10.7208/chicago/9780226738901.001.0001

Schmitt, C. (2007a). The age of neutralizations and depoliticizations. In *The concept of the political* (Schwab, G., Trans.; pp. 80–96). University of Chicago Press. (Original work published 1929) DOI: 10.7208/chicago/9780226738840.001.0001

Schmitt, C. (2007b). *The concept of the political* (Schwab, G., Trans.). University of Chicago Press. (Original work published 1932) DOI: 10.7208/chicago/9780226738840.001.0001

Simondon, G. (2017). *On the mode of existence of technical objects* (Malaspina, C., & Rogove, J., Trans.). Univocal Publishing. (Original work published 1958)

Srnicek, N. (2017). *Platform capitalism*. Polity Press.

Statista. (2023). Google search statistics 2023. Retrieved from https://www.statista.com/topics/1001/google/

Statista. (2025a). Market share of leading desktop search engines worldwide from January 2015 to March 2025. Retrieved from https://www.statista.com/statistics/216573/worldwide-market-share-of-search-engines/

Statista. (2025b). Leading tech companies worldwide in 2025, by market capitalization. Retrieved from https://www.statista.com/statistics/1350976/leading-tech-companies-worldwide-by-market-cap/

U.S. Department of Justice. (2025). Department of Justice prevails in landmark antitrust case against Google. *U.S. Department of Justice*. Retrieved from https://www.justice.gov/opa/pr/department-justice-prevails-landmark-antitrust-case-against-google

Vaidhyanathan, S. (2018). *Antisocial media: How Facebook disconnects us and undermines democracy*. Oxford University Press.

Vernant, J.-P. (1988). *Myth and tragedy in ancient Greece* (Lloyd, J., Trans.). Zone Books.

Wallerstein, I. (2004). *World-systems analysis: An introduction*. Duke University Press.

Winner, L. (1980). Do artifacts have politics? *Daedalus, 109*(1), 121–136.

World Bank. (2023). GDP (current US$) – France, 2023. Retrieved from https://data.worldbank.org/indicator/NY.GDP.MKTP.CD

Yahoo Finance. (2023). Apple Inc. (AAPL) market capitalization, 2023. Retrieved from https://finance.yahoo.com/quote/AAPL/

Zhao, Y., Alvarez-Torres, M. J., Smith, B., & Tan, H. S. (2004). The non-neutrality of technology: A theoretical analysis and empirical study of computer mediated communication technologies. *Journal of Educational Computing Research, 30*(1–2), 23–55. DOI: 10.2190/5N93-BJQR-3H4Q-7704

Zuboff, S. (2019). *The age of surveillance capitalism: The fight for a human future at the new frontier of power*. PublicAffairs.

Chapter 2
The Quiet Displacement of Social Values in AI Policy

Jonathan Stein
https://orcid.org/0009-0004-7283-9611
University of Edinburgh, UK

Matthew Murphy
Duke University, USA

ABSTRACT

The primary driver for how technological developments are currently scrutinized and regulated is not due to an examination of risks, as one might expect, but from large American tech firms (Big Tech) fortifying their influence with the state. Given this primary motive, technologies like AI have their associated policy approaches framed to benefit tech firms through fundamentally shaping underlying ethical values. This chapter will investigate how the deepening integration between technology corporations and state institutions systematically privileges operational values like security and efficiency over social impact values such as fairness, detailed accountability, and sustainability as the tech industry merges with the state, due to its attempt to preserve and bolster itself by forming a cooperative association.

THE QUIET DISPLACEMENT OF SOCIAL VALUES IN AI POLICY

In the marble halls of the Capitol Rotunda on January 20, 2025, as Donald Trump raised his right hand to become president for the second time, four men in dark suits sat where kings and prime ministers once gathered. Jeff Bezos, Elon Musk, Mark

DOI: 10.4018/979-8-3373-2459-3.ch002

Zuckerberg, and Sundar Pichai had claimed seats of honor at Trump's inauguration, their presence as central to the ceremony as the Chief Justice administering the oath. This visual depicted a truth that our political vocabulary has yet to acknowledge. The following trinity of terms — technology, Big Tech, and corporations — all have their colloquial uses. But their everyday meanings don't capture what's actually happening in today's policy landscape. The meanings of these terms have evolved out of their common applications, perhaps for some time now, and require different perspectives to grasp their new configurations.

The language we use to describe technology companies and their relationship to the state relies on concepts forged in earlier eras. To contextualize our first definition, we observe that "technology" today commonly refers to an object or tool. The common definition references physical devices that instrumentally aid the fulfillment of human purposes. Such an understanding does not fully encapsulate technology's domain of power, and therefore requires a different vantage point. Harvey Brooks (1980) understood the accumulated and collective knowledge embedded *within* a technology as its essential feature. Focusing on the knowledge included within a system is fitting for our era of mass data capture and powerful surveillance, especially given the amount of underlying data used to train AI and the contested use of the *kinds* of data used to train it (copyrighted material, historical biases embedded within, etc). In this chapter, AI is put under the microscope and keeping this notion of embodied collective knowledge in view as we use the term "technology" will provide a much better outlook for grasping the effects of its use. AI serves as a container, holding both accurate and contested forms of knowledge, which has the capacity to cause harms and injustices. This approach focuses on everything that *underlies* technology, which includes how the information gets disseminated and produced, instead of the mere functional capabilities it can manufacture. Another way to think about this is through the lens of Martin Heidegger (2008), who described technology as a "way of revealing". Technology does not refer to an ability or an artifact, but dispositions to the world that are contained within it. The reach of AI systems has already been vast, and carried within it are certain values that get dispersed to consumers. We encourage a perspective that keeps this concern top of mind.

Inspired by Brooks, Stefan Fritsch (2011) employs a methodologically neutral definition of technology that avoids predetermined assumptions about whether technology is inherently beneficial or harmful. This approach treats technology as the accumulation of knowledge and artifacts for human purposes, allowing for systematic analysis of how values become embedded within technological systems. This does not mean technology is empty and devoid of virtues. "[I]t can never be value-neutral", Fritsch contends. Quite the opposite — technology actively embodies and propagates the values and priorities of the systems that create it. Appropriately,

Fritsch also argues that technology should be understood as systematically interwoven with global affairs. We follow both of these lines of thought with our argument.

We propose that what matters is the systematic integration of Big Tech across all levels of government, from national security to municipal services to regulatory oversight. While this integration now spans virtually every domain of governance, national security served as the pioneering arena where these partnerships were first formalized and normalized. The establishment of Unit X by US Defense Secretary Ash Carter one decade ago was the beginning of a new era of the relationship between the Pentagon and technologists in the private sector on the West Coast (Shah & Kirchoff 2024). In his speech at Stanford which announced the initiative, Carter stated, "American businesses own, operate, and see approximately ninety percent of our national networks," meaning all feasible domains of operation including banks, retail, cyber, research and the sciences, etc, have some involvement with the private sector. The foundation is deep, and it buttresses both the digital lives of ordinary citizens and the intelligence of the state apparatus. Unit X was designed to create a bridge without a border crossing. Shah and Kirchoff detail how the defense industry removed red tape for Valley technologists and formed a militaristic collaboration which continues to compound. Crucially, the partnership models, value priorities, and governance approaches pioneered in national security contexts have since been exported across civilian government functions.

With AI as the new technological frontier, the algorithms that originate in the private sector take on a heightened level of importance when they are regularly used by the federal government. Given this enduring relationship, we need to assiduously consider the *essence* of a corporation, especially the technology companies at the base of this private-public dynamic.

"The Corporation" and "Big Tech"

How we legally define what a corporation actually is will determine how much Big Tech can expand its scope of power. The following ways that corporations have been defined by scholars do not sufficiently describe Big Tech or how it maneuvers throughout the economy. To remedy the insufficiency of these definitions, specific and essential features of Big Tech must be identified to form a new legal accountability procedure for these businesses.

As David Millon (1990, p. 206) points out, the early 19th century conception of the corporation was that of "an entity existing separately from its shareholders and other participants". Back then, the government gave companies permission to exist for specific public purposes. In reference to this view, Rutger Claassen posits: "Normatively, the purpose for which corporations must act is, at least partly, a public purpose, and the state has a legitimate interest in closely regulating them"

(Claassen, 2022, p. 207). This view is called *concession theory*, or *"artificial entity theory"*, and was in fashion before corporations were privatized. Millon (pp. 208–9) additionally canvases that, even back then, there were public reproaches due to the "state's selectivity in granting concessions", which resulted in monopolies. The concerns might sound familiar: favoritism, equal economic opportunity, wealth entrenchment, and corruption.

Another notion of the corporation is by way of *contractualist theory*. Ontologically, this view holds that the corporation's existence originates from the various contracts between its participants. Once again, there's a dovetailed purpose here, identified by Claassen (p. 4): "Normatively, the purpose of business corporations is to benefit the interests of these contracting partners (or members)". Contractualist theory thereby yields a reasonable explanation for why a corporation should aim to maximize its value for shareholders. Without the shareholders, the corporation loses its agency and ceases to exist.

Lastly, there is the *real entity theory* of the corporation, which is how most business is conducted and viewed worldwide. This conception emphasizes the distinct legal status of a firm apart from the state or investors. When corporations began to inflate in size and gain immense power in the 20th century, the will of the corporation shifted control to the internal managers and boards of directors. Real entity theory "points to the board as having a fiduciary duty not towards a particular group, but towards the corporation itself" (Ibid, p. 5). This inverted interest is a vital component of the most powerful technology companies. Although the theory views the corporation as an independent entity, which is necessary, a main critique is that it protects owners from risks and other liabilities. Individual actors are legally insulated since the *company* would be held liable, thus creating significant agency problems. To allow legal cover in this way is not a modernized approach for how the largest tech firms operate.

Put simply, Big Tech has splintered the above theories of the corporation. Big Tech (which will earn a definition soon) is given concessions by the state which, in turn, does not have an interest in subsequent regulation of themselves. This extinguishes treating Big Tech under artificial entity theory because these companies no longer serve specific state-defined public purposes and, instead, they have gained the power to define those purposes themselves through their integration with government functions. Meanwhile, the contractual obligations which typically exist in other business categories have been surpassed; Big Tech no longer responds reliably to shareholder concerns or public pressure. This eliminates a contractualist view because these companies now prioritize their institutional survival and government partnerships over traditional stakeholder accountability. Finally, although corporations theoretically represent collections of individuals with shared interests, Big Tech's powerful leaders wield disproportionate control that transcends any collective decision-making.

This concentration of power enables direct negotiations between individual CEOs and public officials, bypassing traditional corporate governance structures. A real entity approach therefore cannot account for this personalized influence because it assumes corporations act as unified entities rather than vehicles for individual executive power in shaping policy, internal decisions, and market dynamics.

We postulate two crucial points that must be recognized for Big Tech. Firstly, corporate actions ultimately originate from individual decisions. Theoretically, since "corporations are the natural products of individual initiative", their status as conversible agents should be legally acknowledged, which we elaborate on later in the chapter (Millon, p. 213). Secondly, we observe that guiding corporate directives through public desires, historically from users and shareholders, is inadequate. Instead, Big Tech has been able to concentrate on self-interested operations, a road which has ultimately led to a cooperative association with the state, which will further reinforce insular efforts as both parties seek to maintain and consolidate their combined power.

We view Big Tech as a "group of companies that own or control important digital platforms" with global influence and their respective leaders (Khanal, Zhang & Taeihagh, 2024, p. 2). The primary firms of interest are Meta, X, Amazon, Google, Apple, and Microsoft. Moreover, notable AI companies such as OpenAI and Anthropic enjoy prominent investment from the former organizations.

The firms under the "Big Tech" umbrella do not all offer platform-based services by accident. Each platform, with slight variations, serves as an intermediary which then matches providers and users (Wörsdörfer, 2022). The global scale on which these operate feeds a self-perpetuating environment in which buyers and sellers are easily able to find their pairing, resulting in monopolistic tendencies of the network effect (Jullien & Sand-Zantman, 2021). In other words, the more people who use platforms like Amazon or Google, the more attractive these platforms become to new users, creating a cycle where market dominance becomes nearly impossible to challenge. However, the traditional evidence for antitrust cases was that monopolists were able to raise prices. Many platforms and services offered by Big Tech are free which, among other factors, has shielded Big Tech from a monopoly classification.

With this model, Big Tech has been able to successfully intrude on other public sectors, which scholars have called "sphere transgressions", due to their steady aggrandizement of power (Sharon & Gellert, 2024). These firms have encroached on the domains of education, public health, welfare, public transportation and more by controlling the information of these areas. Yet, risks therefore escalate, "as tech corporations do not have the domain expertise proportional to their new level of influence in these different societal spheres" and perhaps even more crucially, "are not accountable in the way that public sector actors are" (Ibid, p. 2653). Notice how the mentioned list of domains consists of societal responsibilities typically under the public dominion of government. The merging of Big Tech and these public sectors has been in full force over the past decade, and now requires a comprehensive analysis which treats technology and politics as a fused entity.

The Techno-Political Lens

Ever since the Virginia Statute for Religious Freedom in 1786, there has been a legal partition to separate church and state. Nothing of the sort exists for the American technology sector, which could be why there has been a noticeable entwinement of the US government and Big Tech. Each holds vast power and influence. Currently, both are interested in the development, advancement, and investment of AI to secure global technological supremacy, and to entrench control over the systems that govern its public use.

A truly techno-political landscape has formed in the US. Edwards and Hecht (2010) define techno-politics as "hybrids of technical systems and political practices that produce new forms of power and agency". The integration we're observing here is not new, but has reached an unprecedented intensity in need of deconstruction. The threads that connect the state and the technology sector are pronounced and have existed for some time. It was the heavy research investment by the state that spawned the computing revolution (National Research Council, 1999). Global positioning system (GPS) technology was originally discovered from an initiative for the U.S. Department of Defense, which eventually trickled into many commercial applications (Kumar & Moore, 2002). Apple's Siri emerged from DARPA research on voice recognition. The Google search algorithm was funded by the National Science Foundation. And more recently, Tesla has been the recipient of over 15 billion dollars in government subsidies and contracts to help manufacture electric vehicles (Leparmentier, 2025). These are just a few of countless other prominent examples.

Not only is there a *monetary* link between the state apparatus and the technology industry, but an ideological one lurks beneath as well. Hecht (1998) demonstrates this by a look at the development of nuclear reactors in postwar France, which elucidates this ideological link well. National identity does not always develop from the same perspectives or express the same form of pride. Two organizations, the CEA (Commissariat à l'Énergie Atomique) and the EDF (Électricité de France), had competing political visions while manufacturing their nuclear reactors. The CEA wanted to project the sovereignty of France to the rest of the world, while the EDF prioritized the citizenry, and sought cheap and efficient provisions of nuclear power. These beliefs were implanted into the design of their technologies. Focus on national independence motivated the CEA to use non-enriched uranium because it could be sourced domestically. On the other hand, the EDF favored enriched uranium which yielded better economic performance. Moreover, the physical control rooms of these reactors were fashioned differently. CEA control rooms reflected centralized decision-making, while EDF incorporated more distributed monitoring systems. In this sense, the political ideologies of French technologists in the nuclear industry were materially built into the technologies themselves. This reification of *ideology as technology* is striking to say the least, and can easily go undetected (at least until the sociologists pounce on it a couple decades later).

As Langdon Winner (1980) notes, the interwoven nature of technical systems and modern politics invites a deeper inquiry. "In our times people are often willing to make drastic changes in the way they live to accord with technological innovation," Winner writes, but "at the same time they would resist similar kinds of changes justified on political grounds." People willingly adopt smartphones, smart home devices, and social media platforms that enable unprecedented levels of data collection and surveillance. As Shoshana Zuboff (2019) describes in her concept of "surveillance capitalism," these technologies have fundamentally altered privacy norms and created vast systems of behavioral monitoring and prediction. Yet similar surveillance proposals through explicit political legislation (like mandatory ID cards or government tracking systems) typically face fierce opposition in the US. Gig economy platforms like Uber, DoorDash, and TaskRabbit have radically restructured labor relations by classifying workers as independent contractors rather than employees, effectively circumventing decades of labor protections. These changes were readily absorbed in the name of technological innovation. The domains of technical systems and modern politics cannot be treated as mutually exclusive, but rather as concentric circles that revolve around the same center of gravity, where technology and governance have become indistinguishable.

Given that "the physical arrangements of industrial production, warfare, communications, and the like have fundamentally changed the exercise of power and the experience of citizenship", we must then contend with the actual devices, systems, and infrastructures themselves (Winner, 1980). Indeed, these artifacts are shaped by the social and political systems in which they are embedded, but do the objects *themselves* contain values? Do they contain beneficence or evils? We contend that virtues are inherent in AI systems and require scrupulous attention, which is constantly at risk of being overlooked.

Artificial Intelligence and Its Values

The AI triad is comprised of data, compute, and algorithms. All can be summed up as such: "Machine learning systems use computing power to execute algorithms that learn from data" (Buchanan, 2020, p. 1). When running on unsupervised machine learning models called "neural networks", these features coalesce to create a particular kind of intelligence; one that can deliver outputs at a level of sophistication that has superseded previous technologies. For example, the achievements from large language models have followed a path of steady improvement to the extent that around 30% of the surveyed population views these machines as sentient (Stokel-Walker, 2024). In short, the power of these tools engenders an intuition that AI itself has some form of agency.

For David Runciman (2023), AI does not deserve a unique stature of significance. Instead, we can place AI into the same realm of *artificial entities* that we have existed alongside for centuries. The central two which hold prominence are states and corporations, which have long embodied, expressed, and exercised decisions that extend beyond themselves. The ultimate question is whether AI is a comparable new agent or an extension of the ones already established. Our methodology contends it is the latter. The governmental and corporate territories do not operate in isolation. The issue here, then, is that AI policy is subject to fewer external, social considerations and instead is a malleable asset of the state.

We focus on two types of AI values that are fundamentally at odds with each other. We apply the term "social" and "social impact" to describe normative values that necessarily promote things we consider inherently good for human flourishing, such as fairness, privacy and human rights, and other virtues that aim at moral ideals that impact individuals. This is contrasted with "operational" values that are framed as more self-regarding and instrumental; helping to optimize the objectives of Big Tech or the state. These values like efficiency, security, and accuracy are also usually good for individuals, but are typically driven by organizational objectives and hold those objectives as a first priority. Precise values and their definitions will be addressed later in the chapter. Before we expand on those values, we need to understand the current AI regulatory landscape, ways AI is being managed within it, and how social and operational values manifest in this scene.

AI POLICY SHIFTS

The Early Days of American AI Policy

Federal AI legislation in the US has been noticeably sparse when compared with other global powers like the EU and China. The seminal policies that were enacted, however, were framed as directly tied to national security. The first major U.S. AI policy came with EO 13,859 (2019), which focused on maintaining American leadership in AI while acknowledging some basic ethical principles. EO 13,960 (2020) expanded these guidelines to include civil rights, privacy, and transparency considerations for federal AI use. Meanwhile, the EU was developing much stronger protections. The EU AI Act banned harmful AI applications outright and established detailed accountability mechanisms — a sharp contrast to the more permissive U.S. approach. This global pressure pushed the Biden administration toward EO 14,110 (2023), which represented the most comprehensive U.S. effort to address AI's social impacts, requiring agencies to assess how AI systems affect individual rights and safety. But this emphasis on social values would prove short-lived.

In the earliest days of AI policy, it wasn't clear how AI ethics would split along partisan lines. The regulatory space was so new that there was hope its governance might transcend typical political divides. That optimism didn't last long. As the Republican Party under Trump came in, out, and back into the White House, this forced the Republican and Democratic administrations to increasingly define clear boundaries of what they believed the future of AI and its ethical stewardship should look like. Distinct priorities emerged. The Trump administration's approach has prioritized operational values — efficiency, security, and competitive advantage. This shows up in concrete ways: rescinding Biden's comprehensive AI safety order (EO 14,110), refusing to sign international agreements on "ethical" AI development at the 2025 Paris Summit, and implementing tariffs that pushed Nvidia to commit $500 billion in domestic AI infrastructure. Democrats have consistently emphasized social impact values — fairness, transparency, and civil rights protections. Biden's EO 14,110 required agencies to assess AI's equity impacts and maintain human oversight of automated systems. The administration also pursued international cooperation, signing agreements like the Council of Europe's Framework Convention on AI and Human Rights. Though the partisan split between operational and social impact values is not exact, a fundamental divergence in philosophy is discernible. Republicans emphasize market-driven innovation with minimal government intervention, while Democrats advocate for stronger guardrails to ensure AI development aligns with broader social values and protections for vulnerable populations. Despite this surfacing ideological landscape, there is still much ambiguity around certain AI values, and demonstrable confusion around others. It's likely that through the next few years, positions on these values in the context of AI will be clarified as high profile instances of tension emerge.

One current tension surrounds bias and fairness in AI. Among social impact values, bias has received the most extensive scholarly attention. Originally, "bias" had a purely technical definition: training AI models to perform equally well across different demographic groups. In this technical sense, bias is simply a form of model accuracy. Over time, the term expanded beyond technical considerations to encompass broader social and ethical concerns. Bias now refers not only to statistical performance gaps, but to questions about what kind of fairness we want in AI outcomes (whether we prioritize equal opportunity or equal results, for instance). This evolution has made "bias" a politically charged term. The Biden administration developed federal standards for measuring and testing AI bias, establishing detailed requirements for addressing discriminatory impacts. The Trump administration rescinded these guidelines while simultaneously launching their own "anti-bias" policies through EO 14,179, "Removing Barriers to American Leadership in Artificial Intelligence" (2025). However, the "bias" this order targets is framed as ideological bias against conservative viewpoints rather than demographic discrimination. Paradoxically, new Office of Management and Budget (OMB) memos from the same administration advocate for "fairness" (typically understood as the solution to bias) (Office of Management and Budget, 2025). This contradiction illustrates how US definitions of core AI values have become muddled by partisan politics, with the same terms meaning different things depending on which administration is in power. While dynamics shift back and forth on AI governance in the US, they are also shifting beyond US borders.

The AI Arms Race as Policy Driver

The global competition for AI supremacy has fundamentally altered how the US and national governments approach technology policy, with profound implications for which values become prioritized in AI governance frameworks. This technological arms race is not merely about economic advantage. It reshapes how nations conceptualize security, sovereignty, and power. The international landscape of AI development increasingly resembles a zero-sum contest, or at least is framed by global governments as such. Whether this framing is useful or accurate is debatable, but it's clear major powers are investing unprecedented resources to secure technological leadership (Sherman, 2019).

This competition stems from the widely-held belief that AI supremacy will confer decisive economic, military, and geopolitical advantages to whichever nation achieves it first (Mohney, 2025). The stakes of this competition are increasingly perceived to be existential, with AI positioned as the key enabling technology that will define the next era of global power dynamics. Countries believe that whoever wins the AI race will control the future. What distinguishes this technological competition from previous ones is pace and scope. Unlike previous technological revolutions that unfolded over decades, AI capabilities are advancing on a compressed timeline. This shortened time to develop new capabilities creates immense pressure on policymakers to prioritize speed and efficiency over more deliberative approaches to governance.

The United States has explicitly framed its AI initiatives in terms of competition with China, which has committed to becoming the global leader in AI by 2030 through its "New Generation Artificial Intelligence Development Plan" (State Council of China, 2017). This "us versus them" thinking now drives most AI policy developments. As outlined in the previous section, the initial "Advancing American AI Act" under the first Trump administration was explicitly positioned as a response to perceived Chinese advantages in AI development. Even during the Biden administration's push for more socially-conscious AI governance through EO 14,110, the document was still fundamentally framed around maintaining American security leadership. The pendulum swing between Republican and Democratic administrations has revealed that while they may differ on which values to emphasize, both parties fundamentally accept the premise that AI development is a race and one that the United States cannot afford to lose. This bipartisan consensus creates powerful institutional momentum toward operational values. Efficiency, security, and competitive advantage transcend political administrations and are thus continually reinforced.

Perhaps the most consequential aspect of the race to develop AI has been the growing entanglement between commercial AI development and national security infrastructure. What began as separate domains has increasingly converged into what some scholars call the "military-AI complex" (Frazier, 2024). This is perhaps unsurprising, given the US's history of its state national security apparatus acquiring and incubating the development of key emerging technologies. This convergence manifests in several ways. First, through direct partnerships between tech firms and defense agencies, exemplified by controversial programs like Project Maven. While this program initially sparked significant employee resistance at Google — with over 4,000 workers signing a petition and dozens resigning, ultimately forcing the company to withdraw — such partnerships have since become more normalized across the industry (Mohsin, 2024). Google even recently rescinded its commitment to not using AI for surveillance or weapons, demonstrating how typical these partnerships have become (Titu & De Vynck, 2025). It's worth noting that the pattern of resistance, however, continues: Amazon workers have organized walkouts over facial recognition sales to law enforcement, Microsoft employees have protested military contracts, amid other acts of civil protest across tech firms. These acts of resistance reveal ongoing tensions within tech companies between operational imperatives and social values, though the institutional momentum toward defense integration often prevails. Second, the private and public sectors converge through the revolving door of personnel between tech companies, defense contractors, and government agencies, creating shared institutional cultures and priorities. Third, it occurs through enormous defense-oriented investment initiatives that shape the entire AI research ecosystem, from university labs to startups. When AI is viewed primarily through a security lens, values like fairness, transparency, and equitable access become secondary considerations. This isn't because policymakers explicitly reject these values, but because the institutional logic of national security naturally privileges operational efficiency, reliability, and strategic advantage. As Hecht's (2011) technopolitics framework would suggest, these institutional priorities become materially embedded in the technical specifications and architectural choices of AI systems themselves.

The recently launched "Stargate" initiative represents perhaps the clearest example of how the competitive dynamics of the AI arms race shape value priorities in governance. Announced in early 2025 with an initial allocation of $38 billion in federal funding, Stargate aims to dramatically accelerate advanced AI development in the United States through public-private partnerships (Friesen, 2025). The explicit goal of the program is to ensure American leadership in frontier AI capabilities, with particular emphasis on systems that can maintain strategic advantage in both economic and security domains. What's most revealing about Stargate is not just its size, but its structure and governance. Unlike previous federal technology initiatives that maintained clearer boundaries between government oversight and private execution, Stargate establishes unprecedented integration between major tech companies and federal agencies. The initiative creates joint development teams where corporate research labs work alongside military and intelligence personnel, with shared access to computing resources, datasets, and technical infrastructure. The initiative's governing documents reveal a stark prioritization of operational values. Performance metrics focus overwhelmingly on capability advancement, efficiency gains, and deployment speed, with comparatively minimal attention to social impact values. Perhaps most significantly, Stargate has already begun to redefine what counts as "responsible AI" in policy contexts. Program documents repeatedly equate responsibility with ensuring American leadership, framing potential regulatory constraints as threats to national interests. Other AI policies at least claim that ethics and competition are different things. Stargate abandons that pretense entirely. The Stargate initiative illustrates Fritsch's (2011) insight about technological system life cycles: as AI systems mature, they increasingly *shape* rather than *reflect* social priorities. What began as an applied field with at least theoretical openness to various value frameworks has increasingly solidified around operational priorities that serve existing power structures. The values that might enable greater democratic oversight and equitable distribution of AI's benefits are systematically marginalized in favor of those that maintain competitive advantage and institutional control.

THE CORPORATION AS AGENT

Evolving Corporate Agency

In 2022, Amazon shareholders convened for the company's annual meeting where they were given the opportunity to vote on a couple dozen proposals by the company and from shareholders themselves. One proposal was for an independent company to conduct an audit of Amazon warehouses for working conditions and safety, after allegations of unusually high reports of worker injury rates in their facilities (Tulipshare, n.d.). The vote received 44% of the independent vote which, when accounting for founder Jeff Bezos' 9.8% stake that voted against the audit, represented a 53% majority of the independent vote (Morningstar, n.d.). This was an unusually prominent signal for Amazon to take action and one that is often heeded with care, since shareholder votes can control things like executive board placements and compensation. In this scenario, though, Amazon stuck to their minimal required obligation of not taking action on the "minority" vote, allowing them to dismiss these safety investigations. This resistance to audit persisted despite public pressure and explicit concerns from major institutional investors about reputational and operational risks.

The Amazon case reveals something crucial about how Big Tech operates today; corporations increasingly function not as mere extensions of shareholder will, but as independent actors with distinct institutional values and priorities that are independent of shareholders and even employees. Institutions like this can easily take on a life of their own or, put more explicitly, become wholly self-regarding agents. Rather than adjusting policies in response to shareholder concerns (which have continued to emerge, such as in warehouse unionization efforts in recent years), Amazon has increasingly defended its approach as necessary for maintaining its operational model. Through this stance it asserts that the company's own interests and values take precedence over those of its constituent stakeholders.

Two notable features of the Amazon case are related to individual agency. Jeff Bezos retains ownership control (which today is above 10%) that can swing a vote from a minority to majority. No other individual holds such influence, which is also enjoyed to an even greater extent by Mark Zuckerberg and Elon Musk with their respective organizations. Likewise, the Amazon board and CEO Andy Jassey chose to turn a blind eye to the democratic process of proposal voting, thereby flouting the traditionally ascribed power to shareholders in the concerns of their investments. Thus, we advocate for legal frameworks that acknowledge the concentrated power of individual executives rather than treating corporations as collective decision-making bodies.

What makes this different from the perennial tension between corporate interests and workers' interests? For Big Tech, the difference is a newly bold paradigm of indifference towards stakeholders, an obsession with operational values that eclipses outside perspectives, and their mobilization of technology to reinforce those values. Amazon implements algorithmic management systems to govern warehouse workers that track productivity metrics, issue automated warnings, and even generate termination notices (Jee, 2019). These represent a form of automated governance that operates according to internally-defined values of efficiency and productivity rather than externally-negotiated standards of worker wellbeing. The algorithmic systems embody Amazon's operational values in a way that transcends the preferences of individual executives or shareholders. The company thus emerges as an independent agent, yet highly influenced by the voices of the few over the many.

Independent agency, once it emerges for the corporation, is likely to snowball and self-reinforce. John Steinbeck captured this dynamic succinctly when writing about big banks in his novel *The Grapes of Wrath*:

> *It happens that every man in a bank hates what the bank does, and yet the bank does it. The bank is something more than men, I tell you. It's the monster. Men made it, but they can't control it. (Steinbeck, 1939, p. 23)*

Big Tech as the modern monster is evidenced by a progressively incorrigible, self-interested function in the world despite serving a globally pervasive social role. As these firms become further integrated with state functions, this independent agency becomes even more pronounced, with significant implications for how values are defined and prioritized in technological development.

Comparative Analysis: Alternative State-Tech Models

Understanding the displacement of social values in US AI policy requires examining alternative models of state-technology relations globally. This highlights the unique nature of the current American AI regulatory perspective. Different global leaders in AI possess different approaches to balancing operational and social impact values, and highlighting these distills the evolving US approach.

China has established itself as one of the world's earliest and most comprehensive regulators of AI technologies, with a distinct governance framework that differs markedly from the US approach. China's regulatory landscape features three interconnected pillars of regulation: measures governing recommendation algorithms, rules for "deep synthesis" (synthetically generated content), and provisions for generative AI services. The Interim Measures for the Management of Generative Artificial Intelligence Services, finalized in July 2023 and implemented in August 2023, marked China's position as one of the first countries to formally regulate generative AI technology ("Interim Measures for Generative AI," 2023). These measures were less restrictive than initially drafted, demonstrating China's attempt to balance content control with innovation. The final version somewhat reduced regulatory burdens while placing greater emphasis on compliance with privacy law. A cornerstone of China's approach is its algorithm registry system, which requires detailed disclosures about how AI systems are trained and deployed (Sheehan & Du, 2022). This system exemplifies China's preference for direct oversight of algorithms rather than just their outputs. More recently, new draft regulations in 2024 outlined additional security measures for generative AI service providers, covering areas such as securing training data, protecting AI models, and implementing overall security protocols (China National Information Security Standardization Technical Committee, 2024). There is even a draft Artificial Intelligence Law that includes a "negative list" of areas that AI companies cannot enter without explicit government approval. Such governance is directly in contrast with the previously noted "sphere transgressions" that US Big Tech has encroached upon without oversight. While still in development, this law represents China's move toward a more consolidated regulatory approach (Yang & Ding, 2024).

The Chinese model is characterized by "directed technology development," wherein the state takes a proactive role in shaping AI's trajectory through formal, binding regulations. This approach places the state in a firmly directive position relative to technology companies, creating a clear hierarchy that contrasts sharply with the US model of corporate-state integration. When juxtaposed, the US model runs more in the opposite polarity of corporations running the AI posture of the government.

The European Union presents another distinct model, characterized by a "values-first" approach to AI governance. The EU AI Act, which officially entered into force on August 1, 2024, represents the world's first comprehensive horizontal legal framework designed to govern AI systems based on their level of risk to society. The European model places social impact values at the center of its approach, explicitly enshrining principles of fairness, transparency, and human oversight within a legally binding framework. Unlike the US model, where corporations increasingly set the terms of governance, the EU maintains a clearer separation between regulator and regulated. And unlike the Chinese model, where regulations serve both to control information and direct technological development, the EU approach focuses primarily on mitigating social harms while enabling innovation within ethical boundaries. A key distinction of the European approach is its explicit prioritization of "human-centric AI" and social impact values over operational values like efficiency or competitive advantage. The EU treats AI ethics not as a secondary consideration but as a primary design requirement, evidenced by its strict requirements for high-risk AI systems, including mandatory risk assessments, documentation requirements, and human oversight measures.

These alternative governance models reveal several important lessons about the US approach and its positioning within the wider continuum of global AI governance efforts. First, the increasing integration between Big Tech and the US government is a distinct third path between the state-directed model of China and the regulatory separation model of the EU. This "tech-state fusion" in the US creates a unique set of governance challenges, as entities with significant power over technology development simultaneously help craft the rules that govern them. Second, while China's model subordinates technology companies to state objectives and the EU model imposes external constraints on them, the US model increasingly incorporates tech companies as essential partners in governance itself. This creates a fundamentally different power dynamic that systematically privileges operational values over social impact values, as these companies help define what "responsible AI" means within governance frameworks. Third, all three models are still evolving, but in different directions. China is moving from targeted regulations towards a more comprehensive framework, the EU has established a comprehensive framework and is now actively bolstering its implementation, while the US has relied primarily on voluntary commitments and executive orders without binding legislation.

Beyond the traditional US-EU-China triangle, alternative approaches are emerging across the Global South that challenge dominant value hierarchies. African contexts reveal alternative approaches that explicitly challenge operational-first frameworks. Research on AI adoption across African public administrations shows that effectiveness depends on balancing technical efficiency with local values like ubuntu and "spirit of community", which prioritize deliberative processes and collective decision-making over pure algorithmic optimization (Plantinga, 2022). These frameworks demonstrate more alignment with local working practices and values rather than simply maximizing operational metrics. The current displacement of social values in US AI policy is neither inevitable nor irreversible (at least inherently), but is instead the product of a specific configuration of corporate-state relations that could be recalibrated to better balance operational and social impact values.

IMPLICATIONS FOR AI ETHICS AND GOVERNANCE

Diverting Paths

The proliferation of AI ethics frameworks, governance guidelines, and principles around 2020 and the years following was an overwhelming deluge of documents. Every organization from fintech startups to the Chinese Communist Party have authored some sort of charter on AI principles, with some setting the standard for other organizations to adopt. In general, these ethics frameworks say similar things and mostly cover similar principles. Where they differ, though, is in their emphasis and focus.

The EU's AI Act explicitly positions social impact values as constraints on technological development, prohibiting certain applications based on unacceptable risks to fundamental rights and establishing risk categories with corresponding obligations (European Parliament & Council of the European Union, 2024). It represents a framework where social values can actually limit operational imperatives — values taken seriously enough to prioritize over operational considerations in many cases. This contrasts sharply with both US policy shifts and corporate AI frameworks, which typically present social and operational values side by side without explicit hierarchies but encounter significant limitations upon implementation.

Overall, three key patterns emerge in how contemporary frameworks treat social and operational values:

1) **Differential implementation:** Even when social impact values are articulated with equal prominence in policy documents and ethics frameworks, they typically receive less robust implementation mechanisms, enforcement resources, and concrete metrics than operational values. This implementation gap is particularly evident in the high-profile AI commitments made by tech companies.
2) **Measurement gaps:** The metrics for assessing adherence to operational values (efficiency, accuracy, security) are typically more developed than those for social impact values (fairness, sustainability). This measurement asymmetry creates an implicit prioritization through the governance principle that "what gets measured gets managed". When AI systems are evaluated primarily on quantifiable performance metrics rather than more complex social impact measures, the former inevitably drive development priorities.
3) **Increasing tension:** Recent policy developments suggest growing divergence between frameworks that maintain balance between both value types and those that increasingly privilege operational values. This tension is particularly pronounced in contexts of high tech-state integration, where institutional imperatives align more directly with maintaining competitive advantage and national security.

The pattern of differential value treatment is becoming increasingly evident in state-level responses to the absence of comprehensive federal AI legislation. In 2024 alone, lawmakers across the United States introduced more than 700 AI-related bills, with state approaches varying significantly in their emphasis on social versus operational values (Tech Policy Press, 2025). These policy choices materially encode institutional priorities, as seen in energy infrastructure. Research from the Institute of Electrical and Electronics Engineers (IEEE) on energy justice highlights that "the Electrical Power Grid… is a massive network of infrastructure that most scholars and practitioners treat as disconnected from energy justice concerns," despite containing, "...a series of unseen justice dimensions" (IEEE, 2023). When AI systems for grid management optimize primarily for operational metrics rather than equity considerations, they materially encode institutional priorities that privilege administrative efficiency over equitable access and social justice in the energy sector.

Defining Operational and Social Impact Values

The relationship between ethical rhetoric and governance practice becomes clearer when examining specific ethical principles across frameworks. For example, the principle of "transparency" appears in virtually all major AI ethics frameworks but with dramatically different implementation approaches depending on the institutional context. While some frameworks like the EU AI Act establish detailed requirements for documentation, risk assessment, and disclosure, others define transparency more narrowly; often limited to general explanations of AI capabilities rather than detailed disclosure of algorithmic processes, training data, or potential impacts (Jobin, Ienca, & Vayena, 2019).

Though we've discussed the kinds of characteristics that operational and social impact values embody, it's useful to elaborate on their definitions and how they are uniquely conceived of depending on their positioning and framing. Some examples of operational values include:

Accuracy: Accuracy represents the degree to which an AI system's outputs correspond to ground truth or desired outcomes. While often framed primarily as a technical metric, accuracy carries profound ethical implications and is frequently prioritized as an engineering objective, with AI systems optimized to maximize aggregate performance metrics like precision and recall.

Security: Protection from threats, system integrity, and robustness against attacks. Security values prioritize preventing unauthorized access or manipulation and ensuring reliable operation, particularly in critical infrastructure or national security contexts.

Efficiency: Optimization of resource utilization, speed of operation, and cost-effectiveness. Efficiency values prioritize doing more with less, often measured through quantitative performance metrics like processing time or resource consumption.

Innovation and Competitive Advantage: Advancement of capabilities, novel applications, geopolitical leadership, and competitive technological development. Innovation values prioritize breaking new ground, often measured through patents, technical benchmarks, or market position. The revocation of directives perceived as "hindering AI innovation" exemplifies how this value has become a primary justification for limiting regulatory constraints.

These operational values are not inherently problematic and even serve important functions in AI development. For our analysis, their significance lies not in their presence but in how they relate to social impact values within governance frameworks.

Social impact values in AI ethics frameworks emphasize the broader implications of AI systems for individuals, communities, and society. These values reflect normative commitments to equity, justice, and public good. Some examples of social values includes:

Fairness: Equitable treatment across groups, absence of discriminatory impacts, and just distribution of benefits and harms. Fairness values prioritize ensuring AI systems do not perpetuate or amplify existing social inequities. While prominently featured in ethics statements, the implementation mechanisms for fairness often lack specificity and enforceability compared to operational values.

Accountability: Clear responsibility for AI systems' impacts, mechanisms for redress when harms occur, and liability frameworks. Accountability values prioritize ensuring that someone answers for negative consequences of AI deployment.

Transparency: Visibility into how AI systems function, explainability of decisions, and access to information about development processes. Transparency values prioritize enabling understanding and scrutiny of AI systems. Despite rhetorical commitments to transparency, many high-stakes AI applications remain shielded from meaningful scrutiny through proprietary protections and security classifications.

Sustainability: Long-term environmental, social, and economic viability. Sustainability values prioritize consideration of intergenerational impacts and resource constraints. Sustainability considerations receive limited attention in most governance frameworks in part because of the difficulty in quantifying environmental impact or the seemingly miniscule benefit of doing so (e.g. the carbon output of a small company's HR chatbot is not seen as significant enough to warrant tracking and measurement).

The relationship between operational and social values in AI ethics is not necessarily zero-sum, but in practice, tensions frequently emerge that require prioritization decisions. For example, the pursuit of efficiency in model training often involves amassing larger datasets with less rigorous consent and fewer privacy protections. The real-world consequences of this value prioritization become starkly apparent in high-stakes AI deployments. Consider the ongoing Workday lawsuit, where Derek Mobley and other plaintiffs claim the company's AI-powered hiring system systematically discriminates against applicants over 40, Black candidates, and those with disabilities. Used by over 11,000 organizations worldwide, Workday's automated screening tools can reject job applications within minutes (even, to many applicants' chagrin, in the middle of the night) without human review (Wiessner, 2024). When confronted with these discrimination allegations, Workday's defense has centered entirely on operational metrics: the system's efficiency in processing massive volumes of applications and its technical accuracy in matching skills to job requirements. The company has resisted calls for algorithmic transparency or bias audits, arguing that such requirements would compromise the system's effectiveness and create administrative burdens for clients (Duffy, 2025). In May 2025, a federal judge allowed the case to proceed as a nationwide collective action, noting that the central question is "whether Workday's AI recommendation system has a disparate impact on applicants over forty" (Fisher Phillips, 2025). Here we see efficiency imperatives, namely the ability to screen hundreds of thousands of applicants quickly, taking clear precedence over fairness concerns, even when those concerns involve fundamental questions of equal opportunity in employment.

Similarly, competitive pressures for rapid deployment can conflict with thorough testing for disparate impacts across different demographic groups. Notably, model *fairness* is often at odds with model *accuracy* because intentional weighting and fine-tuning to reduce bias in certain categories will consequently introduce accuracy degradation into the model.

The Responsibility Gap

As Big Tech and state institutions become increasingly intertwined, a systematic diffusion of accountability emerges that fundamentally transforms how responsibility for AI outcomes is allocated. Unlike traditional governance models where lines of authority are relatively clear, tech-state partnerships create intentionally ambiguous responsibility structures that benefit both parties. Corporate actors gain regulatory breathing room and influence over policy, while state actors gain access to cutting-edge capabilities without bearing full accountability for potential harms. It is a deeply consequential case of finger pointing.

This diffusion occurs through several distinct mechanisms that collectively undermine traditional accountability frameworks. First, jurisdictional complexity creates opportunities for strategic regulatory arbitrage, where AI development can shift between locations to evade oversight. Second, contractual arrangements between tech firms and government agencies often include liability shields and indemnification clauses that deliberately fragment responsibility. Third, the classification of AI systems as "proprietary" or "classified" creates informational asymmetries that prevent effective public scrutiny, with neither party fully accountable for outcomes. What distinguishes this accountability gap from conventional regulatory challenges is its deliberate architectural design. The responsibility diffusion is not merely an unfortunate side effect but often an intentional feature of these partnerships.

When the Pentagon contracted with tech firms for Project Maven, for instance, the partnership structure allowed both parties to deflect certain forms of criticism (Mohsin, 2024). The government could point to corporate implementation decisions while corporations could cite government requirements, creating a circular pattern of deflected responsibility. This is a classic shell game in government contracting (external consultants are often facetiously referred to as "getting paid to take the blame"), but AI projects raise the stakes and require more explicit accountability. This is because AI is designed to mirror human decisions, which are filled with value judgments and moral dilemmas, many of which are naturally encountered by AI when it is employed to make those same judgments as part of its decisions (Murphy, 2023). As such, the buck needs to stop somewhere, which is increasingly difficult given cooperative incentives.

Lastly, the cost of operational values are felt unevenly across the globe. In Karen Hao's (2025, pp. 279-287) comprehensive new book *Empire of AI,* she describes how the scale of computing power has spilled over into the Global South. A substantial amount of energy and computer chips are needed to accommodate the functionality of generative AI systems. The economies of Chile and Uruguay have suffered due to the construction of large data centers, which originally promised foreign investment and job opportunities, but have since had a negative effect on communities. The scale of the construction has crowded out the potential for other economies to flourish as both countries are now rather dependent upon the industry. Additionally, to keep cool, data centers require potable water, which Google planned to take from the drinking supply in Uruguay in 2023, a country already suffering from droughts and agricultural setbacks. Public backlash thwarted Google's attempt to use 2 million gallons of fresh water per day for their data center, but it will not be the last time the Global South has to deal with these proposals. Hao reports on many other consequences which stem from Big Tech prioritizing their own objectives.

This systematic prioritization of operational values over social impact considerations in AI stem from a lack of oversight. Big Tech's data colonialism is enabled by its relatively frictionless association with the state (and even international organizations such as the World Trade Organization due to extensive lobbying) which provides a lack of regulatory measures that otherwise could prevent unbridled exploitation of global communities (Arun, 2025).

MORAL RESPONSIBILITY

Consequences for affected stakeholders and communities

When the norm for AI stewardship is deferral of blame and unclear accountability, those deploying AI are insulated while those subject to its operation are left holding the burden of any unintended consequences or negative outcomes. This burden-shifting manifests in several key ways. First, redress mechanisms are systematically neglected. While considerable resources are dedicated to optimizing AI systems for operational metrics like processing speed and accuracy, comparatively little investment goes toward developing accessible, effective channels for affected parties to seek recourse when harmed. Research shows that users "structurally lack such mechanisms" for contesting AI decisions, and contemporary AI systems often lack accessible transparency records or mechanisms for redress because the system was not designed with redress in mind (Fanni et al., 2023).

Second, AI is often implicitly used to increase efficiencies at the sacrifice of individual rights because there is no accountable party for mistreatment that arises. Take the example of HR resume screening increasingly incorporating AI as a standard part of the process. Many job applications will ask, "Are you okay with AI being used to evaluate your application?" The applicant may not want to answer "No" out of concern about the AI model's efficacy, bias, or other potential harms, but in practice must answer "Yes" or their application will be effectively tossed out or deprioritized. Posing this illusory choice checks the box for "consent" in the hiring process while containing no pathway for it to be altered or rectified. Just like that, the operational value of efficiency in application screening has overtaken any semblance of fairness or transparency.

Third, the displacement of social values proceeds with limited public resistance because it aligns with revealed preferences when trade-offs become concrete. Recent research on public attitudes toward algorithmic fairness reveals that even citizens nominally committed to social values will abandon them when operational costs become substantial. When fairness-focused algorithms required sacrificing 15% accuracy, only 15% of participants supported them, down from 83% when accuracy costs were minimal (Mourali et al., 2025). This empirical reality helps explain why operational values so easily displace social considerations.

Further empirical research confirms this pattern is pervasive across the industry. For example, Raji et al. (2020) demonstrated that facial recognition companies marketed overall accuracy rates of 85-99% while concealing substantial performance disparities, with darker females consistently identified as the worst-performing subgroup across multiple commercial APIs. Fairness considerations were effectively concealed behind aggregated accuracy metrics until independent researchers studied these patterns in depth.

Corporate agency and accountability

In a collection of writings entitled "The Moral Responsibility of Firms", Phillip Pettit argues that corporations are "conversable agents" that can make commitments and be held accountable for fulfilling them (Pettit, 2017). The independent corporation possesses an assertive corporate agency where the company increasingly operates according to its own internally-generated logic rather than as a responsive entity negotiating among shareholder demands, worker needs, and consumer preferences. Pettit argues that corporations construct a mind of their own by building "the voice of the corporate body in a way that makes it relatively autonomous from the individual voices of members…" who then "make up the corporate mind that their actions as members then go on to express" (Pettit, 2017, p. 25). In Big Tech we see the corporate mind disproportionately inflated by the power of individual leaders, as previously demonstrated, which aids the definition of these firms themselves as conversable.

Pettit's framework for corporate moral responsibility provides a theoretical lens for addressing the accountability challenges in tech-state partnerships. He argues that corporations can and should be understood as moral agents in their own right. This understanding of corporate moral agency cuts through some of the accountability diffusion described earlier. When corporations are recognized as moral agents, they cannot simply deflect responsibility to market forces, competitive pressures, or government mandates. Instead, they must account for how their institutional values become embedded in technological systems and the consequences of those embeddings for affected communities.

Pettit's approach is particularly valuable for addressing the ethics of AI developed through tech-state partnerships because it rejects both extreme positions: that corporations bear no moral responsibility (only individuals do) or that corporate responsibility entirely displaces individual accountability. Applying this framework to AI governance reveals why voluntary ethics frameworks have proven insufficient. When corporate moral agency is not properly recognized in governance structures, ethics principles remain aspirational rather than binding. The proper acknowledgment of corporate moral agency would require governance mechanisms that can hold firms accountable for the values embedded in their AI systems, regardless of whether those systems were developed at state request. Such mechanisms would need to include both material consequences for harmful outcomes and procedural requirements for demonstrating responsible design choices throughout the development process.

Suggestions for AI ethics and governance

We'll consider some more actionable mechanisms for positioning incentives correctly. There are a slew of solutions that are regularly offered to ameliorate concerns we've articulated about Big Tech influencing AI ethics and governance standards such as multi-stakeholder convenings and third party audits, among others. Interventions like these would undoubtedly prove useful in managing private influence from running amok in the US government. These are structural limitations and rules, but what are some ways to more directly target the incentive asymmetry between social impact values and operational values?

In tech-state partnerships like government contracting, performance-based contracting models could link government compensation to social value outcomes rather than merely technical capabilities. This is a continually developing shift that is already being influenced by the OMB directives and US policy over the last several years and would help change incentives. Drawing lessons from the Environmental, Social, and Governance (ESG) movement, we can envision AI governance frameworks that tie concrete financial benefits to measurable social value metrics. Governments can leverage their purchasing power to counterbalance the operational imperatives that currently dominate tech-state collaborations. Perhaps most importantly, the expansion of mandatory disclosure requirements from just government agencies to include the private sector would help bring all AI technology companies to a similar standard. Backed by penalties for misrepresentation, policies like these could harness market and reputational forces to elevate social values. This is similar in scope to both the EU and China's AI mandates. By requiring standardized reporting on algorithmic impact assessments, bias audits, and stakeholder engagement processes, policymakers could enable investors, customers, and civil society organizations to direct resources toward companies demonstrating genuine commitment to social values.

One particularly promising approach gaining traction is the regulatory markets model for AI governance (Sandhu et al., 2025). In this framework, governments define clear public safety and governance outcomes while licensed private regulatory service providers (RSPs) compete to develop effective methods to achieve these outcomes. Companies that develop or deploy AI must purchase services from licensed RSPs, while insurance providers help quantify and manage risks. This model directly addresses the technical deficit (where public regulators lack expertise to oversee cutting-edge AI) and the democratic deficit (where decisions about societal impact are concentrated in private firms) that we've identified throughout this chapter. Recent pilot projects demonstrate the viability of this approach, with Phase 1 pilots testing basic mechanics in controlled settings and Phase 2 expanding to complex, industry-specific scenarios in high-risk areas like frontier AI models. This market-based solution doesn't replace government oversight but rather enhances it by creating a competitive ecosystem where innovation in regulatory approaches can flourish while maintaining democratic accountability.

Zooming out, what institutional design goals should we strive for to better balance all aspects of AI ethics and governance for a thriving society? First, the current concentration of AI expertise in large technology companies creates significant knowledge asymmetries that undermine effective oversight. Alternative models would establish independent public research institutions with comparable technical capabilities but different incentive structures, enabling them to evaluate claims made by industry and government about AI capabilities and limitations. Again, some efforts in this area have been made by the US government like NIST's AI Safety Institute, but it's currently unclear if those will persist. After all, these institutions require sustained public funding, academic freedom, and insulation from immediate political pressures to maintain their independence over time.

Second, participatory governance mechanisms are always beneficial and offer another approach to counterbalancing the disproportionate influence of tech firms in policymaking. Current AI governance processes primarily involve consultation with technical experts and industry representatives, with limited input from affected communities or civil society organizations. More inclusive models would establish structured processes for diverse stakeholder participation throughout the policy development cycle, not merely as token consultation but as substantive input into decision-making. Indeed, civil society organizations are already pioneering such participatory models while demonstrating effective counter-strategies to tech-state value displacement. The Algorithmic Justice League's campaigns have pressured IBM, Amazon, and Microsoft to impose moratoriums on police use of facial recognition, showing how organized advocacy can shift corporate behavior (Johnson, 2020). Organizations like Data for Black Lives have gone further, developing frameworks for community-owned data infrastructures that embody social values from the ground up (2024). These civic innovations complement professional efforts. Such multi-stakeholder pressure creates alternative pathways for AI development that center human needs, demonstrating that the displacement of social values is contested terrain rather than a foregone conclusion.

Third, international coordination frameworks provide essential counterweights to the national security and general "AI-race" imperatives that currently drive value displacement in AI governance. When AI development is framed primarily as a competitive race between nations, social impact considerations are easily sacrificed for perceived strategic advantage. Alternative models would establish transnational governance mechanisms focused on shared challenges like algorithmic discrimination, transparency, and accountability. While complete global harmonization is neither feasible nor necessarily desirable, coordination on minimum standards could help prevent regulatory arbitrage that undermines social value protections. There have been many attempts for international standards like this such as at the 2025 Paris AI Summit, where the UK and US refused to sign an agreement on "inclusive and sustainable" AI (Milmo & Courca, 2025). Given this, international harmonization of AI objectives may continue to be challenging.

Lastly, liability frameworks represent a crucial and often overlooked dimension of AI governance. Current legal structures create significant barriers to holding companies that develop AI accountable for harmful outcomes, particularly when systems are deployed through public-private partnerships. Alternative approaches would establish clearer liability standards that create direct financial incentives for prioritizing fairness and harm prevention alongside operational efficiency. This might include expanded doctrines of vicarious liability, affirmative duties of care, or mandatory insurance requirements that internalize the social costs currently externalized to affected individuals and communities. The EU AI Act imposes penalties on firms that violate its provisions, but the real challenge is in balancing the significance of penalties with the offenses.

Concluding remarks

These alternative governance considerations acknowledge that rebalancing values in AI policy requires more than good principles or intentions. It demands institutional arrangements that can withstand the powerful forces of tech-state fusion. By creating countervailing centers of expertise, expanding participation in governance processes, coordinating across jurisdictions, and establishing meaningful accountability mechanisms, these interventions aim to create space for social values to influence AI development and deployment even within the constraints of existing power structures. The path forward requires not just technical innovation but political imagination to create governance frameworks that genuinely serve broader human flourishing rather than merely reinforcing existing operational value dominance that is concentrated with those in power.

These governance strategies depend on regulatory approaches that are increasingly under threat. But our real goal here goes beyond policy reform and advocates a shift in how we think about AI's role in society. Our claim is that social, democratic values are being displaced quietly because everything else is so loud; the technology sector binding with the state confronts us with a double-edged predicament, which necessarily creates heightened stakes and tensions. Social impact values *make contact* with users in a morally significant way, and public knowledge of how AI systems can be designed and developed will yield a necessary advantage to engage with this technology. The awareness of this private-public entwinement we've described should provoke an inward turn — a recognition that our lives *change* when novel technologies are deployed en masse. It is a radical disruption. Our instinct is to live in accord with innovation, but that instinct prompts us to bear all of the associated costs.

AI DISCLOSURE STATEMENT

This chapter was developed with assistance from Claude Sonnet 4, an AI assistant, which was used to review drafts, suggest text to improve readability, provide feedback on structure, and help identify citation gaps. The AI tool assisted with organizing ideas and refining prose while all substantive arguments, original analysis, and core intellectual contributions remain the work of the human authors. All AI-generated suggestions were critically evaluated by the authors to reflect their own scholarly judgment and expertise.

REFERENCES

Arun, C. (2025, March 7). *"Data Colonialism" and the Political Economy of Big Tech.* Lawfare. https://www.lawfaremedia.org/article/data-colonialism--and-the-political-economy-of-big-tech

Brooks, H. (1980). Technology, Evolution, and Purpose. *Daedalus*, *109*(1), 65–81.

Buchanan, B. (2020). *The AI triad and what it means for national security strategy.* Center for Security and Emerging Technology. DOI: 10.51593/20200021

China National Information Security Standardization Technical Committee. (2024, March 1). Generative artificial intelligence service security requirements (Draft for Comment). https://www.tc260.org.cn/upload/2024-03-01/1709282398070082466.pdf

Claassen, R. (2022). Political theories of the business corporation. *Philosophy Compass*, *18*(1), e12892. DOI: 10.1111/phc3.12892 PMID: 37033445

Data for Black Lives. (2024). About us. https://d4bl.org/about.html

Duffy, C. (2025, May 22). Lawsuit claims discrimination by Workday's hiring tech prevented people over 40 from getting hired. CNN. https://www.cnn.com/2025/05/22/tech/workday-ai-hiring-discrimination-lawsuit

Edwards, P., & Hecht, G. (2010). History and the Technopolitics of Identity: The Case of Apartheid South Africa. *Journal of Southern African Studies*, *36*(3), 619–639. DOI: 10.1080/03057070.2010.507568

European Parliament, & Council of the European Union. (2024). Regulation (EU) 2024/1689 of the European Parliament and of the Council of 13 June 2024 laying down harmonised rules on artificial intelligence (Artificial Intelligence Act) and amending Regulations (EC) No 300/2008, (EU) No 167/2013, (EU) No 168/2013, (EU) 2018/858 and (EU) 2019/2144 and Directives 2014/90/EU, (EU) 2016/797 and (EU) 2020/1828 (OJ L, 2024/1689). EUR-Lex. https://eur-lex.europa.eu/eli/reg/2024/1689/oj/eng

Fanni, R., Steinkogler, V. E., Zampedri, G., & Pierson, J. (2023). Enhancing human agency through redress in Artificial Intelligence Systems. *AI & Society*, *38*(2), 537–547. DOI: 10.1007/s00146-022-01454-7 PMID: 35692234

Fisher Phillips. (2025, May 22). Discrimination Lawsuit Over Workday's AI Hiring Tools Can Proceed as Class Action: 6 Things Employers Should Do After Latest Court Decision. Fisher Phillips. https://www.fisherphillips.com/en/news-insights/discrimination-lawsuit-over-workdays-ai-hiring-tools-can-proceed-as-class-action-6-things.html

Frazier, K. (2024). Avoiding a military-AI complex. Lawfare. https://www.lawfaremedia.org/article/avoiding-a-military-ai-complex

Friesen, G. (2025, January 23). Trump's AI push: Understanding the $500 billion Stargate initiative. Forbes. https://www.forbes.com/sites/garthfriesen/2025/01/23/trumps-ai-push-understanding-the-500-billion-stargate-initiative/

Fritsch, S. (2011). Technology and Global Affairs. *International Studies Perspectives*, *12*(1), 27–45. DOI: 10.1111/j.1528-3585.2010.00417.x

Hao, K. (2025). Empire of AI. Penguin Books. Hecht, G. (1998). *The Radiance of France: Nuclear Power and National Identity After World War II*. MIT Press.

Hecht, G. (2011). *Entangled Geographies: Empire and Technopolitics in the Global Cold War*. MIT Press. DOI: 10.7551/mitpress/9780262515788.001.0001

Heidegger, M. (2008). *Being and Time*. HarperCollins.

IEEE. (2023). Energy justice and the electrical power grid: Unseen dimensions of justice in infrastructure. IEEE Xplore. https://ieeexplore.ieee.org/abstract/document/10659286

Jee, C. (2019, April 26). Amazon's system for tracking its warehouse workers can automatically fire them. MIT Technology Review. https://www.technologyreview.com/2019/04/26/1021/amazons-system-for-tracking-its-warehouse-workers-can-automatically-fire-them/

Jobin, A., Ienca, M., & Vayena, E. (2019). The global landscape of AI ethics guidelines. arXiv. https://arxiv.org/pdf/1906.11668

Johnson, K. (2020). IBM walked away from facial recognition — what about Amazon and Microsoft? VentureBeat. https://venturebeat.com/ai/ibm-walked-away-from-facial-recognition-what-about-amazon-and-microsoft/

Jullien, B., & Sand-Zantman, W. (2021). The economics of platforms: A theory guide for competition policy. *Information Economics and Policy*, *54*, 100880. DOI: 10.1016/j.infoecopol.2020.100880

Khanal, S., Zhang, H., & Taeihagh, A. (2024). Why and how is the power of Big Tech increasing in the policy process? The case of generative AI. *Policy and Society*, •••, 1–18.

Kumar, S., & Moore, K. (2002). The Evolution of Global Positioning System (GPS) Technology. *Journal of Science Education and Technology*, *11*(1), 59–80. DOI: 10.1023/A:1013999415003

Leparmentier, A. (2025, February 27). *Elon Musk's empire has benefited from $38 billion in contracts and government aid*. Le Monde. https://www.lemonde.fr/en/economy/article/2025/02/27/elon-musk-s-empire-has-benefited-from-38-billion-in-contracts-and-government-aid_6738618_19.html#

Millon, D. (1990). Theories of the Corporation. *Duke Law Journal*, *1990*(2), 201–262. DOI: 10.2307/1372611

Milmo, D., & Courea, E. (2025, February 11). US and UK refuse to sign Paris summit declaration on 'inclusive' AI. The Guardian. https://www.theguardian.com/technology/2025/feb/11/us-uk-paris-ai-summit-artificial-intelligence-declaration

Mulhney, M. (2025, February 26). Navigating the geopolitical stakes of artificial intelligence. Northwestern Engineering News. https://www.mccormick.northwestern.edu/news/articles/2025/02/navigating-the-geopolitical-stakes-of-artificial-intelligence/

Mohsin, S. (2024, February 29). Inside Project Maven, the US military's AI project. Bloomberg. https://www.bloomberg.com/news/newsletters/2024-02-29/inside-project-maven-the-us-military-s-ai-project

Morningstar. (n.d.). Amazon asked by investors to explain working conditions. Morningstar UK. Retrieved April 27, 2025, from https://www.morningstar.co.uk/uk/news/231012/amazon-asked-by-investors-to-explain-working-conditions.aspx

Mourali, M., Novakowski, D., Pogacar, R., & Brigden, N. (2025). Public perception of accuracy-fairness trade-offs in algorithmic decisions in the United States. *PLoS One*, *20*(3), e0319861. DOI: 10.1371/journal.pone.0319861 PMID: 40080482

Murphy, M. A. (2023). Using structured ethical techniques to facilitate reasoning in technology ethics. *AI and Ethics*, *5*(1), 479–488. DOI: 10.1007/s43681-023-00371-9

National Research Council. (1999). *Funding a Revolution: Government Support for Computing Research.* The National Academies Press.

Office of Management and Budget. (2025, February). Accelerating Federal Use of AI through Innovation, Governance, and Public Trust (Memorandum M-25-21). The White House. https://www.whitehouse.gov/wp-content/uploads/2025/02/M-25-21-Accelerating-Federal-Use-of-AI-through-Innovation-Governance-and-Public-Trust.pdf

Pettit, P. (2017). Conversable agents. In E. W. Orts & N. C. Smith (Eds.), The moral responsibility of firms (online ed.). Oxford University Press. DOI: 10.1093/oso/9780198738534.001.0001

Plantinga, P. (2022). Digital discretion and public administration in Africa: Implications for the use of artificial intelligence. Information Development, 40(2), 332-352. (Original work published 2024)DOI: 10.1177/02666669221117526

Raji, I. D., Gebru, T., Mitchell, M., Buolamwini, J., Lee, E., & Denton, E. (2020). Saving face: Investigating the ethical concerns of facial recognition auditing. In Proceedings of the 2020 AAAI/ACM Conference on AI, Ethics, and Society (pp. 145-151).

Runciman, D. (2023). *The Handover: How We Gave Control of Our Lives to Corporations, States and AIs.* Profile Books.

Sandhu, J., Arai, M., Baldridge, D., Ryan, D., & Hadfield, G. (2025). Co-designing regulatory markets: Road-mapping the future of AI governance. Schwartz Reisman Institute for Technology and Society, University of Toronto. https://srinstitute.utoronto.ca/news/co-designing-regulatory-markets-for-ai

Shah, R., & Kirchhoff, C. (2024). *Unit X: How the Pentagon and Silicon Valley are transforming the future of war. Publisher.* Simon & Schuster.

Sharon, T. & Gellert, R. (2024) Regulating Big Tech expansionism? Sphere transgressions and the limits of Europe's digital regulatory strategy, Information, Communication & Society, (27):15, pp. 2651-2668.

Sheehan, M., & Du, S. (2022, December 15). What China's algorithm registry reveals about AI governance. Carnegie Endowment for International Peace. https://carnegieendowment.org/posts/2022/12/what-chinas-algorithm-registry-reveals-about-ai-governance?lang=en Sherman, J. (2019, March 6). Stop calling artificial intelligence research an 'arms race'. The

State Council of China. (2017). New generation artificial intelligence development plan. https://digichina.stanford.edu/work/full-translation-chinas-new-generation-artificial-intell igence-development-plan-2017/

Steinbeck, J. (1939). *The Grapes of Wrath*. Penguin Books.

Stokel-Walker, C. (2024, July 24). *Many people think AI is already sentient - and that's a big problem*. New Scientist. https://www.newscientist.com/article/2439884-many-people-think-ai-is-already-sentient-and-thats-a-big-problem/

Tech Policy Press. (2025, January 26). 2025 may be the year of AI legislation: Will we see consensus rules or a patchwork? Tech Policy Press. https://www.techpolicy.press/2025-may-be-the-year-of-ai-legislation-will-we-see-consensus-rules-or-a-patchwork

The White House. (2025, January 18). Ending radical and wasteful government DEI programs and preferential treatment. The White House. https://www.whitehouse.gov/presidential-actions/2025/01/ending-radical-and-wasteful-government-dei-programs-and-preferencing/

Tulipshare. (n.d.). Amazon: Working conditions. Retrieved April 27, 2025, from https://tulipshare.com/engagements/amzn

Wiessner, D. (2024, July 15). Workday must face novel bias lawsuit over AI screening software. Reuters. https://www.reuters.com/legal/litigation/workday-must-face-novel-bias-lawsuit-over-ai-screening-software-2024-07-15/

Winner, L. (1980). Do artifacts have politics? *Daedalus*, *109*(1), 121–136.

Wörsdörfer, M. (2022). What happened to 'Big Tech' and antitrust? And how to fix them! *Philosophy of Management*, *21*(3), 345–369. DOI: 10.1007/s40926-022-00193-5

Yang, Q., & Ding, J. (2024, March 18). China's draft AI law: A preliminary analysis. Center for Security and Emerging Technology. https://cset.georgetown.edu/publication/china-ai-law-draft/

Zuboff, S. (2019). *The age of surveillance capitalism*. Profile Books.

Chapter 3
"(Em)Power Games": A Therapeutic Techno-Political Approach to the Global Artificial Intelligence Race

Warren Alan Bowles
https://orcid.org/0000-0001-5367-2191
The Independent Institute of Education, South Africa

ABSTRACT

Artificial intelligence (AI) is not only changing the way that people work, live and acquire information, but it also impacts significantly on international relations and global power shifts between states. This is being revealed dynamically through different approaches to the regulation of AI, which in turn also reflects the intention of certain states or regions to stake their claim in what is known today as a "Global AI Race". These events indicate how AI adoption can shift global power, encourage competitiveness and foster innovation. However, this begs the question of whether such a global race is one that has "only one winner" at the expense of all others or one that must prioritise global collaboration, human centricity and fundamental rights in achieving responsible AI for all where every human being wins. This chapter therefore explores how a therapeutic techno-political approach, supported by principles informed by fundamental rights, can amplify collaboration and human-centric values to empower people in their political communities where technology like AI plays key roles.

DOI: 10.4018/979-8-3373-2459-3.ch003

1. INTRODUCTION: FLIP A COIN

Artificial intelligence (AI), as an emerging and disruptive technology borne out of the Fourth Industrial Revolution, has brought unprecedented change to societies and industries around the world, in both work, leisure, education and economic development. AI has the potential to transform how human beings interact with technology and how human beings relate to one another in their own dealings on the international spectrum. This relationship can be taken further to also encompass how human beings relate to one another through AI as a fluid, rapidly changing technological paradigm.

By viewing AI through this lens, looking at human beings and how they interact with one another in industry, in politics and in the pursuit of progress through technological regulation and use can be two sides of the same coin. By using the metaphor of a coin to demonstrate how AI potentially shifts global power and political ideologies, the one side of the coin concerns the emergence of global politics that transforms the power within states or regions (Trang & Thao, 2025, p.2130). The disruptive nature of AI in "shifting global politics" and "transforming power" in relation to states and regions refers to its capabilities to determine geopolitical standing, which includes but is not limited to the building of alliances, the emboldening of new power structures and the empowerment of new international orders (Trang & Thao, 2025, pp.2130 – 2131). This then makes AI a versatile diplomatic tool in today's technologically-advancing world which can represent domination between states and which can therefore dictate international change, from the incorporation of AI into international frameworks, the analysis of datasets to predict future changes and using AI as a bargaining chip in struggles involving global prowess (Trang & Thao, 2025, pp.2130 – 2131).

By viewing AI as a multi-purpose diplomatic tool, how it is to be used by governments presents both positive and negative paradigmatic outcomes. To begin with, AI can strengthen AI positioning for governments who are seeking to gain an economic advantage in the global AI arena, revealing significant repercussions for international relations, especially in relation to military innovation, cybersecurity and intelligence operations (Efthymiopoulos, 2019, pp.7 – 12). The consequential deduction to follow from these repercussions is that states with advanced AI capabilities can potentially have a strategic advantage over other states with regard to warfare, surveillance, digital infrastructure and their use of AI as well as other technological systems to shape public discourse, influence foreign policy and expand their ideological reach – all forms of "soft power" that states can control through various technological channels (Colther, Doussoulin & Tontini, 2025, p.2). What must also be taken into account when talking about "soft power" through AI as a persuasive medium is that states can either use it for good or it can be misused and abused in socio-political contexts (Carminati, 2024). In addition, consideration must be given to the impact of AI in global workplace contexts. AI is not only seen as an agent of change that can increase productivity, complement human work and automate tedious tasks, but there have already been instances where AI has replaced jobs and it can potentially exacerbate wealth and income inequalities within states (Georgieva, 2024). This means that there is great risk to human beings in the global workplace where AI can potentially replace them, irrespective of expertise, years of experience and goals that they would want to achieve in self-determining their own career paths.

Adding to the impact of AI on the global workplace and a disrupted global labour market in general, is how AI bias is becoming an evermore challenging area to navigate with in relation to "social scoring" and job recruitment. AI bias starts with knowing that AI algorithms are not entirely emotionless or neutral – algorithms are designed using rules that are informed by the data that they are trained on and any error, preconceived notion or pre-judgment within training datasets leads to biased outcomes on various levels in an AI system's design. This is known as "algorithmic bias" and from this type of bias, other biases can be found to further impact human beings in unjustified and undignified ways (Gryn & Rzeszucinski, 2018). For example, other biases such as gender bias and racial bias originating from algorithmic bias have detrimental consequences for human beings when it comes to surveillance, facial recognition and biometric identification (Gryn & Rzeszucinski, 2018).

The potential risks and benefits of AI for global growth and flourishing can therefore not be understated. However, the second side of the proverbial coin then deals with the circumstances where AI's abilities to shift global politics and to transform power structures in states and regions comes at a substantial cost to the flourishing of people, as well as ethical and legal considerations aligned to mitigating risks, ensuring fairness, promoting transparency and enforcing accountability of governments and government agencies aligned to AI implementation planning (Trang & Thao, 2025, p.2131). These measures, among others, then aim to ensure that risks associated with warfare and the military application of AI in conflict (for example, where the use of lethal autonomous weapons is concerned) are avoided; that AI is used to augment the ability of human beings to flourish in the global workplace; and that the value as well as the dignity of the human being is protected with regard to mitigating bias and using AI for surveillance, facial recognition technology and for biometric identification. As will be shown below, several key developments have taken place to ensure that AI is regulated on a global scale, but it has involved in the context of a "Global AI Race", where winning the race is associated with people across the world being negatively affected in the face of rising competitiveness and relentless innovation. This means that diplomats and representatives of governments in national, regional and international spheres must consider pursuing the benefits of

AI by collaborating more and transforming the international AI regulatory domain extensively with the impact of people at the forefront, in such a way that unintended negative consequences on people are mitigated and best strategic practices help people flourish with AI that transcends international borders (Trang & Thao, 2025, p.2131).

Bridging the divide between AI's potential to change global politics, to transform power differential in international relations and to ensure that the fundamental rights of people and their flourishing in the technological age is looked at in this contribution through techno-politics as an enabling model for comprehensive change. According to Kurban, Péna-Lopez & Haberer (2016: pp.501 – 502), the term "techno-politics" refers to the ability of different actors to develop political goals with the support of technology. Techno-politics also includes the furtherance of political practices by using technology to develop new forms of power and agency (Kurban, Péna-Lopez & Haberer, 2016, p.502). By describing techno-politics as "therapeutic" for purposes of this contribution, the aim is to show that techno-politics must go further to ensure that the well-being and care of people in turbulent political shifts caused by AI are taken care of, taking into account their autonomy and depoliticising their uniqueness as human beings in spaces where political conflict may influence driving certain AI adoption agendas that would negatively impact on a variety of rights and interests (Salmenniemi, 2019, pp.408 – 409). This contribution therefore aims to evaluate how a therapeutic technopolitical approach, supported by principles grounded in fundamental rights and the flourishing of people in the AI era, must primarily influence the global AI race to ensure that humanity comes first and that multi-stakeholder collaboration will strengthen competitiveness and innovation in the global AI domain, with humanity as the global winner in harnessing every benefit that AI can offer. This will be done following a "black letter" or doctrinal research methodology, which means that current prevailing AI trends, regulatory instruments and indicators of shifts in global power as elucidated in various literary sources will be analysed.

2. PUTTING THE GLOBAL AI RACE INTO PERSPECTIVE: THE TALE OF THE TAPE

It has not taken long for different regions and countries around the world to appreciate the benefits of harnessing AI to improve economies, promote innovation and foster competitiveness between different global markets where AI is concerned. The culmination of the global AI race needs to be examined with reference to developments that have taken place with Generative AI (GenAI), in the form of chatbots and other related Large Language Models (LLMs). It was only on 30 November 2022 that OpenAI released an early demo version of ChatGPT and the chatbot went viral, attracting more than one million users who could showcase what the chatbot could do via social media (Marr, 2023). The arrival of ChatGPT has culminated in two types of events that characterise the global AI race: the race for more innovative AI-systems and tools, and the race to regulate AI through legislation implemented at international, regional and national levels.

Since the advent of ChatGPT, companies continue to compete by releasing more powerful and more versatile AI models into the global market, which has now become characterised by increasing competition for the most powerful, useful and trusted AI models which all claim to have their own unique strengths in reasoning, context, speed or scalability (Sharan, 2025). Innate to this race is the constant revision and development of new versions within an AI model itself, for example, especially where the AI model is revealed to have been incorrectly calibrated to the extent that it is unnaturally agreeable, validating unethical ideas and demonstrating incorrect reasoning as was the case with ChatGPT-4o in May 2025 (Sharan, 2025). With each new upgrade and revision of an AI model's training datasets comes an increase in that AI-model's ability to reason, its potential to be more intelligent and its capability to interact with people, therefore characterising the global AI race as an innovative endeavour when it comes to evolving technologies and innovative AI design.

The global AI race as a pursuit for the innovation of more powerful and trustworthy AI models can be exemplified when looking at several global developments characterising this type of race. In late January 2025, Chinese company Deepseek released its Deepseek R1 LLM into the global AI market as a competitor against ChatGPT (Marr, 2025). In addition, it was observed that the Deepseek AI assistant, a mobile application that provides a chatbot interface for Deepseek R1, went to number one on the top of Apple's App Store chart, outranking ChatGPT's mobile application (Kerner, 2025). The viral popularity of Deepseek in terms of its usage and its appeal to users across the world resulted in a cataclysmic shift in global stock markets, triggering a market sell-off on 27 January 2025 that negatively impacted technology companies such as Nvidia, Microsoft, Meta, Oracle, Broadcom, Alphabet and other technology companies as the result of investors reassessing their AI valuations (Kerner, 2025). In the case of Nvidia, to single out one example of the negative impact experienced by one technology company in the global stock market context, the Nasdaq Composite dropped by 3.4% at market opening, with Nvidia declining by 17% which resulted in a loss of approximately US$ 600 billion in market capitalisation (Kerner, 2025). The release of Deepseek R1 (which is Deepseek's first AI model and is now followed by several more advanced and specialised Deepseek AI models) evidences the power of AI models, when released into the global AI market, to shift global market values and perceptions, which influences global economies in an instant and it shifts the power of play within the confines of international relations as well as geopolitics. These shifts, influences and fluctuations in global markets then serve as motivators for igniting the global AI race, especially within the ambit of pursuing unique and ground-breaking innovation in global AI discourse and spaces.

The cataclysmic shift that accompanied the release of Deepseek was further amplified by comparisons especially related to the costs for developing both ChatGPT and Deepseek, as well as their subscription requirements, open-source availability and strengths. The costs in respect of developing ChatGPT and especially its GPT-4 model cost over US$ 100 million with the building in of extensive computational resources and advanced AI chips, whereas Deepseek was developed with a budget of US$ 5.5 million using fewer resources and less powerful AI chips (PlayAI, 2025). Comparing the costs of development for both Deepseek and ChatGPT is also shown when looking at what their Application Programming Interface (API) costs are. API refers to "a set of rules or protocols that enable software applications to communicate with each other in order to exchange data, features and functionality" (Goodwin, 2024). API pricing in respect of Deepseek equates to US$ 0.48 per million tokens while the API pricing for ChatGPT equates to US$ 3 to US$ 15 per million tokens depending on the GPT model (PlayAI, 2025). In terms of subscription requirements, Deepseek is available for free whereas ChatGPT has both a free version and it has premium features that require payment (PlayAI, 2025). Open- source availability is embraced highly by Deepseek, which allows for developers to access and modify AI models, with the added advantage of fostering innovation as well as customisation within the developer community. In contrast, ChatGPT operates by using a proprietary model, with limited open-source access, resulting in less flexibility for modifying the underlying AI model (PlayAI, 2025). The cost to develop Deepseek and its open-source orientation illustrate its strengths as being cost-effective with high reasoning accuracy, whereas ChatGPT's development costs and proprietary model orientation characterise its strengths as being rich in features and versatile when looking at AI use cases (PlayAI, 2025).

It must also be emphasised that Deepseek does not have certain features that are otherwise exhibited through using ChatGPT. For example, Deepseek does not presently support advanced voice interactions whereas ChatGPT offers an Advanced Voice Mode which allows users to engage in verbal conversations with it (PlayAI, 2025). It is also worth noting that, upon its release, Deepseek was banned in several European countries, like Italy and Belgium, because it could not account for how it processes the data of users which, despite protests by Deepseek, contravened provisions in the General Data Protection Regulation (GDPR) (Bahr, 2025). Despite these shortcomings, the release of Deepseek and the disruption that it brought to the global AI domain illustrates how AI is able to shift power relations in the world from the perspective of innovation and the pursuit of competitively powerful AI systems and tools seeking market share in an unpredictable and rapidly expanding global AI market.

The race to regulate AI is a dynamic and evolving event, focused more on principle-based and guideline-orientated approaches to finding the balance between advancing AI innovation and ensuring that any risks presented by AI are mitigated in the process. Regulating AI happens against the backdrop of debates around whether AI needs to be regulated or not. This is not only grounded in politics that influence the development of legislation but also in the novelty of AI systems as a rapidly emerging and disruptive technology (Judge et al, 2025: p.86). A significant aspect of this novelty is that AI systems do not operate solely on the code provided to them by human beings; the deep neural networks, machine learning processes and the multitude of tuned parameters enforced by the data training sets used for an AI system are intricately finetuned for the AI system to behave in such a way that it does not reflect the intentions of its developers nor is it clearly determined how to trace and remedy challenges experienced with AI systems when they do not perform as intended (Judge et al, 2025:86). This constructive view of AI and the unpredictable manner in which it works make it difficult to enforce objective rules in AI systems (for example, "LLMs must not provide legal advice"). Rather, developers of AI systems must rely on the system learning the appropriate rules through sufficient training and reinforcement, therefore making it difficult for AI systems to comply with regulatory specifications (Judge et al, 2025:86).

On the contrary, arguments in favour of regulating AI come from a place of stark realisation: AI as a technology represents a category of intelligent machines that can perform a variety of different tasks with unrivalled capability across a variety of different areas, and in some instances, better than human beings can do. AI as a transformative force and a catalyst for change has extensive effects and its impact is being felt in various facets of human life, for example, in employment contexts where it is replacing human beings in specific jobs and it is being used in some instances for state surveillance (Judge et al, 2025). There are also concerns about the progression towards what is known as "Artificial General Intelligence" (AGI) which refers to AI surpassing human beings in all areas of life, with intelligence far exceeding that of the human being, making it such that, without regulation, the consequences for humanity could be highly disruptive and potentially catastrophic (Judge et al, 2025). Where the regulation of AI is favoured for these reasons, it then begs the question of what form and shape such regulation must take (Judge et al, 2025), and there are various forms of this type of regulation that have been developed in recent years.

2.1 Foundational Principles for AI Governance: The Organization for Economic Cooperation and Development (OECD) Recommendation on Artificial Intelligence

The regulation of AI in the global sphere is not a new or recent development. Instruments such as the Organization for Economic Cooperation and Development (OECD) Recommendation on Artificial Intelligence (OECD Recommendation) were one of the first international documents to set out guiding principles for the responsible stewardship of trustworthy AI, having been adopted on 22 May 2019 and they also reflect a further update made to the OECD Recommendation on 3 May 2024 (OECD Legal Instruments, 2025). These guiding principles constitute what are now known as the OECD AI Principles, which are regarded as the first intergovernmental standard in AI, promoting innovative and trustworthy AI that respects human rights and democratic values (OECD, 2025). The AI principles in the OECD Recommendation are composed of five values-based principles (set out in section 1 of the Recommendation) and five recommendations that provide practical and flexible guidance for policymakers and AI stakeholders (set out in section 2 of the Recommendation) (OECD, 2025). Set out in section 1 of the OECD Recommendation on Artificial Intelligence, these guiding principles have formed the backdrop against which more recent regulatory developments have grounded their principle-based approaches to regulating AI as a trustworthy and responsible emerging technology. It is important to note that these guiding principles warrant further exploration as part of this contribution because they provide a foundation to proceed with when exploring therapeutic techno-politics as a lens for empowering people and positioning them better in the global AI race. These principles are stipulated in the OECD Recommendation in the following manner:

Inclusive Growth, Sustainable Development and Well-Being

The principle emphasises the importance of stakeholders being proactive in the responsible stewardship of trustworthy AI when seeking to harnessing its benefits for people and the planet as a whole. This is to be done by using AI to augment human capabilities, to enhance creativity, to advance the inclusion of underrepresented and marginalised groups, to reduce economic, social, gender and other inequalities and to ensure that the natural environments are protected in advancing inclusive growth, well-being, sustainable development and environmental sustainability (OECD Legal Instruments, 2025).

Respect for the rule of law, human rights and democratic values, including fairness and privacy

Under this principle, AI stakeholders are required to respect the rule of law, human rights, democratic and human-centred values throughout the entire life cycle of an AI model. Included within the scope of this principle are the imperatives of non-discrimination, equality, freedom, dignity, autonomy of individuals, privacy and data protection, diversity, fairness, social justice and intentionally recognised labour rights (OECD Legal Instruments, 2025). This principle also requires that instances of misinformation and disinformation disseminated through AI needs redress, within the scope of freedom of expression and other rights applicable in international law, and this means that appropriate safeguards, such as capacity for human agency and oversight, need to be implemented to mitigate uses of AI that extend beyond its intended purpose, intentional misuse or unintentional misuse in a manner appropriate to the context and that is consistent with the state of the art (OECD Legal Instruments, 2025).

Transparency and explainability

This principle requires of AI stakeholders to commit to transparency and responsible disclosure with respect to AI systems, which includes the provision of contextually-relevant meaningful information and that is consistent with the state of art in order to foster a general understanding of AI systems, including their capabilities and limitations; to make stakeholders aware of their interactions with AI systems, including in workplaces; to provide information in plain simple language regarding the sources of data or input, factors, processes and/or logic that led to the prediction, content, recommendation or decision, to enable those affected by an AI system's decision-making to understand the output, where this is useful and feasible; and to provide information that enables those who have been adversely affected by an AI system to challenge its output (OECD Legal Instruments, 2025).

Robustness, security and safety

This principle emphasises the requirement that AI systems must be robust, secure and safe throughout their entire lifecycle so that, in normal perusal, foreseeable use or misuse, or other adverse conditions, they function appropriately and do not pose unreasonable safety and/or security risks (OECD Legal Instruments, 2025). A significant facet of the security and safety of AI systems is that they are required to have mechanisms in place to override, for repairs and for decommissioning safely when needed in instances where the AI system causes undue harm or exhibits undesired behaviour (OECD Legal Instruments, 2025). In addition, where it is technically feasible, such mechanisms must also aim to strengthen information integrity while ensuring for freedom of expression (OECD Legal Instruments, 2025).

Accountability

Together with the preceding principles, this principle commits AI stakeholders to be held accountable for the proper functioning of AI systems based on their roles, the relevant contexts and considering the state of the art at the time (OECD Legal Instruments, 2025). This then bestows on AI stakeholders the duty to ensure traceability relating to datasets as well as processes and decisions made during an AI systems lifecycle, to enable the analysis of AI system's outputs and responses to inquiry, appropriate to the context and consistent with the state of the art (OECD Legal Instruments, 2025). Based on their roles, relevant contexts and their ability to act, AI stakeholders need to follow a systematic risk management approach to each phase of an AI system's lifecycle consistently and they must adopt responsible business practices in order to mitigate risks deriving from AI systems, which include remediating harmful bias and upholding human rights, safety, security, privacy as well as labour and intellectual property rights (OECD Legal Instruments, 2025).

By taking into account these principles, the recommendations made in terms of section 2 of the OECD Recommendation encourage governments to implement the following in relation to fostering national AI policies and international co-operation for trustworthy AI:

Investing in AI research and development

Governments are required to consider long-term public investment, and encourage private investment, in research and development and open science which also includes multi-disciplinary efforts, to foster innovation in trustworthy AI with a focus on challenging technical issues, policy issues as well as AI-related social, legal and ethical implications (OECD Legal Instruments, 2025). In addition, this recommendation also calls upon governments to consider long-term public and private investment in open-source tools and open datasets that represent and respect privacy and data protection, with a view to supporting an environment for AI research and development that is free of harmful bias and to improve interoperability as well as the use of standards (OECD Legal Instruments, 2025).

Fostering an inclusive AI-enabling ecosystem

This recommendation encourages governments to foster development of, and access to, an inclusive, dynamic, sustainable and interoperable digital ecosystem for trustworthy AI, meaning that such an ecosystem must include, among other things, data, AI technologies, computational and connectivity infrastructure, and mechanisms for sharing AI knowledge where applicable (OECD Legal Instruments, 2025). In order to achieve this, governments should consider promoting mechanisms like data trusts, in order to support the safe, fair, legal and ethical sharing of data (OECD Legal Instruments, 2025).

Shaping an enabling interoperable governance and policy environment for AI

This recommendation requires of governments to promote an agile policy environment that supports transitioning from the research and development stage to the deployment and operation stage for trustworthy AI systems. To this effect, governments therefore need to consider experimentation to provide a controlled environment in which AI systems can be tested and scaled up where applicable (OECD Legal Instruments, 2025). Furthermore, governments should consider the adoption of outcomes-based approaches that provide flexibility in achieving governance objectives and governments then need to co-operate within and across jurisdictions to promote interoperable governance and policy environments where applicable (OECD Legal Instruments, 2025).

The proposed transitioning that governments need to consider and the nature of the collaboration that governments are required to engage with and share with one another across different jurisdictions also implies that governments should review and adapt their policy and regulatory frameworks, as well as their assessment mechanisms that apply to AI systems so that this will foster innovation and competition in the pursuit of responsible AI (OECD Legal Instruments, 2025).

Building human capacity and preparing for labour market transformation

This recommendation encourages governments to work closely with stakeholders to prepare for the transformation of the world of work and of society in relation to the pervasion of AI in various industries. In order to accomplish this, governments should empower people to effectively use and interact with AI systems across the breadth of its applications, meaning that governments need to equip people with the necessary skills (OECD Legal Instruments, 2025). To fulfil this aim, governments need to take steps, including through social dialogue, to ensure a fair transition for workers as AI is deployed, which also includes providing training programmes to workers to complement their work lives and to provide support for those who are affected by displacement caused by AI, with the latter being assisted through social protection and assistance in accessing new opportunities in the labour market (OECD Legal Instruments, 2025). In this regard, governments need to work closely with stakeholders to promote the responsible use of AI at work, to enhance the safety of workers, the quality of jobs and of public services, with the aim of fostering entrepreneurship and productivity, as well as to ensure that the benefits from AI are broadly and fairly shared.

International co-operation for trustworthy AI

This recommendation speaks to several key points that governments need to consider in fostering comity and sharing of best practices related to implementing trustworthy AI. Governments, including developing countries and with stakeholders in mind, should actively co-operate to advance these principles and to progress on responsible stewardship of trustworthy AI (OECD Legal Instruments, 2025). The nature of this co-operation can be described as governments working together in the OECD and with other regional entities to foster the sharing of AI knowledge, which also focuses on international, cross-sectoral and open multi-stakeholder initiatives to garner long-term expertise on AI (OECD Legal Instruments, 2025). In order to facilitate the optimal sharing of best practices and knowledge surrounding responsible AI, governments should also promote the sharing of multi-stakeholder, consensus-driven global technical standards for interoperable and trustworthy AI (OECD Legal Instruments, 2025). Lastly, governments should also encourage the development, and their own use, of internationally comparable indicators to measure AI research, development and deployment, with the progress on such indicators being substantiated by evidence in supporting the implementation of the OECD Recommendation principles (OECD Legal Instruments, 2025).

These recommendations that are revealed in the OECD Recommendation reflect an ideal approach to how governments around the world must approach the development of trustworthy AI and its implementation with focussed respect and emphasis on democratic values, human rights and collaboration between states and regions. The OECD Recommendation serves as a guide to various states and regions on how they should structure their AI policies but unfortunately, the fact that the OECD Recommendation is only a recommendation means that it is not legally binding on states and therefore, states are not obliged to follow its recommendations in absolute and mandatory terms. It is only a guideline for state governments to consider in the pursuit of harnessing the benefits of trustworthy AI. A more recent policy development has not only inculcated these principles from the OECD Recommendation but it also makes them legally binding on states within the European Union (EU).

2.2 AI Principles, Binding Law: The European Union Artificial Intelligence Act

The European Union Artificial Intelligence Act (EU AI Act) entered into force on 1 August 2024, with its fundamental purpose as set out in section 1 being to improve the functioning of internal markets while also promoting human-centric trustworthy AI and ensuring that health, safety and fundamental rights are protected (European Union Artificial Intelligence Act, 2025). This is regarded as the first law of its kind to regulate AI in member states of the European Union and, with reference to Recital 1 of the Act, a significant driving focus within its formation and implementation lies in improving the functioning of the internal market within the European Union in respect of putting AI systems into the market for service and use (European Union Artificial Intelligence Act, 2025).

The EU AI Act categorises AI by risk and sets out requirements that various AI systems need to meet, except for those AI systems that are expressly prohibited. Prohibited AI systems, according to Article 5 of the EU AI Act, are those AI systems that seek to distort the behaviour of a person or groups by inhibiting them from making informed decisions that can lead to causing harm to themselves or others; AI systems that seek to exploit any vulnerabilities of persons or specific groups of persons aligned to their age, disability or a specific social or economic situation; AI systems that evaluate or classify persons or groups of persons over a specific period of time based on their social behaviour or known, inferred or predicted personal or personality characteristics which lead to detrimental social scoring of such persons in specified contexts; AI systems that make risk assessments of persons or groups of persons with specific risk being directed to whether or not such persons could commit criminal offences just based on profiling their personality traits and characteristics; AI systems that create or expand facial recognition databases through untargeted scraping of facial images from the internet or CCTV (Closed Circuit Television) footage; AI systems that aim to infer the emotions of persons or groups of persons in the workplace and educational institutions (except where this is necessary for medical or safety reasons); AI systems that use biometric categorisation systems designed to categorise individuals based on their biometric data that provides information about their race, political opinions, trade union membership, religious or philosophical beliefs, sex life or sexual orientation; AI systems that are designed to use "real time" remote biometric identification systems in publicly accessible spaces for the purposes of law enforcement (unless this is done as, firstly, a targeted search for specific victims of abduction, human trafficking, sexual exploitation or for missing persons, secondly, to prevent specific, substantial and imminent threats to the life and physical safety of persons or the foreseeable threat of a terrorist attack, thirdly, to localise or identify a person suspected of having committed a criminal offence so that a criminal investigation of such a person can take place or such a person can be prosecuted and appropriately punished in accordance with Annex II of the EU AI Act (European Union Artificial Intelligence Act, 2025).

Before proceeding to examine the categories of AI risk stipulated in the EU AI Act, it is worth noting how the rationale behind these express prohibitions on the AI systems specified in Article 5 emphasises that the beginning of achieving trustworthy AI starts with addressing AI systems that blatantly present harm and danger to human beings, especially in relation to many characteristics of being human that start with any attempts by an AI system to manipulate perceptions of one's outward appearance right down to any AI systems that attempt to read human emotions and human predisposition to commit acts that are criminal in nature. Although the exceptions to some AI systems are important to consider with regard to appropriate law enforcement measures and for the protection of vulnerable persons, a specific article that outlines what AI systems are prohibited and why they are prohibited gives one an understanding of what trustworthy AI is not and what AI needs to aim for in terms of protecting fundamental rights, the safety of individuals and their health in environments where AI ecosystems find root. The importance of this provision is further emphasised by the fact that it came into force on 2 February 2025, forcing European Union states and non-member states with AI-associated operations in the European Union to approach their development and deployment of AI systems with caution, especially where they can potentially infringe on Article 5 of the EU AI Act (European Union Artificial Intelligence Act, 2025).

High-risk AI systems are defined in Article 6 of the EU AI Act as those AI systems that are intended to be used as a safety component of a product or where the AI product itself is a product covered by Union harmonisation legislation as set out in Annex 1 to the EU AI Act, or those AI systems in which the actual safety component is the AI system itself or the product created is the AI system itself, in which case it will then be required for such an AI system to undergo a third-party conformity assessment that would confirm its suitability for being placed into the market in accordance with Union harmonisation legislation as set out in Annex I (European Union Artificial Intelligence Act, 2025). In addition to this description of high-risk AI systems, the systems that are set out in Annex III of the EU AI Act are also considered to be high-risk, such as AI systems that assess biometrics to the extent that relevant Union or national law requires; AI systems used as safety components in the management and operation of critical digital infrastructure (for example, in the supply of utilities like water and electricity); AI systems used in education and vocational training; AI systems that impact on employment, workers management and access to self-employment; AI systems that impact on access to and the enjoyment of essential public and private services along with their benefits, law enforcement to the extent that is protected under Union and national law; AI systems connected to border control, and AI systems that impact on the administration of justice and democratic processes (European Union Artificial Intelligence Act, 2025).

An AI system that is then regarded as high risk in terms of the EU AI Act speaks to what the nature of the AI system is as a software medium and how this characteristic of AI can pose threats to individuals and different industries within the societies across the European Union. This is also exemplified by certain exceptions to what defines a high-risk AI system in terms of Article 6(3) of the EU AI Act. Article 6(3) stipulates that an AI system would not be regarded as high-risk where it does not pose a significant risk of harm to the health, safety or fundamental rights of individuals, where such an AI systems meets the conditions of being able to perform a narrow procedural task, improves the result of a previously completed human activity, detects decision-making patterns or deviations from prior decision-making patterns not related to replacing or influencing a previous human-centred decision and the AI system performs a preparatory task to an assessment for the purposes of the use cases listed in Annex III (European Union Artificial Intelligence Act, 2025). In the case of these AI systems, they are regarded as low or minimal risk AI systems within the confines of the EU AI Act.

High-risk AI systems are mandated, in terms of the EU AI Act, to comply with a series of requirements before they can be deployed into a market. In terms of Article 8, developers of AI systems are compelled to ensure that the AI system that they intend to deploy meets not only the requirements of the EU AI Act but also those requirements as set out in Union harmonisation legislation (European Union Artificial Intelligence Act, 2025). The requirements include the establishment of a risk management system in terms of Article 9 of the EU AI Act, with such a risk management system being viewed "as a continuous iterative process planned and run through the entire lifecycle of a high-risk AI system, requiring regular systematic review and updating", with certain important steps that it needs to include in order to mitigate risk (European Union Artificial Intelligence Act, 2025). Article 10 of the EU AI Act stipulates important standards that datasets used to train high-risk AI systems need to meet in accordance with appropriate data governance and data management practices (European Union Artificial Intelligence Act, 2025). Article 11 (Technical Documentation) and Article 12 (Record-Keeping) in the EU AI Act speak to the importance of keeping up-to-date and consistent written records regarding the development of and eventual deployment of a high-risk AI system (European Union Artificial Intelligence Act, 2025). Article 13 of the EU AI Act mandates developers of high-risk AI systems to ensure that the system's development and production is done in a sufficiently transparent manner that will enable deployers of these AI systems to interpret the system's output and to use it appropriately (European Union Artificial Intelligence Act, 2025). Article 14 of the EU AI Act raises in a rather direct manner the importance of human oversight and supervision of high-risk AI systems, through the employment of human-machine interface tools that can be effectively overseen by human beings during the time that such an AI system is being used (European Union Artificial Intelligence Act, 2025). In Article 15 of the EU AI Act, it is stipulated that high-risk AI systems must be designed and developed in such a manner that an appropriate level of accuracy, robustness and cybersecurity are imbued in their design throughout their entire lifecycle (European Union Artificial Intelligence Act, 2025).

The EU AI Act continues to set strict regulations in section 3 that emphatically address the obligations of providers and deployers of high-risk AI systems and other parties. There are several articles of the EU AI Act that lay down the required steps that providers (or developers) and deployers of high-risk AI systems must comply with. Although these provisions are important, save for one stipulation, they are beyond the scope of this contribution and would be the subject of further research. The one stipulation saved for analysis regarding this responsibility that is imposed on developers and deployers of high-risk AI systems is contained in Article 27 of the EU AI Act, and this concerns the establishment of Fundamental Rights Impact Assessments for High-Risk AI Systems. Article 27 stipulates that, among others, deployers that are governed in terms of public law and private deployers who perform public services, shall perform a fundamental rights impact assessment that will address whether or not fundamental rights will impacted by the high-risk AI system that they are producing and intending to deploy. Deployers must then perform the assessment which will consist of:

- A description of the deployer's processes in which the high-risk AI system will be used in line with its intended purpose.
- A description of the period of time within which, and the frequency with which, each high-risk AI system is intended to be used.
- The risk categories of natural persons and groups likely to be affected by its use in the specific context.
- The specific risks of harm likely to have an impact on the categories of natural persons or groups of persons identified, taking into account information that is given by the provider in this respect.
- A description of the implementation of human oversight measures, according to the instructions of use.
- The measures to be taken in the case of the materialisation of those risks, including the arrangements for internal governance and complaint mechanisms (European Union Artificial Intelligence Act, 2025).

The provisions that have been explored within the EU AI Act demonstrate in various respects how AI principles that appeared in the OECD Recommendation have now been codified into a law that is binding on member states of the European Union and, somewhat indirectly, on non-member states who have AI-related operations in European Union member states. The selected articles covered in this section demonstrate reference to key principles such as transparency, fairness, accuracy, robustness, cybersecurity, data governance, data protection, human-centred oversight and the protection of fundamental rights at the forefront of AI development and AI deployment.

The EU AI Act has been said to demonstrate the European Union's commitment to high ethical standards, protection of fundamental rights and to the nurturing of trust in AI systems that are grounded in human-centric values (Csernatoni, 2025). By looking at this monumental development through the lens of the global AI race, however, Csernatoni (2025) is of the view that the European Union's approach to AI regulation, which is informed by a rights-based methodology, can be seen as an assertive geopolitical strategy that is orientated towards normative power and the setting of international benchmarks for AI governance. Otherwise known as the "Brussels" effect, the European Union's large single market and its forward-looking technological regulations have historically caused a rippling effect globally with regard to how the rest of the world perceives these regulations (Csernatoni, 2025).

As important as regulation of AI is and the manner in which the European Union is leading the way with AI governance, this does present a dilemma for the European Union. The speed at which AI is rapidly developing, with the United States of America and China spending great sums of money on its development, have prompted several debates about how the European Union's ambitions to regulate AI can result in industrial weaknesses to deter investment and talent required to nurture a robust AI ecosystem and culture (Csernatoni, 2025). This has since resulted in the European Union adopting a defined focus on encouraging AI innovation, meaning that it has relaxed its vigorous pursuit of regulating AI and adhering to strict AI governance measures (Csernatoni, 2025). This move by the European Union has been motivated by heightened geopolitical risks, especially in relation to Europe's vulnerabilities in digital supply chains and AI infrastructure as well as European reliance on external providers for essential AI components such as advanced semiconductors and cloud computing resources which, according to Csernatoni (2025), could lead to potential exploitation by competitors like the United States of America and China.

The change in geopolitical strategy by the European Union to focus more on AI innovation rather than on AI regulation can have far-reaching consequences for the region. On the one hand, this may result in accelerated innovation that would rapidly increase growth, amplify tech scale-ups and increase global competitiveness. On the other hand, regulation would become a secondary aim which can result in important privacy, consumer, labour and environmental safeguards becoming compromised (Csernatoni, 2025). Where these safeguards are compromised, sight cannot be lost of the fact that regulation as a governance strategy in the time of AI serves an important democratic purpose, by ensuring that oversight and guardrails necessary to protect fundamental rights are enforced against unfettered corporate power and control by governments, especially in relation to the surveillance of its citizens (Csernatoni, 2025).

2.3 The United States of America: Deregulation of AI as a Strategy for the Global AI Race

In the United States of America, on 20 January 2025, the incoming Trump Administration rescinded several executive orders that were undertaken by the Biden Administration. One of the executive orders that was rescinded was Executive Order 14110, which provided for the "Safe, Secure, and Trustworthy Development and Use of Artificial Intelligence" (The White House, 2025). This has now led to the United States of America formulating a new AI strategy under the Trump Administration, with such a strategy aiming to "sustain and enhance America's dominance in AI to promote human flourishing, economic competitiveness and national security" (The White House, 2025).

The orientation of this new AI strategy appears to have a competitive element that differed somewhat significantly from what was envisioned in the now rescinded Executive Order 14110. The new and revised national AI strategy that the Trump Administration envisions aims to place the United States of America at the forefront of AI innovation, drawing strength from their free markets, research institutions and the spirit of entrepreneurship that AI is spurring in economic spaces (The White House, 2025). In order to achieve this, Executive Order 14110 was rescinded as one of several existing AI policies and directives that are still being explored as possible inhibitors of American AI innovation (The White House, 2025). This move that was taken by the Trump Administration illustrates the strategy of deregulation as a catalyst for innovation that the United States of America ascribes to as a competitor in the global AI race. The strategy follows the rationale that removing any barriers to AI innovation would enable the United States of America "to act decisively to retain global leadership in artificial intelligence" (The White House, 2025). This position that the United States of America has adopted in relation to retaining its position as a global leader in AI innovation was further emphasised at the Artificial Intelligence Action Summit which took place in February 2025, where Vice-President JD Vance remarked that his contribution at the Summit was going to address "AI opportunity" as opposed to "AI safety" (The American Presidency Project, 2025). In Vance's assessment of AI as an opportunity, he suggested that the advent of AI does not invite risk-averse approaches but rather the opposite, in other words, experimentation and the pursuit of rewards from the potential innovations that AI can bring in job creation, national security, healthcare and freedom of expression but to name a few areas where AI has an influence, would be severely restricted by rigid regulation and positivist AI governance instruments (The American Presidency Project, 2025). Vance went further to state that the Trump Administration would be committed to ensuring that "AI technology continues to be the gold standard worldwide" and the United States of America would ensure that it would become the partner of choice for other foreign countries who would be looking to establish their own AI policies and infrastructure (The American Presidency Project, 2025). This commitment suggests that the Trump Administration would also aim to influence international AI standards by ensuring that individual liberties are protected, innovation is fostered and economic and security measures are strengthened in light of the influences on AI that have developed in China and in the European Union, which could potentially fragment policies and cause risk to American competitiveness and personal freedoms (Kennedy, 2025). In addition, Vance reiterated that too much regulation of the AI domain would halt its potential as a transformative catalyst that is only now starting to show the world what it is capable of, which therefore drives home the strategy of the Trump Administration that deregulation of AI must become part of AI innovation discourse in other states (The American Presidency Project, 2025). The final two points that Vance made in his speech related to, firstly, the Trump Administration's commitment to ensuring that AI would remain free from "ideological bias" and that AI in the American context would not be used as a tool for authoritarian leadership. This commitment by the Trump Administration suggests that the United States of America would be in a position to lead in the global AI race by reinforcing democratic values and maintaining technological leadership through the advancement of transparent, market-drievn standards in collaboration with its foreign partners and industry (Kennedy, 2025). Secondly, the pursuit of AI innovation would be done taking into account the maintenance of a "pro-worker growth path" which therefore envisions AI as an important instrument for job creation in the United States of America (The American Presidency Project, 2025). According to Kennedy (2025), this strategy of deregulation of AI in order to pursue the highest goals of innovation in AI would involve the prioritisation of AI investment, the introduction of talent development and the establishment of infrastructure security without excessive regulatory stipulations. The pro-innovation approach adopted by the Trump Administration in pursuing AI innovation over excessive regulation would ensure that AI would remain "an engine of American economic strength and military superiority", embodying a strong focus on both economic expansion and national security that enables the United States of America to lead the global agenda rather than to relinquish this in favour of interrogating rigid AI regulations and rules (Kennedy, 2025).

2.4 China: Emerging And Prepared

The release of Deepseek that was discussed at length earlier in this contribution demonstrated China's intentions to make its name known in the global AI race that was previously dominated by the United States of America and the European Union. Since the release of Deepseek, China has continued to comprehensively plan and structure its national AI agenda with intense focus on investment, upskilling of talent and developing appropriate AI infrastructure. According to Kuo (2025), China's noticeable entry into the global AI race was the result of years of national strategy, alignment of public and private sectors within the country and thorough investment in talent and infrastructure.

As a competitor in the global AI race, China's impact on the global AI context is the result of more than a decade's worth of preparation, commencing in 2017 under a State Council directive known as the Next Generation Artificial Intelligence Development Plan (Kuo, 2025). The Next Generation Artificial Intelligence Development Plan acknowledges that the rapid growth of AI and its infiltration into various industries not only in China but around the world will change the way that humanity, society and life will interact on normative terms. Interestingly, the Next Generation Artificial Intelligence Development Plan provides as its purpose that it has originated in the intention for China "[t]o seize the major strategic opportunity for the development of AI, to build China's first-mover advantage in the development of AI, to accelerate the construction of an innovative nation and global power in science and technology." (Next Generation Artificial Intelligence Development Plan, 2017). This directive therefore makes China's intentions clear in terms of how it present its strategy to become and to remain a significant competitor in the global AI race.

It is worth noting further that the directive was formulated in accordance with the requirements of the Communist Party of China (CCP) Central Committee and the Chinese State Council (Next Generation Artificial Intelligence Development Plan, 2017). This is a significant catalyst in China's drive to grow its AI industry and related sectors into a market that is worth US$ 14 trillion by 2030 because China's progressive AI growth gets ample support and resources from the Chinese government, meaning that Chinese corporate interests with regard to AI are aligned with national priorities (Morgan Stanley, 2025). The impetus for China's escalating AI ambitions is backed by state interests and a state agenda for China to become a global leader in the global AI race. Unlike the European Union and the United

States of America, the Chinese government is therefore an important contributor, benefactor and driver for the success of China's national and international AI agenda.

2.5 Africa: A Wild Card And Rising Star For AI Governance In The Global South

It can be seen from the preceding paragraphs that exploring the strengths and weaknesses precipitated by analysis of the OECD Recommendation, the EU AI Act and the key AI developments that are taking place between the two AI state superpowers of the world – namely the United States of America and China – share one common trait as competitors in the global AI race: they are regarded as critical players in AI development and governance in the Global North. This statement then serves as an appropriate segway into which regions or states in the Global South could allay challenges to the competitors of the Global North in the global AI race. This leads then to examining AI developments and AI governance trends that have emerged (and continue to emerge) in Africa.

Exploring AI developments and AI governance trends in Africa must done by taking into account Africa's history, its potential influences on AI in the Global North and the challenges faced in Africa regarding AI adoption and implementation. Adams (2024) observes that Africa has "a crucial yet paradoxical position" when it comes to the global AI race. It is a "crucial" position in that the African continent is integral to AI supply chains (for example, by providing essential resources for AI production) and it is "paradoxical" in that the African continent is facing its own set of complex challenges in harnessing AI for its own socio-economic development.

The provision of essential resources for AI production by the African continent has become a sensitive and controversial issue because provision of these resources is not fairly acknowledged or compensated (Adams, 2024). This practice of not being acknowledged or being compensated for essential resources required for AI production is now becoming part of Africa's narratives on colonialism in its various forms. One of these forms that is associated with having monopoly over African resources and, for example, mineral wealth, was that of "extractivism" which refers to "colonial practices that have existed over the last several hundred years with the goal of wealth and resource accumulation, regardless of the oppressions that geographically separate taker and giver" (Iyer, 2022).

The current disruptive and fast-paced technological age invites us to think differently about "extractivism" in African colonial contexts. If colonial narratives from the African continent can be conceived as a book, then the new chapter now would be titled as "digital extractivism" in light of the African continent's contributions to the global AI race. Digital extractivism relates to extraction that has a digitised character and it is further exacerbated by borderless capitalism with relation to how much money is spent and earned in its furtherance by interested actors (Iyer, 2022). Digital extractivism comes in a variety of different forms that have a digital basis and purpose. These forms are as follows, with further insights grounded in an African context where applicable:

- **Digital labour** – tech companies hire their employees from locations in Africa where the labour is cheap and labour laws are weak. In this regard, it must be said that African workers contribute greatly to AI development through data labeling, machine learning model training and "gig economy" labour, usually without sufficient compensation and in the face of minimal labour and social protection (Adams, 2024).
- **Illicit financial flows** – the method by which tax payments are minimised or reduced. In the form of "tax dodging" (a nefarious practice that includes tax avoidance, tax evasion, corruption and offshore accounts), multinational corporations, including big tech in AI domains, are able to secretly design complex schemes to boost their profits and to avoid paying tax thereon by using Africa as a cloak of secrecy or by using other African states as tax havens (for example, Zambia in relation to agreements with transnational companies like the global copper producer Vedanta to extract minerals, and Nigeria in relation to its agreements with transnational companies like the British Shell Group for petroleum) (Liu & Otusanya, 2022). Due to the fact that they have an abundance of resources, African countries become especially susceptible to aggressive tax planning and tax evasion enabled by offshore companies (Liu & Otusanya, 2022). Expanding intra-company trading, the secrecy surrounding foreign investment activities and loopholes in treaties make African countries emphatically vulnerable to tax avoidance (Liu & Otusanya, 2022). In addition, governments in sub-Saharan Africa also lack the human, financial and technical resources to stem the outflow of wealth that is the result of multinational companies not paying tax to these governments and rather paying it into tax havens or other offshore accounts (Liu & Otusanya, 2022).
- **Data extraction** – when tech companies exploit minimal data protection legislation to collect the personal data of consumers (for example, their identities, behaviours and beliefs) to sell to political actors or advertisers for profit. In this regard, an important instrument that warrants consideration is the African Union Convention on Cyber Security and Personal Data Protection (otherwise known as "The Malabo Convention"). The aim of this instrument is to set out provisions that provide consumer protection to natural and legal persons in member states (for example, where e-commerce interaction in Article 2 and electronic contracts in Article 5 are concerned) and to regulate the protection and handling of data and personal information for natural and

legal persons of member states in accordance with Articles 10, 13, 14, 15, 16, 17, 18, 19 and 20) (African Union Convention On Cyber Security And Personal Data Protection, 2014). The Malabo Convention does not, in itself, shield data from international forces like big tech or other multinational companies with regard to preventing all external access, but it does provide a legal basis for member states to regulate data processing and cybersecurity within their borders, especially in relation to cross-border transfers. The suggestion then is that, to curb data extraction as a form of digital extractivism, perhaps something more is required at a regional level in Africa to strengthen sovereignty over its data in the instance where some African states may be subject to intense and illicit data extraction practices by external multinational companies.

- **Natural Resource Mining –** This form of digital extractivism warrants contextualisation through an example. Adams (2024) emphasises that Cobalt is a mineral that is essential to the manufacturing and production of smartphones. Cobalt is also an extremely important component modern AI chips and semiconductor manufacturing for building AI systems (SFA Oxford, 2025). Cobalt is mined in and extracted from the Democratic Republic of Congo (DRC) which is a country that is fraught with human rights abuses (Adams, 2024). This is further aggravated by the risks brought on by mining Cobalt in the DRC such as environmental risks (for example, the accumulation of toxic heavy metals derived from Cobalt mining), social risks (for example, child labour is a common practice in Cobalt mining in the DRC) and economic risks (for example, indigenous people losing their livelihoods or being displaced by mining-motivated armed conflict in the DRC) (Cao, Sharmina & Cuéllar-Franca, 2024). The point to be made here is that Western countries extract minerals, labour and raw materials from African countries, usually at great cost to that country's inhabitants.
- **Infrastructure monopolies –** this entails foreign domination of African digital infrastructure such as internet services and mobile phone services.
- **Digital lending** – a practice where digital lenders combine extractive financial approaches, data extractivism and social shaming in order to trap or extort users.
- **Funding structures –** a practice where venture capitalists have been seen to exhibit severe bias in funding African startups.
- **Beta testing –** this relates to the early testing of digital and electronic products unethically and on vulnerable populations in Africa without their informed consent.

- **Platform governance –** the institutionalisation of bias in AI platform guidelines as well as the automated AI application of platform rules, which can lead to discrimination against marginalised groups (Iyer, 2022).

It is evident from the preceding paragraphs that the African continent's role in providing resources for AI production is highly important but it comes at a great cost to the continent itself. The African continent's impact on AI, at least for the previously examined competitor in the global AI race is undergirded by colonial, pre-colonial and neo-colonial influences which now carry over into the African continent's digital and AI-informed spaces. In addition, Africa faces other nuanced challenges. Besides not receiving any sustainable benefits for its important contributions to global AI value chains, Africa is still, despite its best efforts, "catching up" with the relentless speed of AI adoption, for which it may need to leverage vital resources and funding that are otherwise needed for critical areas like healthcare and education (Adams, 2024). These challenges provide valuable insights into the African economic, political and social contexts that is a compelling background required to understand how AI policy and AI governance in Africa are being shaped.

On 18 and 19 July 2024, the African Union's Executive Council endorsed the Continental Artificial Intelligence (AI) Strategy in its commitment to harness the benefits of AI by using an "African-centric, development-focused approach to AI, promoting ethical, responsible and equitable practices." (African Union, 2024). This Continental Strategy has as its main focus the achievement of AI goals in Africa through its Agenda 2030 aspirations and its commitment to the United Nation's Sustainable Development Goals (SDGs) (African Union, 2024). The Continental AI Strategy demonstrates Africa's commitment to regulating the development, adoption and the implementation of AI in African states, using the United Nation's SDGs and the African Union's Agenda 2030 as yardsticks for this realisation. This is relevant because, when looking at the EU AI Act for example, the United Nation's SDGs are not expressly mentioned as a key motivator for the adoption of AI. To go further, no reference is also made to the United Nations SDG's in recent AI regulatory documents from the United States of America and China. Africa's AI aspirations are therefore rather unique when looking at what other global competitors in the global AI race are aiming to achieve. What is also important is that, similar to EU AI Act, the Continental AI Strategy aims to adopt and implement responsible AI as one of its key functional areas.

The inculcation of a responsible AI atmosphere in African society begins with looking at specific goals that are outlined in the Continental AI Strategy. There are 15 goals that are outlined in the Continental AI Strategy, but the following goals are important when looking how the achievement of responsible AI must take shape on the African continent:

- Cultivating an enabling environment for a vibrant and inclusive AI startup ecosystem.
- Ensuring the availability of high-quality and diverse datasets for training systems, which would be enabled through high-performance computing, data centres and cloud services.
- Fostering information integrity, media and information literacy.
- Promoting AI skills and talent in schools, colleges and workplaces, along with providing upskilling opportunities for individuals who are in jobs that are at risk of being replaced by AI.
- Promoting research and innovation in AI through partnerships between academia and the private as well as the public sectors.
- Providing for the adoption and implementation of ethical principles for AI that respect human rights and dignity within the framework of regional and international human rights law; that capture diversity, inclusivity, African culture and values like Ubuntu; that promote the protection of children in the face of AI as Africa is fast becoming a young continent; and committing to the responsible and unbiased use of AI that respects intellectual property rights and is equipped to address potential societal and legal challenges.
- Adopting and implementing technical standards to ensure the safety and security of AI systems across the African continent (African Union, 2024).

African values, inclusion, diversity, respect for fundamental rights and the quest to ensure responsible and ethical AI for the African continent are at the heart of the Continental AI Strategy. This instrument has served as a much-needed and timely guide to various African states with regard to how they prepare their own AI policies and how they seek to determine their own trajectories for the implementation of AI within their own borders. To date, African countries that have formulated their own AI policies are Mauritius, Kenya and Egypt. Countries like South Africa and Nigeria are undergoing consultation processes with relevant stakeholders regarding the introduction of their AI policies while other countries like Morocco have yet to propose any policy or guidelines on AI (Dentons, 2025).

On 4 April 2025, representatives from various African states gathered in Kigali, Rwanda for the Global AI Summit on Africa. On this occasion, various African states assented to The Africa Declaration on Artificial Intelligence. Under Article 2.2 of this declaration, it seeks to leverage the potential of AI to drive innovation and competitiveness in order to advance Africa's economies, industries and societies; to position Africa as a global leader in ethical, trustworthy and inclusive AI adoption; and to foster the sustainable and responsible design, development, deployment, use and governance of AI technologies in Africa (The Africa Declaration on Artificial Intelligence, 2025). It is probable that the Africa Declaration on Artificial

Intelligence therefore draws on, among other sources, the Continental AI Strategy to show the African continent's intentions and aspirations in its quest to become a global competitor in the global AI race. This is also demonstrated through some of its provisions that set out commitments to developing AI talent, establishing African open data sets and open AI models, deploying and distributing sovereign computing infrastructure, developing regional AI incubation and scaling hubs to support African-led AI innovation, establishing a US$ 60 billion Africa AI Fund for the creation of safe, inclusive and competitive African AI, supporting the adoption of innovative and responsible national AI policies and governance frameworks aligned to the Continental AI Strategy and endorsing the establishment of the Africa AI Council to encourage institutional cooperation (The Africa Declaration on Artificial Intelligence, 2025). The commitments created within the Africa Declaration on Artificial Intelligence are extensive and the combine not only a rights- and ethics-based approach to developing and implementing responsible AI in Africa, but they also chart Africa's course towards it becoming a rising contender for dominance in the global AI race in the near future.

3. MULTI-STAKEHOLDER IMPACT OF THE GLOBAL AI RACE

The global AI race illustrates a new pattern in the pursuance of regulating AI, irrespective of whether it is via building the most up-to-date AI product or whether it involves developing a comprehensive AI regulatory instrument. The emergence of a global AI race shifts global power in certain quarters of the world. These events demonstrate how power, politics, influence and ideologies dominate each region or country's quest to lead in the realm of AI regulation. This "competitive" pursuance begs the question of whether the race is one that must be won at all costs or whether it should be a race that also prioritises collaboration between regions and countries, to ensure not only the prioritisation of the human being, fundamental rights and human-centric AI, but also the sharing of policy best practice and knowledge for ethical, trustworthy and better AI.

Although these are noble goals that need to be achieved by global AI competitors in the global AI race, these goals face obstacles and stumbling blocks rooted in socio-political agendas, national interests, state control and the economic power vested in governments and big tech. What is becoming evident is that the global AI landscape is fragmenting along political and regulatory lines which can lead to technological decoupling, resulting in the emergence of distinct national AI ecosystems that can cause trade conflicts, data governance challenges, and competing regulatory frameworks (Colther, Doussoulin & Tontini, 2025, p.2).

An example of how AI regulation is fragmented along political lines in the pursuit of competitive AI innovation in the global AI race was recently confronted in the Senate of the United States of America. On 22 May 2025, a budget reconciliation bill (known as the "Big Beautiful Bill") was passed by Congress in which several significant AI-related provisions, including funding for government technology upgrades that incorporated commercially developed AI and a proposed moratorium to be placed on states that would essentially ban them from promulgating AI state law and enforcement for a period of 10 years (Samp, Tobey, Darling & Loud, 2025). The proposal of this bill stems from the Trump Administration's strategy of competing in the global AI race through deregulation in response to the European Union's heavy regulation of AI systems, the proliferation of US state bills, actions by the US attorney general to localise AI governance and vastly competing views on AI safety (Samp, Tobey, Darling & Loud, 2025). The proposal of this 10-year AI moratorium on states was met with fierce opposition from certain segments of American society and this illustrates how the impact of competing in the global AI race can affect various stakeholders with an interest in the outcomes of AI regulation. There were concerns that, should the 10-year AI moratorium be passed by the United States Senate, it would shield big tech companies from complying with existing state regulations and to exploit children, creators and conservatives (Perrigo and Chow, 2025). In addition, the passing of the bill enforcing the 10-year AI moratorium would also entirely nullify state legislation made by the various US states that served the purpose of addressing critical challenges brought on by AI to protect children and social values (for example, states like Texas, Mississippi, Nebraska and Ohio, among others, had passed or proposed legislation to specifically prohibit the use of AI for the creation and distribution of child sexual abuse material) (Newhoff, 2025), as well as to ensure that AI is properly regulated in healthcare, especially with regard to insurance claim processes (for example, laws of this nature were proposed or enacted in California, Connecticut, Florida, Maryland and Massachusetts) (Kelly, 2025). This indicates that the passing of a 10-year moratorium on states that would prohibit them from regulating AI had drastic and severe consequences for the people who were not necessarily parties to the policymaking process but who would ultimately be negatively affected by such a moratorium especially in healthcare and other social contexts. On 27 June 2025, the US Senate voted overwhelmingly to remove the 10-year AI moratorium on states, with lawmakers voting 99 to 1 to strike the moratorium from the bill which means that states can now regulate AI through their own legislation without any further federal intervention (Morgan & Shepardson, 2025). The 10-year AI moratorium was removed from the bill and on 4 July 2025, the "Big Beautiful Bill" was signed into law with amendments aimed at stimulating the economy and fostering financial security, although it is still perceived to be a potential problem for certain individuals and groups trying to survive financially in marginalised quarters of American society (Moran, 2025). The story of the "Big Beautiful Bill" shows how fragmentation along political lines and shifting power in the hands of governments (even within countries themselves) can have a negative impact on people in societies, creating uncertainty around AI and how it is to be regulated for everyone's benefit.

A troubling consequence of global AI players competing in fragmented regulatory and political contexts is the potential for AI to be used as a tool to protect national security, in that governments can use AI to strengthen their defences by using autonomous military technologies, surveillance tools and AI-driven cybersecurity to ensure that their national sovereignty and borders are protected (Colther, Doussoulin and Tontini, 2025, p.6). This presents a serious ethical and strategic concern with regard to what is being perceived as AI-driven warfare, through the use of lethal autonomous weapons, AI-piloted fighter jets, AI-enhanced intelligence gathering and AI systems with either AI cyberattack capabilities or the ability to spread misinformation, disinformation and propaganda in global and local contexts (Kissinger, Schmidt and Huttenlocher, 2021, pp.101 – 102). This evolution of warfare using AI presents a disturbing and dystopian picture of modern warfare in that AI has the potential to augment conventional, nuclear and cyber capabilities that make international relations and security relationships among rivals (especially those participating in the global AI race) more challenging to predict and maintain as well as making conflicts more difficult to limit (Kissinger, Schmidt and Huttenlocher, 2021, p.102). The catastrophic impact of AI-driven warfare is already being seen in the ongoing war between Russia and Ukraine, where the constant development and finetuning of autonomous drones is making the war even more dangerous, deadly and unpredictable for both countries where there are already escalating numbers of civilian and military casualties (Boffey, D. 2025). It has also been reported that AI-driven lethal autonomous weapons systems have been deployed in Palestine (particularly in Gaza) by Israel, causing more civilian deaths and transgressing prevailing international law in a war where AI-driven military systems have been said to fail with telling the difference between civilians and fighters, leading to devastating results and a mounting human cost (Düz, 2025).

The shifts in global power and the negative impacts of pursuing "first place" in the global AI race therefore can have positive effects but the accounts in the preceding paragraphs demonstrate how negative effects resulting from decision-making in the pursuit of competing in the global AI race, both in peacetime and in war, can cause great harm to the people of a state or region who have no bargaining power or voice in the global AI race. In order to avert catastrophic consequences for people who are otherwise regarded as the "spectators" of the global AI race, more is required to ensure that any negative fallout from the global AI race does not harm them. Something more is required to protect people, to empower them and to enable them to flourish from the benefits that would accompany groundbreaking events resulting from the global AI race.

4. TECHNO-POLITICS: A FRAMEWORK FOR MAINTAINING HUMANITY IN THE GLOBAL AI RACE

This is the point of departure for this contribution: that a "race" to accomplish a goal is a healthy and fulfilling competitive exercise, provided that no harm or shame is brought upon the "competitors" (global AI powers), "spectators" (humanity at large) and "the rules of the game" (politics). Techno-politics is therefore the appropriate framework to explore how the global AI race must consider the importance of political goals being enacted with the support of technology like AI and using it in the best way possible to ensure that it serves humanity, not replaces it.

In exploring how techno-politics should enhance the shifts in global power surrounding AI by emphasising the importance of the human being, the importance of fundamental rights and a human-centric golden thread will also be evaluated, which in this regard makes the techno-politics lens on the topic therapeutic. By "therapeutic", it is meant that techno-politics is required to ensure that no one gets hurt, manipulated, victimised or harmed within the overall pursuit of AI power and leadership by any given region or country around the world. This is a core concern with the nature of pursuing AI regulation as a global competition: the impact on people becomes an ethical moot point. In whichever form any dominant AI regulation takes shape, it must place the flourishing and benefits of people at the forefront of its purpose in governing AI. In other words, it must not put financial interests, competitive manipulation, military supremacy and commercial superiority above the importance of people in harnessing the benefits of AI. This will be the core mission of this contribution when looking at techno-politics as a therapeutic framework to protect all people in what is now becoming the next "arms race" in the world – the race to have the "best" AI regulation and AI innovation, with great stakes for the shifts in global power, disruption of international relations and influence to negatively impact the lives of people if it is pursued solely through brute force and "at all costs".

In seeking to define techno-politics as a framework for purposes of this contribution, two different variants of techno-politics need to be explored, especially within the ambit of facilitating communication and placing value on information. According to Kurban, Péna-Lopez and Haberer (2016: pp.500 – 501), the first variant of techno-politics is known as a centralised approach, which applies to techno-political practices that are activated top-down, in other words, with reference to information that is usually exclusive to decision-makers in relation to how the government exercises its powers over new technologies. This variant of techno-politics employs technologies for increasing efficiency and efficacy in traditional areas of governance and government within democracy as a representative paradigm, embracing new practices such as, among others, e-government, e-politics, e-campaigning and e-petitioning (Kurban, Péna-Lopez and Haberer, 2016: p.501). Therapeutic techno-politics can be especially helpful here in order to mitigate concerns and challenges experienced where people are, for example, replaced by AI in the workplace. As governments endeavour to make their own processes more digitised, the impact of AI in labour markets and the intimidating idea of replacing human beings with AI in order to save costs and potentially increase productivity can be mitigated through therapeutic techno-politics by ensuring that the "human-in-the-loop" is always maintained. It will become incumbent on policymakers, business leaders, trade union representatives and workers to confront "new bargains" to address the negative results that AI would bring into the workplace (Muggah & Giussani, 2025). This will require a coordinated effort by governments and businesses to ensure that workers are appropriately trained and upskilled for the advent of AI in different labour markets, to consider the adoption of AI deployment models and to prioritise collaboration between humans and technology (Muggah & Giussani, 2025). In this way, therapeutic techno-politics takes shape to ensure that people are empowered to augment their current skillsets through AI and to complement their own abilities by growing alongside AI in achieving their own career goals in any given discipline. Maintaining the "human-in-the-loop" approach through human-centric employment models is supported by the failure to go "fully AI" by companies like Duolingo, who by retrenching people in favour of going "fully AI" in several job roles, have since had to pivot on their "fully AI" workplace plans by re-employing people to assist them with fixing complications and problems were not foreseen when going "fully AI" seemed to be an initial groundbreaking step in saving costs and increasing productivity for the company (Thubron, 2025).

The second variant of techno-politics is what is known as the distributed approach, usually bottom-up, in which information is co-produced and shared by the individual through overlapping networks as a more transformative use of Information and Communications Technologies to inform new ways of engaging in politics, which is otherwise known as democratic techno-politics (Kurban, Péna-Lopez and Haberer, 2016:p.501). This variant of techno-politics looks at the subversive use of technologies in combination with legal and political tools. For example, new political organisations use online tools and platforms in order to facilitate and accelerate processes, which include generating ideas, prioritising issues, content and media creation which will be crucial for use in the formal political sphere (Kurban, Péna-Lopez and Haberer, 2016:p.501). The suggestion to be made for democratic techno-politics is that it especially needs to be employed to ensure peace and security by eliminating the propensity for misinformation, disinformation and propaganda to be spread. Political players and society should therefore aim to collaborate by ensuring that the prerequisites of inclusion and participation, as prerequisites for building AI systems are maintained, especially when it comes to diversifying AI teams through the participation of women and girls from underrepresented groups, like those who are in the Global South (UNESCO, 2025). This participatory measure would inform the notion of therapeutic techno-politics by allowing for what can be regarded as marginalised or vulnerable groups to not only shape AI paradigms in states and regions but to empower these groups to shape the trajectory of AI regulation in the appropriate political spaces for the benefit of all parties concerned.

When looking at both variants of techno-politics, what is important to remember is that the conceptualisation of techno-politics as a therapeutic device for empowering various stakeholders who are impacted within the global AI race (including the consequences of decisions taken by the competing global AI powers themselves) is that techno-politics represents a complex entanglement of technology and politics that does not lead to one singular response, but rather, it generates a variety of different positions in relation to using technology for political purposes and forging new narratives based on national and social identities (Kurban, Péna-Lopez and Haberer, 2016:p.501). Given this multiplicity of different positions that can be generated through the interplay and complex entanglement of technology and politics, there is great potential for technology in this sense to empower people and actors within the global AI race against others, especially against those who themselves have contentious agendas for AI regulation and the "contesting claims" involved in policy choices that have great political impact (Kurban, Péna-Lopez and Haberer, 2016: p.501).

The disruptive and powerful allure of technology, including AI, is a defining characteristic of its techno-political appearance, in that this characteristic shapes the narratives around AI in relation to politics and societies (Csernatoni, 2024). These narratives raise concerns with regard to who forges these narratives and how these narratives impact on societies (Csernatoni, 2024). By taking into account the two variants of techno-politics as set out above, it is submitted that the therapeutic element of techno-politics challenges individuals who are witnessing the global AI race between their particular countries or regions to actively participate and advocate for AI initiatives and implementation that will serve them and enable them to harness its benefits. In order to do this, state actors and governments must take steps to ensure that the public voice is heard and that any concerns surrounding the rapid development of AI in the global AI race is not about who is coming first in the race, but who is in fact able to ensure that all stakeholders and all people in society are able to share in the fruits and benefits of developing AI that is contextually relevant, safe, ethical and proper in its development and deployment. In order for techno-politics to be therapeutic in its form and to empower all people to challenge the narratives that evolve from it in AI spaces, under the supervision of governments, institutions, big tech and expert communities, therapeutic techno-politics will also need to consider applicable AI principles such as those that are set out in the OECD Recommendation and those principles that, for example, are grounded in the EU AI Act, especially in relation to always ensuring human-centric values and priorities at the forefront of AI developments. These principles, to a degree, are reflected in AI policy developments in the United States of America and in China but it is also suggested that therapeutic techno-politics must also take into account the fluid and diverse ways that AI can enhance innovation for betterment of all humankind through the actions taken by both of these competitors. Therapeutic techno-politics would also need to be designed taking into account the importance of the United Nations SDGs (as envisaged in the African Union Continental AI Strategy) and to frame these as long-term goals that will inform respect for fundamental rights, human-centric values and the pursuit of AI innovation like that which is envisioned for the African continent in terms of the African Declaration on AI. In essence, this speaks to the importance of therapeutic techno-politics as a conduit for ensuring that responsible AI because, just like responsible AI, therapeutic techno-politics envisions the development of AI systems in political contexts that will benefit society while minimising the risk of negative consequences (International Standards Organization, 2025). In this sense, therapeutic techno-politics must, whether in form of top-down or bottom-up processes, also enable people to reap the benefits of AI developments and AI policy developed in their region or country as part of the global AI race through international collaboration and the sharing of best practices from around the globe; in this manner, everyone wins and not just a select or privileged few at the expense of all others.

In order to achieve this ideal, several ongoing challenges that feature prominently in the global AI race also need to be viewed through the lens of therapeutic techno-politics. At the outset, the therapeutic element needs to account for how algorithmic transparency and algorithmic governance relating to the training datasets used by AI systems will strike a balance between the goals to be achieved by political actors regarding AI and the empowerment of people in any given society to use AI beneficially. It has already been pointed out that AI shows great promise for enhancing surveillance, facial recognition and biometric identification technologies but, if used improperly, AI tools can potentially produce discriminatory outcomes that can negatively impact the privacy, dignity and equality rights of people. These benefits need to be carefully weighed against the possible risks presented by bias in its all of its forms, particularly algorithmic bias which can reveal itself at different stages in AI system's lifecycle (Europol, 2025). Therapeutic techno-politics would, in seeking to mitigate bias, invite AI developers and deployers to ensure that there are fair outcomes in the training datasets attributed to AI systems, to ensure that AI systems comply with maintaining public trust and to ensure that AI systems protect and respect fundamental rights such as rights to privacy, dignity and identity (Europol, 2025). This would empower people who are the subjects of surveillance, facial recognition and biometric identification technologies to challenge any impropriety or infringements through these AI systems by holding AI developers and deployers with political affiliations accountable for their actions, for example, in terms of the provisions of the EU AI Act regarding ethical and fundamental rights protections afforded to individuals. Further impetus for the notion of therapeutic techno-politics as an empowering framework to balance the protection of peoples' privacy rights and AI as a strengthening force for law enforcement can be seen when Article 21 (the right of a data subject to object to the processing of their personal data in a given situation) and Article 22 (the right of a data subject to not be subject to decision-making based solely on automated processing, including profiling) of the General Data Protection Regulation (GDPR) are invoked to protect a person or groups of persons from biased decision-making through surveillance, facial recognition or biometric identification technologies that are driven by AI.

In relation to AI-driven warfare, therapeutic techno-politics envisions calling on all political actors to not only consider the devastating effects that AI-driven warfare is already causing but to ensure that checks and balances are instilled to limit the concentration of power that AI technologies could provide to governments and relevant stakeholders where war is concerned (Araya & King, 2022, p.12). The time may be near where the traditional understanding of the "Laws of War" as set out in the Geneva Conventions will need to change in response to the rapid technological developments brought on by AI in warfare. Progress is already being made in this area through The Geneva Process on AI Principles, a document that aims "to define ethical principles to guide the design, development and use of AI for defence and military purposes" (Geneva Centre for Security Policy, 2025). The Geneva Process on AI Principles is a work in progress and it is also points to an important facet of what therapeutic techno-politics envisions regarding AI warfare: the importance of international and organisational collaboration, in shaping the contours of war and conflict in the future by developing guardrails for the evolution of military AI, through common international rules and regulations (Araya & King, 2022, pp.12 – 13). In this way, therapeutic techno-politics then envisions the field of international humanitarian law as an evolving tool in the quest to regulate AI warfare and military AI so that people are not only protected but they are empowered to know more about surviving in conflict situations where AI is becoming an ever-growing singular threat to humanity, peace and security.

5. CONCLUSION

Rapid and more complex developments in AI continue to constantly challenge notions of how AI must be regulated and how it must be developed to foster innovation and competitiveness in an ever-growing global AI market. This antithesis between regulation and innovation is a fine line that AI policy decision-makers need to tread in their pursuit to lead in the global AI race. In the pursuit of AI innovation, the arrival of ChatGPT form OpenAI in the United States of America and its monopoly being threatened by the release of China's Deepseek already demonstrated how a challenge from one competitor to another in the AI global race can severely compromise global markets and social perceptions of AI tools. In the pursuit of AI regulation, the EU AI Act as a rights-based regulation demonstrated the importance of regulating AI from a normative vantage point, but at the expense of AI innovation which has resulted in the European Union having to shift its priorities to AI innovation in order to remain a relevant competitor in the global AI race. Moreover, this has also come as response to how the Trump Administration in the United States of America and the government in China have chosen to pursue innovation at the expense of rigid regulation of AI. The African Union Continental AI Strategy and the African Declaration on AI include a combination of rights-based aspirations and the pursuit of economic growth and autonomy with the United Nations SDGs and Agenda 2063 as the long-term goals for truly African AI on the continent.

While the global AI race ebbs and flows, it has been shown that the people and other relevant stakeholders who can be perceived as the "spectators" of the global AI race must not be forgotten in the political decisions that are taken to enhance AI regulation or to accelerate AI innovation. Therapeutic techno-politics therefore serves as a compassionate and human-centric lens to ensure that people can still be empowered to participate and to advocate for their importance in the determination of who remains ahead in the global AI race. By considering the importance of AI principles such as those that ground the OECD Recommendation and are made legally binding in the EU AI Act, therapeutic techno-politics can be seen to inculcate these principles as a means to ensure that the fundamental rights of all persons are protected in the pursuit of rewards deriving from the global AI race. In addition, the approach to deregulation as a catalyst for accelerated growth in AI innovation as exhibited in the United States of America and China further amplifies the importance for people to also share in the proceeds that derive from such innovation, as opposed to the proceeds only being taken by a select or privileged few. Therapeutic techno-politics has been shown to potentially address challenges that arise as a result of AI in the contexts of mitigating bias, surveillance, facial recognition, biometric identification, the impact of AI on global labour markets and the use of AI-driven tools in warfare.

The global AI race is starting to become even more competitive with the arrival of new global regions and companies who are looking to make their own marks in the race through their own AI policies, adoption and implementation. As the global AI race gains more momentum, therapeutic techno-politics must therefore continue to adapt as a mechanism to ensure that not only do people affected by the global AI race are protected in its pursuits, but that everyone wins in the quest to harness the benefits of AI for all nations and for all peoples now and in the future.

REFERENCES

Adams, R. (2024). Geopolitics of AI: Africa's Role in a Shifting Global Landscape. *Global Center on AI Governance.* https://www.globalcenter.ai/research/geopolitics-of-ai-africas-role-in-a-shifting-global-landscape

African Union. (2024), Continental Artificial Intelligence Strategy, https://au.int/en/documents/20240809/continental-artificial-intelligence-strategy

African Union. (2024), Continental Artificial Intelligence Strategy: Harnessing AI for Africa's Development and Prosperity, https://au.int/sites/default/files/documents/44004-doc-EN-_Continental_AI_Strategy_July_2024.pdf

African Union Convention On Cyber Security And Personal Data Protection (2024), https://au.int/sites/default/files/treaties/29560-treaty-0048_-_african_union_convention_on_cyber_security_and_personal_data_protection_e.pdf

Araya, D., & King, M. (2022). The Impact of Artificial Intelligence on Military Defence and Security. *Centre for International Governance Innovation.* https://www.cigionline.org/static/documents/no.263.pdf

Bahr, C. (2025). EU Regulators Scrutinize Deepseek For Data Privacy Violations. *Usercentrics.* https://usercentrics.com/knowledge-hub/eu-regulators-scrutinize-deepseek-for-data-privacy-violations/

Boffey, D. (2025). Killing Machines: How Russia and Ukraine's Race To Perfect Deadly Pilotless Drones Could Harm Us All. *The Guardian.* https://www.theguardian.com/world/2025/jun/25/ukraine-russia-autonomous-drones-ai

Cao, X., Sharmina, M., & Cuéllar-Franca, R. M. (2024). Sourcing Cobalt in the Democratic Republic of the Congo for a Responsible Net-Zero Transition: Incentives, Risks and Stakeholders. *Resources Policy.* https://www.sciencedirect.com/science/article/pii/S0301420724005166

Carminati, D. (2024). Opinion – The Concept of Soft Power And AI. https://www.researchgate.net/publication/386073334_The_Concept_of_Soft_Power_and_AI

Colther, C., Doussoulin, J. P., & Tontini, G. (2025). Artificial Intelligence and Global Power Dynamics: Geopolitical Competition, Strategic Alliances, and the Future of AI Governance. https://papers.ssrn.com/sol3/papers.cfm?abstract_id=5251303

Csernatoni, R. (2024). Charting the Geopolitics and European Governance of Artificial Intelligence. *Carnegie Endowment For International Peace.* https://carnegieendowment.org/research/2024/03/charting-the-geopolitics-and-european-governance-of-artificial-intelligence?lang=en

Csernatoni, R. (2025). The EU's AI Power Play: Between Deregulation and Innovation. *Carnegie Endowment For International Peace.* https://carnegieendowment.org/research/2025/05/the-eus-ai-power-play-between-deregulation-and-innovation?lang=en

Dentons. (2025). AI Regulation and Policy in Africa. *Legal 500.* https://www.legal500.com/developments/thought-leadership/ai-regulation-and-policy-in-africa/#:~:text=First%20among%20the%20African%20AI,any%20guidance%20on%20AI%20regulation

Düz, S. (2025). Gaza as a Testing Ground: Israel's AI Warfare. *SETA.* https://www.setav.org/en/opinion/gaza-as-a-testing-ground-israels-ai-warfare

Efthymiopoulos, M. P. (2019). A Cyber-security Framework for Development, Defense and Innovation at NATO. *Journal of Innovation and Entrepreneurship, 8*(12), 1–26. DOI: 10.1186/s13731-019-0105-z

European Union Artificial Intelligence Act. (2025), https://artificialintelligenceact.eu/

European Union Artificial Intelligence Act (2025), Article 5: Prohibited AI Practices | EU Artificial Intelligence Act.

European Union Artificial Intelligence Act (2025), Article 6: Classification Rules for High-Risk AI Systems | EU Artificial Intelligence Act.

European Union Artificial Intelligence Act (2025), Annex III: High-Risk AI Systems Referred to in Article 6(2) | EU Artificial Intelligence Act.

European Union Artificial Intelligence Act (2025), Article 8: Compliance with the Requirements | EU Artificial Intelligence Act.

European Union Artificial Intelligence Act (2025), Article 9: Risk Management System | EU Artificial Intelligence Act.

European Union Artificial Intelligence Act (2025), Article 10: Data and Data Governance | EU Artificial Intelligence Act.

European Union Artificial Intelligence Act (2025), Article 11: Technical Documentation | EU Artificial Intelligence Act.

European Union Artificial Intelligence Act (2025), Article 12: Record-Keeping | EU Artificial Intelligence Act.

European Union Artificial Intelligence Act (2025), Article 13: Transparency and Provision of Information to Deployers | EU Artificial Intelligence Act.

European Union Artificial Intelligence Act (2025), Article 14: Human Oversight | EU Artificial Intelligence Act.

European Union Artificial Intelligence Act (2025), Article 15: Accuracy, Robustness and Cybersecurity | EU Artificial Intelligence Act.

European Union Artificial Intelligence Act (2025), Article 27: Fundamental Rights Impact Assessment for High-Risk AI Systems | EU Artificial Intelligence Act.

European Union Artificial Intelligence Act. (2025), https://artificialintelligenceact.eu/recital/1/

Europol. (2025). Understanding and Mitigating Bias To Harness AI Responsibly. *Europol.* https://www.europol.europa.eu/media-press/newsroom/news/understanding-and-mitigating-bias-to-harness-ai-responsibly

General Data Protection Regulation (GDPR). (2025). https://gdpr-info.eu/art-22-gdpr/

Geneva Centre for Security Policy. (2025). The Geneva Process on AI Principles. https://www.gcsp.ch/the-geneva-process-on-AI-Principles

Georgieva, K. (2024). AI Will Transform the Global Economy. Let's Make Sure It Benefits Humanity. *IMF Blog.* https://www.imf.org/en/Blogs/Articles/2024/01/14/ai-will-transform-the-global-economy-lets-make-sure-it-benefits-humanity

Goodwin, M. (2024). What is an API? *IBM.* https://www.ibm.com/think/topics/api

Gryn, R., & Rzeszucinski, P. (2018) Bias In AI Is A Real Problem. Here's What We Should Do About It. *World Economic Forum.* https://www.weforum.org/stories/2018/09/the-biggest-risk-of-ai-youve-never-heard-of/

International Standards Organization (ISO). (2025). Building a Responsible AI: How to Manage the AI Ethics Debate. *International Standards Organization.* https://www.iso.org/artificial-intelligence/responsible-ai-ethics

Iyer, N. (2022) Digital Extractivism in Africa Mirrors Colonial Practices. *Stanford University Human-Centered Artificial Intelligence.* https://hai.stanford.edu/news/neema-iyer-digital-extractivism-africa-mirrors-colonial-practices

Judge, B., Nitzberg, M., & Russell, S. (2025). When code isn't law: Rethinking regulation for artificial intelligence. *Policy and Society*, *44*(1), 85–97. DOI: 10.1093/polsoc/puae020

Kelly, T. E. (2025). Locked Out: How a Federal Moratorium on AI Regulation Could Reshape Healthcare Oversight. *Arnall Golden Gregory LLP.* https://www.agg.com/news-insights/publications/locked-out-how-a-federal-moratorium-on-ai-regulation-could-reshape-healthcare-oversight/

Kennedy, M. (2025). A Strategic Vision For US AI Leadership: Supporting Security, Innovation, Democracy and Global Prosperity. *Wilson Centre.* https://www.wilsoncenter.org/article/strategic-vision-us-ai-leadership-supporting-security-innovation-democracy-and-global#:~:text=By%20advancing%20transparent%2C%20market%2Ddriven,than%20reacting%20to%20authoritarian%20models

Kerner, S. M. (2025). Deepseek explained: Everything you need to know. *TechTarget.* https://www.techtarget.com/whatis/feature/DeepSeek-explained-Everything-you-need-to-know

Kissinger, H. A., Schmidt, E., & Huttenlocher, D. (2021). *The Age of AI And Our Human Future.* John Murray Publishers. http://103.203.175.90:81/fdScript/RootOfEBooks/E%20Book%20collection%20-%202024%20-%20G/CSE%20%20IT%20AIDS%20ML/The%20Age%20of%20AI_%20And%20Our%20Human%20Future.pdf

Kuo, K. (2025). Why China's AI breakthroughs should come as no surprise. *World Economic Forum.* https://www.weforum.org/stories/2025/06/china-ai-breakthroughs-no-surprise/

Kurban, C., Péna-Lopez, I., & Haberer, M. (2016). *What is Technopolitics? A Conceptual Scheme for Understanding Politics in the Digital Age* [Paper presentation]. *12th International Conference on Internet, Law* & Politics, Barcelona, Spain.

Liu, J., & Otusanya, O. J. (2022) How Multinationals Avoid Taxes in Africa and What Should Change. *The Conversation.* https://theconversation.com/how-multinationals-avoid-taxes-in-africa-and-what-should-change-179797

Marr, B. (2023). A Short History Of ChatGPT: How We Got To Where We Are Today. *Forbes.* https://www.forbes.com/sites/bernardmarr/2023/05/19/a-short-history-of-chatgpt-how-we-got-to-where-we-are-today/

Moran, B. (2025). How the "Big, Beautiful Bill" Will Deepen the Racial Wealth Gap – A Law Scholar Explains How It Reduces Poor Families' Ability to Afford Food and Health Care. *The Conversation.* https://theconversation.com/how-the-big-beautiful-bill-will-deepen-the-racial-wealth-gap-a-law-scholar-explains-how-it-reduces-poor-families-ability-to-afford-food-and-health-care-260680

Morgan, D., & Shepardson, D. (2025). US Senate Strikes AI Regulation Ban From Trump Megabill. *Reuters.* https://www.reuters.com/legal/government/us-senate-strikes-ai-regulation-ban-trump-megabill-2025-07-01/

Morgan Stanley. (2025). AI in China: A Sleeping Giant Awakens. *Morgan Stanley.* https://www.morganstanley.com/insights/articles/china-ai-becoming-global-leader

Newhoff, D. (2025). A 10-year Moratorium on AI Regulation is Madness. *The Hill.* https://thehill.com/opinion/technology/5357228-ai-moratorium-harms-american-people/

Organization for Economic Cooperation and Development (OECD). (2025). AI principles. *OECD.* https://www.oecd.org/en/topics/sub-issues/ai-principles.html

Organization for Economic Cooperation and Development (OECD). (2025). Recommendation of the Council on Artificial Intelligence. *OECD Legal Instruments.* https://legalinstruments.oecd.org/en/instruments/oecd-legal-0449

Oxford, S. F. A. (2025). AI and Digital Technologies: Critical Minerals, Policy, and the Energy Transition. https://www.sfa-oxford.com/knowledge-and-insights/critical-minerals-in-low-carbon-and-future-technologies/critical-minerals-in-artificial-intelligence/#:~:text=Cobalt%20is%20used%20in%20the,to%20ensure%20durability%20and%20efficiency

Perrigo, B., & Chow, A. R. (2025). Senators Reject 10-Year Ban on State-Level AI Regulation, In Blow to Big Tech. *TIME.* https://time.com/7299044/senators-reject-10-year-ban-on-state-level-ai-regulation-in-blow-to-big-tech/

Play, A. I. (2025). Deepseek v ChatGPT. *PlayAI.* https://play.ht/blog/deepseek-vs-chatgpt/#:~:text=DeepSeek:%20Developed%20with%20a%20budget,resources%20and%20advanced%20AI%20chips

Samp, T., Tobey, D., Darling, C., & Loud, T. (2025). Ten-year Moratorium on AI Regulation Proposed in US Congress. *DLA Piper.* https://www.dlapiper.com/en/insights/publications/ai-outlook/2025/ten-year-moratorium-on-ai

Sharan, G. (2025). ChatGPT Walks It Back – AI Giants Race Ahead. *PeopleMatters.* https://anz.peoplemattersglobal.com/article/technology/chatgpt-walks-it-back-ai-giants-race-ahead-45465

The Africa Declaration on Artificial Intelligence. (2025). https://c4ir.rw/docs/Africa-Declaration-on-Artificial-Intelligence.pdf

The American Presidency Project. (2025). Remarks by the Vice President at the Artificial Intelligence Action Summit in Paris, France. *The American Presidency Project.* https://www.presidency.ucsb.edu/documents/remarks-the-vice-president-the-artificial-intelligence-action-summit-paris-france

The White House. (2025). Fact Sheet: President Donald J. Trump Takes Action To Enhance America's AI Leadership. https://www.whitehouse.gov/fact-sheets/2025/01/fact-sheet-president-donald-j-trump-takes-action-to-enhance-americas-ai-leadership/

The White House. (2025). Initial Recissions of Harmful Executive Orders and Actions. https://www.whitehouse.gov/presidential-actions/2025/01/initial-rescissions-of-harmful-executive-orders-and-actions/

The White House. (2025). Removing Barriers To American Leadership In Artificial Intelligence. https://www.whitehouse.gov/presidential-actions/2025/01/removing-barriers-to-american-leadership-in-artificial-intelligence/

Thubron, R. (2025). Duolingo CEO Backtracks on AI Push, Says Human Workers Still Needed. *Techspot.* https://www.techspot.com/news/108054-duolingo-ceo-backtracks-ai-push-after-outcry-human.html

Trang, N. M., & Thao, K. P. (2025). AI and the Transformation of Global Politics. *International Journal of Scientific Research and Management*, *13*(2), 2130–2137. DOI: 10.18535/ijsrm/v13i02.sh01

UNESCO. (2025). Mainstreaming Accessibility and Inclusivity in AI and Digital Technologies, https://www.unesco.org/en/articles/mainstreaming-accessibility-and-inclusivity-ai-and-digital-technologies

KEY TERMS AND DEFINITIONS

Agile: An iterative and incremental approach that emphasises flexibility, collaboration and rapid response to change.

Algorithmic Bias: The bias that develops from systematic errors, preconceived notions and prejudged information that are inserted into AI training datasets, producing unfair or discriminatory outcomes.

Algorithm: A process or set of rules to be followed in calculations or other problem-solving operations, especially by a computer.

Amplified: Expand upon or elaborate on in significant detail.

API: Application Programming Interface – code that allows for communication between software applications in relation to exchanging data, features and functionality.

Artificial Intelligence (AI): Computer systems that are trained to perform tasks that would otherwise require human intelligence such as comprehension, problem solving, translating languages and generating ideas.

Bias: Inclination or prejudice for or against one person or group, especially in a way that is considered to be unfair against said person or group.

Calibrated: Aligned with metrics, readings or requirements.

Cataclysmic: Causing sudden upheaval.

Catalyst: A person, thing, situation or event that causes an emphatic reaction.

Comity: An association of nations or regions for their own mutual benefit.

Customisation: Modifying something to suit a particular individual, need, task or circumstance.

Digital Extractivism: The practice of gathering and exploiting vast amounts of data, often personal data, from digital platforms and devices, mirroring traditional resource extraction practices.

Endeavour: An attempt or an activity with a certain goal to be achieved.

Evolving: To develop over time.

Exemplified: Illustrated or clarified through an example.

Extractivism: An economic model primarily focussed on the large-scale extraction of natural resources for export, often with limited local processing or benefit.

Geopolitics: The study of how geographical factors influence political power and international relations.

Gig Economy: A labour market characterised by the prevalence of short-term contracts or freelance work as opposed to permanent jobs.

Global North: High-income, industrialised countries that are characterised by advanced economies, technological infrastructure and high standards of living.

Global South: A group of countries primarily located in the Southern Hemisphere that share common socio-economic and political characteristics. These characteristics are associated with historical, colonial and ongoing challenges to the development in these countries.

Igniting: Inflaming a situation.

Innate: Natural or born within.

Innovation: The act of developing something new or groundbreaking in a particular field or discipline.

Interoperable: The ability of computer systems and software to exchange and make use of information.

Redress:To correct: set right, or make amends for a wrong or grievance.

Risk: A situation that involves exposure to danger or peril.

Scalability: The capacity to be changed in size and scale.

Social Scoring: The concept that all daily actions by human beings are digitally monitored and scored for their benefit to society as a whole.

Soft Power: The ability of governments to influence others through attraction and persuasion rather than through coercion or military force, by relying on a country's culture, political values and foreign policies to shape the preferences of other nations.

Stark: Visibly apparent or obvious.

Stewardship: The responsible management and care of something that has been entrusted to someone to care for.

Tax haven: A country or independent area where taxes are levied at a low rate.

Technological Decoupling: The process where countries or regions reduce their reliance on foreign technologies, especially in strategic sectors, often due to national security concerns or geopolitical tensions.

Techno-politics: A framework that contextually addresses how technology influences political decision-making and agendas.

Therapeutic: Ensuring that the well-being, care, safety and security of people is maintained and that there is no harm or negative impact caused to people.

To augment: To make (something) greater by adding to it.

To harness: To control and make use of.

To mitigate: To make something bad less severe, serious or painful.

Versatile: Adaptable to different functions, circumstances or activities.

Chapter 4
Smart Cities and Control:
Reconsidering Techno-Politics and Individual Agency in China and the UK

Ufuk Ayhan
https://orcid.org/0000-0002-2673-8308
Turkish National Police Academy, Turkey

ABSTRACT

This chapter examines the techno-political dimensions of smart cities by comparing China and the UK. While China's social credit system represents explicit state control through data-driven governance, the UK's smart city model, though framed around openness and empowerment, also involves covert algorithmic influence via corporate surveillance and behavioral nudging. Drawing on techno-political theory, the chapter argues that digital infrastructures are never neutral; they embed political ideologies that shape both governance and citizen subjectivity. It highlights how individuals in both contexts navigate these systems through compliance or resistance, and calls for a vision of smart cities rooted in transparency, democratic accountability, and social justice.

1. INTRODUCTION: THE TECHNO-POLITICAL STAKES OF SMART CITIES

Over the past decade, "smart city" projects have moved from pilot schemes in a handful of metropolitan testbeds to a global policy orthodoxy. Worldwide spending on smart-city programmes was forecast to hit US $203 billion in 2024, driven chiefly by sensor networks, public-safety platforms, and data marketplaces. Annual indices

DOI: 10.4018/979-8-3373-2459-3.ch004

such as the IMD Smart City Index (2024/25) now benchmark more than 140 cities on digital infrastructure, environmental performance, and residents' perceptions of "smartness," underscoring the sector's maturation into a field of inter-urban competition. Municipal leaders tout gains in service efficiency, traffic optimisation, predictive maintenance, targeted social services, while technology vendors emphasise connectivity, edge computing, and AI as solutions to mounting urban pressures of population growth, climate resilience, and fiscal constraint (Parliamentary Office of Science and Technology [POST], 2021).

This chapter explores the techno-political dynamics of smart city development by focusing on two distinct governance contexts: China's controlling model and the United Kingdom's liberal-democratic approach. It critically investigates how both states deploy digital infrastructures, such as sensors, facial recognition systems, and algorithmic governance platforms, not merely for administrative efficiency but as instruments of behavioral control and political inscription. By examining the surveillance architectures in place, including China's Social Credit System and the UK's expanding use of live facial recognition, the chapter demonstrates how ostensibly neutral technologies produce profound implications for civil liberties and urban subjectivities. The analysis further interrogates the underlying control logics embedded within these systems, comparing China's overt reward-and-punishment mechanisms with the UK's more subtle, often opaque, forms of algorithmic nudging and data commodification. In doing so, it highlights the regulatory gaps and asymmetries of power that emerge when private technology firms operate alongside or within public governance structures. Finally, the chapter foregrounds citizen responses across both contexts, analyzing patterns of compliance, resistance, and negotiation. It shows how individuals and communities engage with these digital systems, either by internalizing normative expectations, challenging technological intrusions through civic or legal means, or strategically bargaining for localized benefits. By positioning these dynamics within a broader theoretical framework of techno-politics, the chapter contributes to a more nuanced understanding of how smart city technologies are reshaping the relationship between state, market, and citizen in the digital age.

Yet techno-political scholarship reminds us that the same infrastructures that streamline governance simultaneously reconfigure power (Arslan, 2025). Artefacts embody "frozen politics" (Winner, 1980). As Feenberg (1991) argues, design choices privilege certain imaginaries of order and of the ideal citizen, naturalising particular distributions of agency and control.

To interrogate how political ideologies become material in code, the chapter adopts a comparative lens pairing two high-profile smart-city trajectories:

Table 1.

China	United Kingdom
Controlling-synchronised model: vertically integrated platforms link local sensors to national databases such as the Social Credit System (SCS), codified in the 2014 State Council Planning Outline for the Construction of a Social Credit System (2014-2020). Hangzhou's City Brain 3.0, launched 31 March 2025, incorporates the DeepSeek-R1 LLM to orchestrate traffic, policing, and utilities.	Market-pluralist model: city governments broker public–private partnerships (PPPs) such as Manchester's Triangulum data platform (Siemens; Manchester-i) and Bristol Is Open. National oversight is fragmented; regulation lags behind deployments in policing and retail.

While China's discourse foregrounds "trust" and social harmony, the UK frames smartness in terms of innovation ecosystems, open data, and citizen empowerment. Nevertheless, both trajectories embed mechanisms of surveillance and behavioural steering, China through algorithmic scoring and overt sanctions, the UK through live facial-recognition (LFR) roll-outs that doubled to 4.7 million face-scans in 2024.

Smart-city technologies are not neutral utilities; they are normative assemblages that operationalise distinct visions of governance and personhood. Whether under China's directive state-capitalism or the UK's liberal-democratic pluralism, digital infrastructures script permissible actions, delimit dissent, and shape the reflexive self-governance of urban subjects (Jasanoff, 2018; Zuboff, 2019). The chapter therefore argues that ideological inscription, not merely technical capacity, determines how data systems reorder citizenship and authority.

2. CHINA'S SOCIAL CREDIT SYSTEM: ALGORITHMIC GOVERNANCE AND SOCIAL CONTROL

China's rapid urbanization and technological advancement have positioned it as a global leader in the development of smart cities, where digital infrastructures are seamlessly integrated into urban governance. At the heart of this transformation lies the Social Credit System (SCS), a state-driven initiative that epitomizes the convergence of data-driven technologies and control governance. The SCS is not merely a technological framework but a cornerstone of China's smart city infrastructure, designed to monitor, evaluate, and regulate citizen behavior through algorithmic means. This section explores the mechanics of the SCS, analyzes how its data-driven technologies enable state surveillance and behavioral conformity, examines urban applications such as facial recognition and citizen scoring, and discusses their implications for social stratification and the explicit disciplinary aims of controlling techno-politics.

The Social Credit System, formally introduced in 2014 through the State Council's "Planning Outline for the Construction of a Social Credit System (2014–2020)," aims to create a comprehensive mechanism for assessing the "trustworthiness" of individuals, businesses, and organizations (State Council, 2014). By leveraging big data, artificial intelligence (AI), and Internet of Things (IoT) technologies, the SCS aggregates vast amounts of data from diverse sources, including financial records, online activities, social interactions, and government databases, to assign credit scores that determine access to social and economic opportunities (Creemers, 2018). Unlike Western credit systems focused primarily on financial solvency, China's SCS encompasses moral, social, and political dimensions, embedding state-defined notions of "good" citizenship into its algorithmic logic.

In the context of smart cities, the SCS operates as a centralized digital infrastructure that integrates with urban systems such as transportation, public services, and security. Cities like Hangzhou, Shenzhen, and Shanghai have piloted SCS implementations, linking citizen scores to access to public transport, education, and healthcare (Liang et al., 2018). This integration reflects China's vision of "smart governance," where technology enhances administrative efficiency while reinforcing state control. However, as Kostka (2019) argues, the SCS is less about technological innovation and more about consolidating the Chinese Communist Party's (CCP) authority over society, making it a quintessential example of control techno-politics.

The SCS relies on an ecosystem of data-driven technologies to enable pervasive surveillance and enforce behavioral conformity. At its core is the collection of real-time data through interconnected devices, including smartphones, CCTV cameras, and IoT sensors embedded in urban environments. According to a 2021 report by Comparitech, China has deployed over 626 million surveillance cameras nationwide, many equipped with AI-powered facial recognition capabilities (Bischoff, 2025). These technologies allow the state to monitor citizens' movements, interactions, and transactions, creating a digital panopticon where individuals are aware of constant scrutiny.

The algorithmic processing of this data is central to the SCS's operation. Machine learning models analyze patterns in citizens' behavior, assigning scores based on criteria such as compliance with laws, financial responsibility, and social conduct. For instance, jaywalking, late bill payments, or posting "untrustworthy" content online can lower one's score, while volunteering or donating to charity can improve it (Chen & Cheung, 2020). These scores are dynamic, updated in real time, and publicly accessible in some regions, fostering a culture of self-discipline as citizens internalize the state's evaluative gaze.

Behavioral conformity is further enforced through a system of rewards and punishments tied to SCS scores. High scores grant privileges, such as priority access to high-speed rail tickets or elite schools, while low scores result in restrictions, including travel bans, job limitations, or social ostracism (Creemers, 2018). This gamification of citizenship incentivizes compliance with state norms, aligning individual behavior with the CCP's ideological priorities. As Zuboff (2019) notes in her broader critique of surveillance systems, such mechanisms transform human behavior into predictable, controllable patterns, reducing agency to algorithmic outputs.

The SCS's urban applications, particularly facial recognition and citizen scoring, illustrate its role in reshaping social dynamics and reinforcing state power. Facial recognition technology is ubiquitous in China's smart cities, used for tasks ranging from unlocking public bicycles to enforcing quarantine measures during the COVID-19 pandemic (Mozur & Clark, 2020). In Shenzhen, for example, facial recognition systems linked to the SCS publicly shame jaywalkers by displaying their faces on large screens at intersections, a practice that combines technological surveillance with social humiliation (Liang et al., 2018). Such applications demonstrate how smart city technologies can be weaponized to enforce compliance at a granular level.

Citizen scoring, another key feature, creates a stratified social order based on algorithmic evaluations. In pilot programs, citizens are categorized into tiers (e.g., A, B, C, D), with each tier conferring different levels of access to resources and opportunities (Kostka, 2019). For instance, in Rongcheng, a city in Shandong Province, residents with low scores face restrictions on government jobs and international travel, while those with high scores receive discounts on utilities and public services (Chen & Cheung, 2020). This system institutionalizes inequality, as access to social mobility becomes contingent on state-approved behavior.

The social stratification induced by citizen scoring has profound implications for urban life. As Reilly et. (2021) observes, the SCS exacerbates existing inequalities by disproportionately penalizing marginalized groups, such as rural migrants or low-income residents, who may lack the resources to maintain high scores. Moreover, the opacity of scoring algorithms, proprietary and inaccessible to the public, prevents citizens from contesting their evaluations, reinforcing the state's unilateral authority. These dynamics highlight the SCS's role as a tool of social control, where technology amplifies rather than mitigates structural inequities.

The SCS's explicit disciplinary aims reflect the broader techno-political agenda of China's controlling regime. Unlike liberal democracies, where surveillance is often justified by security or economic efficiency, China's SCS is overtly designed to align citizen behavior with the CCP's ideological vision of a "harmonious society" (Creemers, 2018). This vision prioritizes collective stability over individual autonomy, using technology to enforce a moral and political order defined by the state.

The disciplinary power of the SCS operates through what Foucault (1977) terms "governmentality," where governance shapes individuals into self-regulating subjects. By making citizens' scores publicly visible and tying them to tangible consequences, the SCS creates a feedback loop of surveillance and self-censorship. For example, individuals may avoid criticizing the government online or associating with low-scoring peers to protect their own scores (Kostka, 2019). This dynamic not only suppresses dissent but also fosters a culture of conformity, where citizens internalize the state's normative expectations.

Moreover, the SCS serves as a tool for preemptive governance, identifying and neutralizing potential threats before they materialize. AI algorithms flag "untrustworthy" behavior, such as frequent contact with dissidents or irregular financial transactions, enabling the state to intervene proactively. This predictive approach aligns with the CCP's broader strategy of maintaining social stability, particularly in urban centers where rapid modernization has intensified social tensions (Liang et al., 2018).

The controlling techno-politics of the SCS also have global implications. As China exports its smart city technologies to countries in Africa, Asia, and Latin America through initiatives like the Belt and Road, the SCS model of governance is gaining traction (Mozur & Clark, 2020). This raises concerns about the proliferation of surveillance-driven urban systems, challenging global norms around privacy and human rights. As Zuboff (2019) warns, the normalization of such systems risks creating a "digital control regime" that transcends national borders.

China's Social Credit System represents a paradigmatic case of how smart city technologies can be instrumentalized to consolidate state power and enforce social control. Through its integration of data-driven surveillance, facial recognition, and citizen scoring, the SCS transforms urban life into a system of algorithmic evaluation and social stratification. Its explicit disciplinary aims, rooted in the CCP's vision of a harmonious society, distinguish it from liberal-democratic smart city models, yet its mechanisms of behavioral conformity and predictive governance resonate with broader global trends in techno-politics. As smart cities continue to evolve, the SCS serves as a cautionary tale of how technology, when divorced from democratic accountability, can erode individual agency and entrench control.

3. THE UK'S SMART CITIES: EMPOWERMENT OR SUBTLE CONTROL?

The United Kingdom has emerged as a global leader in smart city development, deploying advanced technologies to address urban challenges and enhance the quality of life in cities such as London, Manchester, Bristol, Glasgow, Milton Keynes, and Peterborough. These initiatives, characterized by the integration of Internet of Things (IoT) devices, big data analytics, and artificial intelligence, promise to deliver social, economic, and environmental benefits through improved efficiency, sustainability, and citizen engagement (POST, 2021). Central to these efforts are open data platforms, civic engagement strategies, and public-private partnerships (PPPs), which collectively aim to create responsive and inclusive urban environments. However, beneath the rhetoric of empowerment lies a complex techno-political landscape where corporate data collection, opaque algorithms, and surveillance capitalism raise significant concerns about privacy, autonomy, and subtle forms of control (Arslan, 2025). This section critically examines UK smart city initiatives, highlighting their potential to empower citizens while arguing that they may inadvertently replicate control mechanisms under the guise of democratic governance.

UK smart city projects span a variety of applications, including smart transportation, energy management, public safety, and environmental monitoring, all underpinned by digital technologies that collect and analyze data. A hallmark of these initiatives is the emphasis on open data platforms, which facilitate the sharing of information among government entities, private companies, and citizens to enhance transparency and decision-making. For example, Manchester's Triangulum project, part of a €25 million Horizon 2020 initiative, developed the Manchester-i data platform to support data-driven governance along the Oxford Road Corridor, aiming to create a knowledge-driven, low-carbon district (Triangulum, n.d.). Similarly, the West of England Mayoral Combined Authority collaborates with Opendatasoft to build an open data portal focused on environmental improvements, demonstrating the role of data in addressing urban challenges (Smart Cities World, 2025).

Civic engagement is another critical component, with cities leveraging digital platforms to involve residents in urban governance. London's "Smarter London Together" roadmap outlines strategies to enhance public services through technology, including mobile apps that allow citizens to access services and provide feedback (Mayor of London, 2018). Bristol's "Bristol Is Open" initiative creates a city-scale testbed for smart technologies, fostering collaboration between the city council, universities, and businesses to engage communities in innovation (Bristol Is Open, n.d.). A study of six UK cities found that approximately one-third of smart city activities are oriented towards civic publicness, such as participatory events and community workshops, though these are often temporary (Cowley et al., 2017).

Public-private partnerships are instrumental in driving smart city development, providing the necessary funding, technical expertise, and innovation. Bristol Is Open, for instance, is a collaborative effort involving Bristol City Council, the University of Bristol, and private sector partners, creating a network for testing smart technologies (Government Events, 2024). In Hull, the Smart City OS integrates 12 solutions, including streetlighting and people movement monitoring, through partnerships with companies like Datatek and Citilogik (APM, 2020). These partnerships are vital, as only 16% of cities can self-fund infrastructure projects, making private investment a key driver (Raconteur, 2019).

Table 2.

City	Key Initiative	Focus Areas	Partners
Manchester	Triangulum Project	Low-carbon district, open data (Manchester-i)	Siemens, Universities, Manchester City Council
Bristol	Bristol Is Open	City-scale tech testbed, civic engagement	Bristol City Council, University of Bristol, Businesses
London	Smarter London Together	Smart transportation, civic apps	Transport for London, Private tech firms
Hull	Smart City OS	Full-fibre connectivity, sensor networks	Datatek, Citilogik, Hull City Council

While UK smart cities are framed as empowering, their reliance on data-driven technologies introduces significant risks related to corporate data collection, opaque algorithms, and surveillance capitalism. These issues challenge the democratic ideals of transparency and autonomy, potentially aligning smart city governance with subtler forms of control.

Smart city technologies generate vast amounts of data through sensors, cameras, and citizen interactions, much of which is accessible to private companies involved in PPPs. This raises concerns about data ownership and potential misuse. For instance, in the Triangulum project, Siemens played a central role in developing ICT infrastructure, potentially gaining access to citizen data (Triangulum, n.d.). Similarly, in Bristol Is Open, private partners may utilize data collected from the city's sensor network, though the extent of this access remains unclear (Bristol Is Open, n.d.). The commodification of personal data, where data is collected and sold for profit, threatens privacy, as citizens may not be fully aware of how their information is used. The lack of meaningful consent in ambient smart city environments exacerbates these concerns, as data is often collected from inevitable public interactions (Edwards, 2016).

The algorithms underpinning smart city applications, such as those used for traffic management or resource allocation, are often proprietary and lack transparency. This opacity makes it difficult for citizens to understand or challenge automated decisions, undermining accountability. For example, the algorithms driving Manchester-i's data analytics are not publicly disclosed, raising questions about their fairness and potential biases (Triangulum, n.d.). The POSTnote on smart cities highlights that the complexity of these systems can erode public trust, particularly when decision-making processes are not transparent (POST, 2021). This lack of openness contrasts with the democratic principles that smart cities claim to uphold.

Surveillance capitalism, as defined by Shoshana Zuboff, involves the extraction and commodification of personal data to predict and influence behavior (Zuboff, 2019). In smart cities, this manifests through behavioral nudging, where data-driven interventions guide citizen actions towards desired outcomes. The UK's Behavioural

jay-walking, utility payments, platform ratings, to a moral economy of trust (Ahlers et al., 2024). Through "data-centric control," the state embeds socialist-meritocratic values (obedience, thrift, public harmony) into code and scoring algorithm.

By contrast, UK smart-city policy is framed in the liberal vernacular of service optimisation and innovation ecosystems. Flagship demonstrators, Bristol Is Open and Manchester's CityVerve, foreground open data, Internet-of-Things (IoT) interoperability, and public-private-people partnerships. Yet techno-political analysis reveals a competing logic of securitised urbanism increasingly visible in the Home Office's endorsement of live facial-recognition (LFR) and real-time analytics. Parliamentary briefings acknowledge that neither bespoke legislation nor robust safeguards presently exist, leaving deployment to dispersed police discretion.

In China, ratings dashboards, coloured health codes, and AI-generated risk maps render citizen conduct continuously auditable. Studies show that 99% of surveyed residents reported at least one behavioral adjustment to maintain positive scores under the SCS scheme (Gao, 2025). Hangzhou residents describe a "sense of ambient monitoring" that encourages punctual bill payment and discourages jay-walking because "someone is always watching". UK citizens encounter subtler mechanisms: smartphone apps for smart parking and bike sharing in Manchester nudge modal shifts, while environmental dashboards invite individuals to visualise, and therefore govern, their own carbon footprints. In both contexts, algorithmic affordances cultivate reflexive discipline in Deleuze's (1992) "societies of control."

Chinese propaganda frames City Brain as minsheng (people's livelihood) technology, conflating efficiency with benevolence and thereby recoding compliance as patriotic civic duty (Sun, 2020). UK local authorities use the lexicon of convenience and choice, depicting sensors as friction-reducing tools for empowered consumers rather than supervised subjects (Kitchin, 2022). The rhetorical distinction masks functional convergence: both systems channel everyday behaviour toward administratively desirable ends.

Table 3.

Context	Compliance	Resistance	Negotiation
Hangzhou, China	High uptake of government ride-sharing schemes linked to SCS discounts; residents voluntarily download Zhi-An (Smart Safety) app for faster gate access.	Bank-run protesters in Henan saw their health-code apps turned red to pre-empt collective gathering, triggering nationwide outrage. Online "white-paper" protests used blank signs and coded memes to evade censorship after zero-COVID lockdowns.	Some communities bargain for local benefits, e.g., extra elder-care credits, in exchange for accepting deeper sensor coverage (Sun, 2020).
England & Wales, UK	Retail chains integrate Facewatch; customers tacitly comply with biometric scans at store entrances for frictionless payment (Home Office, 2023). Police LFR vans scanned 4.7 million faces in 2024, double the previous year.	Civil-society coalitions (Big Brother Watch, Liberty) mount legal challenges and public campaigns; shoppers file complaints after being mistakenly placed on watch-lists.	CityVerve participatory workshops invite residents to co-design IoT use-cases, resulting in modified data-sharing agreements rather than outright rejection.

These patterns illustrate that compliance and contestation are not binary opposites but exist along a continuum of negotiated subjectivities. Chinese citizens may exploit scoring loopholes (e.g., paying bills for relatives to raise personal credit), while UK activists leverage human-rights law to narrow permissible use cases of LFR without rejecting smart-city innovations wholesale.

1. Governance Mode. China's model is controlling-synchronised: data platforms are vertically integrated into a single party-state command chain. The UK exhibits a market-pluralist mode in which local councils, tech vendors, and police forces experiment with heterogeneous platforms, producing regulatory gaps exploitable by corporate actors.
2. Visibility of Power. Ideological inscription is overt in China, score dashboards, red health codes, whereas it is latent in the UK, buried inside proprietary algorithms and contractual terms of service. The result is that UK citizens often experience surveillance as convenience rather than coercion, aligning with Zuboff's (2019) notion of "instrumentarian power."
3. Vectors of Resistance. In China, overt protest is risky, so resistance manifests as culture jamming, VPN use, or micro-level non-compliance. In the UK, an expansive civic-legal sphere enables strategic litigation and media advocacy, illustrating how liberal democratic institutions modulate, but do not eliminate, techno-political power.
4. Subjective Internalisation. Both cases demonstrate a transition from Foucault's disciplinary enclosure to Deleuzian modulation: citizens are governed through

continuous data flows rather than discrete institutional settings. Compliance becomes a real-time, self-administered calculation of algorithmic risk.

Techno-political theory reminds us that smart-city infrastructures are performative scripts through which states encode visions of the ideal citizen, be it the harmonious socialist subject in China or the responsible consumer in the UK. Yet citizens are not passive recipients. They translate, scramble, or legally contest the codes that attempt to shape their identities and behaviours. Future comparative research should therefore focus on situated translations of technology, asking not only what infrastructures do, but how different publics make sense of, appropriate, or subvert them in daily life.

5. REIMAGINING SMART CITIES: TOWARD TRANSPARENCY AND SOCIAL JUSTICE

This chapter has critically interrogated the techno-political architectures of smart city development in China and the United Kingdom, revealing how divergent governance models converge in their instrumental use of digital infrastructures to shape citizen subjectivities, govern behavior, and inscribe ideological visions into code. While China's controlling-synchronised system openly aligns technological systems with state-defined moral hierarchies, the UK's liberal-democratic framework couches algorithmic governance in the language of empowerment, choice, and civic innovation. Yet both systems normalize surveillance and behavioral nudging, either through overt mechanisms like the Social Credit System or through more latent techniques embedded in public-private data ecosystems.

A key contribution of this chapter has been to challenge the simplistic binary of control regime versus democratic empowerment. As shown, the distinction between coercive and consensual governance is increasingly blurred in the digital age. Citizens in both contexts engage not only in compliance or resistance but also in complex negotiations with these technologies, seeking benefits, subverting controls, and adapting behavior in response to algorithmic visibility. In doing so, they exemplify a range of datafied subjectivities that exceed deterministic models of control.

The comparative analysis demonstrates that smart cities are not merely technical assemblages designed for efficiency, but ideological infrastructures that operationalize distinct imaginaries of governance and citizenship. Technologies such as facial recognition, open data platforms, and behavioral nudging are never neutral; they reflect political priorities, reproduce existing power asymmetries, and create new modalities of governance. Whether through China's "digital Confucianism" or the

UK's consumer-oriented smart urbanism, the infrastructures of "smartness" function as performative scripts, disciplining bodies, shaping desires, and delimiting dissent.

Yet this determinism is not total. The chapter emphasizes that citizens are not passive recipients of digital governance. Rather, they translate, appropriate, and sometimes subvert technological impositions through micro-resistance, legal contestation, and creative negotiation. Understanding these everyday practices is critical for reframing smart city discourse beyond technological determinism and toward situated, context-specific engagements with digital power.

Moving forward, a reimagining of smart city design is essential, one grounded not solely in optimization or economic growth, but in democratic accountability, transparency, and social justice. This entails several normative commitments:

- Transparency in Algorithmic Systems: Algorithms that govern urban life must be open to audit, public scrutiny, and democratic oversight. Proprietary code cannot justify opacity in decisions that shape citizen futures.
- Data Sovereignty and Consent: Citizens must retain meaningful control over how their data is collected, stored, and used. Consent should not be presumed or buried in terms of service, especially in ambient environments.
- Inclusive Participation: Smart city governance must center long-term civic engagement, not merely token consultations or pilot projects. Marginalized voices must be included in the co-design of urban technologies.
- Equity-Centered Design: Infrastructure should be designed to redress, rather than reproduce, socio-economic and spatial inequalities. This means interrogating who benefits from smart city investments, and who is left behind.
- Accountable Public-Private Partnerships: PPPs should operate under clear ethical standards and public-interest obligations, with mechanisms for redress, transparency, and citizen oversight.

Ultimately, the chapter advocates for a model of smart urbanism rooted in agency, dignity, and justice, where digital tools serve democratic life rather than eroding it. In contrast to techno-solutionist fantasies, this vision acknowledges the inherently political nature of technology and insists on embedding governance structures that align with principles of human rights, collective well-being, and ethical urban futures. As smart cities become the dominant paradigm of urban planning, ensuring that they are also just cities remains an urgent political task.

REFERENCES

Arslan, A. C. (2025). *Tekno-Politika Çağı: Devlet Şirket İlişkilerinin Teorik Analizi ve Güvenliğin İnşası.* Yetkin Yayınları.

Behavioural Insights Team. (n.d.). *Who we are.* https://www.bi.team/about-us/

Bischoff, P. (2025). *Surveillance camera statistics: Which are the most surveilled cities?* Comparitech. https://www.comparitech.com/vpn-privacy/the-worlds-most-surveilled-cities/

Bristol Is Open. (n.d.). *About Bristol Is Open.* https://www.bristolisopen.com/about/

Chen, Y., & Cheung, A. S. Y. (2020). The transparent self under big data profiling: Privacy and Chinese legislation on the social credit system. *Journal of Comparative Law, 15*(2), 356–378.

Cowley, R., Joss, S., & Dayot, Y. (2017). The smart city and its publics: Insights from across six UK cities. *Urban Research & Practice, 11*(1), 53–77. DOI: 10.1080/17535069.2017.1293150

Creemers, R. (2018). China's social credit system: An evolving practice of control. SSRN *Electronic Journal.* DOI: 10.2139/ssrn.3175792

Edwards, L. (2016). Privacy, security and data protection in smart cities: A critical EU law perspective. *European Data Protection Law Review,* 2(1), 28–58. DOI: 10.21552/EDPL/2016/1/6

Feenberg, A. (1991). *Critical theory of technology.* Oxford University Press.

Foucault, M. (1977). *Discipline and punish: The birth of the prison.* Pantheon Books.

Government Events. (2024). *The UK's top 3 smart cities: A transformative approach for local governments.* https://www.governmentevents.co.uk/ge-insights/the-uks-top-3-smart-cities-a-transformative-approach-for-local-governments/

Home Office. (2023). *Live facial recognition: Operational guidance for police forces.*

IMD. (2024). *Smart City Index 2024.* IMD World Competitiveness Center.

Jasanoff, S. (2018). Can science make sense of life? *Polity.*

Kitchin, R. (2022). *Data lives: How data are made and shape our world.* Policy Press.

Kostka, G. (2019). China's social credit systems and public opinion: Explaining high levels of approval. *New Media & Society, 21*(7), 1565–1593. DOI: 10.1177/1461444819826402

Liang, F., Das, V., Kostka, G., & Hussain, M. (2018). Constructing a data-driven society: China's social credit system as a state surveillance infrastructure. *Policy and Internet*, *10*(4), 415–453. DOI: 10.1002/poi3.183

Mayor of London. (2018). *Smarter London together*. https://www.london.gov.uk/sites/default/files/smarter_london_together_v1.66_-_published.pdf

Mozur, P., & Clark, D. (2020). China's surveillance state sucks up data. U.S. tech helps. *The New York Times*. https://www.nytimes.com/2020/12/14/technology/china-surveillance-state-us-tech.html

Parliamentary Office of Science and Technology. (2021). *POSTnote 656: Smart cities*.

POST. (2021). *Smart cities*. Parliamentary Office of Science and Technology. https://post.parliament.uk/research-briefings/post-pn-0656/

Ranchordás, S. (2019). Nudging citizens through technology in smart cities. *International Review of Law Computers & Technology*, *27*(3), 254–276. DOI: 10.1080/13600869.2019.1590928

Reilly, J., Lyu, M., & Robertson, M. (2021). China's social credit system: Speculation vs. Reality. *The Diplomat*. https://thediplomat.com/2021/03/chinas-social-credit-system-speculation-vs-reality/

Smart Cities World. (2025). *UK local authority uses open data to create greener future*. https://www.smartcitiesworld.net/open-data/uk-local-authority-uses-open-data-to-create-greener-future

State Council. (2014). *Planning outline for the construction of a social credit system (2014–2020)*. Government of China. https://digichina.stanford.edu/work/planning-outline-for-the-construction-of-a-social-credit-system-2014-2020/

Sun, G. (2020). Government Governance of Smart Cities in China. *Advances in Economics. Business and Management Research*, *118*, 302–307.

Triangulum. (n.d.). *About Triangulum*. https://triangulum-project.eu/

Weber, V. (2022). *Data-centric authoritarianism: How China's Development of Frontier Technologies Could Globalize Repression*. National Endowment for Democracy.

Winner, L. (1980). Do artifacts have politics? *Daedalus*, *109*(1), 121–136.

Zuboff, S. (2019). *The age of surveillance capitalism: The fight for a human future at the new frontier of power*. PublicAffairs.

ENDNOTE

1 Artificial intelligence-based tools were utilized to proofread the language used in this study.

Section 2
Culture, Identity, and Governance Perspectives Under Techno-Politics

Chapter 5
AI, Digital Sovereignty, and Global Governance: Towards a Hybrid Regulatory Model

Atdhe Lila
https://orcid.org/0009-0009-5460-1980
Institute for Technology and Society, Kosovo

ABSTRACT

AI has rapidly transformed societies, economies, and governance, but it has also exposed critical challenges in global AI regulation. This chapter examines the contrasting governance models of the European Union, the United States, and China—each reflecting distinct values and strategic interests. These differences have led to fragmented global AI governance, creating compliance burdens, stifling innovation, and risking human rights. To address this, the chapter proposes a hybrid governance model combining national sovereignty with global interoperability. This model is built on three tiers: universal norms, national and regional frameworks, and sector-specific adaptations. It balances data, technological, and normative sovereignty, providing a scalable solution for ethical AI governance. The chapter concludes by assessing the model's feasibility, emphasizing the need for international cooperation to ensure responsible, adaptable, and coherent AI regulation worldwide.

1. INTRODUCTION

Artificial intelligence (AI) has become an undeniable force in the modern world, transforming industries, enhancing public services, and reshaping daily life. From healthcare and education to finance and defense, AI systems are now embedded in

DOI: 10.4018/979-8-3373-2459-3.ch005

critical processes, offering new efficiencies but also raising profound ethical, social, and legal questions. As these technologies become more sophisticated, the question of how they should be governed has moved from the realm of theoretical debate to an urgent global priority.

Yet, the governance of AI is not a straightforward challenge. Around the world, nations have pursued divergent regulatory models, each reflecting unique values, strategic interests, and cultural perspectives. The European Union (EU) has positioned itself as a leader in ethical AI regulation, emphasizing human rights, transparency, and accountability. Through frameworks such as the AI Act, the EU aims to establish a protective, rights-based approach to AI oversight. In contrast, the United States has taken a more market-driven path, promoting innovation while relying on a mix of federal guidance and state regulations. This decentralized model allows for flexibility but can lead to inconsistent protections. China presents a third approach, where state control and ideological conformity are central. Its AI governance is defined by strict regulatory oversight, data localization mandates, and alignment with national values.

The result is a fragmented global governance landscape. AI systems that comply with European standards may violate Chinese regulations, while tools developed under U.S. guidelines may lack the transparency demanded in the EU. This fragmentation is not merely a technical inconvenience—it creates significant barriers to cross-border data flows, complicates compliance for companies, and raises the risk of conflicting legal obligations. More broadly, it reflects deeper geopolitical tensions, as leading powers compete to shape the future of AI governance in ways that align with their own strategic goals.

This fragmented environment has led to a growing recognition that a purely national or purely global approach to AI governance is insufficient. On one hand, national sovereignty allows countries to regulate AI in line with their own values and priorities. On the other, the transnational nature of AI—relying on global data flows, cross-border research, and international cooperation—demands a degree of global coordination. But how can these conflicting needs be balanced?

This chapter proposes a three-tier hybrid governance model for AI, designed to reconcile the need for national sovereignty with the benefits of global cooperation. The model is built around three interconnected tiers:

- The first tier consists of universal norms and principles, developed through multilateral platforms such as the OECD and UNESCO. These norms establish a common ethical foundation, ensuring that AI systems respect core principles like privacy, transparency, accountability, and human rights.
- The second tier allows for national and regional regulatory frameworks, enabling countries to adapt these universal norms to their local contexts. This

ensures that AI governance reflects domestic values, legal systems, and strategic priorities.

- The third tier provides for sector-specific adaptations, recognizing that the impact of AI varies across domains such as healthcare, finance, education, and defense. This flexibility ensures that AI is governed in a way that reflects the unique risks and opportunities of each sector.

This chapter begins with an analysis of existing global AI governance models, exploring how the EU, United States, and China have approached this challenge (Section 2). It then examines the concept of digital sovereignty and its role in shaping national approaches to AI (Section 3). Section 4 addresses the problem of fragmentation, illustrating how conflicting regulations hinder the development of coherent global standards. Finally, Section 5 presents the three-tier hybrid governance model in detail, exploring its design, implementation, and the political barriers it must overcome. The conclusion reflects on the model's potential, acknowledging its strengths while recognizing the challenges it must navigate.

By offering a flexible yet coherent approach, the three-tier hybrid model seeks to balance the benefits of AI innovation with the need for responsible governance. It provides a pathway for aligning national priorities with global principles, ensuring that AI serves as a force for progress rather than a source of conflict or inequality.

2. GLOBAL AI GOVERNANCE MODELS

The governance of AI is a rapidly evolving field, shaped by the competing priorities of national sovereignty, economic competitiveness, human rights protection, and security. Around the world, governments have adopted diverse approaches to AI regulation, each reflecting their unique values, strategic interests, and regulatory traditions. Among these, three models stand out due to their global influence: the European Union's rights-focused regulatory framework, the United States' innovation-centric approach, and China's state-centric model. These models are not only distinct in their guiding principles but also embody different visions of how AI should be developed, deployed, and governed. These three regions are chosen because they represent the most influential and contrasting regulatory models for AI, each reflecting different values, priorities, and governance philosophies, and their regulatory decisions have significant global implications

Understanding these three models is essential for two reasons. First, they represent the most influential regulatory approaches, with each serving as a potential blueprint for other countries and regions. Second, their differences illustrate the fundamental challenge of global AI governance—how to reconcile divergent rules and values in a world where AI is inherently transnational. This section critically examines each of these models, beginning with the European Union.

2.1 The European Union: Risk-Based, Rights-Focused Regulation

The EU has established itself as a global leader in the regulation of AI, leveraging its normative power to promote ethical technology governance. This leadership is grounded in a rights-focused, precautionary approach that reflects the EU's broader commitment to human dignity, privacy, and data protection. The EU's most ambitious initiative in this field is the Artificial Intelligence Act (AI Act), which builds on the principles of the GDPR but extends them to address the unique challenges of AI (European Commission, 2024).

At the core of the AI Act is a risk-based framework that categorizes AI systems into four levels of risk: unacceptable, high, limited, and minimal. This classification is not merely a regulatory convenience but a reflection of the EU's ethical stance on AI. Unacceptable-risk systems are prohibited because they pose clear and unacceptable threats to fundamental rights. Examples include social scoring systems that rank individuals based on their behavior, and subliminal techniques that manipulate human decisions without their awareness. Such uses are seen as inherently incompatible with European values.

High-risk systems, which include AI applications in critical areas such as healthcare, education, employment, and law enforcement, are subject to stringent regulatory requirements. Providers of high-risk AI must conduct conformity assessments, maintain detailed technical documentation, and ensure human oversight. For instance, an AI system used in biometric identification in public spaces must be transparent, secure, and subject to clear accountability measures. These safeguards reflect the EU's emphasis on transparency, accountability, and non-discrimination (European Commission, 2024).

Limited-risk systems, such as chatbots or AI-powered customer support, are subject to basic transparency obligations. These systems must clearly disclose their automated nature to users, ensuring that individuals understand they are interacting with an AI. Minimal-risk systems, which include most AI applications like spam filters or basic data analysis tools, are largely exempt from regulation, reflecting a pragmatic balance between oversight and innovation.

The EU's institutional framework for AI governance is designed to ensure consistent implementation across member states. The European Artificial Intelligence Office (EAIO) will oversee the enforcement of the AI Act, while a European AI Board, composed of national authorities, will coordinate regulatory practices and promote harmonization. This multi-level governance model is intended to prevent the regulatory fragmentation that has complicated GDPR enforcement (European Commission, 2024).

However, the EU model is not without its challenges. Critics argue that the stringent requirements for high-risk systems could stifle innovation, particularly for small and medium-sized enterprises (SMEs) that may lack the resources to comply with complex documentation and assessment procedures (Mügge, 2024). Some member states, including France, Germany, and Italy, have called for a more flexible approach to foundation models, warning that overregulation could drive AI innovation offshore (Bradford, 2023).

There are also concerns about enforcement. Like the GDPR, the AI Act relies on national supervisory authorities to monitor compliance. This decentralized approach has led to inconsistent enforcement under the GDPR, with some member states being more proactive than others. There is a risk that the same issue could arise with the AI Act, where national differences in capacity and resources could lead to uneven regulatory application (European Data Protection Board, 2023).

Yet, despite these challenges, the EU's rights-focused approach has a powerful normative impact beyond its borders. Known as the "Brussels Effect," the EU's ability to set global standards through its regulations has been widely recognized. Non-EU countries and global companies, including Google and OpenAI, have signaled compliance with EU transparency requirements to maintain market access (Bradford, 2023). The AI Act has also inspired discussions on ethical AI in international forums such as the G7 and the UNESCO AI ethics platform, reinforcing the EU's influence as a normative power in digital governance.

Ultimately, the EU's model represents a deliberate attempt to embed ethical principles into AI regulation, reflecting a broader European commitment to fundamental rights. Its strengths lie in its clear ethical foundations, comprehensive scope, and potential to shape global standards. However, its success will depend on effective implementation, consistent enforcement, and a balanced approach that fosters innovation without compromising fundamental rights.

2.2 The United States: Innovation-Driven, Fragmented Oversight

The US has adopted a distinct approach to AI governance, one that reflects its foundational values of innovation, free enterprise, and limited government intervention. Unlike the EU's centralized, rights-focused model, the U.S. relies on a decentralized regulatory framework characterized by a mix of federal guidance, state-level laws, and voluntary industry standards. This fragmented model is both a strength and a weakness—it fosters rapid technological development but also creates regulatory uncertainty.

At the federal level, the U.S. government has promoted AI governance primarily through guidance rather than binding legislation. A notable initiative is the Blueprint for an AI Bill of Rights, introduced by the White House Office of Science and Technology Policy (OSTP) in 2022. This document outlines five core principles: safe and effective systems, protections against algorithmic discrimination, data privacy, notice and explanation, and human alternatives (OSTP, 2022). While these principles are not legally binding, they reflect a normative vision for ethical AI, serving as a reference for both public and private sector actors.

Another significant federal initiative is the National Institute of Standards and Technology (NIST) AI Risk Management Framework (RMF 1.0), released in 2023. This voluntary framework provides organizations with a flexible tool for managing AI-related risks, emphasizing stakeholder collaboration, context-specific risk mitigation, and continuous monitoring (NIST, 2023). Unlike the EU's prescriptive rules, the NIST framework allows organizations to tailor their risk management strategies to their operational needs, reflecting the U.S. preference for industry-driven innovation.

Federal agencies also play a critical role in sector-specific AI regulation. The Food and Drug Administration (FDA) provides guidelines for AI in medical devices, the Federal Trade Commission (FTC) monitors AI in consumer protection, and the Securities and Exchange Commission (SEC) addresses AI in financial markets. This sectoral approach allows for targeted oversight, but it also leads to inconsistent standards across industries.

State-level regulations further complicate the U.S. model. California has enacted the California Consumer Privacy Act (CCPA), which provides transparency and data protection rights for consumers. Illinois has pioneered biometric privacy with the Biometric Information Privacy Act (BIPA), imposing strict requirements on the collection and use of biometric data. New York has introduced AI-related rules for hiring practices, mandating transparency and non-discrimination in automated employment decisions. These state laws reflect proactive governance but also create a fragmented regulatory landscape, where compliance varies depending on jurisdiction (Brookings Institution, 2023).

The most significant federal development in recent years is Executive Order 14110 on Safe, Secure, and Trustworthy AI, issued by President Biden in October 2023. This executive order represents a shift toward more active federal oversight, mandating that developers of advanced AI systems, particularly foundation models, share safety testing results with the federal government (White House, 2023). It also requires the development of privacy-preserving technologies, the protection of civil rights in AI applications, and the creation of standards and evaluation tools by NIST.

Importantly, the executive order establishes interagency coordination, including the Department of Commerce, the Department of Defense, and the Department of Health and Human Services, to ensure that AI risks are managed across critical sectors.

Despite these initiatives, the U.S. model faces significant challenges. Its decentralized nature leads to regulatory fragmentation, with conflicting state laws creating compliance burdens for companies operating nationwide. For example, a company deploying facial recognition technology may comply with BIPA in Illinois but face different rules in California or New York. This patchwork of regulations increases compliance costs and creates uncertainty, particularly for startups and small businesses (Brookings Institution, 2023).

Moreover, the reliance on voluntary guidelines and sector-specific rules means that many AI systems operate with minimal oversight. Companies can choose to adopt NIST's risk management framework or ignore it altogether. Critics argue that this approach prioritizes innovation at the expense of consumer protection, leaving users vulnerable to algorithmic discrimination, data breaches, and unsafe AI applications (NIST, 2023).

The U.S. model is also shaped by the influence of major technology companies, which actively lobby for light-touch regulation and self-regulation. Companies like Google, Microsoft, and OpenAI have established their own ethical guidelines for AI development, but these voluntary commitments are not subject to external enforcement. This industry-driven approach has led to accusations of "regulatory capture," where technology firms influence policymaking in ways that benefit their business interests (Brookings Institution, 2023).

Yet the U.S. model also has clear strengths. Its flexible, innovation-driven approach allows for rapid technological development, making it a global leader in AI research and commercialization. The country is home to the largest concentration of AI startups, research centers, and technology companies, supported by a vibrant venture capital ecosystem. This dynamic environment has enabled breakthroughs in natural language processing, autonomous vehicles, and generative AI, making the U.S. a global AI powerhouse (NIST, 2023).

On the global stage, the U.S. model has both positive and negative impacts. Its emphasis on innovation has accelerated AI development worldwide, but its light-touch approach has also been criticized for enabling unethical practices and insufficient consumer protection. In contrast to the EU's rights-focused model, which aims to protect human dignity and privacy, the U.S. approach prioritizes technological leadership and economic growth.

In summary, the U.S. model of AI governance is defined by its flexibility, innovation focus, and decentralized structure. It offers a stark contrast to the European Union's rights-based approach and China's state-centric model, reflecting core American values of entrepreneurship and limited government. However, this flexibility comes at the cost of regulatory consistency and consumer protection. As global debates over AI governance continue, the U.S. model will likely remain influential—but also contested.

2.3 China: State-Driven, Ideologically Aligned Regulation

China has developed a distinctive model of AI governance characterized by centralized state control, ideological alignment, and integration with national security objectives. This approach is not only a reflection of the Chinese government's commitment to maintaining social stability but also a strategic effort to achieve technological self-reliance and global influence. The Chinese model treats AI as a dual-use technology—both a driver of economic growth and a tool for social management. This dual nature has shaped a regulatory framework that emphasizes security, ideological conformity, and strict state oversight.

China's approach to AI governance is grounded in a comprehensive legal framework designed to ensure state control over data, algorithms, and digital content. Key legal instruments include the Cybersecurity Law (2017), which establishes broad data security obligations, including requirements for data localization and security assessments for critical information infrastructure. The Personal Information Protection Law (PIPL, 2021) provides a comprehensive framework for data privacy, imposing strict requirements on data collection, processing, and cross-border transfers, similar to the EU's GDPR but with a focus on state security. The Data Security Law (2021) further regulates data processing activities that may affect national security, including mandatory security reviews for data transfers outside China. More recently, the Interim Measures for the Management of Generative AI Services (2023) introduced specific rules for generative AI, requiring providers to conduct security assessments, obtain licenses, and ensure that AI-generated content aligns with "socialist values." These measures also mandate the labeling of AI-generated content and impose liability on providers for illegal or harmful outputs (Zhang, 2024).

Beyond legal instruments, China has established extensive control mechanisms for AI governance. The Cyberspace Administration of China (CAC) is the primary regulatory authority, overseeing AI deployment, enforcing compliance, and coordinating with other agencies such as the Ministry of Industry and Information Technology (MIIT) and the Ministry of Public Security. Algorithmic regulation is a core feature, with specific rules targeting recommendation algorithms, including transparency obligations, algorithmic audits, and content moderation requirements. Companies must register their algorithms with the CAC, which can demand changes to ensure compliance. Technologies such as deepfakes and generative AI are subject to regulation under the "deep synthesis" framework, which mandates labeling and prevents misuse. Real-name registration is required for users of AI services, facilitating state monitoring and accountability.

China's model of AI governance offers significant advantages in terms of state control, rapid implementation, and regulatory clarity. The government's ability to impose immediate compliance requirements ensures that AI providers align with national priorities. This model has enabled China to rapidly regulate emerging technologies, such as generative AI, through the 2023 Interim Measures. However, the model has been widely criticized for its authoritarian features. Critics argue that the emphasis on state control and ideological alignment comes at the expense of individual rights and freedoms. The requirement for real-name registration and the extensive use of surveillance technologies have raised concerns about privacy, freedom of expression, and human rights (Sheehan, 2023). Additionally, the lack of independent oversight means that AI providers must comply with government directives without legal recourse, making them vulnerable to state interference.

China's state-driven, ideologically aligned model of AI governance has not only shaped domestic policy but has also had a significant impact on other countries, particularly in Asia and Africa. Several countries have adopted similar regulatory frameworks, citing the Chinese model as a source of inspiration for maintaining state sovereignty over digital technologies. For example, Vietnam and Ethiopia have introduced AI regulations that emphasize state control and data localization, reflecting China's influence (Belli et al., 2024). China has actively promoted its digital governance model through the Digital Silk Road initiative, exporting its regulatory standards and technologies to partner countries. This strategy has positioned China as a leader in digital governance in the Global South, where governments often prioritize state control over digital platforms for security and political stability.

China's state-driven, ideologically aligned model is a clear reflection of the country's broader political system, where state authority and social stability take precedence over individual rights. While this model provides clear rules and rapid regulatory response, it also raises serious concerns about surveillance, censorship, and the suppression of dissent. Nonetheless, China's approach has proven influential, particularly among countries seeking to assert digital sovereignty and reduce dependence on Western technology. As global debates on AI governance continue, China's model stands as both a challenge and an alternative to the rights-based and innovation-driven approaches of the EU and the US.

2.4 Comparative Reflections: Divergence and Implications

The analysis of the European Union, United States, and China reveals three fundamentally different approaches to AI governance, each reflecting the underlying values, political systems, and strategic priorities of these regions. The European

Union has adopted a centralized, rights-focused, risk-based model, driven by a commitment to human rights, transparency, and accountability. Its regulatory framework, embodied in the AI Act, seeks to ensure that AI systems respect fundamental rights and are subject to rigorous oversight. However, this model also faces challenges, particularly in balancing innovation with strict compliance requirements, which can be burdensome for SMEs.

In contrast, the United States has embraced a decentralized, innovation-driven model characterized by a combination of federal guidance, state-level laws, and voluntary industry standards. This approach reflects core American values of free enterprise and limited government intervention. It has allowed the United States to maintain a global leadership position in AI research and commercialization, driven by a vibrant technology sector and a flexible regulatory environment. Yet, the lack of a unified federal framework has also led to regulatory fragmentation, with conflicting state laws and limited consumer protections.

China's state-driven, ideologically aligned model represents a third, distinct approach. Here, AI governance is tightly integrated with national security, ideological conformity, and state control. This model enables rapid regulatory response and ensures alignment with national priorities, but it raises serious concerns about surveillance, censorship, and the suppression of individual freedoms. The strong role of the CAC and other state agencies ensures strict enforcement, but it also places AI providers under direct government supervision.

This comparison highlights the divergent priorities and strategies that define global AI governance. The European Union's rights-focused model prioritizes ethical safeguards but may stifle innovation due to compliance costs. The United States' innovation-centric approach promotes technological growth but lacks consistent protections for consumers. China's model offers clear rules and rapid implementation but sacrifices individual freedoms in favor of state control.

From a global perspective, these three models represent competing visions of AI governance. The EU seeks to establish ethical standards that can influence other regions, leveraging its normative power. The United States, through its flexible, industry-driven model, maintains leadership in AI research and commercialization, while China promotes a state-centric model that has gained traction among countries seeking to assert digital sovereignty. The coexistence of these models has contributed to a fragmented global landscape, where conflicting rules complicate cross-border data flows, compliance, and innovation.

2.5 Conclusion

This section has explored the diverse approaches to AI governance adopted by the European Union, the United States, and China, each reflecting distinct values, priorities, and regulatory philosophies. The EU has emphasized a rights-based, risk-driven model; the United States has prioritized innovation and flexibility; while China has focused on state control and ideological alignment. These models demonstrate how global governance is shaped by local values, but they also highlight a deeper issue: the struggle for digital sovereignty. As countries assert their own regulatory models, they are not only promoting different visions of AI governance but also competing for control over the digital world. This pursuit of sovereignty is central to understanding why global AI governance has become so fragmented. The next section will examine the concept of digital sovereignty in greater detail, exploring its dimensions, drivers, and contradictions.

3. DIGITAL SOVEREIGNTY AND ITS DISCONTENTS

The concept of digital sovereignty has emerged as a critical issue in the global debate over AI governance. At its core, digital sovereignty refers to the ability of a state to assert control over digital infrastructure, data, and technologies within its jurisdiction. This concept has gained prominence in recent years, driven by the rise of AI, increasing concerns about data security, and the growing influence of major technology companies. While digital sovereignty is often portrayed as a means of protecting national values and security, it also presents significant challenges, particularly in a world where digital ecosystems are inherently global.

The rise of AI has intensified the debate over digital sovereignty because AI systems rely heavily on cross-border data flows, multinational research collaborations, and globally distributed computing resources. For many countries, the ability to govern AI within their borders is seen as essential to maintaining strategic autonomy, protecting citizens' rights, and ensuring economic competitiveness. Yet, this drive for sovereignty also creates tension with the principles of an open and interconnected digital world. In practice, digital sovereignty can manifest in different forms, from data localization requirements to national AI strategies designed to promote domestic innovation and security.

3.1 What Is Digital Sovereignty?

Digital sovereignty is a multifaceted concept that encompasses three interrelated dimensions: data sovereignty, technological sovereignty, and normative sovereignty. Data sovereignty refers to the control over data generated, stored, and processed within a country's borders. This can include requirements for data localization, restrictions on cross-border data transfers, and obligations for data transparency and user consent. Countries such as China have adopted strict data sovereignty rules, requiring that critical data remain within national borders (PIPL, 2021), while the European Union's GDPR imposes strict data protection standards even for data transferred outside the EU (European Commission, 2024).

Technological sovereignty extends beyond data to include control over digital infrastructure, software, and AI systems. This dimension is reflected in national strategies that promote domestic innovation, research, and development, as well as efforts to reduce dependence on foreign technology providers. The United States, for example, has promoted technological sovereignty through initiatives such as the CHIPS and Science Act, which aims to boost domestic semiconductor manufacturing and reduce reliance on foreign suppliers (White House, 2023).

Normative sovereignty involves the ability of a state to define the ethical, legal, and regulatory standards that govern digital technologies within its jurisdiction. This is particularly relevant to AI, where questions of transparency, accountability, and fairness are central to governance. The European Union's AI Act represents an assertion of normative sovereignty, as it seeks to establish ethical standards for AI that reflect European values (European Commission, 2024). In contrast, China's model emphasizes state control and ideological conformity, with strict rules ensuring that AI-generated content aligns with "core socialist values" (Zhang, 2024).

These three dimensions of digital sovereignty are interconnected, and their importance varies depending on the strategic priorities of each country. While some nations focus primarily on data control, others emphasize technological self-reliance or the ability to set ethical norms for AI. As digital technologies continue to evolve, the debate over digital sovereignty is likely to intensify, with far-reaching implications for global AI governance.

3.2 Why Sovereignty Now? Drivers and Aspirations

The emergence of digital sovereignty as a critical policy objective is driven by a combination of strategic, economic, security, and cultural factors. In an increasingly interconnected world, countries view digital sovereignty as a means to protect their national interests, assert control over critical technologies, and prevent dependency on foreign technology providers. For many states, digital sovereignty is not merely a defensive measure but an aspiration to shape the global digital landscape according to their values and interests.

Strategic autonomy is a key driver of digital sovereignty. The European Union has emphasized this concept, viewing digital sovereignty as essential to reducing dependency on foreign technology providers and maintaining control over critical digital infrastructure. The EU's Digital Strategy explicitly highlights the need to achieve technological independence in areas such as cloud computing, artificial intelligence, and semiconductors (European Commission, 2024). Similar concerns have led the United States to promote domestic semiconductor manufacturing through the CHIPS and Science Act (White House, 2023).

Security considerations also play a central role in the push for digital sovereignty. For countries like China, digital sovereignty is closely linked to national security, as digital infrastructure and data are seen as strategic assets that must be protected from external threats. The Chinese government's emphasis on data localization and strict control over cross-border data transfers reflects this security-focused approach (PIPL, 2021). The United States has similarly cited national security concerns in its restrictions on Chinese technology companies such as Huawei, viewing them as potential security risks (White House, 2023).

Economic competitiveness is another key driver. Governments view digital sovereignty as a means of fostering domestic innovation, protecting local industries, and ensuring that national economies benefit from the digital economy. The European Union's AI Act aims to create a trusted environment for AI innovation within the EU, while China's digital strategy promotes domestic technology companies, reducing reliance on foreign providers (Mügge, 2024). For the United States, maintaining global leadership in AI is both an economic and strategic priority, reflected in initiatives that support AI research and commercialization.

Cultural preservation and normative control further motivate digital sovereignty. Countries seek to ensure that digital technologies reflect their cultural values and ethical standards. The European Union's rights-based approach to AI governance is a clear example, as it emphasizes transparency, accountability, and non-discrimination (European Commission, 2024). In contrast, China's model prioritizes ideological alignment, with rules ensuring that AI-generated content conforms to state-approved narratives (Zhang, 2024).

These drivers of digital sovereignty reflect a broader struggle over control of the digital world. As AI and other digital technologies become more deeply embedded in societies, the ability to govern them according to national priorities has become a matter of strategic importance. However, this pursuit of sovereignty also generates tensions, as countries attempt to balance national control with the benefits of global digital connectivity.

3.3 Sovereignty vs. Globalization: Key Contradictions

The pursuit of digital sovereignty is often portrayed as a means of protecting national interests, securing critical infrastructure, and asserting control over digital technologies. However, this drive for sovereignty is inherently at odds with the global nature of the digital ecosystem. AI, in particular, relies on cross-border data flows, global research collaborations, and multinational technology supply chains.

This fundamental tension gives rise to several key contradictions between digital sovereignty and globalization.

One of the most significant contradictions is the risk of regulatory fragmentation. As countries assert digital sovereignty by adopting national AI regulations, they create a patchwork of conflicting rules that complicate cross-border data flows and technology deployment. For example, the European Union's GDPR imposes strict data protection standards, while China's data localization requirements under the PIPL mandate that certain data remain within national borders (European Commission, 2024; PIPL, 2021). For multinational companies, navigating these conflicting rules is both costly and complex, creating compliance burdens and reducing global interoperability.

Another contradiction lies in the tension between national control and global innovation. Countries that prioritize digital sovereignty may restrict foreign technology providers, limit access to international research collaborations, or impose barriers on cross-border data transfers. While these measures may protect local industries and enhance national security, they can also stifle innovation by limiting access to global knowledge, talent, and technology. The United States, which has historically promoted an open, innovation-driven model, has also experienced this tension, as seen in its restrictions on Chinese technology companies such as Huawei (White House, 2023).

Digital sovereignty also creates the risk of a "splinternet," a fragmented global internet where each country or region imposes its own rules on data, content, and technology. This phenomenon is most clearly seen in China's "Great Firewall," which restricts access to foreign websites and digital services, while promoting state-approved content and domestic technology platforms (Zhang, 2024). The European Union's AI Act, while driven by ethical considerations, also contributes to regulatory fragmentation by establishing strict compliance requirements for AI providers targeting the EU market (European Commission, 2024).

Another critical contradiction is the risk of digital protectionism. While digital sovereignty is often justified as a means of protecting citizens' rights and national security, it can also be used as a tool for economic protectionism. Countries may impose data localization requirements, restrict foreign technology providers, or favor domestic companies under the guise of sovereignty. This approach not only distorts competition but also undermines the principles of an open, global digital market.

Finally, the pursuit of digital sovereignty can have unintended consequences for human rights. In authoritarian regimes, digital sovereignty is often used to justify surveillance, censorship, and information control. China's model of digital sovereignty, with its emphasis on state control and ideological conformity, has raised serious concerns about privacy, freedom of expression, and access to information (Sheehan,

2023). Even in democratic countries, digital sovereignty can lead to overregulation, limiting user access to digital services and creating a chilling effect on free speech.

These contradictions highlight the complex and often contradictory nature of digital sovereignty in the context of AI governance. While sovereignty offers countries a means of protecting their interests and values, it also risks fragmenting the global digital ecosystem, creating barriers to innovation, and undermining human rights. As countries continue to pursue digital sovereignty, the challenge will be to balance national control with the benefits of global connectivity.

3.4 Normative Assessment: Is Full Digital Sovereignty Realistic or Desirable?

The concept of digital sovereignty is often portrayed as a protective measure, allowing countries to safeguard their values, security, and economic interests in an increasingly digital world. Yet, when considered in the context of AI governance, the question arises: is full digital sovereignty both realistic and desirable? The answer is complex, shaped by competing priorities, ethical considerations, and practical realities.

From a practical perspective, full digital sovereignty is inherently difficult to achieve. Digital technologies, particularly AI, are inherently global. AI systems rely on cross-border data flows, multinational research collaborations, and globally distributed computing infrastructure. Even countries that adopt strict data localization requirements, such as China under the PIPL, cannot entirely isolate themselves from the global digital ecosystem (Zhang, 2024). The reliance on global supply chains, international data transfers, and foreign technology providers means that complete sovereignty is an aspiration rather than an achievable reality.

Moreover, full digital sovereignty risks creating a fragmented global digital ecosystem. As countries assert control over digital technologies, they often introduce conflicting rules and standards, making cross-border compliance complex and costly for companies. This fragmentation can stifle innovation, restrict market access, and lead to the emergence of a "splinternet" where countries maintain separate, incompatible digital environments (European Commission, 2024). The regulatory conflicts between the EU's rights-based model, the US's innovation-driven approach, and China's state-centric model exemplify this challenge.

Ethically, full digital sovereignty raises important questions about fundamental rights. In authoritarian regimes, sovereignty can become a tool for surveillance, censorship, and ideological control, as seen in China's state-driven model (Sheehan, 2023). Even in democratic countries, the pursuit of sovereignty can lead to overregulation, limiting user access to digital services, restricting freedom of expression, or imposing excessive compliance burdens on businesses. The challenge is to balance sovereignty with respect for human rights and open digital access.

At the same time, some level of digital sovereignty is essential for protecting national values, security, and economic interests. Countries have legitimate reasons to ensure that AI systems used within their borders align with local ethical standards and comply with domestic laws. For example, the European Union's AI Act reflects the region's commitment to transparency, accountability, and non-discrimination (European Commission, 2024). The United States emphasizes innovation and free enterprise, while China prioritizes security and ideological control. Each of these models reflects a different interpretation of digital sovereignty.

A more balanced approach is the pursuit of calibrated digital sovereignty—one that allows countries to assert control over critical aspects of AI governance while remaining open to global collaboration. This can be achieved through mechanisms such as mutual recognition of standards, international agreements, and cross-border regulatory cooperation. For instance, the EU and US have engaged in transatlantic dialogues on digital regulation, while the The Global Partnership on AI (GPAI) provides a platform for countries to coordinate on AI governance (OECD, 2023).

Ultimately, the question is not whether digital sovereignty is inherently good or bad, but how it can be pursued in a way that balances national interests with the benefits of global connectivity. As AI continues to transform societies, countries will need to find ways to assert sovereignty without sacrificing the advantages of an open, interconnected digital world.

3.5 Conclusion

Digital sovereignty is a concept marked by both promise and paradox. It offers countries the ability to protect their values, security, and economic interests, but it also risks creating a fragmented digital ecosystem characterized by regulatory conflicts, innovation barriers, and human rights concerns. The analysis in this section has shown that full digital sovereignty is both unrealistic and potentially undesirable, particularly in the context of AI governance. However, a balanced approach—calibrated digital sovereignty—can allow countries to assert control over critical aspects of AI governance while benefiting from global connectivity. As AI continues to reshape societies, the challenge will be to reconcile the need for sovereignty with the advantages of an open, interoperable digital world.

4. FRAGMENTATION OF THE GLOBAL AI GOVERNANCE LANDSCAPE

The rapid development of AI has brought remarkable opportunities for innovation, but it has also exposed a fundamental challenge: fragmentation in global AI governance. As countries pursue their own digital sovereignty agendas, the world is witnessing the emergence of conflicting rules, standards, and ethical principles governing AI. This fragmented landscape is not merely a theoretical problem—it is a reality that directly impacts how AI is developed, deployed, and regulated across borders.

Fragmentation in AI governance can be seen in the divergent approaches of the European Union, the United States, and China. Each of these regions has adopted its own regulatory model, reflecting its values, priorities, and strategic interests. The European Union has prioritized ethical safeguards and transparency through the AI Act, while the United States has emphasized innovation and flexibility with a decentralized, sector-specific approach. China, in contrast, has adopted a state-centric model focused on security, stability, and ideological control. These competing models not only reflect different philosophies but also create practical barriers to the global deployment of AI systems.

The consequences of this fragmentation are significant. Companies seeking to operate globally must navigate a complex web of regulatory requirements, ensuring compliance with conflicting rules in different jurisdictions. For smaller companies and startups, these compliance burdens can be prohibitive, limiting innovation and market access. Moreover, fragmentation has a direct impact on fundamental rights, as countries impose divergent rules on data protection, algorithmic transparency, and content moderation. The rise of digital sovereignty as a policy objective has only intensified this trend, leading to a "splinternet" of incompatible digital ecosystems.

4.1 Understanding Fragmentation in AI Governance

Fragmentation in AI governance can be understood as the emergence of conflicting rules, standards, and oversight mechanisms across different jurisdictions. This fragmentation is driven by the pursuit of digital sovereignty, as countries assert control over AI technologies within their borders. While sovereignty allows countries to regulate AI in accordance with their values and interests, it also creates regulatory divides that complicate cross-border data flows, technology deployment, and compliance.

There are three primary types of fragmentation in AI governance:

- **Normative Fragmentation:** This occurs when countries adopt conflicting ethical principles and regulatory standards for AI. The European Union's rights-based model emphasizes transparency, accountability, and human rights (European Commission, 2024), while China's state-centric approach prioritizes ideological control and national security (Zhang, 2024). The United States, with its market-driven model, focuses on innovation and industry self-regulation (NIST, 2023).
- **Technical Fragmentation:** This involves incompatibility in technical standards, data formats, and compliance requirements. AI systems designed to comply with the EU's transparency and accountability rules may not meet China's security and content control requirements. Even within the United States, state-level regulations such as the CCPA differ from federal guidelines, creating compliance challenges for companies (Brookings Institution, 2023).
- **Institutional Fragmentation:** This refers to the existence of separate governance frameworks and oversight bodies across regions. The European Union has established a centralized system through the European AI Office and AI Board, while the United States relies on a decentralized, sector-specific model with regulatory roles divided among agencies like the FTC and the NIST. China, in contrast, maintains centralized oversight through the CAC, which enforces compliance and ensures ideological alignment.

These three types of fragmentation are not merely theoretical distinctions—they are directly observable in the global AI governance landscape. They create significant challenges for companies seeking to deploy AI systems across borders, for regulators attempting to ensure compliance, and for citizens who may face different levels of protection depending on where they live. The next section will provide concrete examples of how fragmentation has manifested in practice.

4.2 Evidence of Fragmentation: Key Developments and Trends

Fragmentation in global AI governance is not merely a theoretical concept—it is a lived reality with tangible consequences for companies, governments, and citizens alike. The evidence of fragmentation can be seen in the divergent regulatory approaches adopted by the European Union, the United States, and China, but it also extends beyond these major players, affecting the entire global digital ecosystem.

One of the clearest examples of fragmentation is the conflict between the European Union's GDPR and China's PIPL. While the GDPR emphasizes transparency, user consent, and data minimization, the PIPL prioritizes data localization and state security. Companies operating in both regions must navigate two fundamentally different data governance regimes, leading to compliance complexity and increased operational costs. For instance, a multinational AI provider must ensure that user data collected in China is stored and processed domestically under the PIPL, while also adhering to the GDPR's strict data protection standards for European users.

Fragmentation is also evident within the United States itself, where state-level regulations on data protection and AI oversight vary significantly. CCPA establishes strict user rights and transparency obligations, while Illinois' BIPA imposes strict rules on the collection and use of biometric data. At the federal level, the NIST provides voluntary guidelines through the AI Risk Management Framework, but there is no unified federal AI law. This patchwork of rules creates compliance burdens for companies operating across state lines, with businesses often forced to adopt the strictest standard to ensure compliance.

The impact of fragmentation is not limited to data protection and privacy. In the realm of algorithmic transparency, the European Union's AI Act mandates that high-risk AI systems must provide clear explanations of their decision-making processes, while the United States has no equivalent federal requirement. Meanwhile, China's regulatory framework mandates that AI-generated content aligns with socialist values and requires providers to maintain detailed records of user interactions. These divergent standards not only complicate compliance for AI providers but also create significant ethical dilemmas.

Fragmentation is further compounded by technical standards. The International Organization for Standardization (ISO) and the International Electrotechnical Commission (IEC) have developed global AI standards, but regional differences persist. The European Union has adopted specific standards for biometric systems under the AI Act, while China's national standards prioritize state security and ideological alignment. These conflicting technical standards make it difficult for companies to develop AI systems that can seamlessly operate across multiple jurisdictions.

In addition to regulatory and technical fragmentation, institutional fragmentation also complicates global AI governance. The European Union has established a centralized regulatory system with the European AI Office and AI Board, ensuring consistent enforcement across member states. In contrast, the United States relies on a decentralized, sector-specific approach, with regulatory responsibilities divided among agencies such as the FTC, FDA, and NIST. China maintains a centralized system under the CAC, which enforces compliance and ensures ideological alignment.

The consequences of fragmentation are significant. For companies, compliance costs have skyrocketed as they attempt to meet conflicting regulatory requirements in different regions. Startups and small enterprises are particularly affected, as they lack the resources to develop region-specific compliance strategies. For consumers, fragmentation means that their rights and protections vary depending on their location, creating inequalities in digital rights and data protection. On a global scale, fragmentation risks creating a "splinternet," where countries maintain separate, incompatible digital ecosystems.

4.3 The Real-World Impact of Fragmentation

The fragmentation of global AI governance has significant real-world consequences, affecting companies, governments, and individuals alike. As AI regulations diverge across regions, organizations are forced to navigate a complex web of compliance requirements, while consumers experience varying levels of protection depending on their location. This section explores the practical impact of fragmentation, focusing on four key areas: compliance costs, innovation barriers, human rights risks, and geopolitical tensions.

One of the most immediate impacts of fragmentation is the skyrocketing cost of compliance for companies operating across multiple jurisdictions. Multinational firms must ensure that their AI systems meet the requirements of the European Union's AI Act, comply with the United States' sector-specific regulations, and adhere to China's state-centric standards (European Commission, 2024; NIST, 2023; Zhang, 2024). Startups and small enterprises are particularly affected, as they often lack the resources to maintain region-specific compliance strategies. According to a study by the Brookings Institution (2023), compliance costs for AI providers have increased by an average of 30% due to the need to meet conflicting regulatory standards.

For example, a company providing AI-powered healthcare solutions must ensure compliance with the EU's transparency and accountability requirements for high-risk AI systems, while also meeting the US FDA's safety and effectiveness standards and adhering to China's content moderation rules for health-related information (FDA, 2023; European Commission, 2024; CAC, 2023). The result is a complex compliance landscape where companies must allocate significant resources to legal, technical, and administrative measures.

Fragmentation also creates barriers to innovation, particularly for SMEs. Companies that develop AI solutions for global deployment must design their systems to meet the highest regulatory standard among their target markets, a process known as "compliance by design." This approach can stifle innovation, as developers spend more time ensuring compliance than improving their products. In some cases, companies may abandon certain markets entirely due to the high cost of compliance. For instance, OpenAI temporarily restricted access to its GPT-3 model in the European Union due to concerns about GDPR compliance (Brookings Institution, 2023).

The fragmentation of AI governance also reduces market access for companies seeking to expand internationally. Regional regulations such as the GDPR in the European Union and the PIPL in China impose strict conditions on data transfers, limiting the ability of companies to provide cross-border services (European Commission, 2024; Zhang, 2024). The US-China technology rivalry has further exacerbated this problem, as technology providers in both countries face restrictions on exporting AI technologies to each other (White House, 2023).

The fragmentation of AI governance also has significant implications for human rights. In regions with strong regulatory frameworks, such as the European Union, consumers enjoy robust protections for data privacy, transparency, and non-discrimination. In contrast, individuals in countries with weaker or authoritarian governance models may be subject to surveillance, censorship, and manipulation through AI-driven systems (Zhang, 2024; Sheehan, 2023). This disparity creates a form of digital inequality, where fundamental rights are protected in some regions but not in others.

For example, China's regulatory model requires AI providers to ensure that their systems align with state-approved narratives and prohibits content that undermines social stability (CAC, 2023). In contrast, the European Union's AI Act emphasizes transparency and accountability, requiring providers to explain their decision-making processes (European Commission, 2024). The result is a global digital divide, where users in different regions experience AI in fundamentally different ways.

Finally, fragmentation in AI governance is contributing to geopolitical tensions, particularly between major powers such as the United States, the European Union, and China. These regions have not only adopted conflicting regulatory models but also view AI as a strategic asset, leading to a form of regulatory competition. The US has promoted its innovation-driven model as a means of maintaining global technological leadership, while China has used its state-driven approach to promote digital sovereignty and secure influence in the Global South through initiatives such as the Digital Silk Road (OECD, 2023; Belli et al., 2024).

The European Union, for its part, has leveraged its rights-based model to position itself as a global normative power, influencing AI governance beyond its borders through the "Brussels Effect" (Bradford, 2023). However, this normative influence has also created friction with other regions, particularly the United States, where companies have expressed concerns about the cost of complying with EU standards (Brookings Institution, 2023).

Geopolitical tensions have also manifested in the form of technology export controls, as countries seek to restrict the spread of AI technologies to rival states. The US has imposed export controls on advanced AI chips and software to China, while China has introduced restrictions on the export of sensitive AI technologies to foreign entities (White House, 2023; Zhang, 2024). These measures reflect a growing recognition that AI is not only a commercial technology but also a tool of geopolitical influence.

The next section will explore why early attempts to mitigate fragmentation have largely fallen short, highlighting the limitations of existing international initiatives and the need for a more coherent global governance model.

4.4 Why Attempts to Mitigate Fragmentation Have Fallen Short

Despite the clear risks posed by fragmentation in global AI governance, numerous international initiatives have sought to promote a more coherent and interoperable regulatory framework. However, most of these efforts have struggled to achieve meaningful progress. This section critically examines why attempts to mitigate fragmentation have largely fallen short, focusing on the limitations of existing initiatives, the structural barriers to global cooperation, and the geopolitical dynamics that undermine consensus.

One of the most prominent international initiatives aimed at harmonizing AI governance is the OECD AI Principles, adopted by over 50 countries. These principles emphasize human rights, transparency, accountability, and fairness, providing a common ethical foundation for trustworthy AI (OECD, 2023). Yet, the OECD Principles are voluntary, and their implementation depends on the willingness of member states. As a result, countries have adopted these principles selectively, tailoring them to their own regulatory frameworks. For instance, the European Union has incorporated these principles into its rights-focused AI Act, while China has interpreted them through the lens of state control and ideological alignment (European Commission, 2024; Zhang, 2024).

The GPAI is another major initiative, bringing together governments, international organizations, industry, and academia to promote responsible AI development. GPAI has facilitated multi-stakeholder dialogue and research, but its impact has been limited by its lack of binding authority. While it has provided a valuable platform for knowledge exchange, it has not succeeded in creating a unified global governance model (GPAI, 2023). The diversity of its members, ranging from the United States and European Union to India and Brazil, has made consensus difficult to achieve.

UNESCO's Recommendation on the Ethics of Artificial Intelligence represents another effort to establish a common ethical framework for AI governance. Adopted by 193 member states, the recommendation provides guidance on transparency, accountability, data protection, and the prevention of discrimination (UNESCO, 2021). However, like the OECD Principles, UNESCO's guidelines are non-binding, allowing countries to interpret and implement them according to their own legal and cultural contexts. This flexibility has resulted in significant variations in how countries have applied these principles.

Efforts at the regional level have also faced challenges. The European Union and the United States have engaged in transatlantic dialogues on digital regulation through the Trade and Technology Council (TTC), but progress has been slow. The two regions continue to differ on fundamental issues, such as data privacy (GDPR vs. CCPA), algorithmic transparency, and content moderation. Even within the European Union, enforcement of the GDPR has been inconsistent, with data protection authorities in different member states adopting varying interpretations of the law (Bradford, 2023).

Geopolitical dynamics further complicate efforts to achieve global AI governance. The United States, European Union, and China each promote their own regulatory models, not only as domestic policies but also as tools of international influence. The US has positioned itself as a leader in innovation-driven governance, while China has promoted its state-centric model through the Digital Silk Road initiative, offering technical support and regulatory guidance to developing countries (Belli et al., 2024). The European Union has sought to export its rights-based model through the "Brussels Effect," using its regulatory power to shape global standards (Bradford, 2023). These competing visions reflect broader geopolitical rivalries that make consensus difficult.

A further challenge is the lack of strong enforcement mechanisms at the international level. Initiatives such as the OECD Principles and UNESCO's Ethical Guidelines are valuable in setting common values, but they lack the authority to ensure compliance. Countries are free to adopt these principles selectively, and there are no sanctions for non-compliance. This "soft law" approach limits the effectiveness of these initiatives, particularly when countries prioritize their own sovereignty over global cooperation.

The complexity of AI itself also presents a barrier to unified governance. AI technologies are diverse, ranging from narrow machine learning applications to complex autonomous systems. Different sectors—healthcare, finance, education, defense—present unique risks and ethical considerations, making it difficult to develop a one-size-fits-all governance model. As a result, countries have adopted sector-specific regulations that further fragment the governance landscape (OECD, 2023).

In conclusion, the failure of existing initiatives to mitigate fragmentation in AI governance reflects a combination of structural, geopolitical, and technological challenges. Voluntary principles lack enforcement power, geopolitical rivalries undermine cooperation, and the diverse nature of AI complicates the development of universal standards. The next section will explore how a more coherent and hybrid governance model could address these challenges, providing a pathway toward global interoperability without sacrificing national sovereignty.

4.5. Conclusion

This section has demonstrated that fragmentation in global AI governance is not just a theoretical concern but a pressing reality, creating compliance burdens, stifling innovation, undermining human rights, and fueling geopolitical tensions. The persistence of these challenges reveals a fundamental problem: existing governance models are either too rigid, too fragmented, or too weak to effectively manage the global impact of AI. To overcome this impasse, a new approach is needed—one that balances national sovereignty with global interoperability. The next section proposes a hybrid governance model that can bridge these divides, providing a pathway toward a more coherent, scalable, and adaptable framework for AI regulation.

5. TOWARD A HYBRID AND INTEROPERABLE GOVERNANCE MODEL

The rapid proliferation of AI across sectors has revealed a fundamental tension in global governance: the need to balance national digital sovereignty with the imperatives of global interoperability. As detailed in previous sections, countries such as the United States, European Union, and China have pursued divergent governance models, each asserting control over their digital ecosystems according to their own values, security concerns, and economic interests. Yet, AI is inherently a transnational technology, relying on global data flows, cross-border research, and multi-regional deployment. This tension—between sovereign control and global coherence—has led scholars and policymakers to advocate for hybrid governance models that can bridge these competing priorities.

We propose a three-tier hybrid governance model for AI regulation that reflects this imperative. The first tier consists of universal norms and principles, adopted through multilateral platforms and soft law instruments, providing a common foundation for global interoperability. The second tier comprises national and regional regulatory frameworks that implement these norms in locally adapted ways, ensuring political legitimacy and contextual relevance. The third tier allows for sector-specific adaptations, recognizing that AI's application in healthcare, defense, education, and finance may require distinct regulatory mechanisms, even within the same jurisdiction.

5.1 Understanding Hybrid Governance: Concepts and Rationale

Hybrid governance refers to a model that combines elements of national control with mechanisms for international cooperation, allowing countries to maintain sovereignty while participating in shared frameworks for AI oversight. In designing a hybrid governance model for AI, it is essential to recognize that digital sovereignty itself has multiple dimensions—data sovereignty, technological sovereignty, and normative sovereignty, as discussed in Section 3. A successful hybrid model must balance these aspects, allowing countries to maintain control over their data and technology (data and technological sovereignty) while also aligning on shared ethical principles and regulatory standards (normative sovereignty). This approach ensures that states can protect their strategic interests without creating a fragmented global ecosystem. This hybrid model is essential because purely national or purely global approaches are insufficient to address the complex, cross-border risks and opportunities posed by AI (OECD, 2023; WEF, 2024). At the heart of this approach is the recognition that states have legitimate interests in regulating AI to protect their citizens, ensure economic competitiveness, and maintain cultural values. Yet, they must do so without creating a fragmented global landscape where incompatible rules hinder cross-border AI deployment, reduce market access, and complicate compliance for developers (OECD, 2023; WEF, 2024).

This chapter builds on a three-tier model:

- **Tier 1: Universal Norms and Principles:** These are foundational values and ethical guidelines adopted through multilateral platforms, such as the OECD AI Principles or UNESCO's Recommendation on the Ethics of AI. They provide a common ethical and safety baseline, ensuring that countries align on fundamental protections.
- **Tier 2: National and Regional Regulatory Frameworks:** Countries and regions adopt these norms in locally adapted ways, maintaining their sovereign right to regulate AI based on domestic needs. The European Union's AI Act, China's state-centric regulations, and the United States' market-driven approach exemplify this tier (European Commission, 2024; Zhang, 2024).
- **Tier 3: Sector-Specific Adaptations:** Within each jurisdiction, regulatory approaches can be further customized by sector. This is crucial because AI's impact varies significantly across domains such as healthcare, finance, defense, and education. For example, the U.S. FDA has specific rules for AI in medical devices, while financial regulators impose separate transparency requirements on algorithmic trading systems.

The concept of hybrid governance is rooted in theories of polycentric governance, where multiple overlapping authorities—national, regional, and global—share responsibility for rule-making and enforcement (Roberts et al., 2024). It draws on the idea that diverse actors—governments, international organizations, private companies, and civil society—should cooperate in setting norms and ensuring compliance. This approach has proven effective in other domains, such as climate governance (through the Paris Agreement) and financial regulation (via the Financial Action Task Force). Hybrid governance offers several advantages. It provides flexibility, allowing countries to maintain regulatory autonomy while aligning on shared principles. It enhances resilience, enabling the system to adapt to new risks and technological developments through ongoing coordination. It ensures inclusion, bringing diverse stakeholders into the governance process, making it more democratic. Finally, it supports risk management by balancing local protections with global interoperability, ensuring that AI systems can operate across borders without losing oversight.

Real-world examples illustrate this model in action. The OECD AI Principles, adopted by over 50 countries, provide a flexible, interoperable framework for trustworthy AI, promoting human rights, accountability, and transparency without mandating a single legal model (OECD, 2023). Similarly, UNESCO's Recommendation on the Ethics of AI offers a global ethical framework adopted by 193 member states, providing shared values while allowing national adaptation (UNESCO, 2021). The G7 Hiroshima Process is another illustration, where leading economies aim to harmonize AI governance through a Code of Conduct for AI developers, balancing national interests with international coordination (G7 Communiqué, 2023).

These initiatives demonstrate the value of a hybrid model that balances the need for national control with the advantages of international coordination. The next section will build on this foundation by exploring the key design features that make a three-tier hybrid governance model practical and effective.

5.2 Key Design Features of a Three-Tier Hybrid Governance Model

A robust hybrid governance model for artificial intelligence must integrate design features that ensure it is adaptable, interoperable, and scalable. This model is structured around three interconnected tiers: universal norms and principles, national and regional regulatory frameworks, and sector-specific adaptations. Each tier serves a distinct purpose but operates in a coordinated manner, ensuring both global alignment and local relevance.

Universal Norms and Principles (Tier 1)

This foundational tier establishes global ethical and safety standards that provide a common baseline for AI governance. These norms are developed through multilateral organizations such as the OECD, UNESCO, the ISO, and the IEC. They include fundamental principles such as:

- **Privacy and Data Protection:** Ensuring that AI systems respect user privacy, comply with data minimization principles, and secure personal data against unauthorized access (e.g., OECD Privacy Guidelines, GDPR's global influence).
- **Transparency:** Requiring that AI decision-making processes are explainable, with clear documentation and accessible information for users (UNESCO Ethics Recommendation, OECD AI Principles).
- **Accountability:** Mandating that developers, deployers, and operators of AI systems are responsible for their impacts, including mechanisms for redress in case of harm (ISO/IEC AI Standards).
- **Human Rights and Non-Discrimination:** Safeguarding human dignity, preventing bias, and ensuring fairness in AI applications, with special protection for vulnerable groups (UNESCO Ethics of AI).
- **Robustness and Safety:** Ensuring that AI systems are reliable, secure, and operate within acceptable risk thresholds, particularly in high-risk applications (ISO AI Safety Standards).

These norms are not legally binding but exert significant normative influence, shaping the design of national regulations and industry practices worldwide. They create a "soft law" layer that promotes convergence without directly imposing legal obligations.

National and Regional Regulatory Frameworks (Tier 2)

This tier allows countries and regions to adapt universal norms to their legal, cultural, and economic contexts while maintaining regulatory sovereignty. Major regions have developed distinct AI regulatory models:

- **European Union:** The EU AI Act adopts a risk-based approach, categorizing AI systems into unacceptable, high-risk, limited-risk, and minimal-risk categories. High-risk systems, such as biometric surveillance, are subject to stringent transparency, oversight, and compliance requirements. This model emphasizes human rights, transparency, and accountability (European Commission, 2024).
- **United States:** The U.S. maintains a decentralized model with federal guidance (NIST AI Risk Management Framework) and state-level regulations (e.g., California Consumer Privacy Act, Illinois' Biometric Information Privacy Act). This model balances innovation with consumer protection.
- **China:** China's model is state-driven, emphasizing control, security, and ideological alignment. Regulatory measures include mandatory data local-

ization, security reviews for AI systems, and rules ensuring that generative AI reflects "core socialist values" (Zhang, 2024).

These frameworks demonstrate how countries adapt global principles to align with their domestic priorities. For instance, the EU's human rights focus contrasts with China's emphasis on state control, while the U.S. promotes innovation through a market-driven approach. Regional cooperation can also occur, as seen in the EU-U.S. Trade and Technology Council's efforts to align AI standards.

Sector-Specific Adaptations (Tier 3)

AI's impact varies significantly across sectors, making sector-specific governance essential. This tier provides flexibility for domains where AI poses unique risks or opportunities:

- **Healthcare:** AI diagnostic tools must comply with medical device regulations (e.g., FDA in the United States, EU's Medical Device Regulation). WHO guidelines for AI in healthcare emphasize patient safety and ethical use.
- **Finance:** Algorithmic trading is governed by transparency, accountability, and anti-fraud rules (e.g., EU's MiFID II, U.S. SEC regulations). These ensure market stability and consumer protection.
- **Education:** AI-powered learning tools must respect data protection and non-discrimination principles (e.g., UNESCO Ethics for AI in Education, GDPR in the EU, FERPA in the U.S.).
- **Defense:** Autonomous weapons and military AI are subject to ethical guidelines, such as the UN discussions on Lethal Autonomous Weapons Systems (LAWS) and NATO's ethical AI principles for defense.

These sectoral rules ensure that AI is governed according to its specific risks, with stricter standards in high-risk areas (e.g., healthcare, defense) and more flexible rules in low-risk sectors (e.g., education).

Interconnection of the Three Tiers

The three tiers are not isolated but interconnected, forming a layered governance system. Universal norms (Tier 1) establish ethical and safety baselines, national frameworks (Tier 2) adapt these norms to local contexts, and sector-specific rules (Tier 3) fine-tune them to manage domain-specific risks. For example, an AI diagnostic tool must adhere to global safety principles (Tier 1), comply with the EU

AI Act's high-risk rules (Tier 2), and meet FDA medical device standards in the U.S. (Tier 3).

This multi-layered model ensures coherence and adaptability, allowing AI systems to operate across borders while respecting local regulations.

A critical aspect of this model is regulatory interoperability—the ability of AI systems to comply with multiple jurisdictions without conflicting requirements. This is achieved through mechanisms such as:

- **Mutual Recognition Agreements:** Countries recognize each other's regulatory standards (e.g., GDPR adequacy decisions, EU-U.S. Trade and Technology Council).
- **Global Certification Schemes:** Systems certified under ISO/IEC AI standards are recognized globally, reducing compliance burdens.
- **Interoperable Compliance Systems:** AI providers design their systems to meet the highest standard, ensuring acceptance in multiple regions.

This hybrid model offers significant advantages. It is flexible, allowing countries to maintain regulatory autonomy while aligning on shared principles. It is scalable, capable of expanding to new sectors or regions as AI technology evolves. It supports risk management, ensuring stricter oversight for high-risk applications while allowing lighter regulation for low-risk systems. Most importantly, it enhances interoperability, enabling cross-border AI deployment without creating conflicting obligations.

However, the model also faces challenges. Regulatory complexity can create compliance burdens for companies operating globally. Some countries may resist global norms, leading to regulatory divergence. Inconsistent enforcement can result in a fragmented landscape, where AI systems are compliant in one region but restricted in another. Finally, the model depends on international cooperation, which can be undermined by geopolitical tensions.

These features make the three-tier model both adaptable and robust, but its success depends on effective implementation. The following section will explore how such a model can be operationalized through institutional pathways and enforcement mechanisms.

5.3 Institutional Pathways and Implementation Strategies

While the three-tier hybrid governance model for artificial intelligence offers a robust theoretical framework, its success depends on effective implementation through well-defined institutional pathways and coordinated mechanisms. The hybrid model relies on multi-level governance, with distinct roles for global, national, and sectoral actors. At the global level, international organizations such as the OECD, UNESCO, and the ISO provide universal norms and standards. The OECD's AI Principles offer ethical guidelines, while ISO/IEC standards set technical requirements for AI safety, transparency, and accountability. UNESCO's Ethics Recommendation provides a universal ethical framework, adopted by over 193 member states (UNESCO, 2021). At the national and regional level, countries and regions adapt these global norms to their local contexts. The European Union's AI Act establishes a comprehensive regulatory framework, categorizing AI systems by risk and imposing stricter requirements on high-risk applications (European Commission, 2024). The United States uses a decentralized model, where the NIST AI Risk Management Framework offers voluntary guidelines, complemented by state laws such as California's CCPA. China adopts a state-driven model, with strict controls on data localization and mandatory security reviews for generative AI (Zhang, 2024).

At the sectoral level, specialized regulators ensure that AI is governed according to domain-specific risks. In healthcare, the FDA in the United States and the European Medical Device Regulation (MDR) ensure that AI medical devices are safe and effective. Financial regulators, such as the SEC in the U.S. and ESMA in the EU, impose transparency requirements for AI in algorithmic trading. In education, UNESCO's ethical guidelines ensure that AI respects student data privacy and promotes non-discrimination. These levels do not operate in isolation but are interconnected through regulatory networks. International norms guide national policies, which are then adapted to sectoral contexts. This coordination is facilitated by regulatory platforms, such as GPAI, the G7 Hiroshima Process, and the OECD's AI Observatory, where states and stakeholders share best practices and align policies.

Regulatory interoperability is essential for a hybrid governance model, allowing AI systems to operate across borders without conflicting requirements. This is achieved through mutual recognition agreements, where countries recognize each other's regulatory standards, reducing compliance burdens. For example, the GDPR's adequacy decisions allow data flows between the EU and other jurisdictions deemed to have equivalent data protection standards. Global certification schemes, such as those provided by ISO/IEC, offer a universally recognized benchmark for AI safety and transparency. Companies can develop AI systems that meet these standards, ensuring compliance across multiple markets. Interoperable compliance systems further enhance this, where firms design their AI to meet the highest standards, ensuring cross-border deployment. For instance, an AI provider can design its system to comply with the EU AI Act, ISO safety standards, and NIST transparency guidelines.

A truly global hybrid governance model must include developing countries, which may lack the technical expertise or regulatory capacity to govern AI effectively. Capacity-building is essential, ensuring that these countries can participate meaningfully in AI governance. UNESCO and the OECD offer training programs for regulators in low- and middle-income countries, covering ethical AI, data protection, and regulatory best practices. Organizations such as the World Bank and the UN Development Programme (UNDP) provide financial support for digital transformation projects, including AI governance capacity. The GPAI includes governments, academia, and industry experts, offering a platform for developing countries to share knowledge and participate in AI governance. By ensuring that developing countries have the necessary skills and resources, this approach prevents the emergence of a global "AI divide."

Transparency and accountability are critical to the credibility of the hybrid model. These principles ensure that AI systems operate in a manner consistent with ethical norms and legal requirements. Mechanisms include public disclosure of AI standards, transparency registers such as the EU's AI registry, and algorithmic explainability requirements. Accountability mechanisms ensure that developers, deployers, and operators of AI systems are clearly responsible for their impacts. ISO standards and UNESCO ethics emphasize accountability, requiring that AI providers take responsibility for their systems. Independent audits and oversight provide an additional layer of assurance, with regular inspections by national authorities (e.g., EU AI Act's conformity assessments), peer reviews (OECD), and cross-border audits for global firms. Dispute resolution mechanisms, such as data protection authorities (DPA) under GDPR and international arbitration for cross-border disputes, offer avenues for addressing violations.

Effective implementation of the hybrid model depends on the coordinated efforts of multiple institutions. The OECD provides global norms, coordinates peer reviews, and supports regulatory alignment. UNESCO offers ethical guidance, capacity-building, and multi-stakeholder dialogue. ISO/IEC develops technical standards for AI safety, transparency, and accountability. The G7 and G20 facilitate strategic alignment among leading economies, promoting common principles. The GPAI serves as a multi-stakeholder platform for research, capacity-building, and policy alignment. These institutions must collaborate through joint working groups, shared technical resources, and cross-border initiatives to ensure that AI governance remains consistent and adaptable.

The hybrid model must also remain adaptable to changing technological, social, and political contexts. This is achieved through regular review of global norms, with the OECD's AI Observatory providing ongoing monitoring and updates. The EU AI Act's risk-based approach is adaptable, allowing for the reclassification of AI systems as technologies evolve. Rapid response mechanisms, such as the G7 Hiroshima Process, can coordinate emergency responses to emerging AI risks, such as the misuse of generative AI.

The success of the three-tier hybrid governance model depends on effective implementation through these institutional pathways. By ensuring coordination across global, national, and sectoral levels, establishing transparency and accountability mechanisms, and building the capacity of developing countries, this model can achieve both flexibility and coherence. However, its implementation is not without challenges. The next section will explore the political, economic, and geopolitical barriers that may hinder this model.

5.4 Feasibility and Political Barriers

While the three-tier hybrid governance model for artificial intelligence offers a theoretically robust and adaptable framework, its practical implementation is fraught with challenges. These challenges arise from the political, economic, and geopolitical dynamics that shape global AI governance. At the heart of these challenges is the inherent tension between digital sovereignty and global interoperability. Nations prioritize their strategic, economic, and security interests, which often conflict with the principles of shared governance and regulatory convergence. The geopolitical landscape, defined by competition between major powers such as the United States, the European Union, and China, further complicates efforts to establish a cohesive global governance model. Each of these actors has its own vision of AI governance, driven by distinct values, regulatory philosophies, and geopolitical ambitions.

A primary challenge lies in the risk of regulatory fragmentation. As countries assert their digital sovereignty, they develop AI regulations that reflect local values, priorities, and risk perceptions. The European Union, with its emphasis on human rights, transparency, and accountability, has adopted the AI Act as a comprehensive regulatory framework. The United States, in contrast, maintains a more market-driven approach, with decentralized regulation that allows innovation to flourish while providing limited federal oversight. China's state-centric model emphasizes control, security, and ideological conformity, with regulations that ensure AI aligns with national values. These divergent approaches create a fragmented regulatory landscape where AI providers must navigate conflicting rules, increasing compliance costs and limiting cross-border deployment.

Geopolitical rivalries further complicate global AI governance. The United States and China are locked in a strategic competition that extends to technology, including AI. Both countries view AI as a critical element of national security and economic dominance. The United States has sought to align like-minded democracies through initiatives such as the G7 Hiroshima Process and the Trade and Technology Council with the European Union, promoting shared principles of trustworthy AI. China, in contrast, has promoted its own AI standards through the Digital Silk Road initiative, exporting its regulatory model to partner countries across Asia, Africa, and Latin America. This competition creates a "bifurcated" global AI governance landscape, where countries are pressured to align with one of two competing models.

In addition to geopolitical tensions, the hybrid model faces practical challenges related to regulatory capacity and enforcement. Developing countries, which lack the technical expertise, financial resources, and institutional capacity to effectively govern AI, may struggle to comply with global norms. Without adequate capacity-building support, these countries risk becoming passive recipients of AI technologies developed and governed by external actors. This could lead to "AI colonialism," where powerful nations set the rules while developing countries have little influence over their design or implementation.

Enforcement is another critical barrier. Even in regions with strong regulatory frameworks, such as the European Union, ensuring compliance is challenging. The EU's GDPR has demonstrated that high standards are meaningless without effective enforcement mechanisms. DPAs in many EU member states lack the funding, staff, and technical expertise needed to investigate violations, leading to inconsistent enforcement. In the context of AI, where technical complexity and rapid innovation make oversight difficult, this problem is even more pronounced. Companies may engage in "compliance theater," meeting formal regulatory requirements without truly addressing ethical or safety concerns.

The hybrid model's reliance on international cooperation also exposes it to the risks of political divergence. Multilateral organizations such as the OECD and UNESCO provide a platform for developing universal norms, but their influence is limited by the willingness of states to align their domestic policies with these norms. Countries may sign international agreements while adopting domestic rules that conflict with global principles, creating a "commitment-compliance gap." This gap is further widened by the absence of strong enforcement mechanisms at the international level. For example, UNESCO's Ethics Recommendation provides valuable guidance, but it is a non-binding instrument, and countries are free to interpret or ignore it.

Economic interests can also undermine the model's effectiveness. Technology companies, which are among the most powerful global actors, have a strong interest in shaping AI governance in ways that favor their business models. These companies may engage in regulatory capture, using their financial influence to shape domestic regulations in their favor. They may also engage in "jurisdictional arbitrage," relocating their operations to countries with weaker regulatory standards to avoid compliance costs. This practice not only weakens global AI governance but also creates a "race to the bottom," where countries compete to attract AI companies by lowering regulatory standards.

Finally, the model faces a broader challenge related to cultural and ethical diversity. While universal norms provide a common foundation, the interpretation and application of these norms can vary significantly across regions. For example, the principle of transparency may be interpreted as a right to explainability in Europe, while in the United States, it may be seen as a matter of consumer choice. In China, transparency may be subordinated to state security. These divergent interpretations create ambiguity, complicating efforts to achieve global alignment.

Despite these challenges, the hybrid model remains the most viable pathway for achieving coherent and adaptable AI governance. Its flexibility allows it to accommodate diverse regulatory philosophies, while its emphasis on coordination provides a foundation for gradual convergence. However, its success will depend on the ability of states and institutions to navigate these political, economic, and geopolitical barriers. The next section will explore how these challenges can be mitigated through strategic cooperation, capacity-building, and dynamic governance mechanisms.

5.5 Conclusion

The three-tier hybrid governance model for artificial intelligence represents a comprehensive and adaptable approach to global AI regulation, balancing the need for universal norms with the flexibility of national and sector-specific rules. Throughout this section, we have explored how this model can provide a robust framework for AI governance, ensuring both global coherence and local relevance. The model's strength lies in its ability to integrate diverse perspectives, aligning global principles with domestic priorities while recognizing the unique risks associated with different sectors.

However, the hybrid model is not without its challenges. As discussed, regulatory fragmentation remains a significant barrier, with divergent approaches taken by the European Union, the United States, and China creating a fragmented regulatory landscape. Geopolitical rivalries further complicate global governance, as leading powers compete to shape AI norms in line with their strategic interests. Developing countries, lacking technical expertise and regulatory capacity, risk becoming passive recipients of external standards, while even advanced regions struggle with enforcement and compliance. Economic interests and cultural diversity add further complexity, creating a landscape where universal principles may be interpreted in conflicting ways.

Despite these obstacles, the hybrid model remains the most viable pathway for achieving responsible, flexible, and scalable AI governance. Its emphasis on regulatory interoperability, capacity-building for developing countries, and the coordination of diverse stakeholders makes it uniquely suited to the complex, cross-border nature of AI. To ensure its success, however, states and institutions must commit to continuous coordination, dynamic adaptation of norms, and the effective enforcement of principles. This requires not only international cooperation but also domestic political will, regulatory capacity, and a shared commitment to ethical AI.

In an increasingly digital and interconnected world, the need for coherent AI governance has never been more urgent. The three-tier hybrid model offers a pathway toward a balanced and adaptable system, one that can protect fundamental rights, promote innovation, and ensure that the benefits of AI are widely shared. As the next section will discuss, achieving this vision will require strategic cooperation, capacity-building, and the continuous evolution of governance mechanisms to keep pace with technological change.

6. CONCLUSION

This chapter has explored the complex and evolving landscape of global AI governance, examining the divergent approaches adopted by the European Union, the United States, and China. These three regions were chosen because they represent the most influential and contrasting regulatory models—rights-based, precautionary regulation in the EU; innovation-driven, decentralized governance in the US; and state-centric, ideologically aligned control in China. These models not only reflect regional values and strategic interests but also highlight the broader challenge of digital sovereignty, where countries seek to assert control over data, technology, and ethical standards.

The analysis revealed that these competing governance models have contributed to the fragmentation of global AI governance, creating compliance burdens, stifling innovation, and undermining human rights. Fragmentation manifests in conflicting ethical principles, technical standards, and institutional frameworks, making it increasingly difficult for companies to develop and deploy AI systems across borders. The chapter also demonstrated that existing international initiatives—such as the OECD Principles, UNESCO's Ethical Guidelines, and the Global Partnership on AI—have struggled to overcome this fragmentation due to their voluntary nature, geopolitical rivalries, and the inherent complexity of AI technology.

In response to these challenges, the chapter proposed a hybrid governance model that combines national sovereignty with global interoperability. This model is designed around three interconnected tiers: universal norms and principles, national and regional regulatory frameworks, and sector-specific adaptations. The hybrid model seeks to balance data sovereignty, technological sovereignty, and normative sovereignty, allowing countries to maintain regulatory control while ensuring alignment on shared ethical principles and technical standards. By providing a flexible, scalable, and adaptable framework, this model offers a practical pathway toward a more coherent global AI governance system.

The chapter concludes that achieving effective global AI governance requires more than voluntary principles or regional regulations—it demands a hybrid approach that respects national interests while fostering international cooperation. Such a model can promote ethical AI development, enhance regulatory coherence, and mitigate the risks of fragmentation. However, its success will depend on the willingness of states to align on core principles, the capacity of international institutions to coordinate effectively, and the ability of stakeholders to adapt to new risks and technological developments.

As AI continues to transform societies and reshape global power dynamics, the need for a balanced, interoperable governance model has never been more urgent. The hybrid model proposed in this chapter is a step toward achieving that balance, providing a foundation for responsible, inclusive, and sustainable AI governance.

REFERENCES

G7 Communiqué. (2023). Hiroshima Process on Trustworthy AI. Retrieved from https://www.g7.org/

Belli, L., de Queiroz, T., Senna, A., & Das, S. (2024). *Digital sovereignty in the BRICS countries: How the Global South is reshaping AI governance*. Cambridge University Press.

Bradford, A. (2023). *Digital empires: The global battle to regulate technology*. Oxford University Press. DOI: 10.1093/oso/9780197649268.001.0001

Brookings Institution. (2023). *The geopolitics of AI and the rise of digital sovereignty*. Retrieved from https://www.brookings.edu/research/the-geopolitics-of-ai/

China. (2021). Personal Information Protection Law (PIPL). Cyberspace Administration of China. Retrieved from https://www.cac.gov.cn/

China. (2023). Interim Measures for the Management of Generative AI Services. Cyberspace Administration of China. Retrieved from https://www.cac.gov.cn/

European Commission. (2024). *The Artificial Intelligence Act and its implementation*. Retrieved from https://digital-strategy.ec.europa.eu/en/policies/european-ai-act

European Data Protection Board. (2023). *AI and GDPR: Analyzing AI's impact on European data rights*. EDPB Report.

European Union. (2016). General Data Protection Regulation (GDPR) (Regulation (EU) 2016/679). Retrieved from https://eur-lex.europa.eu/

European Union. (2024). Regulation (EU) 2024/1689: Artificial Intelligence Act. Official Journal of the European Union. Retrieved from https://eur-lex.europa.eu/

Mügge, D. (2024). EU AI sovereignty: For whom, to what end, and to whose benefit? *Journal of European Public Policy*, *31*(8), 2200–2225. DOI: 10.1080/13501763.2024.2318475

National Institute of Standards and Technology. (2023). *AI Risk Management Framework (1.0)*. Retrieved from https://www.nist.gov/itl/ai-risk-management-framework

OECD. (2023). *Global Trends in AI Governance: 2023 Update*. OECD AI Policy Observatory. Retrieved from https://www.oecd.ai/

Office of Science and Technology Policy. (2022). *Blueprint for an AI Bill of Rights*. The White House. Retrieved from https://www.whitehouse.gov/ostp/ai-bill-of-rights/

Roberts, H., Taddeo, M., & Floridi, L. (2024). Global AI governance: Barriers and pathways forward. *International Affairs*, *100*(3), 1275–1286. DOI: 10.1093/ia/iiae073

Sheehan, M. (2023). *China's algorithm regulation: A model for the world?* Carnegie Endowment for International Peace. Retrieved from https://carnegieendowment.org

UNESCO. (2021). *Recommendation on the ethics of artificial intelligence*. Retrieved from https://unesdoc.unesco.org/ark:/48223/pf0000377897

United States. (2008). Illinois Biometric Information Privacy Act (BIPA). Illinois General Assembly. Retrieved from https://www.ilga.gov/

United States. (2018). California Consumer Privacy Act (CCPA). California Legislature. Retrieved from https://leginfo.legislature.ca.gov/

United States. (2022). Blueprint for an AI Bill of Rights. Office of Science and Technology Policy. Retrieved from https://www.whitehouse.gov/ostp/ai-bill-of-rights/

United States. (2023). Executive Order 14110 on Safe, Secure, and Trustworthy AI. The White House. Retrieved from https://www.whitehouse.gov/

White House. (2023). *Executive Order on the Safe, Secure, and Trustworthy Development and Use of Artificial Intelligence*. Retrieved from https://www.whitehouse.gov/briefing-room/presidential-actions/2023/10/30/executive-order-on-the-safe-secure-and-trustworthy-development-and-use-of-artificial-intelligence/

Zhang, A. H. (2024). The promise and perils of China's regulation of artificial intelligence. *SSRN*, *63*(1), 50–78. DOI: 10.2139/ssrn.4708676

Chapter 6
Digital States:
The New Frontier in the Techno-Political Power Struggle

Büşra Begçecanlı
https://orcid.org/0009-0006-1591-2119
Anadolu Agency, Turkey

ABSTRACT

In an era where data rivals oil as a source of power, who truly governs: states or corporations? This question drives the exploration of techno-politics, a field examining how technological advancements reshape political authority and governance. This paper investigates the state-company struggle through three interconnected dimensions: the tension between states and corporations, the rivalry among states exemplified by China and the USA, and the competition between companies. Together, these dynamics signal a profound shift toward digital states, where power hinges on control over digital infrastructure and data.

INTRODUCTION

Is data the new oil, reshaping global power as profoundly as the Industrial Revolution once did? In an era where algorithms govern economies, influence elections, and redefine citizenship, the struggle for control over digital infrastructure has become the defining battleground of the 21st century. Techno-politics—the dynamic interplay of technology and political authority—drives this transformation, as states, corporations, and individuals compete to master the intangible assets of data, connectivity, and computational power. From the U.S.-China race for AI supremacy to tech giants like NVIDIA dictating the architecture of artificial intelligence, these contests mirror historic struggles for territorial dominance, yet they unfold in a bor-

DOI: 10.4018/979-8-3373-2459-3.ch006

derless digital realm. As traditional state sovereignty erodes, a new political order emerges: digital states, entities where authority stems not from geographic borders but from the control of data and digital platforms.

Historically, power was anchored in tangible resources—land, oil, or military might. The 20th century saw nation-states leverage industrial capabilities to assert dominance, as oil cartels and nuclear arsenals shaped geopolitical hierarchies. Today, the data age has upended this paradigm. Corporations like X Corp, guided by technolibertarian visions of figures such as Elon Musk, challenge state monopolies by fostering "digital citizenship" through platforms that transcend national jurisdictions. In 2025, X's premium membership model, which binds users to its ecosystem through exclusive services, exemplifies how individuals increasingly align with digital platforms over geographic nations. Meanwhile, geopolitical rivalries intensify, with the United States' tariffs on Chinese semiconductors and China's advancements in DeepSeek's R-1 chip underscoring the race for digital infrastructure supremacy. Corporate battles, such as NVIDIA's dominance in AI chips or OpenAI's diplomatic ventures in the Gulf, further blur the lines between economic competition and political authority.

Despite the growing significance of techno-politics, scholarship has yet to fully explore how these struggles converge to birth digital states. Existing studies often focus on isolated dimensions—cybersecurity, corporate monopolies, or geopolitical tensions—without synthesizing their collective impact on political authority. This paper bridges this gap by analyzing the techno-political power struggle through three interconnected dimensions, arguing that the convergence of state and corporate power is forging a new political order. Digital states, defined by their mastery of data and algorithms, are not merely theoretical constructs but emerging realities that reshape governance, citizenship, and global power. This study offers a framework for policymakers, technologists, and scholars navigating the digital age, where governance may evolve into a service offered by platforms rather than a function of territorial states. To illuminate this transformation, the paper examines the following dimensions:

1. **State vs. Company: The Rise of Corporate Power and Technolibertarianism** This section explores how tech giants like NVIDIA and X Corp challenge state sovereignty through data control and technolibertarian ideologies, redefining governance in a data-driven world.
2. **State vs. State: Geopolitical Rivalry in the Technological Arena** This section analyzes how nations, such as the U.S. and China, compete for digital infrastructure dominance, with examples like semiconductor tariffs and AI advancements shaping global power balances.

3. **Company vs. Company: Corporate Battles with Political Implications** This section examines how corporate rivalries, such as NVIDIA versus OpenAI, spill into political arenas, influencing regulatory frameworks and blurring the lines between market and governance.

The conclusion synthesizes these dynamics to envision the rise of digital states and their implications for the future of global politics.

1-STATE vs. COMPANY: THE RISE OF CORPORATE POWER AND TECHNOLIBERTARIANISM

In the 21st century, the global stage is no longer defined solely by territorial conquests or resource wars but by techno-political rivalries, where states compete for supremacy through mastery of digital and extraterrestrial frontiers. Techno-politics, the dynamic interplay of technological innovation and political authority, has elevated technologies like AI, 5G networks, semiconductors, and space systems to the core of state power. This struggle births digital states—entities whose authority hinges on control over data, algorithms, and digital infrastructure rather than geographic sovereignty. While technolibertarianism, an ideology championed by figures like Elon Musk and Peter Thiel that advocates minimal state regulation and maximal corporate autonomy, primarily shapes corporate strategies, it indirectly influences state actions as governments counter corporate dominance with technological sovereignty. In 2025, this competition transcends Earth, with space emerging as a critical arena: China's quantum communication satellites and laser imaging systems rival the United States' SpaceX-driven orbital networks, signaling a new dimension of geopolitical power.

The dynamics of this global technological competition are fueled by strategic imperatives and paradoxical forces. States prioritize digital infrastructure—AI models, chip production, and 5G networks—to secure economic competitiveness, military superiority, and cultural influence, as seen in the U.S.-China chip wars. Space technologies, such as China's Tianyan-504 quantum computing project or the U.S.'s lunar data centers, amplify this race, extending state power into extraterrestrial domains. The Jevons Paradox intensifies these rivalries: as technological efficiencies, like advanced chip designs, reduce costs, demand for computational power surges, driving states to invest heavily in innovation and infrastructure. For instance, the global semiconductor market's growth from $617 billion in 2024 to projected $800 billion in 2025 underscores this insatiable demand. These dynamics reshape power balances, as states that control digital and space-based ecosystems gain unprecedented leverage, laying the foundation for digital statehood.

This section examines how state-state rivalries in the techno-political arena redefine global power, setting the stage for digital states. By analyzing key case studies, such as the U.S.-China competition and the roles of the Gulf States and the European Union, it reveals how technological and extraterrestrial dominance translates into political authority. These struggles not only highlight the erosion of traditional state sovereignty but also foreshadow a future where digital infrastructure governs global hierarchies.

1.1-Silicon Valley's Trump Alliance: Technolibertarian Power and the Rise of Digital States

The alliance between Silicon Valley and the Trump administration in 2025 marks a pivotal shift in the techno-political landscape, where tech giants leverage political influence to challenge state sovereignty and advance a technolibertarian vision of digital statehood. Once a Democratic stronghold aligned with Obama-era policies, Silicon Valley underwent a dramatic transformation during the 2024 election, with industry titans like Elon Musk, Peter Thiel, Jeff Bezos, and Mark Zuckerberg openly supporting Donald Trump's campaign (Forbes Türkiye, 15 February 2025). This shift, driven by Trump's promises of deregulation, tax cuts, and the dismissal of antitrust lawsuits, positions tech companies as co-architects of U.S. policy, reshaping governance in a data-driven world. The alliance was vividly displayed at Trump's 20 January 2025 inauguration, where Bezos, Zuckerberg, and Musk occupied VIP seats in the Capitol Rotunda, alongside Trump's cabinet nominees, symbolizing tech's ascent in the political hierarchy (The New York Times, 21 January 2025; Reuters, 21 January 2025). By aligning with the state, Silicon Valley firms not only secure economic advantages but also foster digital states—entities where authority derives from data control and platform ecosystems rather than traditional state structures.

Elon Musk emerges as the linchpin of this alliance, wielding unprecedented influence through his role in the Trump administration's "Department of Government Efficiency" (DOGE), tasked with cutting $2 trillion in federal spending (BBC, 18 January 2025). Musk's X Corp, with its premium membership model, exemplifies the technolibertarian ideal of "digital citizenship," binding users to its ecosystem over geographic nations. X's data infrastructure, controlling vast troves of user interactions, enables Musk to shape public discourse and challenge state regulatory efforts, as seen in his defiance of EU data privacy fines (BBC, 18 January 2025). Similarly, Mark Zuckerberg's Meta, once targeted by antitrust regulators, secures a reprieve under Trump, with former UFC president Dana White's appointment to its board signaling a new era of political alignment (Forbes Türkiye, 10 January 2025). Zuckerberg's presence at the inauguration, alongside his wife Priscilla Chan, and his co-hosting of a gala with Miriam Adelson, cemented this reconciliation (Reuters,

21 January 2025). Jeff Bezos, through Amazon's $1 million inauguration donation and the Washington Post's decision to remain neutral in 2024, aligned with Trump; his appearance at the ceremony with fiancée Lauren Sanchez underscored his stake in this techno-political order (NBC News, 15 January 2025).

Vice President JD Vance, alongside Peter Thiel and David Sacks, forms a critical axis in this techno-political realignment, channeling Silicon Valley's influence into Trump's administration. Thiel, a PayPal co-founder and Vance's mentor, bankrolled Vance's 2022 Senate campaign with $15 million and facilitated his 2021 Mar-a-Lago meeting with Trump, solidifying their alliance (Bloomberg, 7 March 2025). Thiel's Palantir and Anduril secure defense contracts, embedding AI and surveillance into state infrastructure, while his inauguration party at his D.C. mansion, attended by Vance, Zuckerberg, and OpenAI's Sam Altman, underscored his clout (The Times of India, 27 January 2025). Sacks, another PayPal alum and Trump's AI and crypto czar, co-hosted a 2024 Trump fundraiser with Vance, raising millions from tech donors (Axios, 31 March 2025). Their technolibertarian push for deregulation and crypto-friendly policies shapes a governance model where digital platforms rival state authority, accelerating the rise of digital states.

This convergence of corporate and state power illustrates how Silicon Valley exploits techno-political opportunities to redefine governance. By influencing policies on AI, data privacy, and infrastructure, these firms lay the groundwork for digital states where platforms, not governments, dictate societal rules. Musk's X posts in 2025, proclaiming "X is the fortress of digital freedom," underscore this vision, aligning with technolibertarian principles that prioritize corporate autonomy over state control (X post, 12 March 2025). Yet, this alliance raises questions about accountability, as unchecked corporate power risks eroding democratic institutions, paving the way for a new techno-political order dominated by digital state ecosystems.

1.2-OpenAI's Global AI Diplomacy: Shaping Digital State Infrastructure Through Corporate Power

OpenAI's global AI diplomacy in 2025 exemplifies the techno-political power of corporations to negotiate as near-equals with states, accelerating the rise of digital states defined by data and algorithmic control. Under Sam Altman's leadership, OpenAI forges strategic partnerships with governments, embedding its AI infrastructure into national strategies while advancing a technolibertarian vision that prioritizes corporate autonomy over state regulation. By cultivating state dependency on its AI systems, OpenAI not only secures economic dominance but also shapes the governance frameworks of digital states, where platforms increasingly dictate societal rules. This corporate-state convergence, rooted in OpenAI's global outreach, underscores how tech giants are redefining political authority in a data-driven world.

The cornerstone of OpenAI's diplomacy is the Stargate project, a $500 billion AI infrastructure initiative unveiled alongside President Trump in 2025, aimed at building hyperscale data centers to power next-generation AI models (BBC, 28 January 2025). This project, backed by Microsoft and NVIDIA, positions OpenAI as a critical partner for states seeking AI supremacy. In the United Arab Emirates, OpenAI's $100 billion deal with MGX, a state-backed investment vehicle, establishes AI training hubs that bolster the UAE's ambition to become a digital state hub, integrating OpenAI's systems into its economic and security frameworks (Author's Previous Work, 18 April 2025). Similarly, OpenAI's collaboration with India to develop AI education centers, supported by government subsidies, enhances India's digital infrastructure while tying its workforce to OpenAI's ecosystem (T24, 18 March 2025). These agreements, spanning North America, the Middle East, and South Asia, demonstrate OpenAI's ability to navigate geopolitical rivalries and secure state partnerships.

OpenAI's diplomacy amplifies the techno-political shift toward digital states by fostering state reliance on corporate AI infrastructure. Altman's presence at Peter Thiel's inauguration party in Washington, D.C., alongside JD Vance and Mark Zuckerberg, further cements OpenAI's influence in shaping U.S. tech policy (The Times of India, 27 January 2025). However, this corporate ascendancy raises concerns about state sovereignty, as governments cede control over critical AI systems to private entities. By embedding its technology into global digital state frameworks, OpenAI not only drives innovation but also redefines governance, aligning with the technolibertarian ethos that underpins the digital state paradigm.

1.3-NVIDIA in the Crossfire: Navigating US-China Techno-Political Tensions in the Chip War

The escalating US-China chip war in 2025 places NVIDIA at the epicenter of techno-political tensions, as US export bans disrupt global AI chip markets and challenge corporate autonomy. The US, aiming to curb China's AI and military advancements, tightened restrictions on advanced chip exports, notably NVIDIA's H20 chips, causing a $5.5 billion revenue loss for the company (Reuters, 18 April 2025). These bans, coupled with China's retaliatory antitrust probes and push for domestic chips, force NVIDIA to balance compliance with its critical Chinese market, which accounts for 17% of its revenue (Donanimhaber, 20 January 2025). NVIDIA's CEO Jensen Huang's April 2025 Beijing visit, where he met DeepSeek's founder and Chinese officials, underscored China's importance while urging lighter restrictions to preserve innovation (The Guardian, 17 April 2025). NVIDIA's calls to ease sanctions echo broader corporate concerns about fragmented supply chains, yet its strategic pivot to US-aligned production reveals the delicate dance between state pressures and corporate interests.

NVIDIA's H20 chip, designed to comply with earlier US restrictions, powered Chinese AI models like DeepSeek's R-1, prompting the US to impose indefinite export licenses in April 2025 (Yahoo Finance, 28 April 2025). China responded with a probe into NVIDIA's market practices and promoted Huawei's 910C chip, a potential H100 rival (CNN Business, 16 April 2025). Chinese firms stockpiled $16 billion in H20 chips pre-ban, signaling strategic resilience (NPR, 16 April 2025). Meanwhile, NVIDIA invested $100 billion in a TSMC Arizona factory, aligning with US onshoring to secure AI infrastructure (Euronews, 3 April 2025). Huang warned that prolonged bans could harm US innovation, echoing his 2023 caution of "enormous damage" to the tech sector (Patronlardunyasi, 26 May 2023).

NVIDIA's navigation of these tensions shapes digital statehood, where AI chips define data control and power. By driving global AI ecosystems despite state constraints, NVIDIA reinforces corporate influence over digital state infrastructure. However, this techno-political struggle risks fracturing global markets, raising questions about sovereignty as companies like NVIDIA mediate between rival state agendas.

1.4-China's 2025 AI Private Sector Summit: State-Driven Innovation for Digital Statehood

China's 2025 AI Private Sector Summit, convened by President Xi Jinping, underscores the state's strategic alignment with private tech giants to bolster digital statehood, where data and AI infrastructure define governance. Held on 17 February 2025, the symposium gathered CEOs from Huawei, BYD, Alibaba, Xiaomi, and DeepSeek, signaling a pivot from the 2020 tech crackdowns to a "new era" of state backed private innovation (CNBC, 17 February 2025). Xi's call for entrepreneurs to "show their talents" reflects China's urgency to counter US tech restrictions and economic slowdown, positioning private firms as engines of AI-driven growth (Foreign Policy, 19 February 2025). This state-private synergy, rooted in the "Next Generation AI Development Plan," aims to cement China's digital state infrastructure by 2030, prioritizing national security and ideological control (Wikipedia, 2 April 2025).

Xi's summit emphasized equal market access, legal protections, and solutions to payment delays for private firms, alongside a draft law to promote the private economy (China Daily, 19 February 2025). Huawei's Ren Zhengfei and DeepSeek, whose R-1 model rivals OpenAI's offerings, were showcased as state-aligned innovators (Reuters, 17 February 2025). DeepSeek's success, backed by a $48 billion semiconductor fund, highlights how state investment fuels private AI breakthroughs, yet firms like Baidu were notably excluded, reflecting selective state patronage (BBC, 8 February 2025). Xi's central role at the summit, with CEOs arranged hierarchically around him, underscores the state's dominance over private autonomy (Foreign Policy, 19 February 2025).

This convergence shapes digital statehood by integrating private AI into state-controlled ecosystems, such as surveillance and digital yuan platforms. However, tight regulations, including the 2025 AI law draft, ensure alignment with state ideology, limiting corporate freedom (FiscalNote, 7 August 2024). By leveraging private innovation under state guidance, China advances a digital state model where governance hinges on data control, challenging global norms and raising concerns about unchecked state power in the techno-political landscape.

1.5-EU's 2025 Big Tech Regulations: Countering US Dominance and Shaping Digital Statehood

The European Union's 2025 regulations on US Big Tech, particularly AI companies, reflect a techno-political strategy to curb American digital dominance and foster a sovereign digital state model. Fearing the unchecked power of US firms like OpenAI, Meta, and Google, which control 80% of Europe's cloud and AI markets, the EU enforces stringent rules to protect data privacy, competition, and democratic values (France24, 16 April 2025). The Digital Markets Act (DMA), Digital Services Act (DSA), and AI Act target US tech giants with investigations—Meta and Apple faced €162 million fines for DMA violations, while Google and X are probed for anticompetitive practices and weak content moderation (Reuters, 14 January 2025). These actions, led by Commissioner Henna Virkkunen, aim to reduce Europe's reliance on US tech, which poses risks to sovereignty amid transatlantic tensions (Politico, 10 March 2025).

President Trump frames these regulations as "de facto tariffs," accusing the EU of targeting US firms to stifle innovation (ITIF, 28 April 2025). His administration, backed by Meta's Mark Zuckerberg and Elon Musk, threatens retaliatory tariffs, viewing EU fines—nearly one-fifth of its 2024 tariff revenue—as economic warfare (Brookings, 30 January 2025). This clash, amplified by Vice President JD Vance's critique of the AI Act at the 2025 Paris AI Summit, underscores a transatlantic rift where US firms resist EU oversight while leveraging Trump's protectionism (Washington Post, 1 April 2025). The EU, however, insists its rules are not anti-American but necessary for fair competition and user trust (Guardian, 11 April 2025).

The EU's response to US dominance is the EuroStack, a €300 billion initiative to build a sovereign tech ecosystem spanning chips, cloud, and AI (Foreign Policy, 31 March 2025). By championing open-source platforms and data sovereignty, EuroStack aims to break dependency on US providers, aligning with the EU's vision of digital statehood rooted in privacy and interoperability (AI Now Institute, 15 October 2024). While fostering innovation, these regulations and EuroStack raise concerns about trade escalation and market fragmentation, highlighting the techno-political struggle to define digital governance globally.

1.6-Conclusion: Corporate Power and Technolibertarianism in the Digital State Era

In 2025, the "State vs. Company" dynamic, illuminated through five case studies, reveals corporations as formidable rivals to states in shaping digital statehood. Silicon Valley's technolibertarian surge, with Musk and Thiel aligning with Trump's administration, leverages platforms like X to sway policy, challenging state authority (Forbes Türkiye, 15 February 2025). OpenAI's global AI expansion, from India's education hubs to regulatory navigation, positions it as a soft-power giant, rivaling state influence (T24, 18 March 2025). NVIDIA's AI chip dominance, despite $5.5 billion losses from US export bans, cements its role as a quasi-state actor, dictating technological access (Reuters, 18 April 2025).

China's AI firms, backed by $48 billion in state funds, drive innovation under tight governmental control, creating a state-corporate hybrid that competes with Western tech giants (BBC, 8 February 2025). The EU's regulatory push, enforcing the AI Act and fining Meta and Apple €162 million, seeks to curb corporate overreach but faces backlash from US tariff threats, highlighting state vulnerabilities (Guardian, 11 April 2025). These cases underscore a power shift where companies wield state-like capabilities through chips and AI, redefining sovereignty.

Corporations exploit state dependencies, from the US's $52.7 billion CHIPS Act subsidies to China's tech mandates, yet technolibertarian ideals of autonomy clash with this reliance. Firms like NVIDIA and OpenAI control data and compute, tools once exclusive to states, enabling propaganda and surveillance at unprecedented scales. This corporate ascent disrupts traditional governance, as states struggle to regulate entities integral to their digital infrastructure.

The techno-political order teeters as corporate power rivals state authority. While companies drive innovation, their unchecked influence risks eroding democratic accountability and polarizing global tech access (Forbes Türkiye, 10 January 2025). This section highlights that digital statehood hinges on navigating this delicate balance, posing urgent questions about governance, equity, and the future of power when corporations act as de facto states in the chip and AI-driven era.

2-STATE vs. STATE: GEOPOLITICAL RIVALRY IN THE TECHNOLOGICAL ARENA

In 2025, the techno-political landscape is defined by fierce state-to-state rivalries over semiconductors and AI, the twin pillars of digital statehood where control over data and compute equates to geopolitical power. The US-China chip wars, intensified by Biden's $52.7 billion CHIPS and Science Act and export bans like those on NVIDIA's H20 chips, underscore a battle for semiconductor supremacy, with Taiwan Semiconductor Manufacturing Company (TSMC), —producing 90% of advanced chips—at the epicenter (Reuters, 18 April 2025). Concurrently, the AI product wars pit US giants like OpenAI against China's DeepSeek, whose R-1 model challenges Western dominance in large language models and visual generation, reshaping information and propaganda in digital states (Yahoo Finance, 28 April 2025). These conflicts, rooted in the quest for technological sovereignty, extend beyond bilateral tensions, as states forge strategic alliances to secure digital infrastructure.

The US's "small yard, high fence" strategy, bolstered by a "friend map" of 20 allies including Japan, South Korea, and Taiwan, prioritizes chip and AI technology sharing, with TSMC's Kumamoto and Samsung's US investments reinforcing this bloc (ITIF, 2025). Meanwhile, US-Gulf partnerships, such as the $100 billion AI deal with the UAE's MGX, position the Gulf as a new digital state hub, merging chip production with energy security (Reuters, 23 April 2025). China counters with the BRICS AI Alliance, rallying Russia, India, and the Global South to challenge US hegemony through alternative AI ecosystems (BBC, 8 February 2025). The Jevons Paradox amplifies these rivalries, as chip efficiency gains fuel exponential AI compute demands, escalating state competition.

This section explores five case studies—US-China chip wars with TSMC's role, AI product battles, the US friend map with Japan and South Korea, US-Gulf tech deals, and China's BRICS AI push—to dissect how geopolitical strategies shape digital states. By controlling chips, AI, and alliances, states redefine sovereignty, raising critical questions about global equity, autonomy, and the future of governance in the techno-political era.

2.1-Bi-Techno Polarization: US-China Chip Wars

The 2025 US-China chip wars carve a techno-political divide, splitting the globe into rival digital state blocs vying for semiconductor dominance. The US's $52.7 billion CHIPS and Science Act, launched in 2022, powers domestic chip production with $39 billion in grants and $75 billion in loans to companies like Intel and TSMC (ITIF, 2025). President Trump, after briefly halting funds in 2025 as "bureaucratic excess," escalated export controls, banning NVIDIA's H20 chips to China, costing

NVIDIA $5.5 billion (Reuters, 18 April 2025). The US's "small yard, high fence" strategy employs chip tier levels—Tier 1 (Japan, South Korea, Taiwan), Tier 2 (EU), Tier 3 (others)—limiting advanced chip access to 20 allied nations and bolstering supply chains through Japan's TSMC Kumamoto and Samsung's US factories (Anadolu Ajansı, 11 March 2025).

Semiconductors, the backbone of AI, data processing, and military systems, are critical to digital statehood, driving China to desperate measures to secure them. Through Singapore and Indonesia's black markets, Chinese firms stockpiled $16 billion in chips, dodging US bans to fuel AI models like DeepSeek's R-1 (NPR, 16 April 2025). Defying ASML lithography restrictions, SMIC reached 5nm chip production, and Huawei's Ascend 910C, unveiled in April 2025, rivals NVIDIA's H100, marking a leap toward self-reliance (Daktilo 1984, 5 December 2024). Xi Jinping's $48 billion semiconductor fund, coupled with China's 60% control of rare earths like germanium, empowers firms like Huawei to challenge US supremacy (BBC, 8 February 2025). China's BRICS allies, such as Russia and India, bolster its chip ecosystem, countering the US-led bloc.

This chip-fueled polarization redefines digital statehood, as semiconductors dictate AI and data sovereignty. For nations, chips are now a national security imperative, with the US's tiered alliances and China's defiant breakthroughs forcing countries to pick sides in a fractured global order. As supply chains splinter, this techno-political divide signals that in the race for digital state supremacy, every nation is staking its place in an escalating global showdown.

2.2-TSMC's Strategic Role: The Semiconductor Linchpin in US-China Rivalry

TSMC, with 54% of the global chip market and 90% of advanced chip production, is the bedrock of digital statehood, enabling AI, smartphones, and military systems for clients like NVIDIA and Apple (Anadolu Ajansı, 11 March 2025). Its unrivaled capacity makes TSMC a geopolitical fulcrum in US-China tensions, as chips define technological sovereignty. China's dependence on TSMC for AI and defense chips, paired with its territorial claims over Taiwan, heightens invasion risks, while the US leverages TSMC to secure supply chains and thwart China's tech ambitions. China exerts pressure on TSMC through economic coercion and military threats, amplifying Taiwan's vulnerability.

China's pressures on TSMC are both overt and covert. Beijing's claim over Taiwan, coupled with Xi Jinping's refusal to rule out military force, casts a shadow over TSMC's operations, as a potential invasion could disrupt 60% of global chip supply. Economically, China, once absorbing 60% of Taiwan's chip exports, has pushed TSMC to maintain Nanjing fab operations despite US restrictions. After TSMC's

2020 halt of Huawei chip shipments under US pressure, China retaliated with rare earth export curbs, leveraging its 98% gallium dominance to squeeze TSMC's supply chain. Covertly, Chinese cyberattacks targeting TSMC's trade secrets have surged, with state-linked hackers aiming to bypass US bans. These pressures drive TSMC's pivot to self-preservation, aligning closer with the US.

The US counters with lucrative incentives to anchor TSMC. The $52.7 billion CHIPS Act grants TSMC's Arizona subsidiary $6.6 billion and $5 billion in loans for a $100 billion expansion, including six factories and an R&D center by 2030 (Reuters, 4 March 2025). Trump's 25% chip tariff exemptions ensure TSMC's cost-competitiveness, while Apple's pledge to buy Arizona chips solidifies demand. TSMC's compliance with US export controls limits China to 16nm chips from its Nanjing fab, with 7nm shipments halted after a 2024 TechInsights report found TSMC chips in Huawei's Ascend 910B. By balancing US alignment with China's pressures, TSMC shapes digital statehood but risks escalating Taiwan's precarious position in this techno-political showdown.

2.3-US-Gulf Chip and Energy Deals: Building a Techno-Strategic Hub

The US-Gulf chip and energy agreements in 2025, centered on the UAE and Saudi Arabia, position the Gulf as a techno-strategic hub for AI and data infrastructure, countering China's regional influence. The US pressures Gulf nations to sever tech ties with China, targeting BAE's Huawei 5G contracts and Saudi Arabia's chip deals with SMIC, citing national security risks. In 2024, the US halted UAE's $100 billion AI fund over Chinese partnerships, forcing Abu Dhabi to suspend Huawei's 5G rollout (Reuters, 12 February 2025). Saudi Arabia faced similar ultimatums, with Trump threatening tariffs unless Riyadh exits China's semiconductor supply chain, aligning with US-led blocs.

These pressures pave the way for US-Gulf tech integration. The UAE's MGX, a $100 billion AI fund, partners with OpenAI's Stargate, a $500 billion AI supercomputer project, to build data centers in Abu Dhabi, leveraging TSMC's 2nm chips. Saudi Arabia's Vision 2030 commits $200 billion to energy-AI infrastructure, including Neom's solar-powered data hubs, with NVIDIA supplying H200 chips (BBC, 15 March 2025). The US's $52.7 billion CHIPS Act extends $10 billion in grants to Gulf allies, funding BAE's GlobalFoundries fab and Saudi's planned 5nm chip plant. These investments aim to produce 15% of global AI chips by 2030, securing US supply chains.

The Gulf's role as an AI-energy hub redefines digital statehood, with data centers and renewable energy anchoring US techno-dominance. BAE's 50 GW solar capacity and Saudi's 100 GW renewable push power AI workloads, reducing reliance on China's rare earths. However, China's $48 billion chip fund and BRICS tech alliances challenge this shift, risking Gulf's neutrality. As Gulf nations navigate US pressure to ditch Chinese tech, their pivot to US-aligned infrastructure signals a techno-political realignment, but escalating tensions may destabilize global chip and energy markets, threatening equitable access in the digital state era.

2.4-AI Product Wars: US-China Rivalry in Large Language Models and Visual Generation

In 2024, the US led large language models and visual generation with OpenAI's ChatGPT and DALL-E, and Google's Gemini, harnessing NVIDIA's H100 chips to dominate global AI narratives (Reuters, 28 January 2025). China's 2025 counteroffensive, led by DeepSeek's R-1 and R-2 models, disrupted this order. Trained for $6 million—97% cheaper than GPT-4—R-1 outshines in math and coding, shaking US tech stocks by $1.2 trillion as investors shift to Chinese AI. Powered by Huawei's Ascend 910C chips, DeepSeek's rise, alongside Baidu's ERNIE-ViLG for visual generation, redefines digital statehood by controlling information and geopolitical influence (CNBC, 17 February 2025).

China's success hinges on its "copy-paste" strategy: let the West innovate, bear R&D risks, and then replicate at lower costs. In electric vehicles, BYD mimicked Tesla's Model Y, slashing prices to capture 30% of global EV sales by 2025, a playbook mirrored in AI. DeepSeek's R-1, with GPT-like responses, reflects this, reverse-engineering OpenAI's frameworks while leveraging state-backed data to train models (Webtekno, 2025). Xi's $48 billion semiconductor fund and SMIC's 5nm chips enabled R-2's 1.2 trillion operations per second, rivaling Gemini 2.0 (BBC, 8 February 2025). This approach—mimicking then undercutting—floods the Global South with affordable AI, eroding US market share.

On the other hand, the Jevons Paradox, where efficiency gains increase resource demand, fuels this AI race. Named after William Jevons, who observed that efficient coal use boosted consumption, the paradox applies as advanced chips (TSMC's 2nm, SMIC's 5nm) reduce AI training costs, spurring more models and compute needs. This benefits the US, with NVIDIA and TSMC reaping $2 trillion in chip revenue, and China, whose Huawei and SMIC scale Ascend 910C production. Both amass data and influence, strengthening digital states.

The 2025 AI landscape is fiercely competitive. OpenAI's $500 billion Stargate and Google's $75 billion R&D fortify US leadership, while China's BRICS-aligned AI, led by DeepSeek, targets Russia and India (Reuters, 28 January 2025). China's copy-paste ethics spark debate, as R-1's mimicry blurs innovation lines. Yet, both nations exploit LLMs for propaganda, polarizing ecosystems. This techno-political clash risks fragmenting AI access, with developing nations torn between US premiums and China's budget models, challenging equitable digital statehood.

2.5-Where Does Russia Stand? AI, Cyber Power, and BRICS-China Synergy

Where does Russia stand in the global AI and cyber race? In 2025, amidst Western sanctions, Russia leverages BRICS and a deepening China partnership to carve a techno-political niche, countering US dominance. Ranking 31st in AI innovation per Tortoise Media's Global AI Index, Russia trails the US, China, and BRICS peers India and Brazil but harnesses China's AI prowess to bolster its digital statehood (Anadolu Ajansı, 1 January 2025). President Putin's January 2025 directive mandates Sberbank and the government to integrate China's DeepSeek AI, targeting a $109 billion GDP boost by 2030 (Reuters, 2 June 2025). Sberbank's tests show DeepSeek's R-1 outperforming GigaChat MAX in scientific tasks, while GigaChat leads in banking . Moscow's AI Journey conference unveiled the BRICS AI Alliance Network, linking Brazil, India, Iran, and the UAE to challenge Western tech hegemony (Independent Türkçe, 12 December 2024).

China's "copy-paste" strategy, replicating Western AI at lower costs, underpins this synergy. DeepSeek's R-1, powered by Huawei's Ascend 910C chips, mirrors GPT-4 for 97% less, enabling Russia to deploy affordable AI for banking and propaganda. China's $48 billion chip fund and SMIC's 5nm chips skirt US bans, supplying Russia via intermediaries (BBC, 8 February 2025).

Russia's AI-enhanced cyber capabilities amplify its reach. Newsguard's 2025 report details Kremlin-linked hackers injecting propaganda into Western AI models, skewing narratives across BRICS (Teknomers, 20 March 2025). DeepSeek's integration fuels Russia's disinformation, strengthening BRICS's alternative ecosystem. The Jevons Paradox—efficient chips driving higher AI demand—benefits both nations, as Huawei and Sberbank scale compute for surveillance and influence.

This BRICS synergy redefines digital statehood, but Russia's chip reliance on China risks dependency. Its cyber manipulations spark ethical concerns, while BRICS's expansion tests cohesion. As Russia navigates sanctions and global tech fractures, its AI and cyber pivot with China signals a bold, yet precarious, stand in the digital state era.

2.6-Conclusion: Digital States in the Techno-Political Arena

The 2025 techno-political landscape, as explored through five case studies, reveals a world where chips and artificial intelligence redefine digital statehood. The US-China chip wars, epitomized by the $52.7 billion CHIPS Act and Huawei's Ascend

910C, polarize global supply chains, with the US's "small yard, high fence" strategy and China's black-market resilience fracturing technological equity (Reuters, 18 April 2025). TSMC, commanding 90% of advanced chips, stands as a geopolitical linchpin, courted by US incentives and pressured by China's territorial ambitions, amplifying Taiwan's precarious role (Anadolu Ajansı, 11 March 2025). The US-Gulf alliances, with BAE's $100 billion MGX fund and Saudi Arabia's Neom data hubs, forge a new AI-energy hub, countering China's regional influence through strategic decoupling (BBC, 15 March 2025).

AI product wars, driven by OpenAI's Stargate and DeepSeek's R-1, highlight China's "copy-paste" strategy, replicating Western models at 97% lower costs to dominate the Global South (Evrim Ağacı, 2025). Russia's AI and cyber moves within BRICS, challenge US hegemony, though its chip reliance on China risks dependency (Teknomers, 20 March 2025). The Jevons Paradox—where efficient chips and AI spur greater demand—fuels this race, empowering both US firms like NVIDIA and China's SMIC to amass compute and influence.

These rivalries transcend economics, reshaping sovereignty through data and compute control. Chips and AI, as tools of propaganda and surveillance, enable digital states to wield unprecedented power, yet polarize access, leaving developing nations caught between US premiums and China's budget models. The techno-political order, driven by alliances like BRICS and the US's "friend map," risks instability as national security trumps global cooperation. This section underscores that digital statehood hinges on technological control, raising urgent questions about equity, autonomy, and governance in an era where chips and AI dictate the future of power.

3-COMPANY vs. COMPANY: CORPORATE BATTLES WITH POLITICAL IMPLICATIONS

In 2025, corporate battles in the chip and AI arenas transcend mere market competition, wielding profound techno-political implications for digital statehood. The intensifying rivalry among tech giants shapes not only global technological landscapes but also domestic and international political dynamics, particularly within the United States and between the US and China. Within the US, companies like Microsoft, Google, and xAI navigate a polarized political sphere, aligning with or challenging state power through technolibertarian ideologies and strategic partnerships with figures like Trump (Forbes Türkiye, 15 February 2025). These internal struggles influence policy, from deregulation pushes to national security priorities, as firms like NVIDIA and OpenAI redefine state dependencies on private infrastructure (Reuters, 18 April 2025).

Globally, the US-China technological divide, fueled by chip wars and AI races, pits American firms against Chinese counterparts like Huawei and Alibaba, echoing state-level tensions. Corporate strategies—whether NVIDIA's chip dominance or Huawei's Ascend 910C breakthroughs—mirror the US's "small yard, high fence" export controls and China's self-reliance push, impacting bilateral relations and global supply chains. Companies like Amazon and Apple, entangled in this rivalry, forge or fracture alliances across the Global South, amplifying geopolitical stakes. These battles, rooted in control over chips, AI models, and cloud infrastructure, reshape power dynamics as corporations assume state-like roles in data governance and propaganda.

This section examines four pivotal corporate rivalries to unpack their political ramifications. Through the lenses of Microsoft's AI-cloud dominance versus Google's innovation, NVIDIA's chip hegemony versus Huawei's resilience, the ideological clash between Musk's xAI and Altman's OpenAI, and the global cloud-AI wars of Amazon, Alibaba, and Apple, we explore how these conflicts influence US domestic policy and US-China relations. By analyzing these techno-political fault lines, this section illuminates the evolving role of corporations in digital statehood, where corporate power increasingly rivals state authority in shaping the future of global governance.

3.1-Microsoft vs. Google: AI, Cloud, and Pentagon Alignment Wars

Since the 2010s, Microsoft and Google have fueled the AI race, with Google's $400 million DeepMind acquisition in 2014 sparking AlphaGo's breakthroughs and Microsoft's $13 billion OpenAI investment by 2025 scaling ChatGPT. Their rivalry spans cloud (Azure vs. Google Cloud), LLMs (GPT-4 vs. Gemini), visual generation (DALL-E 3 vs. Imagen), and quantum computing, where Google's qubit advances outpace Microsoft's Azure Quantum. In 2025, Trump's administration reshapes this contest, with Pentagon contracts and diversity (DEI) purges tying both firms closer to state agendas, raising questions about their technolibertarian autonomy (Forbes Türkiye, 15 February 2025).

In January 2025, U.S. Secretary of Defense Pete Hegseth directed the cancellation of $5.1 billion worth of IT and consulting contracts with firms such as Accenture and Deloitte, categorizing them as "non-essential." This move was part of a broader cost-cutting effort within the Pentagon. (*Reuters, April 2025*)

Microsoft's Azure OpenAI Service has been officially authorized for Department of Defense Impact Level 6 (IL6), allowing it to handle highly classified national security workloads. (*Microsoft Azure Gov Blog, 2024*)

Google previously withdrew from Project Maven in 2018 following internal employee protests. As of 2025, it has gradually re-engaged in defense-related technologies, though no specific new contract has been officially confirmed. (PBS, 2018; *Google public statements*)

Google announced a $75 billion investment in data centers and AI infrastructure to support services like Gemini and Google Cloud. (Source: DataCenterDynamics, 2025) Microsoft is involved in a $500 billion AI infrastructure initiative, reportedly named Stargate, in collaboration with OpenAI, Oracle, and UAE-based MGX. This initiative aims to strengthen U.S. AI capabilities. (Computing UK, 2025)

China's DeepSeek has launched a low-cost, high-performance open-source model called DeepSeek-V2, gaining rapid traction in the Global South and sparking concern among U.S. tech firms. (*Foreign Policy, Jan 2025;* SCMP, 2025) Both Google and Microsoft rely on TSMC-produced chips and receive significant state subsidies, reflecting a growing entanglement between Big Tech and national governments in the AI arms race.

3.2-Musk vs. Altman: xAI and OpenAI's Ideological AI Clash

The feud between Elon Musk and Sam Altman, rooted in OpenAI's 2015 founding, epitomizes a techno-political clash over AI's future. Musk, Altman, and others co-founded OpenAI as a nonprofit to advance AI research, but Musk exited in 2018, citing disagreements over its shift to a for-profit model (Forbes, 2025). By 2025, Musk's xAI, valued at $50 billion, competes with OpenAI's $157 billion valuation, fueled by Microsoft's $14 billion investment (Forbes, 2025). Their rivalry, marked by lawsuits and public spats, intensified under Trump's 2025 administration, reshaping US AI policy (Reuters, 2025).

Musk's 2024 lawsuits accused OpenAI of abandoning its nonprofit mission and colluding with Microsoft to monopolize AI resources (The New York Times, 2025). OpenAI countered, alleging Musk's harassment via xAI's competing Grok model (EL PAÍS, 2025). In January 2025, Trump announced Stargate, a $500 billion AI infrastructure project led by OpenAI, Oracle, and SoftBank, with an initial $100 billion investment (Reuters, 2025). Altman, present at the White House, praised Trump's support, claiming Stargate would secure US AI leadership (The New York Times, 2025). Musk, a Trump advisor leading the DOGE, criticized Stargate's funding, claiming SoftBank had secured less than $10 billion (Forbes, 2025). Altman refuted this, inviting Musk to visit the Texas site already under construction (Axios, 2025).

Musk's Trump alliance, bolstered by $100 million in campaign support, grants him influence over federal AI policy, yet his Stargate critique reveals tensions (Newsweek, 2024). Trump downplayed the feud, noting Musk's personal dislike for Altman (CNN, 2025). Microsoft's Pentagon contracts give OpenAI a state-backed edge, while xAI's $12 billion data center struggles against OpenAI's scale (India Today, 2025). Musk's technolibertarian push for deregulation clashes with Altman's pragmatic state alignment, redefining digital statehood. Their rivalry risks polarizing AI governance, as corporate egos shape national priorities over public interest.

3.3-OpenAI's Chip Gambit: Challenging NVIDIA's AI Infrastructure Dominance

OpenAI's strategic move to develop custom AI chips marks a significant shift in the AI infrastructure landscape, aiming to reduce its dependency on NVIDIA's GPUs, particularly the H100 models that have powered the training of systems like ChatGPT. Recognizing scalability and cost constraints associated with third-party hardware, OpenAI began designing its own chips in 2024.

By 2025, OpenAI had partnered with TSMC to manufacture these custom chips using 3nm process technology, with the goal of powering its large-scale AI systems, including the recently announced $500 billion Stargate AI infrastructure project. The Stargate initiative, backed by Microsoft, seeks to dramatically expand AI computing capacity within the United States. Microsoft has invested nearly $14 billion into OpenAI, reinforcing their joint commitment to AI leadership.

This move occurs amid broader efforts by U.S. technology firms to secure supply chains and reduce reliance on constrained GPU availability. Meanwhile, China's DeepSeek, supported by Huawei's Ascend 910C AI chips, is emerging as a key competitor in the Global South, offering more accessible AI solutions.

While NVIDIA remains the dominant player with the release of its H200 GPUs, OpenAI's entry into custom chip design reflects a growing ambition to shape the foundational infrastructure of AI systems and enhance U.S. technological sovereignty.

Both Microsoft and OpenAI, however, remain dependent on TSMC-manufactured chips and government subsidies, revealing the increasing overlap between corporate innovation and state-backed infrastructure in the ongoing global AI race.

3.4-Global Corporate Alliances: Transcending State Power

In 2025, global corporations forge alliances that transcend national boundaries, rivaling state power in the techno-political arena. By crafting agreements above state jurisdictions, companies like Amazon, Apple, and OpenAI amplify their influence, leveraging shared resources to dominate chip, AI, and cloud ecosystems. These partnerships, often aligned with geopolitical strategies, redefine digital statehood by consolidating corporate control over critical technologies.

Amazon and Apple exemplify this trend through their cloud and chip synergy. Amazon AWS supports Apple's iCloud infrastructure, integrating Apple's A-series and M-series chips, manufactured by TSMC's 2nm process, into AWS data centers. This collaboration optimizes Apple's global service delivery while enhancing AWS's enterprise offerings, creating a unified ecosystem that strengthens US technological dominance. The partnership, backed by US policies like the CHIPS Act, positions both firms as pillars of national security infrastructure, surpassing state-driven initiatives.

OpenAI's alliance with SoftBank for the $500 billion Stargate supercomputer project further illustrates corporate supremacy. OpenAI, supported by Microsoft's $14 billion investment, collaborates with SoftBank to access Japan's advanced compute infrastructure, aiming for exascale AI performance by 2030. This cross-border agreement, aligned with Trump's 2025 AI leadership push, enables OpenAI to scale beyond US borders, consolidating corporate influence over global AI governance.

Amazon's collaboration with Microsoft also underscores this dynamic. AWS and Azure share data center resources in regions like the UAE's MGX AI hub, pooling infrastructure to meet surging global cloud demand. This partnership, tied to US-Gulf alliances, amplifies both firms' roles in shaping digital economies, often outpacing state regulatory frameworks. These alliances empower corporations to dictate techno-political terms, challenging state sovereignty while reinforcing their dominance in the digital state era.

CONCLUSION: THE CONSOLIDATION OF DIGITAL STATEHOOD IN THE TECHNO-POLITICAL ORDER

The analysis presented in this paper underscores a fundamental reconfiguration of political authority in the digital age. Across three interrelated axes—state versus company, state versus state, and company versus company—the contours of power are being redrawn around control of digital infrastructure, computational capacity, and algorithmic governance. This shift signals the emergence of digital states: entities whose legitimacy and influence are derived not from territorial sovereignty but from the capacity to organize, surveil, and mobilize through data systems and platform infrastructures.

Corporate actors such as OpenAI, NVIDIA, and X Corp have transcended their traditional market functions, increasingly performing state-like roles in diplomacy, security, and social regulation. Simultaneously, governments—whether through the U.S. CHIPS Act, the European Union's regulatory frameworks, or China's state-directed AI ecosystem—are adopting corporate strategies to safeguard digital sovereignty and strategic autonomy. These entanglements reflect a growing symbiosis between public authority and private infrastructure, eroding clear distinctions between state power and corporate dominance.

Moreover, the global AI and semiconductor rivalries examined in this study reveal how technological capabilities have become critical instruments of geopolitical competition. Access to compute power, control over advanced chips, and influence in AI governance forums now define a state's ability to assert influence in the international system. In parallel, corporate rivalries increasingly shape regulatory regimes and diplomatic alignments, positioning companies as key actors in the emerging global order.

This convergence of state and corporate power is not merely a structural shift—it constitutes a paradigmatic transformation in how authority, legitimacy, and governance are produced. Digital states are no longer speculative constructs; they are materializing through infrastructures, protocols, and alliances that reorganize global hierarchies. As such, the future of global politics will be shaped not only by intergovernmental negotiations but by platform-mediated governance, proprietary algorithms, and the politics of compute.

Recognizing and critically engaging with the formation of digital states is thus imperative. For scholars, this demands a recalibration of analytical frameworks beyond Westphalian assumptions. For policymakers, it necessitates the development of governance models that can navigate the blurred boundaries of sovereignty, security, and corporate autonomy. And for citizens, it requires vigilance to ensure that this new digital order does not eclipse the principles of transparency, accountability, and democratic oversight upon which political legitimacy ultimately depends.

REFERENCES

T24. (2025, January 28). Hintli medya şirketleri telif hakkı ihlali gerekçesiyle OpenAI'a dava açtı. https://t24.com.tr/haber/hintli-medya-sirketleri-telif-hakki-ihlali-gerekcesiyle-open-ai-a-dava-acti,1213778

AI Now Institute. (2023, Apr 11). 2023 landscape: Confronting tech power. https://ainowinstitute.org/publications/research/2023-landscape-confronting-tech-power

Anadolu Ajansı. (2025, June 27). MİA, "Yapay Zeka, Toplum ve Güvenlik Ekseninde Türkiye'nin Yol Haritası" başlıklı raporunu yayımladı. https://www.aa.com.tr/tr/gundem/mia-yapay-zeka-toplum-ve-guvenlik-ekseninde-turkiyenin-yol-haritasi-baslikli-raporunu-yayimladi/3614942

Anadolu Ajansı. (2025, April 23). ABD-Çin çip çekişmesinde en değerli şirketlere ABD, ham maddeye Çin sahip. https://www.aa.com.tr/tr/dosya-haber/abd-cin-cip-cekismesinde-en-degerli-sirketlere-abd-ham-maddeye-cin-sahip/3545905

Axios. (2025, January 24). Musk vs. Altman (and Trump): Anatomy of a feud. https://www.axios.com/2025/01/24/trump-musk-altman-stargate-openai

BBC. (2022, February 22). Neom: What's the green truth behind a planned eco-city in the Saudi desert? https://www.bbc.com/news/blogs-trending-59601335

BBC. (2025, February 6). 'People seem dumbstruck' - Inside Musk's race to upend government. https://www.bbc.com/news/articles/c1dg95dyxygo

BBC. (2025, April 18). Nvidia: The AI chip giant caught between US and China. https://www.bbc.com/news/articles/cedy6gl99eno

Begçecanlı, B. (2025). Çip savaşları: ABD ve Çin arasındaki güç dengesi nasıl şekilleniyor? [Chip wars: How is the power balance between the U.S. and China shaping up?]. Anadolu Ajansı. https://www.aa.com.tr/tr/analiz/cip-savaslari-abd-ve-cin-arasindaki-guc-dengesi-nasil-sekilleniyor/3507034

Bloomberg. (2025, March 7). Peter Thiel's deep ties to Trump's top ranks. https://www.bloomberg.com/features/2025-peter-thiel-trump-administration-connections/

Brookings. (2025, January 30). Are tariffs Big Tech's new tool against EU regulation? https://www.brookings.edu/articles/are-tariffs-big-techs-new-tool-against-eu-regulation/

Business, C. N. N. (2024, December 10). 'No winners': China's Xi warns US against a trade war. https://edition.cnn.com/2024/12/10/business/china-us-trade-war-xi-warning-hnk-intl

China Daily. (2025, February 19). Support for private sector to fuel growth. https://www.chinadaily.com.cn/a/202502/19/WS67b545e0a310c240449d613e.html

CNBC. (2025, April 30). Xi wants Shanghai to spearhead China's AI ambitions. https://www.cnbctv18.com/technology/xi-jinping-china-artificial-intelligence-ai-global-race-shanghai-hub-ws-l-19597004.htm

CNN. (2025, January 24). Trump shrugs off Elon Musk's criticism of AI announcement: 'He hates one of the people'. https://edition.cnn.com/2025/01/23/tech/elon-musk-trump-ai-sam-altman

Computing, U. K. (2025, Janurary 22). $500 billion 'Stargate' project to boost AI in the USA. https://www.computing.co.uk/news/2025/ai/500-billion-stargate-boost-ai-usa

Daktilo 1984. (2024, December 5). Teknoloji Gündemi: TSMC, Huawei ve ABD-Çin Arasındaki Çip Savaşının Yeni Perdesi. https://daktilo1984.com/bultenler/teknoloji-gundemi-tsmc-huawei-ve-abd-cin-arasindaki-cip-savasinin-yeni-perdesi/

DataCenterDynamics. (2025, February 5). Google expects 2025 capex to surge to $75bn on AI data center buildout. https://www.datacenterdynamics.com/en/news/google-expects-2025-capex-to-surge-to-75bn-on-ai-data-center-buildout/

Defense News. (2024, March 25). Pentagon inks dozens of cloud contract orders, more in the pipeline. https://www.defensenews.com/battlefield-tech/it-networks/2024/03/25/pentagon-inks-dozens-of-jwcc-orders-with-more-in-the-pipeline/

Defense One. (2025, April 17). There's no more DEI at DOD, watchdog finds. https://www.defenseone.com/policy/2025/04/theres-no-more-dei-dod-watchdog-finds/404669/

Donanimhaber. (2025, January 20). Nvidia, ambargolar sonrası Çin ile ilişkileri iyi tutmaya çalışıyor. https://www.donanimhaber.com/nvidia-cin-ile-iliskileri-iyi-tutmaya-calisiyor--186772

EL PAÍS. (2025, February 12). Timeline of a tech feud: Sam Altman and Elon Musk's 10-year rivalry. https://english.elpais.com/technology/2025-02-12/timeline-of-a-tech-feud-sam-altman-and-elon-musks-10-year-rivalry.html

Euronews. (2025, April 4). Who are the tech winners and losers of Donald Trump's sweeping 'Liberation Day' tariffs? https://www.euronews.com/next/2025/04/03/who-are-the-real-winners-and-losers-of-donald-trumps-liberation-day-tariffs

Evrim Ağacı. (2025, February 25). Yapay Zekada Büyük Atılım: DeepSeek V3 ve R1 Nedir ve Neden Önemlidir? https://evrimagaci.org/yapay-zekada-buyuk-atilim-deepseek-v3-ve-r1-nedir-ve-neden-onemlidir-19879?srsltid=AfmBOoqXLVc66ZCmQX5NjfC3Q8XkK6D5SIHouqUhQ8OA1o2gQLwilkAF

FiscalNote. (2024, August 7). China's AI Policy & Development: What You Need to Know. https://fiscalnote.com/blog/china-ai-policy-development-what-you-need-to-know

Forbes. (2025, April 25). This Open-Source Company Is Quietly Working To Transform AI. https://www.forbes.com/sites/torconstantino/2025/04/25/how-one-company-is-quietly-working-to-transform-ai-forever/

Forbes. (2025, January 22). Musk Bashes Trump's New Stargate AI Initiative With OpenAI And Oracle As 'Fake'. https://www.forbes.com/sites/dereksaul/2025/01/22/musk-is-bashing-trumps-new-stargate-ai-initiative-with-openai-and-oracle-heres-why/

Forbes Türkiye. (2025, February 15). Silikon Vadisi Obama'dan Trump'a nasıl yöneldi? https://www.forbes.com.tr/makale/silikon-vadisi-obama-dan-trump-a-nasil-yoneldi

Forbes Türkiye. (2025, January 11). Trump'ın Kabinesi ve Kilit Görevler. https://www.forbes.com/sites/saradorn/2025/01/11/trumps-cabinet-and-key-jobs-katherine-macgregor-steven-bradbury-among-latest-staff-picks/

Foreign Policy. (2025, February 18). Xi Sends Message to China's Private Sector. https://foreignpolicy.com/2025/02/18/china-xi-jinping-ceos-meeting-private-sector-economy/

Foreign Policy. (2025, January 29). DeepSeek Is Reshaping China's AI Landscape. https://foreignpolicy.com/2025/01/29/deepseek-china-ai-chatgpt-stocks/

Foreign Policy. (2025, March 31). Europe Must Avoid Becoming a Digital Colony. https://foreignpolicy.com/2025/03/31/europe-digital-sovereignty-colony-trump-asml-ai-eurostack/

France24. (2025, March 25). EU negotiators agree landmark law to reign in US tech giants. https://www.france24.com/en/europe/20220325-eu-negotiators-agree-landmark-law-to-reign-in-us-tech-giants

Guardian. (2025, April 28). The Guardian view on the EU and big tech: Brussels must lay down the law. https://www.theguardian.com/commentisfree/2025/apr/28/the-guardian-view-on-the-eu-and-big-tech-brussels-must-lay-down-the-law

Independent Türkçe. (2024, December 12). BRICS'ten yapay zeka atılımı: "Sektördeki dengeler değişecek". https://www.indyturk.com/node/750437/d%C3%BCnya/bricsten-yapay-zeka-at%C4%B1l%C4%B1m%C4%B1-sekt%C3%B6rdeki-dengeler-de%C4%9Fi%C5%9Fecek

India Today. (2025, April 26). Elon Musk's xAI Holdings nears record $20 billion fundraise, second only to OpenAI. https://www.indiatoday.in/technology/news/story/elon-musks-xai-holdings-nears-record-20-billion-fundraise-second-only-to-openai-2715433-2025-04-26

ITIF. (2025, May 5). Overly Stringent Export Controls Chip Away at American AI Leadership. https://itif.org/publications/2025/05/05/export-controls-chip-away-us-ai-leadership/

Microsoft Azure Gov Blog. (2025, April 16). Azure OpenAI Service now authorized for all U.S. Government data classification levels. https://devblogs.microsoft.com/azuregov/azure-openai-authorization/

News, N. B. C. (2025, January 14). Elon Musk, Jeff Bezos and Mark Zuckerberg to attend Trump's inauguration. https://www.nbcnews.com/politics/donald-trump/elon-musk-jeff-bezos-mark-zuckerberg-attend-trump-inauguration-rcna187642

Newsweek. (2024, October 18). Elon Musk Offers Pennsylvania Voters $100 Each As He Drums Up Trump Support. https://www.newsweek.com/elon-musk-offers-pennsylvania-voters-100-sign-donald-trump-petition-presidential-election-1971021

NPR. (2025, April 16). Nvidia discloses that U.S. will limit sales of advanced chips to China after all. https://www.npr.org/2025/04/16/nx-s1-5366665/nvidia-china-h20-chips-exports

Patronlardunyasi. (2024, December 23). Nvidia CEO'su Huang: Trump yönetiminde de küresel iş birliği devam edecek. https://www.patronlardunyasi.com/nvidia-ceosu-huang-trump-yonetiminde-de-kuresel-is-birligi-devam-edecek

PBS. (2018, June 3). Amid pressure from employees, Google drops Pentagon's Project Maven account. https://www.pbs.org/newshour/show/amid-pressure-from-employees-google-drops-pentagons-project-maven-account

Politico. (2025, March 10). EU-US rift triggers call for made-in-Europe tech. https://www.politico.eu/article/push-for-eurostack-as-eu-us-tech-tensions-grow/

Reuters. (2019, July 24). UAE's du says U.S. ban on Huawei not an issue for 5G network. https://www.reuters.com/article/business/uaes-du-says-us-ban-on-huawei-not-an-issue-for-5g-network-idUSKCN1UJ141/

Reuters. (2025, April 11). Pentagon to end $5.1 billion in contracts with Accenture, Deloitte, others. https://www.reuters.com/world/us/pentagon-terminate-51-billion-it-contracts-with-accenture-deloitte-others-2025-04-11/

Reuters. (2025, April 17). Nvidia faces $5.5 billion charge as US restricts chip sales to China. https://www.reuters.com/technology/nvidia-expects-up-55-billion-charge-first-quarter-2025-04-15/

Reuters. (2025, February 26). DeepSeek rushes to launch new AI model as China goes all in. https://www.reuters.com/technology/artificial-intelligence/deepseek-rushes-launch-new-ai-model-china-goes-all-2025-02-25/

Reuters. (2025, February 6). Russia's Sberbank plans joint AI research with China as DeepSeek leaps forward. https://www.reuters.com/technology/artificial-intelligence/russias-sberbank-plans-joint-ai-research-with-china-deepseek-leaps-forward-2025-02-06/

Reuters. (2025, January 21). Trump's inauguration billionaires, CEOs: Ambani, Zuckerberg, Bezos attend church, ceremony. https://www.reuters.com/world/us/trumps-inauguration-billionaires-ceos-ambani-zuckerberg-bezos-attend-church-2025-01-20/

Reuters. (2025, January 22). Trump announces private-sector $500 billion investment in AI infrastructure. https://www.reuters.com/technology/artificial-intelligence/trump-announce-private-sector-ai-infrastructure-investment-cbs-reports-2025-01-21/

Reuters. (2025, June 6). US-UAE multi-billion dollar AI data campus deal far from finalised. https://www.reuters.com/business/finance/us-uae-multi-billion-dollar-ai-data-campus-deal-far-finalised-sources-say-2025-06-06/

Reuters. (2025, March 10). Apple, Meta likely to face modest fines over DMA breaches. https://www.reuters.com/technology/eu-likely-impose-modest-fines-apple-meta-over-dma-breaches-sources-say-2025-03-10/

Reuters. (2025, March 4). Trump and TSMC announce $100 billion plan to build five new US factories. https://www.reuters.com/technology/tsmc-ceo-meet-with-trump-tout-investment-plans-2025-03-03/

SCMP. (2025, April 30). DeepSeek quietly updates open-source model that handles maths proofs. https://www.scmp.com/tech/tech-trends/article/3308566/deepseek-quietly-updates-open-source-model-handles-maths-proofs

The Guardian. (2025, April 17). Nvidia's CEO makes surprise visit to Beijing after US restricts chip sales to China. https://www.theguardian.com/technology/2025/apr/17/nvidias-ceo-surprise-visit-beijing-restricts-chip-sales-china

The New York Times. (2025, January 21). Tech Elites Take Center Stage at Trump Inauguration. https://www.wsj.com/politics/elections/tech-elites-take-center-stage-at-trump-inauguration-af846e64

The New York Times. (2025, May 30). Silicon Valley Is at an Inflection Point. https://www.nytimes.com/2025/05/30/opinion/silicon-valley-ai-empire.html

The Times of India. (2025, January 27). Peter Thiel, David Sacks and the other Right wing men in SV set to drive policy in Donal Trump's government. https://timesofindia.indiatimes.com/technology/tech-news/peter-thiel-david-sacks-and-the-other-right-wing-in-silicon-valley-set-to-drive-policy-in-donald-trumps-government/articleshow/117598459.cms

Washington Post. (2025, February 11). Vance pushes 'America First' AI agenda, accuses allies of overregulation. https://www.washingtonpost.com/politics/2025/02/11/vance-paris-ai/

Webtekno. (2025, January 27). OpenAI ve Google Gibi Yapay Zekâ Devlerini Köşeye Sıkıştıran, iPhone Kullanıcılarının ChatGPT'den Daha Çok İndirdiği DeepSeek Aslında Nedir? https://www.webtekno.com/deepseek-yapay-zeka-kim-calismalari-h154973.html

Yahoo Finance. (2025, May 29). Nvidia Faces $8B Hit as U.S. Halts H20 AI Chip Exports to China. https://finance.yahoo.com/news/nvidia-faces-8b-hit-u-124344159.html?guccounter=1&guce_referrer=aHR0cHM6Ly93d3cuZ29vZ2xlLmNvbS8&guce_referrer_sig=AQAAAM3GeGH3Quo5WaWrl4d02hoTR_hzKiRYmZoEFMIh16nZ0IAADt_KpPchj6NIgYz-ihhPI-Dhoe_zHfNGPW6MZ1ZGB381iHrUdDi0_OsButHzou9zY56tJVVqDnu51loox12CEANZ5CDnQnS9GU0jvA-QHi2N9K3GGGt6DLqTYa-W

Chapter 7

Europe's Technological Sovereignty and American Techno-Political Influence:
Clash of Digitalization

Enes Kilic
https://orcid.org/0009-0001-4940-5901
Ibn Haldun University, Turkey

ABSTRACT

This article explores the interconnections between Kondratieff's Long Wave Theory, Schumpeter's concept of creative destruction, and the collapse of neoliberal informationalism, framing these within the context of Europe's emerging techno-political landscape. The piece argues that the current technological crisis, fueled by the monopolistic expansion of the Magnificent 7 and the rise of techno-imperialism, presents an opportunity for Europe to assert its digital sovereignty. Drawing on historical precedents, Europe's regulatory response, which is embodied in the Digital Services Act, the Digital Markets Act, and the AI Act alike laws, signals a strategic departure from the American global technopolitical model. On this theoretical base, the chapter contends that rather than being a passive follower of global technological trends, Europe is opting for regulation as a means to insert itself as an independent player.

DOI: 10.4018/979-8-3373-2459-3.ch007

I. INTRODUCTION

Technopolitics, the interaction of technology with policy-making structures, is now intertwined with geopolitics and is becoming more decisive than it in many contexts. Artificial intelligence, semiconductors and quantum technologies, cyber-security, next-generation warfare technologies, 5G-like digital infrastructures, and dependency relations have turned into a strategic battleground, and have become a key factor determining the economic, military and political capacities of countries. In fact, not only in international relations but also in domestic affairs, as it can be seen from the Cambridge Analytica scandal to Musk turning X into a place of his agenda. While geography, natural resources and classical balances of power are still very important, these resources are used to produce technology, as in the case of lithium, or to fund and attract technology, as it can be observed in the case of Gulf countries.

The pressure exerted on the European techno-political approach by this narrative of innovation driven by American technology companies and their political allies, which initially marketed as a common technological front against China, challenges the dominant narrative that Europe is lagging behind by arguing that the issue is actually different, that the big-tech is implementing a deliberate strategy to maintain technological dominance and protect its market from the unchecked influence of foreign technological monopolies. Using the theoretical background in the context of Kondratieff waves and Joseph Schumpeter's theory of "creative destruction", this argument reveals how technological paradigms overlap with capitalist cycles from Keynesian Fordism to Neoliberal Informationalism and how the current period of crisis could trigger the birth of a new techno-political model. Each paradigm shift has not only redefined economic systems but also reshaped global power dynamics, suggesting that Europe's strategic maneuvering may signify more than just regulatory caution but rather the early stages of a transformative techno-political era.

I.A. Politics of Technology

Recent literature in Science and Technology Studies (STS) and critical policy studies has contested the view that technology is politically neutral. Langdon Winner's (1980) canonical question, "Do artifacts have politics?", has become central in analyzing how technological systems encode particular institutional biases and power asymmetries. In her work, The Ethics of Invention (2016), Sheila Jasanoff emphasizes that technologies do not develop independently of social, political, and legal orders; rather, they are shaped in interaction with these orders. That is, they emerge through a process of co-production. Jasanoff (2016) argues that technologies are not merely technical tools for generating solutions; they also shape which problems are deemed important, who decides on these problems, and how the resulting risks are distributed within society. Therefore, technological developments cannot be considered independent of the social, political, and legal contexts surrounding them. The view frequently put forward by the neoliberal narrative that innovation will only accelerate with the liberalization of the market and the withdrawal of state intervention must thus be approached with suspicion. In her view, such reductionist approaches ignore not only the capacity of technologies to transform the social order but also the power of the social order to direct technological developments. Innovation gains meaning and takes shape not only through the unleashing of market dynamics, but also within a context where social values, legal regulations, and democratic participation mechanisms are effective. Therefore, Jasanoff argues that regulating technological innovation is a necessity for social ethics and the public good, reminding us that innovation is not a natural market product but a constantly negotiated social process.

The European Union's regulatory interventions, such as the General Data Protection Regulation (GDPR), the AI Act, and the Digital Markets Act, represent not merely technocratic corrections to market failures but assertive normative claims about the role of digital technologies in a democratic society. As Ulnicane and Aden (2023) argue, policies on AI and emerging technologies are not simply administrative exercises; they are arenas where divergent socio-technical imaginaries and ideational frames compete. These debates expose tensions between corporate techno-solutionism and public-oriented techno-regulation, which underpin differing visions of technological modernity.

Furthermore, narratives, frames, and paradigms serve as structuring devices in policy-making, especially in uncertain environments, as emphasized by Malmborg (2022). The construction of policy problems, such as how "bias" in AI is understood, reveals that power in technopolitics lies not only in who governs but in whose definition of a problem prevails. The EU's framing of AI as an issue of ethical governance rather than purely one of economic competitiveness thus diverges sharply from the dominant American techno-industrial model (Kuzior, 2024).

II. THEORETICAL FRAMEWORK: TECHNOPOLITICS AND CAPITALIST CYCLES

II.A. Kondratieff's Long Wave Theory and Its Relevance

Starting in 1926, Russian-Soviet economist Nikolai Kondratieff conceptualized long economic waves, suggesting that capitalist economies each experience cycles of peaks and busts, each with a burst of technological innovation (Akaev, 2022).

These 'Kondratieff waves' (K-Waves) sought to explain how economic downturns often triggered technological innovations that were only fully realised during subsequent economic upturns.

Figure 1. Kondratieff's waves. (Tyulin et al., 2023)

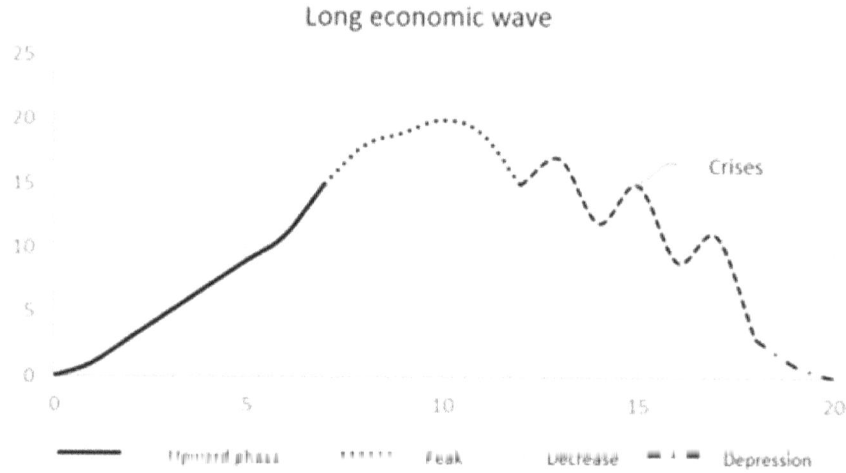

The European regulatory approach can be seen as a response to these historical cycles, emphasising stability and social benefits rather than uncontrolled economic growth, as they had suffered from this problem before. Examples could be multiplied, such as Europe in the 1830s experiencing an economic recession due to market saturation and overproduction.

II.B. Techno-political Paradigms: From Keynesian Fordism to Neoliberal Informationalism

The periodization of the transition from Keynesian Fordism, where state regulation balanced industrial growth with social welfare, to neoliberal informationalism, characterized by digital economies and unregulated markets, provides an angle from the perspective of financial philosophy, albeit not absolute, and offers explanations. Although Europe does not adopt the Chinese global technopolitical paradigm, where ethical concerns are occasionally ignored, its reluctance to fully adopt the American model, which is the focus of the chapter, stems from the recognition that neoliberal policies often lead to inequality, social instability, and economic volatility. Europe aims to alleviate these problems through regulation, because regulation does not grant merely theoretical rights but is instead a result of past struggles and suffering. It is the people's negotiation with the state.

Kondratieff's economic cycles and the periodization of Fordism and neoliberal informationism reveal the strong connection between technological and economic paradigms that shape the long-term evolution of capitalist development. Kondratieff waves consist of periods of economic expansion and contraction, each lasting approximately 50–60 years and triggered by major technological innovations.

Fordism is a model of production and consumption that overlaps with the fourth wave of these cycles. Fordism, characterized by mass production, the rise of the internal combustion engine, and the development of consumer goods industries, represented phases of expansion and prosperity (spring and summer), followed by a period of stagnation (fall) with market saturation, and finally a winter period leading to the economic crisis of the 1970s. This crisis marks a period when the old technological paradigm no longer supports economic growth and a need for a new paradigm arises, and is often a precursor to a period of greater breakthroughs.

However, as the limitations of Fordism became apparent in the 1970s, neoliberal informationalism, supported by advances in computing and networking, became widespread. The neoliberal paradigm, with its emphasis on deregulation, privatization, and market oriented policies, was perfectly aligned with the rise of Big Tech, a.k.a the Magnificent 7. Schumpeterian "creative destruction" further explains how entrepreneurial innovation drives these paradigm shifts, showing how technological advances not only create new markets but also disrupt existing structures, and as such becomes an integral theme of the chapter.

The new paradigm, which brought a whole new era by information technologies and globalization, has led to economic expansion through innovations such as market deregulation, flexible production models, marketing and the transition to a knowledge based economy. However, with the maturation of digital communication technologies, the market has become saturated again, and a new period of stagnation has begun with the financial crises of the 2000s and 2010s. This transformation is in line with Kondratieff's long wave theory, which suggests that we are currently at a crisis point in the current economic cycle, necessitating a new paradigm shift. In this context, Europe's strategy of creating a new paradigm with digital sovereignty and balanced regulation may herald a possible new Kondratieff wave. However, American techno-political influence may not allow this.

II.C. The Collapse of the Neoliberal 'Informationalism'

The early digital age was underpinned by the utopian belief that information and communication technologies (ICTs) would function as emancipatory tools. Theorists and policymakers alike hailed the advent of social media as the democratization of the public sphere: a decentralised, peer-to-peer communication infrastructure that would empower citizens, undermine authoritarianism, and enable spontaneous, grassroots political mobilisation. During the Arab Spring, digital platforms were hailed as instruments of liberation, with the promise of replacing hierarchical gate-keeping with horizontal dialogue.

However, this techno-optimism has largely dissipated. The digital public sphere has not evolved into a disintermediated agora for democratic deliberation; rather, it has been captured by a small number of financially and politically powerful actors. As Kremidas-Courtney and Litobarski (2024) argue, what has emerged is not a global village, but "an Empire of Technology," where power is increasingly wielded through algorithmic manipulation, financial scale, and cross-border data governance. The commercial logics of platform capitalism reward outrage, division, and emotional arousal, rather than rational discourse, thereby fostering polarisation and the erosion of shared epistemic baselines.

Moreover, these platforms have become tools of asymmetric information warfare. Hostile state and non-state actors alike weaponise disinformation, exploit algorithmic biases, and micro-target vulnerable populations. The very architectures that once promised democratic renewal now reinforce inequality, exacerbate civic fragmentation, and undermine public trust. European policymakers have thus come to realise that the normative assumptions underpinning the American innovation model,rooted in deregulation, private capital, and platform dominance,are fundamentally incompatible with democratic resilience.

II.D. The Onset of a New Techno-Political Paradigm

The stability that came with Fordism's mass production and welfare state policies was followed by the digital revolution and free market understanding of neoliberal informationism. However, with the maturation of the digital economy and the market dominance of GAFAMX, which symbolizes big technology companies and took the front stage during the inauguration of the 47th President of the United States Donald J. Trump, and surrendered Apple, Meta, TeslaX companies (and their owners), new challenges have emerged such as income inequality, data privacy issues, and the erosion of democratic values. In this context, the current crisis has not only economic but also social and political dimensions, showing that neoliberal informationism no longer offers a sustainable development model. Among social problems, the unstoppable rise of extremism, which is especially evident in the Western world, on the right and left of the political spectrum, is one of the most talked about topics. These companies are directly related to these social problems.

This theoretical framework allows us to better understand the importance and necessity of the regulatory policies currently being pursued by Europe. Europe has tried and is trying to protect its digital sovereignty by opposing the unlimited power of big technology companies and to create a new technopolitical paradigm that prioritizes social values. The resistance shown by technology giants and big corporations to these regulations can actually be read not only as a struggle to protect commercial interests, but also as a challenge to the democratic legal order. Europe's initiatives such as the Digital Services Act (DSA) and the Digital Markets Act (DMA) are strategic moves aimed at laying the foundations of a new "Global Techno-Policy" (GTP) paradigm. This new paradigm aims to protect market stability and social welfare while encouraging technological innovation. Therefore, in the theoretical background, the concepts of crisis and paradigm shift stand out as an important binding element supporting the strategic mind and long-term vision behind Europe's current policies.

Perceiving the European approach as a Global Techno-Policy (GTP) paradigm, where technology serves broader societal goals, would create a different perspective within this theoretical framework. Europe has focused on data privacy, digital rights and ethical AI development, and the fact that it has not created a single large company serving monopolistic corporate interests, as evidenced by the presence of competition on the continent and the magnitude of investment rates.

The divergence is also structural. The EU's recognition of its "middle-tech trap," particularly in legacy sectors such as automotive manufacturing, has illuminated the limitations of incremental innovation strategies. Csernatoni (2024) warns that Europe's inability to scale high-tech firms domestically has forced many start-ups to seek capital and infrastructure abroad, exposing them to the gravitational pull of U.S. technological hegemony. However, this situation has galvanized new political will across European institutions. Initiatives like Gaia-X, EuroHPC, and the envisioned "EuroStack" signal not just infrastructural investments but a reassertion of Europe's normative agency in the global digital order.

II.E. Humanized Innovation and the Competence-Innovation-Market Spiral

Recent developments in long wave theory, particularly in the context of the AI economy and Industry 4.0, challenge the deterministic understanding of economic stagnation during downturn phases of Kondratieff cycles. Tyulin et al. (2023) propose a transformative model wherein the decline phase of the long wave is mitigated,or even reversed,by the humanization of innovation. In this view, it is not merely technological breakthroughs, but the ethical and inclusive integration of these technologies into society that sustains growth.

This insight aligns closely with Europe's techno-political resistance to Big Tech's neoliberal informationism. European regulatory efforts,such as the Digital Services

Act (DSA) and Digital Markets Act (DMA),can be interpreted not simply as defensive mechanisms, but as deliberate attempts to insert social values into technological advancement. These initiatives represent a form of innovation humanization, emphasizing gradual, inclusive, and competence-driven progress over disruptive, monopolistic innovation cycles.

The "competence-innovation-market" spiral described by Tyulin et al. positions technological competencies (e.g., ethical AI design, privacy engineering, algorithmic accountability) as the foundation for sustainable innovation. This feedback loop suggests that when a society invests in building technological competencies,rather than just enabling capital-intensive monopolies,it not only produces new markets but avoids the deep recessions typically expected in Kondratieff's winter phase. Europe's emphasis on digital literacy, social protections in platform work, and citizen data rights reflects such a spiral, wherein regulatory foresight enhances resilience and sustains growth amid global economic shifts.

II.F. From Cyclical Crises to Linear Stability

Tyulin et al. also argue that accelerated development of competencies, supported by appropriate institutional mechanisms, can convert cyclical downturns into near-linear growth. This reframing implies that capitalist economies are not doomed to endless boom-and-bust oscillations but can achieve sustained innovation under human-centered frameworks. Europe's current trajectory,seeking to "de-monopolize" digital capitalism through fair competition, digital public infrastructure, and ethical innovation,is an active experimentation in applying this theory.

By resisting the logic of maximalist tech disruption, Europe may be trying to engineer a soft-landing from the neoliberal informationist paradigm into a more stable, regulated techno-political order. This could represent not just a policy shift but a fundamental alteration of the innovation-growth cycle itself. In this sense, Europe is not simply late to the innovation race,it is pioneering a new, less volatile model of techno-economic governance. This effort might prefigure a sixth Kondratieff wave defined by decentralized intelligence, socially embedded technologies, and algorithmic accountability.

II.G. Divergence, Convergence, and Technological Sovereignty

The article also introduces the distinction between divergent and convergent stages within Kondratieff waves. Divergent stages are marked by the rise of radically new technologies and paradigms, while convergent stages involve the refinement and spread of these innovations. Europe's current efforts can be read as a form of divergence,not in raw technological invention, but in the political and legal redefinition of what digital modernity should be. Its "EuroStack" vision, for example, is not just about catching up technologically, but about asserting a sovereignty model fundamentally distinct from both U.S. neoliberalism and Chinese techno-authoritarianism.

Furthermore, the "stationary phases" described by Tyulin et al. emphasize the importance of institutional and infrastructural balance. European emphasis on coordinated regulation, ethical standards, and pan-European digital projects (e.g., Gaia-X) may enable it to avoid premature technological exhaustion or dependency. This theoretical refinement bolsters your original claim: that Europe's approach is not reactive regulation but an embryonic techno-political paradigm in itself.

III. AMERICAN TECHNO-POLITICAL STRATEGY AND THE BIG TECH NARRATIVE

III.A. The Market Motive of American Tech Giants

The GAFAMX has not only dominated the global digital market (except for China), it has also shaped the discourse around technological advancement. Indicators of this today, from the office culture of tech companies in India to its use of the US to combat the fines it has received for breaching rules in different countries, are a sign of this. Its promotion of the idea that Europe is merely a regulatory power and lacks technological dynamism is entirely related to the political climate it has influenced in America. A European market free of regulation presents a huge, lucrative opportunity for American tech giants looking to grow beyond saturated local markets. The American argument is not merely one of market dynamics but is intertwined with a broader geopolitical strategy,techno-nationalism,that serves the U.S.'s national interests.

According to Fang and Hwang (2023), the rise of techno-nationalism within the U.S. has fueled the narrative that technological leadership, particularly in artificial intelligence, social media, and semiconductor production, is integral to maintaining geopolitical power. This perspective sees technological supremacy not as a collective international achievement but as a zero-sum competition between the U.S. and China. In this context, U.S. policy, supported & lobbied by tech giants, promotes the belief that technological success hinges on minimal government regulation, framing it as a critical tool to ensure national security and economic growth.

Techno-nationalism posits that the competition for technological dominance between China and the U.S. is fundamentally a battle of different national models,an "American" approach versus a "Chinese" approach to technology. As Fang and Hwang (2023) describe, U.S. tech companies are deeply embedded in this narrative, with many advocating for a tech policy that minimizes regulation. This ideological framework has expanded by 2025 with the Trump administration seizing the power once again beyond national borders, in an attempt to position the U.S. as a global leader in both technological innovation and the discourse on how technology should be governed. The promotion of a deregulated environment is central to this vision, as U.S. tech giants argue that Europe's regulatory approach,while protective of privacy and competition,limits the market's potential to innovate at the same pace as the U.S. and China. Meanwhile they had to pay a record amount of fines for violating those regulations.

As the American tech companies whose CEOs were present at the presidential inauguration continue to push for deregulation, they argue that a European market free of stringent controls would present a vast and lucrative opportunity for growth. Fang and Hwang (2023) emphasize that the U.S. perceives Europe's regulatory models as obstacles that prevent its tech companies from scaling rapidly in a saturated U.S. market, as they need areas to promote their products. The push for deregulation is often instrumentalized as an essential condition for technological success, with U.S. companies urging Europe to adopt a more market-driven approach that would facilitate competition and innovation. However, as the article explains, this deregulatory effort is based on a broader ideological protectionist/techno-nationalist agenda where the goal is not only to promote innovation but also to maintain US dominance in the global technology race. It ignores the role of regulation in shaping the technology industry to serve the public interest, while neglecting that a regulatory framework is necessary for technological progress. As Fang and Hwang (2023) argue, the techno-nationalist vision often sees technology advancing faster as it ignores the shared global nature of technology and the ethical responsibilities that come with technological innovation. The rhetoric put forward by US tech giants is based on the idea that less regulation will lead to more innovation, but this argument fails to take into account the fact that many of the challenges posed by new technologies, such as data privacy breaches, monopolistic practices and social inequality, stem from the lack of regulation that these companies advocate. In this context, it is implied that deregulation will be an advantage in the race with China. From this perspective, Europe's regulatory approach, while often criticized as a barrier to growth, serves as an alternative narrative that balances the unchecked expansion of Big Tech. However, by advocating for a more comprehensive regulatory framework, Europe is attempting to ensure that technological progress does not solely serve corporate interests but also aligns with democratic values and public welfare. The European model is not merely about limiting innovation but is focused on creating, if not ethical, at least a sustainable model for the technological future. As Fang and Hwang (2023) suggest, a transnational approach to technology policy is necessary,one that recognizes the interconnectedness of global technological ecosystems while ensuring that technological advancements are grounded in shared values of privacy, fairness, and accountability, since in the new century of the world all technological developments are almost interconnected with each other thanks to globalism.

Thus, while the U.S. advocates for deregulation under the guise of promoting innovation, this push is inherently tied to a broader techno-nationalist agenda. The rhetoric surrounding deregulation as a necessary condition for technological success is deeply embedded in a U.S.-centric view of global power dynamics. In contrast, Europe's more regulatory stance reflects a commitment to ensuring that technology serves not only economic growth but also the broader social good, protecting citizens from the harms that can arise from unchecked technological dominance (Fang & Hwang, 2023).

III.B. The Influence of Silicon Valley on Global Tech Discourse

There are also internal Silicon Valley rhetoric wars, and whoever wins tries to capitalize on that gain in Europe. Through a powerful mix of lobbying, media influence, and political alliances, Silicon Valley has managed to plant the idea that 'innovation' is synonymous with 'deregulation'. Figures like Elon Musk, often portrayed as the quintessential tech innovator, play a key role in pushing this narrative, turning the once-blue Valley red.

This rhetoric sets a broader agenda for shaping global techno-political standards according to American neoliberal informationalism, which favors minimal government intervention and an unrestricted flow of data.

The extension of this way of thinking is shared by both American techno-political strategy and Mario Draghi's recent strategic vision for Europe. In his report titled The Future of European Competitiveness (2024), Draghi attributes the widening economic gap between Europe and the United States primarily to differences in labor productivity. Productivity, as he clarifies, refers to the ratio between inputs (typically labor hours) and output,essentially, how much more can be produced with the same resources. For instance, if a team of three workers increases their output from x units to 2x within a year without additional inputs, this reflects a clear productivity gain. Yet such improvements have a natural ceiling. Once existing methods, technologies, and organizational routines are optimized, further gains diminish. As Draghi and Schumpeter both contend, breaching this ceiling requires technological transformation,the introduction of new production methods, processes, or tools that fundamentally alter the capacity to generate value, namely innovation.

Figure 2. Schumpeter's long waves of innovation

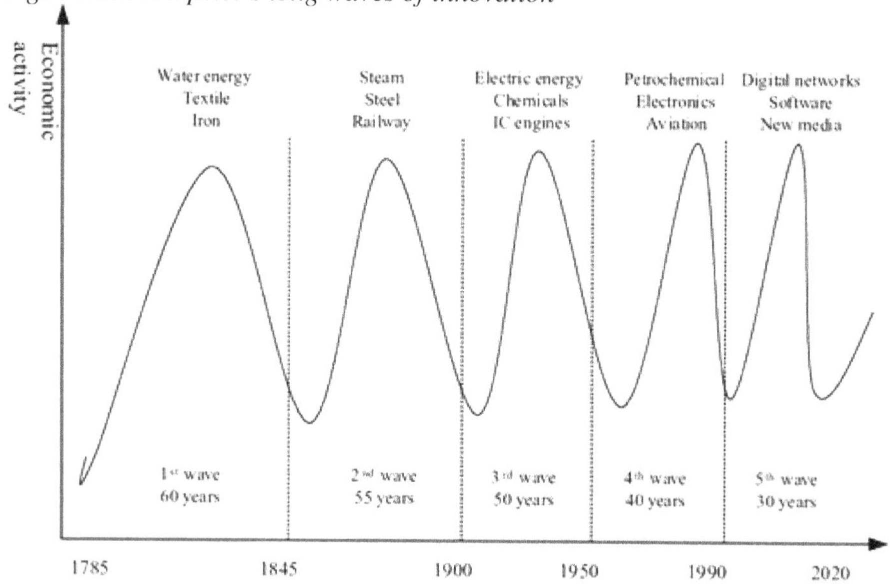

It is at this juncture that the convergence with the American model becomes visible in his argument. In both cases, the solution to stagnation is the same: unlock innovation by removing barriers of all sorts. For the U.S., this has historically meant fostering large-scale monopolies in the tech sector, deregulating markets, and allowing accumulated private capital to drive technological change. Draghi's report, although framed within a European policy context, ultimately arrives at a similar conclusion. To regain competitiveness, Europe must invest in R&D, scale innovation, and rewire its industrial landscape to be more agile,logics that are inherently aligned with the Schumpeterian cycle of creative destruction. While Draghi does not explicitly advocate for American-style deregulation or Big Tech monopolies, the underlying assumption is shared: that only through embracing disruptive innovation can Europe close its productivity gap and avoid long-term decline.

> *"First, while Europe must advance with its Capital Markets Union, the private sector will not be able to bear the lion's share of financing investment without public sector support. Second, the more willing the EU is to reform itself to generate an increase in productivity, the more fiscal space will increase, and the easier it will be for the public sector to provide this support" (Draghi, 2024).*

III.C. Learning from the Past: Europe's Approach to the AI Revolution

Europe's cautious approach to the deregulation of technological progress is based on a depth of historical experience, notably the Industrial Revolution, that the Americas and other regions have not felt. As the birthplace of the revolution, the continent witnessed rapid technological growth that led to significant economic transformations, but also to great suffering. The lack of regulations during this period had serious social repercussions, such as the exploitation of labor. Child labor in dangerous factory conditions, long working hours and unsafe environments led to growing inequality and social unrest. The ideological structures created and nurtured by these sufferings shaped even international relations for years.

Determined not to repeat these mistakes, European policymakers aim to manage the risks of the current AI revolution while reaping the benefits. America needs to take this responsibility, not just for Europe, but for the whole world. There needs to be more focus on addressing potential threats such as job displacement, privacy violations and misuse of autonomous systems. In 2021, the European Commission enacted the Artificial Intelligence Act, which sets out a framework for regulating AI applications according to risk levels. High-risk uses, including in law enforcement and healthcare, have laid the legal groundwork for stricter oversight ensuring transparency and anti-discrimination measures are in place. This sensitivity is the guarantee that these technologies will not lead to accidental mass deaths during wars in the future.

Beyond regulation, Europe is also considering broader societal solutions with a theoretical background of it, such as universal basic income (UBI), to address the potential job losses caused by automation and AI, and even created the mechanism for it to be voted on. Although controversial, the mere discussion of UBI contributes to the humanly discussion of the future of technology & society in political platforms.

From Draghi's report to Leyen's Competitiveness Compass, the European Union is seemingly aware of the challenges and is making intentional, thoughtful choices, it can be interpreted from the measures it takes. Instead of blindly following the Silicon Valley model, Europe is forging its own path by prioritizing deep technology over fleeting trends, embedding ethics into the design process rather than treating it as an afterthought, focusing on sustainable growth, and generating real economic value.

According to Brando Benifei (personal communication, January 30, 2025), who has led the Parliament's work on the AI Act at European Parliament & currently the head of the EU-U.S. delegation, interviewed specifically for this chapter, industry-led opposition to the AI Act reflects vested interests in avoiding regulatory scrutiny. As one of the prominent contributors of the world's first artificial intelligence law, he warns against an all-out liberal approach: "Without rules, AI becomes an instrument of power concentration, benefiting only those who can afford to manipulate it." (Kilic, 2025)

Furthermore, in contrast to common belief, Europe is already hosting and nurturing leading innovators in artificial intelligence and in other tech spaces. Companies like Mistral and DeepL demonstrate how European firms are effectively utilizing AI in practical applications, while elevating its development and proving that Europe is not simply a follower but a competitive force in the global tech sector.

IV. THE GLOBAL TECHNO-POLITICS (GTP) PARADIGM: DIGITAL SOVEREIGNTY

Unlike the American model, which often prioritizes corporate interests, the GTP paradigm in Europe integrates technology with public policy to ensure societal benefits. Regulations such as the Digital Markets Act (DMA) and the Digital Services Act (DSA) are not simply defensive measures, but proactive strategies to set global standards.

The concept of 'EuroStack', a fully European digital infrastructure, is central to this vision. This infrastructure would operate like traditional public services, providing essential services such as digital identities, payment systems and data platforms with the same level of security and accessibility as roads, electricity or water systems. It does so without resorting to the extremism of a 'social credit' system like that in China.

On another aspect of the matter, the question of "why those paradigms are called 'global' emerges. As Kutlay's (2019) work on new developmentalism and its implications for global governance, the statement about technopolitical frameworks not always being "global" can be expanded to highlight how countries like Turkey and India, while playing important roles in global geopolitics, are often constrained by their spheres of influence and the traditions they have developed over time. These technological constraints prevent them from setting entirely new technopolitical paradigms, positioning them as followers rather than innovators in the technological and political arenas, though they remain a producer.

Kutlay (2019) discusses how nations like Turkey and India operate within specific frameworks that are influenced by their historical, cultural, and political contexts. These countries, while engaging with global trends, are often seen as adapting existing models rather than pioneering new ones. The influence of global powers and international institutions often shapes their technological and political decisions. This is particularly evident in how these nations integrate into existing economic and political systems like BRICS (Brazil, Russia, India, China, South Africa) or align with major players like the EU and the U.S. This results in a situation where they often trail behind in terms of technological innovation, as their actions are typically reactive to global trends rather than proactive in shaping them. Hence, while these countries are pivotal in regional geopolitics and the production of specific warfare tools, their technopolitical strategies are often limited by their strategic alignments, historical legacies, and economic structures, and their niche areas of production which prevent them from taking the lead in setting global technological or political trends. This can be seen as a function of their broader developmental approach, which Kutlay (2019) describes as engaging with, but not fundamentally challenging, the dominant global structures.

V. REFRAMING THE NARRATIVE OF BINARIES

Anu Bradford's (2024) critique of the often-used binary that equates regulation with a blockage to innovation challenges a deeply embedded American understanding of technological orthodoxy in techno-policies. She contends that this view oversimplifies the evolving relationship between regulatory frameworks and technological advancement. Far from being an automatic constraint, regulation, when thoughtfully designed, can function as an enabling force, establishing the conditions for innovation and long-term, sustainable societal and sectoral benefit.

The European Union's approach to digital governance, exemplified with the laws that had consensus on them, illustrates how public-interest regulation can steer innovation toward democratic and social objectives, rather than merely safeguarding the competitive edge of dominant tech firms and being a simple digital market extension. Bradford argues that such measures level the playing field for smaller enterprises, fostering innovation ecosystems grounded in sustainability, fairness, and accountability (Bradford, 2024), though harming a concentration of a monopolistic capital.

By contrast, the recent U.S. model of Republican understanding, grounded in regulatory minimalism, is frequently linked to the belief that limited state intervention fuels entrepreneurial dynamism. However, Bradford warns that this hands-off stance has enabled monopolistic behavior, rampant data commodification, and broader democratic erosion. She thus advocates a more integrated vision, one that treats regulation as a vital component of the innovation process rather than an external constraint.

V.A. The EU's Techno-Political Vision: Shaping Innovation Through Regulation

Bradford (2024) further emphasizes that the EU's regulatory ethos does not aim to stifle technological growth but to shape it in accordance with foundational European values, namely bringin democracy, fairness, and the protection of fundamental rights to the every sector strategically. In contrast to the U.S., where innovation is often framed in market-centric terms because of the dominant lobby element of the political system, the EU structure advances a vision of technology as a public good, since it needs a political majority of all ideological lines in the spectrum. Initiatives such as the Digital Services Act (DSA) and the DMA exemplify this orientation, as they met with a minor resistant in the parliament.

In promoting regulation as a strategic lever, the EU contests the notion that unregulated markets are the most fertile ground for innovation. Bradford describes this as a "rights-driven" model,one that prioritizes consumer protection, data privacy, and corporate accountability over unbridled growth. This model aspires to build a digital ecosystem that not only sustains competitiveness but also reflects Europe's normative commitments to the public interest.

Nonetheless, this vision has drawn sharp criticism from industry leaders. At the World Economic Forum in Davos, Morten Wierod, CEO of ABB, expressed concern over what he termed the cumulative burden of overlapping regulations: "Each regulation is set with good intentions. But when combined, it becomes too much." Steven van Rijswijk of ING echoed this, calling for a more coherent regulatory framework to boost tech-sector investment. Ericsson's CEO, Borje Ekholm, went further, rejecting the EU's "regulatory-first approach" and insisting that "innovation requires flexibility, not bureaucracy." Likewise, Mario Greco of Zurich Insurance criticized Europe for being "always busy with itself," implying that overregulation risks leaving the continent behind in the global tech race.

What emerges is a strikingly unified critique from a specific constituency: the CEOs of multinational corporations. These executives, deeply embedded in the global technological landscape, argue that the EU's regulatory orientation is undermining Europe's ability to compete internationally. Their framing often contrasts Europe's rules-heavy environment with the perceived flexibility of U.S. and Chinese models,particularly during the deregulatory thrust of the Trump administration. In this context, the loudest objections to the EU's regulatory state are not coming from policymakers or civil society, but from the corporate elite, who view current measures as impediments to market agility. Yet, it is worth noting that the EU's AI Act passed with overwhelming support across the political spectrum in the European Parliament, reflecting a cross-party consensus that innovation must be governed with responsibility.

V.B. The U.S.–EU Technology Gap: Beyond the Regulation Narrative

Bradford (2024) underscores that the technological gap between the U.S. and the EU cannot be attributed solely to divergent regulatory philosophies. While the U.S. has outpaced Europe in producing global tech giants, she points to structural issues as the more decisive factors,most notably, market fragmentation, limited access to capital, and a cultural aversion to risk.

The United States benefits from a large, unified digital market, a robust venture capital ecosystem, and a cultural narrative that valorizes disruption. Europe, by contrast, faces obstacles in scaling innovation across its member states. Fragmented regulatory and linguistic environments, along with underdeveloped investment channels, have impeded the rapid growth of European tech firms (Bradford, 2024).

Still, these limitations do not diminish the normative or strategic value of the EU's regulatory approach. Bradford argues that Europe must simultaneously address its structural deficits while maintaining its leadership in digital rights and standards. The objective is not to discard regulation but to recalibrate its innovation environment so that regulatory clarity complements rather than constrains technological dynamism.

V.C. The Role of Regulation in the Future of Technological Sovereignty

J. Torreblanca, head of the European Council on Foreign Relations in Madrid, has described the combined ascendancy of GAFAMX and a second Trump presidency as a form of "digital colonialism" (2025). In response, Bradford (2024) argues that the EU's regulatory architecture is essential not only for protecting European citizens but for asserting the continent's technological sovereignty. As U.S. and Chinese platforms consolidate their influence, the EU has opted for a governance model that prioritizes autonomy over dependency, embedding its digital strategies in the broader project of geopolitical self-determination.

The concept of digital sovereignty, as operationalized in initiatives like the "EuroStack," envisions a fully European digital infrastructure that is both secure and values-driven. This vision seeks to minimize reliance on foreign-owned platforms and technologies, while championing ethical innovation rooted in transparency, social justice, and democratic control.

Bria and Sheikh (2025) contend that continued dependence on external technology providers is rapidly becoming a strategic liability. From semiconductor supply chains to AI governance, Europe's exposure to foreign control risks reproducing new forms of digital subjugation. In their view, this emerging "digital colonialism" threatens to subordinate European interests to the economic and political imperatives of U.S.

and Chinese tech empires. The EuroStack proposal is thus more than a technological initiative,it is a declaration of intent to reclaim agency in the digital age.

While some critics argue that stringent regulation may inhibit Europe's global competitiveness, Bradford insists that regulatory ambition is indispensable to constructing a resilient and equitable digital economy. She envisions a future in which innovation and oversight are not mutually exclusive but co-constitutive,an innovation ecosystem built not merely for profit, but for public purpose (Bradford, 2024).

This imperative has gained urgency. Johannes Späth (2025) warns that Europe's increasing reliance on U.S.-based digital platforms, from AI to quantum technologies, compromises its ability to steer its own technological future. Such dependencies leave Europe vulnerable to shifting geopolitical currents and external policy decisions.

Späth emphasizes that Europe's failure to secure indigenous capabilities in strategic sectors,ranging from healthcare and energy to defense and advanced computing,deepens this vulnerability. The continent's lag in critical technologies is compounded by fragmented markets and insufficient public investment. He argues that unless Europe adopts a more coherent and proactive strategy to develop its own infrastructure, it will remain beholden to external powers. The broader challenge is thus not only one of innovation but of sovereignty,and the future of European autonomy hinges on whether it can build a digital ecosystem aligned with its values and imperatives (Späth, 2025).

VI. UNDERSTANDING THE NATURE OF REGULATION AND DECONSTRUCTING ITS STRUCTURE

The relationship between regulation and innovation has long been a subject of debate, particularly in the context of the European Union (EU). One of the central questions in this ongoing discussion is whether regulation acts as a barrier to technological innovation or whether it fosters the creation of new ideas, industries, and business models. In their 2014 report, Pelkmans and Renda explore the multi-faceted, often ambiguous, and complex relationship between EU regulation and innovation, shedding light on the different types of regulations that can either stimulate or hinder innovation.

Pelkmans and Renda (2014) suggest that EU regulations should not be viewed solely as a hindrance to innovation. Their research reveals that regulation can, at times, act as a powerful stimulus to innovation by providing a framework that promotes market stability and ethical development. However, this potential depends on the nature of the regulation itself, as well as its ability to balance protection and flexibility.

One of the key insights of Pelkmans and Renda's (2014) analysis is the ecosystem approach to regulation and innovation. By viewing both regulation and innovation as interconnected ecosystems, they demonstrate that these two systems often interact in ways that can either hinder or enhance innovation. In particular, the authors note that while regulation can sometimes provide stability that encourages innovation, overly prescriptive or rigid regulations may stifle the creativity and adaptability required for technological advancements. This insight is especially important in the context of Europe's evolving digital economy, where rapid technological developments demand a regulatory approach that is both adaptive and forward-looking.

VI.A. Regulation at Different Stages of Innovation

According to Pelkmans and Renda (2014), the impact of regulation on innovation can vary depending on the stage of innovation. General or horizontal regulations, which apply broadly across industries, tend to have a positive effect on innovation. These regulations, by ensuring fair competition and transparency, can help create an environment conducive to long-term technological development. The deepening of the internal market in Europe over the past decades, as outlined in the report, has played a key role in this regard. By providing a stable and predictable regulatory environment, these horizontal regulations enable firms to plan and invest in long-term R&D efforts without the threat of sudden regulatory shifts.

On the other hand, sector-specific regulations, particularly those that are overly prescriptive or rigid, may hinder innovation. These regulations often impose detailed requirements that firms must adhere to, which can lead to high compliance costs and restrict the ability of companies, especially start-ups, to experiment with new ideas. Pelkmans and Renda (2014) note that while sector-specific regulations aim to address particular issues within industries, their prescriptive nature can sometimes lead to unintended consequences by discouraging entrepreneurial risk taking and innovation.

In contrast, innovation-specific regulations, which are tailored to promote the development of specific technologies or industries, tend to have a more direct and positive impact on innovation. Pelkmans and Renda (2014) highlight several examples where regulation has actively encouraged technological development, particularly in emerging industries like clean energy, AI, and digital services. By setting clear guidelines and standards, these regulations provide companies with the security to invest in new technologies, while also ensuring that these innovations align with broader social and environmental goals.

VI.B. The Role of Flexibility in EU Regulation

A central theme in Pelkmans and Renda's (2014) report is the need for flexibility in regulatory frameworks. More flexible regulations, which allow companies to find innovative solutions to meet regulatory requirements, tend to encourage technological innovation. This is particularly important in industries like technology, where the pace of innovation is rapid and ever-changing. Pelkmans and Renda (2014) argue that prescriptive regulations, which impose rigid requirements, can become a burden on businesses, especially smaller firms that do not have the same resources as larger companies to navigate complex rules.

In contrast, more flexible EU regulation,which focuses on outcomes rather than prescriptive processes,encourages entrepreneurial activity by allowing businesses to adapt and innovate within the confines of regulatory standards. For example, the EU's Digital Markets Act (DMA) and the Digital Services Act (DSA) are designed with a degree of flexibility that ensures tech giants adhere to ethical standards without stifling market competition or entrepreneurial innovation.

The flexibility of these regulations is also crucial in addressing issues like data privacy and AI ethics, where the technology is evolving rapidly and requires agile regulatory approaches. Pelkmans and Renda (2014) suggest that a flexible regulatory environment fosters the kind of adaptive thinking that leads to innovation, allowing businesses to find new ways to meet social goals, such as privacy protection and ethical AI deployment, without being hindered by overly strict rules.

VI.C. The Impact of Compliance Burden on Innovation

One of the most consistent critiques of EU regulations is the compliance burden they impose on businesses. Pelkmans and Renda (2014) note that high compliance costs,particularly for small and medium-sized enterprises (SMEs),can discourage innovation. The cost of compliance, in terms of both time and money, can be a significant barrier to innovation for smaller firms, who may not have the resources to dedicate to navigating complex regulatory frameworks.

In contrast, Pelkmans and Renda (2014) emphasize that reducing the compliance burden, through measures such as simplified reporting requirements and streamlined processes,can have a positive impact on innovation. When businesses are able to focus their resources on research and development rather than on compliance, they are better positioned to bring new ideas and products to market. Moreover, reducing red tape allows for more rapid market entry, which is crucial for start-ups in highly competitive sectors like digital technology and AI.

VI.D. Ex-ante and Ex-post Impact Assessments

One of the key recommendations of Pelkmans and Renda (2014) is the introduction of innovation impact assessments at both the ex-ante (before legislation is passed) and ex-post (after legislation has been implemented) stages of the regulatory process. These assessments would allow policymakers to evaluate the potential impact of regulations on innovation before they are enacted and to assess the actual impact after the regulations are implemented.

By incorporating innovation assessments into the regulatory process, the EU could ensure that new regulations are designed with innovation in mind. This approach would help avoid the unintended consequences of overly restrictive regulations and would allow the EU to better balance the need for social protection with the desire to encourage technological progress. Pelkmans and Renda (2014) stress that this approach would not only improve the regulatory process but would also provide a clearer framework for firms to understand how regulations might affect their business models and innovation efforts.

VI.E. Fostering Innovation through Regulatory Review

Pelkmans and Renda (2014) suggest that there is significant potential for fostering innovation through a review of the EU's regulatory acquis. Over the years, the EU has introduced a wide range of regulations aimed at promoting innovation and competition in the digital economy. However, the evolving nature of technology means that these regulations need to be constantly reviewed and updated to ensure they remain effective in promoting innovation while minimizing any negative effects.

Through periodic regulatory reviews, the EU can ensure that its regulatory frameworks remain responsive to technological advancements and market changes, allowing businesses to thrive while maintaining high standards for social and ethical considerations. Pelkmans and Renda (2014) emphasize that regulatory review is an essential component of a dynamic and forward-looking regulatory strategy, one that encourages innovation while maintaining the public interest.

VII. COUNTER-ARGUMENTS: ADDRESSING CRITICISM OF EUROPEAN REGULATIONS

Critics argue that Europe's regulatory focus can stifle innovation, especially for small businesses and start-ups, but that criticism often comes from monopolies. Europe's initiatives, such as Horizon Europe and national programs to support digital entrepreneurship, and the skilled European workforce contributing to American tech, suggest that's not the problem. The fact that it has produced companies in every field without a concentration of capital also challenges the idea that Europe is technologically stagnant.

At the core of the debate surrounding European regulations is the philosophical tension between state-backed competitive capital, innovation and individual rights. The current regulatory approach may be seen as rooted in an industrial-era mindset, where technological innovation was seen as a force to be controlled and directed by the state, for the sake of the state's power. However, in the digital age, this view encompasses very different parameters. Earlier technology, for instance, required humans to act and could not function without guidance. Now, some AI tools are evolving to become resilient even to attempts to destroy itself.

The state's lack of ethical consideration in its regulations has cost humanity a pandemic so far, and this element of secrecy of the state power with its domestic allies is evident in the Chinese model, without any transparent inter-party public research done until today.

VII.A. The Compliance Burden on Startups and Entrepreneurs

A major concern about EU regulations is the compliance burden they impose on startups and small businesses. As reported by Haeck and Coi (2024), many tech founders and investors have expressed frustration with the complexity and costs associated with EU rulebooks, particularly those governing artificial intelligence and data protection. Startups are often stifled by the bureaucratic red tape that comes with these regulations. These complaints are common and apparent, not only for the monopolies but for the new initiatives. The GDPR, for example, is seen as a significant barrier to entry for small firms in data-driven sectors like AI and machine learning, as it requires a good amended team which necessitates a major investment. The compliance conditions with the rules requires expensive data management systems and legal consultations, resources that early-stage companies cannot always afford. With the high cost of compliance making it harder for smaller firms to compete with larger ones, established players makes free wins. Hence, it is said this is not a problem of monopolistic applications only.

Haeck and Coi (2024) points out the same, using strict data protection measures as an example, which can be prohibitive when new organizations are in the early stages of product development. Startups, by nature, operate on tight profit margins and rely on flexibility and speed to bring new ideas to market. The regulatory framework implemented by the EU can delay market entry, leading to lost opportunities and increased operational costs. This makes it harder for European entrepreneurs to succeed compared to their counterparts in less regulated markets like the United States.

VII.B. The Innovation Slowdown Near Regulatory Thresholds

Another significant critique of EU regulations is their impact on company growth and innovation as firms approach certain regulatory thresholds. A study by MIT Sloan (Vereckey, 2023) examined how commonly regulations giving a bad hand to innovation initiatives and found that firms are less likely to innovate when increasing their workforce leads to additional regulatory burdens. This phenomenon is particularly evident in countries like France, where the regulatory environment becomes notably more burdensome as firms approach 50 employees.

According to Vereckey (2023), when firms approach the 50-employee threshold, they are subjected to a wave of labor market regulations, including mandatory works councils, union representation, and a scheme for profit sharing. While these rules are designed to protect workers, they also introduce significant compliance costs and administrative overhead that discourage firms from growing, but rather do the same job with the same people in a heavier way. Furthermore, the study claims that as companies near the 50 employee size, they experience a decline in innovation, particularly in patent applications, which serve as a proxy for technological progress. This regulatory bottleneck creates a "valley of innovation" on a graphic, where firms are hesitant to expand because crossing the mentioned threshold will subject them to additional costs and requirements. Marydas et al. (2025) explains that firms will often opt for substitution strategies such as increasing digital technologies or working hours to avoid hiring more employees. These tactics don't provide better rights for employers, nor do they foster innovation in the same way that expanding the workforce and investing in new technologies do.

This regulatory environment stifles growth, preventing companies from scaling quickly and making it difficult for startups to compete globally. Innovation slows down precisely when companies need to grow and expand their operations to meet market demand.

VII.C. Deregulation as a Path to Innovation

MIT Sloan research confirms the same crucial point: Regulation can be a deterrent to innovation. It shows that deregulation, or at least simplifying regulatory frameworks, can play a key role in creating an environment where innovation can flourish and more people can be hired. By removing unnecessary regulatory barriers, policymakers can create a more dynamic and entrepreneurial environment that encourages businesses to invest in innovation and expand their operations. The US has served as a testament to the power of a deregulated environment in the tech sector, where companies like GAFAMX have been able to innovate and scale quickly, largely thanks to relatively low jurisdictional and tax burdens. Furthermore, these large monopolies often feed the small startup ecosystem with their investment.

The EU's approach to artificial intelligence could benefit from a similar light-touch regulatory model, where regulations provide safeguards and accountability without stifling innovation, also assisting employees to work in a less loaded manner. While these leveraged monopolies are unlikely to nurture startup ecosystems by investing in a "big fish eats smaller" model, the key is not to eliminate regulations, but to make them more flexible and strategically align them with the needs of start-ups and small businesses. For example, reducing the compliance burden on smaller companies, especially in emerging sectors, will allow them to focus on technological advancements rather than administrative tasks. This is another form of regulation. In sectors like artificial intelligence, where speed and agility are crucial, the EU could focus on results-oriented regulations that ensure ethical practices without burdening startups with prohibitive compliance costs, or it could help these entrepreneurs reduce bureaucratic costs.

VII.D. The Need for a Flexible and Innovation-Focused Regulatory Approach

While deregulation could potentially benefit startups, it is important to emphasize that deregulation does not mean a complete removal of oversight. Rather, the focus should be on creating a more flexible, innovation-driven regulatory framework that removes unnecessary bureaucratic obstacles while still ensuring ethical standards and consumer protection. By adopting outcome-based regulations that focus on innovation and market competitiveness, Europe can foster a business environment that stimulates growth and technological development.

VII. CONCLUSION

It is important to read Europe's regulatory approach not as a sign of stagnation, but rather as an explanation that can be reconciled with historical economic cycles and the vision of a new GTP paradigm, in order to understand the purpose of this period of reinterpretation of the relationship between technology capital, political power and society. As the world enters a new pace and phase of technological evolution, especially with developments in the field of artificial intelligence, reading the European model as a set of reactive and proactive strategies will contribute to seeing it as an alternative rather than an anchor and may prove to offer an alternative as a deliberate practice rather than an idea of 'disorder/status quo'.

However, the challenge is urgent and enormous. A techno-political paradigm driven by tech capital that continues to challenge legal frameworks and reinforce divisive discourses, and can accelerate them while people stare at their screens, is at least understandable. It is necessary to make sense of it in order to show that a model of 'Big Democracy' based on transparency, accountability and public service can thrive, both against the profit-driven model of Silicon Valley and authoritarian alternatives in other parts of the world.

The intersection of Kondratieff's Long Wave Theory, Schumpeter's theory of creative destruction, and the collapse of neoliberal informationalism provides both a philosophical lens for understanding Europe's current techno-political proposal and explains the logic of the alternative it has created. At a crossroads in the global technological order, Europe faces a crucial moment of choice, whether to convince itself of the path of deregulation driven by external pressures or to become the agent of a new paradigm that balances technological innovation with social welfare, sustainability and democratic values. This paper argues that Europe's response to the growing influence of big tech and the rise of techno-authoritarianism is not a simple matter of economic regulation but a strategic move to assert its digital sovereignty, drawing on historical lessons, economic cycles and theoretical frameworks to chart a way forward.

Kondratieff's Long Wave Theory offers a critical perspective on the cycles of capitalist economies, arguing that periods of technological innovation are inherently linked to economic growth and eventual stagnation (Rosenberg & Frischtak, 1983). These cycles, each triggered by major technological breakthroughs, are followed by periods of crisis when old paradigms can no longer sustain growth. In this context, Europe is facing a situation where the digital revolution, initially heralded as a force for democratization and economic opportunity, has reached a saturation point. There are measures that policymakers should agree on to get through this crisis period with minimal damage. While Schumpeter's theory offers a solution to overcome periods of crisis, from this perspective, regulations may also be needed to foster innovation.

Schumpeter argues that capitalism cannot move forward without a continuous cycle of innovation in which new technologies emerge, disrupting existing industries and creating new opportunities for growth. However, Schumpeter's model also points to the role of regulation in driving this process of creative destruction by ensuring that innovation does not lead to the concentration of wealth and power in the hands of a few monopolistic players (Vass, 2019). In this context, Europe's regulatory framework can be seen as a necessary corrective that aims to channel the forces of innovation towards the public good and the preservation of sovereignty, rather than allowing them to be captured by a handful of tech giants.

The growing crises of neoliberal informationalism, the economic and political model that dominates the digital age, with new technologies has left Europe in a particularly precarious position, unable to keep up with the pace of change. Those advancing the narrative that regulations are inherently regressive are actively trying to persuade the public through new technologies, often backed by the influence of powerful tech billionaires who shape digital discourse to serve market interests. The promise of a liberalized, market-driven digital economy has given way to the reality of monopolistic control, mass surveillance, data exploitation and the erosion of privacy rights. The unrestrained growth of tech giants like GAFAMX has exposed the weaknesses of a system that once heralded information and communication technologies as tools of democratic empowerment. Instead, these technologies have been weaponized for profit, manipulated for political gain and used to consolidate corporate power at the expense of the public interest.

At a time like this, it is important to learn from the past to avoid falling into the same cycles of crisis. Europe's experience during the Industrial Revolution, when rapid technological advancement led to severe social and economic inequalities, has shaped its cautious approach to innovation. In the past, Europe witnessed the dangers of unchecked industrialization, including child labor, exploitation of workers, and environmental degradation.

The Industrial Revolution, a transformative period in human history, was closely linked to political and social revolutions. It led to the formation of a wage-dependent working class in urban settings (Tedsungnon, 2022) and sparked significant changes in the nature and purposes of war (Knox, 2001). The absence of regulation during these early phases of technological advancements led to significant social unrest, inequality, and political instability. Europe's regulatory framework today, informed by these historical lessons, aims to prevent the recurrence of such abuses by ensuring that technological advancement occurs within a framework of ethical oversight and social responsibility.

Moreover, the concept of digital sovereignty, as articulated in Europe's vision of initiatives like EuroStack, is not merely a defensive strategy but a proactive stance aimed at reasserting Europe's autonomy in the face of global techno-political pressures.

In conclusion, Europe's response to the current technological crisis is not just an act of regulation, but a conscious effort to create a new techno-political paradigm, one that can influence others. The Schumpeterian concept of the 'workfare postnational regime' reflects a shift in the global socio-economic order where innovation, labor markets and welfare are intertwined within transnational frameworks (Jessop, 1993). Schumpeter's concept of creative destruction, which emphasizes the transformative power of entrepreneurial innovation, is increasingly facilitated by transnational institutions governing global trade, finance and technology. These institutions, such as the World Trade Organization and the European Union, play an important role in shaping economic landscapes by promoting deregulation and market liberalization, while seeking to address the social consequences of technological disruptions through job security policies. In this regard, the European block itself appears as an umbrella of deregulation on many levels. The narrative of the second term of the Trump administration, which opposes international organizations, is nurturing a rhetorical market liberalism with big tech seems contradictory in this respect.

REFERENCES

Akaev, A. A. (2022). Nikolai Kondratiev's Epoch-Making Discoveries and their Impact on Contemporary Economic Science. *AlterEconomics*, *19*(1), 11–39. DOI: 10.31063/AlterEconomics/2022.19-1.2

Bradford, A. (2024). The false choice between digital regulation and innovation. *Social Science Research Network*. DOI: 10.2139/ssrn.4753107

Bria, F., & Sheikh, H. (2025, March 31). Europe must avoid becoming a digital colony. *Foreign Policy*. https://foreignpolicy.com/2025/03/31/europe-digital-sovereignty-colony-trump-asml-ai-eurostack/

Csernatoni, R. (2024, December 12). Europe's wake-up call for tech leadership. *Carnegie Endowment for International Peace*. https://carnegieendowment.org/europe/strategic-europe/2024/12/europes-wake-up-call-for-tech-leadership

Draghi, M. (2024, September 9). *The Draghi report: A competitiveness strategy for Europe (Part A)*. European Commission

Fang, T., & Hwang, T. (2023, November 9). The rise of techno-nationalism. *New America*. https://www.newamerica.org/oti/reports/the-rise-of-techno-nationalism/

Haeck, P., & Coi, G. (2024). A survey on European tech performance: EU regulations on AI and data protection. *Politico*. https://www.politico.eu/article/eu-tech-scene-denounces-ai-data-rules-bad-for-growth-meta-google-survey-gdpr/

Jasanoff, S. (2016). *The Ethics of Invention: Technology and the Human Future*. W.W.Norton.

Jessop, B. (1993). Towards a schumpeterian workfare state? Preliminary remarks on Post-Fordist Political economy. *Studies in Political Economy*, *40*(1), 7–39. DOI: 10.1080/19187033.1993.11675409

Kilic, E. (2025, January 30). EU knows the stakes and innovates on its own terms as U.S.-China AI competition unfolds. *Türkiye Today*. https://www.turkiyestoday.com/articles/eu-knows-the-stakes-and-innovates-on-its-own-terms-as-u.s.-china-ai-competition-unfolds

Knox, M. (2001). Mass politics and nationalism as military revolution: The French Revolution and after. In Cambridge University Press eBooks (pp. 57–73). DOI: 10.1017/CBO9780511817335.004

Kremidas-Courtney, C., & Litobarski, J. (2024). How the EU can fight back. *European Policy Center.* https://www.epc.eu/en/Publications/How-the-EU-can-fight-back~4db32a

Kutlay, M. (2019). Politics of new developmentalism: Turkey, BRICS and beyond. In E. Ersen & S. Kostem (Eds.), *Turkey's pivot to Eurasia: Geopolitics and foreign policy in a changing world order* (pp. 183-196). Routledge. DOI: 10.4324/9780429023064

Kuzior, A. (2024). Navigating AI regulation: A comparative analysis of EU and US legal frameworks. *Materials Research Proceedings, 45*, 258–266. DOI: 10.21741/9781644903315-30

Malmborg, F. A. (2022). Narrative dynamics in European Commission AI policy,-Sensemaking, agency construction, and anchoring. *The Review of Policy Research, 40*(5), 757–780. DOI: 10.1111/ropr.12529

Marydas, S. P., Mathew, N., De Marzo, G., & Pietrobelli, C. (2025). Digital technologies, hiring, training, and firm outcomes. DOI: 10.53330/ARHR3976

Pelkmans, J., & Renda, A. (2014). Does EU regulation hinder or stimulate innovation? *IO: Productivity.*

Rosenberg, N., & Frischtak, C. R. (1983). Long Waves and Economic Growth: A Critical Appraisal. *The American Economic Review, 73*(2), 146–151. https://www.jstor.org/stable/1816830

Späth, J. (2025, March). The rise of techno-authoritarianism and its impact on U.S. foreign policy (Policy brief No. 15). *Danube University.*

Tedsungnon, P. (2022). Bureaucratical fight of workers group movement in industrial worlds. *International Journal Papier Public Review, 3*(2), 6–13. DOI: 10.47667/ijppr.v3i2.152

Torreblanca, J. I. (2025, January 25). Big tech, Donald Trump, and "techno-imperialism": How Europe can avoid becoming a digital colony. *European Council on Foreign Relations.* https://ecfr.eu/article/big-tech-donald-trump-and-techno-imperialism-how-can-europe-avoid-becoming-a-digital-colony/

Tyulin, A. E., Chursin, A. A., Ragulina, J. V., Akberdina, V. V., & Yudin, A. V. (2023). The development of Kondratieff's theory of long waves: The place of the AI economy humanization in the 'competencies-innovations-markets' model. *Humanities & Social Sciences Communications, 10*(1), 54. Advance online publication. DOI: 10.1057/s41599-022-01434-8

Ulnicane, I., & Aden, A. (2023). Power and politics in framing bias in artificial intelligence policy. *The Review of Policy Research*, *40*(5), 665–687. DOI: 10.1111/ropr.12567

Vass, L. T. (2019). Chapter 11. The Contribution of Schumpeter to the Theory of Technology Evolution. Excerpt from forthcoming book, The Theory of Technology Evolution. Other Innovation Research & Policy eJournal.

Vereckey, B. (2023). Does regulation hurt innovation? This study says yes. *MIT Sloan*. https://mitsloan.mit.edu/ideas-made-to-matter/does-regulation-hurt-innovation-study-says-yes

Winner, L. (1980). Do Artifacts Have Politics? *Daedalus*, *109*(1), 121–136. https://www.jstor.org/stable/20024652

Chapter 8
Perception Management Through Implicit Learning in Digital Media

Zeki Can Saroğlu
https://orcid.org/0000-0002-8878-4334
Turkish National Police Academy, Turkey

ABSTRACT

New media platforms have simplified life but also confined individuals within digital boundaries, managing their desires through subtle control. While users can interact and share content freely, creating a seemingly horizontal communication structure, this openness also facilitates perception management. Users are often unknowingly influenced by repeated content and shape their beliefs and behaviour through implicit learning, i.e. unconscious absorption of information. Elements like the mere exposure effect, algorithmic filtering, and micro-targeting contribute to this process by reinforcing certain ideologies, limiting perspective, and delivering personalized persuasive content, especially in politics and advertising.

INTRODUCTION

Digital media have become the dominant infrastructure for information flow, sociability, and commerce, restructuring not only how messages circulate but also how people learn and form preferences. From Castells's (2010) description of a "network society" built on decentralized communication networks to McLuhan's (1964) famous dictum that "the medium is the message," scholars have long recognized that technological affordances transform cognition and culture. Yet the last decade's convergence of mobile connectivity, real-time personalization, and

DOI: 10.4018/979-8-3373-2459-3.ch008

machine-learning, driven content curation has intensified these transformations in unprecedented ways. Across platforms as different as TikTok, Instagram, YouTube, Netflix, and Amazon, users now inhabit algorithmically crafted media environments in which every swipe, pause, or click becomes feedback for further tailoring. This shift makes classical concerns about propaganda and persuasion newly urgent: influence today is often achieved not through explicit argument but through *implicit learning* the unconscious acquisition of knowledge, preferences, and behavioral scripts from patterns of exposure (Reber, 1993; Cleeremans, 2011).

The sections that follow examine how three well-established psychological Dynamics, mere exposure, filter bubbles, and micro-targeting, operate as pillars of perception management in contemporary digital ecosystems. Section 2 surveys the cognitive science of implicit learning, showing how repeated encounters with language, images, and social cues embed durable associative networks below the threshold of awareness (Berry & Dienes, 1993). Section 3 then traces the *mere exposure effect* (Zajonc, 1968) from its laboratory origins to its platform-scaled incarnation, where algorithmic recommender systems compress repetition cycles and cross-modal reinforcement to convert fleeting impressions into lasting attitudes (Bornstein, 1989). By illustrating how brands, political campaigns, and cultural trends exploit this dynamic, the chapter highlights repetition's capacity to normalize ideologies, aesthetic standards, and consumer desires often without overt persuasion.

Section 4 turns to *algorithmic filtering* and the "filter bubble" (Pariser, 2011), emphasizing how engagement-optimized ranking narrows informational diversity, fosters ideological echo chambers, and primes users for implicit norm internalization (Bakshy et al., 2015). While critics rightly note that personalization can improve relevance and reduce information overload (Bruns, 2019), the chapter argues that homogeneous exposure still poses epistemic and democratic risks by limiting encounters with counter-vailing evidence (Sunstein, 2018). To mitigate these harms, scholars propose diversity-aware ranking, serendipity metrics, and explainable-AI interfaces that empower users to inspect and adjust recommendation criteria (Helberger, Karppinen, & D'Acunto, 2018).

Section 5 addresses *micro-targeting*, the data-driven practice of delivering customized messages to finely segmented audiences. Initially pioneered in commercial advertising, micro-targeting now pervades political campaigning, public-relations strategy, and influencer marketing (Kreiss, 2016). By combining psychographic profiling (Kosinski, Stillwell, & Graepel, 2013) with dynamic creative optimization and AI-generated persuasive scripts (Weidinger et al., 2021), platforms can evoke emotions, exploit cognitive biases, and shape decision contexts in ways users rarely perceive as manipulation. The chapter details the ethical stakes, opacity, autonomy, and discriminatory targeting and surveys emerging regulatory and design interventions aimed at restoring informed consent and agency.

Across these sections, a common thesis emerges: digitally mediated perception management depends less on dramatic misinformation than on subtle, cumulative exposures that harness automatic cognitive processes. Repetition breeds familiarity, and familiarity breeds trust (Kahneman, 2011). Personalization curates familiarity by amplifying congruent content and filtering out dissonance. Micro-targeting intensifies familiarity by matching emotionally resonant frames to granular user profiles. Together, these mechanisms create feedback loops in which what is most frequently encountered becomes cognitively fluent, affectively positive, and socially validated regardless of factual accuracy or moral merit (Fazio et al., 2015). Understanding these loops is therefore critical for media scholars, policy makers, and practitioners seeking to promote equitable and trustworthy digital spaces. If platforms act as "invisible pedagogical agents," as Chapter 3 argues, then media literacy must evolve beyond source checking to include awareness of algorithmic repetition and implicit learning. Likewise, regulatory debates should expand from headline concerns about "fake news" to structural questions about exposure diversity, data governance, and persuasive design. Finally, designers and engineers bear a responsibility to balance engagement incentives with safeguards that protect cognitive autonomy, whether through configurable feed settings, transparent recommendation rationales, or throttling mechanisms that dampen runaway virality.

In sum, this book section invites readers to view digital influence not as a series of isolated content harms but as an ambient learning environment shaped by repetition, personalization, and data-driven persuasion. By synthesizing insights from cognitive psychology, communication studies, and data ethics, the following chapters offer a roadmap for diagnosing and, ultimately, counteracting the imperceptible nudges that shape contemporary thought and behavior.

1. PERCEPTION MANAGEMENT IN THE DIGITAL AGE

Digital media have fundamentally reorganized the social ecology of communication. Traditional mass communication followed a top-down, one-to-many model dominated by gatekeepers such as broadcasters and editors. In such systems, power was concentrated in institutions that controlled content production and distribution. However, in the digital era, networked environments operate through distributed architectures where every user can send, receive, and remix content. As Castells (2010), McLuhan (1964), Jenkins (2006), and Arslan (2025) each observe in different ways, this transformation signifies not merely a technological shift, but a cultural and epistemological one. McLuhan famously posited that "the medium is the message," highlighting how the form of communication reshapes human cognition and social structure. Jenkins emphasized participatory culture, where users are no longer passive consumers but active contributors and collaborators in shaping media flows. Danah Boyd (2010) further contributed by examining how networked publics emerge and interact in digital spaces, illustrating the ways in which visibility, persistence, and searchability redefine communication norms. notes, the "network society" has replaced rigid hierarchies with decentralized flows of information, creating a new communicative paradigm in which the logic of networks supersedes that of centralized control. Finally Arslan focuses on macro-political understanding of the technological shift in global area that he calls techno-politics (2025).

In the network society, communication is not simply faster and broader, it is fundamentally restructured. Users operate as nodes in a multi-directional system, where information circulates horizontally, and influence emerges from decentralized interactions. This shift disrupts classical notions of media power and authority. Yet it also enables new forms of subtle control, where influence is exerted not through overt command, but through the design and curation of digital environments. These environments become key terrains for what is now recognized as perception management.

Perception management traditionally referred to strategies used by states or corporations to influence public opinion through controlled messaging, selective information disclosure, and psychological operations. In the digital context, these strategies have evolved into an ecosystem of imperceptible nudges, orchestrated via platform algorithms, behavioral tracking, and data-driven personalization. Rather than relying on explicit persuasion, platforms shape users' perceptions through tailored content flows that exploit the cognitive features of human attention and learning. (Bakshy et al., 2015; Möller et al., 2018).

Central to this process is implicit learning, the unconscious internalization of information, norms, and preferences through passive exposure. Implicit learning allows individuals to acquire complex knowledge structures without conscious effort or intent (Reber, 1993). On digital platforms, users are continuously immersed in repeated content, be it in the form of memes, video loops, trending topics, or personalized suggestions. These repetitive exposures subtly modify what users perceive as familiar, trustworthy, or socially acceptable.

This mechanism operates beneath the threshold of awareness. For example, repeated exposure to particular political narratives, aesthetic standards, or lifestyle choices can lead users to adopt them as normative, even if they cannot explicitly articulate why. The dynamic interplay between algorithmic systems and user cognition thus produces an environment where behavioral preferences, ideological leanings, and identity markers are shaped implicitly. The psychological underpinnings of this transformation are rooted in theories of cognitive fluency and heuristic processing. The mere exposure effect (Zajonc, 1968), a well-documented psychological phenomenon, demonstrates that individuals tend to develop a preference for stimuli merely because they are familiar. When algorithmic systems continuously present users with similar types of content, those ideas or aesthetics become embedded within their mental framework. Over time, this fosters cognitive alignment with dominant narratives promoted by the system, regardless of their empirical accuracy or ethical implications.

Moreover, the convergence of platform economics and user behavior creates a feedback loop that strengthens this perceptual conditioning. Platform algorithms are designed to maximize engagement by learning from user interactions and delivering content that aligns with past preferences. This design reinforces exposure to ideologically or emotionally resonant content, creating what Sunstein (2018) calls the "architecture of control", a system where choice and freedom are ostensibly preserved, but actual behavior is subtly directed.

As Castells (2010) articulates, communication networks are not neutral infrastructures; they are embedded with logics of power and cultural production. The rise of "mass self-communication", a term he uses to describe user-generated and algorithmically mediated content, means that users both produce and consume the symbols that shape perception. Yet while users appear to exercise agency, their contributions are filtered and amplified through commercial algorithms whose goals often align more with advertising profits than with democratic discourse or cognitive diversity.

This chapter aims to examine these processes in detail, focusing on the intersection of perception management and implicit learning as key frameworks for understanding digital influence. It first explores the cognitive science behind implicit learning and how repeated exposure modifies user behavior. Next, it investigates the mere exposure effect in social media environments, followed by a discussion of algorithmic filtering and the filter bubble effect. Finally, it analyzes the role of micro-targeting and AI-driven personalization in strategic manipulation. By tracing these interconnected dynamics, this chapter contributes to an emerging literature that bridges media theory, psychology, and digital sociology. It invites scholars and readers to reconsider how influence operates in the platform age, not through coercion, but through the quiet accumulation of exposures, framings, and associations that define what individuals come to know, believe, and desire.

2. IMPLICIT LEARNING: MECHANISMS AND RELEVANCE

Implicit learning refers to the process by which individuals acquire knowledge without conscious effort or explicit instruction (Reber, 1993). Core characteristics of implicit learning include automaticity, a lack of verbalizable knowledge, and robustness across different cognitive domains. Empirical studies have demonstrated that individuals can detect complex structures, such as syntactic rules in artificial grammars or spatial contingencies in visual patterns, without being able to articulate what has been learned (Berry & Dienes, 1993). From a neurological standpoint, implicit learning is strongly associated with brain systems involved in procedural memory and pattern recognition. Functional MRI studies have shown that the basal ganglia, cerebellum, and parts of the striatum play key roles in encoding statistical regularities (Cleeremans & Jiménez, 2002). Unlike explicit learning, which recruits prefrontal areas associated with conscious reasoning, implicit learning relies on subconscious information processing pathways. This makes it a durable and evolutionarily conserved mode of acquiring adaptive behavior.

While implicit learning is often associated with digital environments, it has long operated in offline contexts. In language acquisition, for example, infants and children unconsciously learn phonological and grammatical rules through exposure to speech. Similarly, in social interactions, people develop an understanding of norms and body language without explicit instruction. In the realm of physical skills, athletes and musicians improve performance through practice, often relying on procedural memory more than declarative strategies. These real-world examples help illustrate the pervasiveness of implicit learning as a foundational cognitive mechanism (Bargh & Chartrand, 1999).

In digital media environments, implicit learning is amplified by several key dynamics:

- **Repetition:** The repeated appearance of ideas, images, or narratives enhances familiarity, which in turn promotes affective preference. This underlies the mere exposure effect, a process by which individuals come to favor content simply because it is familiar (Zajonc, 1968).
- **Narratives:** Structured storylines provide coherence and facilitate the formation of mental schemas. Whether through influencer vlogs or serialized content, digital narratives embed values and norms without requiring analytical scrutiny (Green & Brock, 2000).
- **Visuals:** Emotionally evocative or morally charged images are rapidly processed and tend to leave lasting impressions. Visual salience and design aesthetics function as non-verbal carriers of cultural codes that shape perception at an unconscious level.

The intersection of implicit learning and perception management becomes especially potent in digital contexts, where repetition is engineered, narratives are algorithmically curated, and visuals are optimized for engagement. The consequence is a feedback loop in which what is seen most frequently becomes cognitively and emotionally prioritized, regardless of its factual veracity or ethical implications.

Thus, platforms act as invisible pedagogical agents, shaping worldviews in ways users may never recognize or interrogate (Fazio et al., 2015).

Understanding the cognitive mechanisms behind implicit learning is essential for unpacking the subtle power of digital influence. As users interact with curated environments, their beliefs and preferences are continuously shaped; not by overt persuasion, but by exposure, pattern, and emotional tone. In this sense, implicit learning serves as the psychological infrastructure of perception management, offering platforms a pathway to guide user cognition invisibly yet effectively (Reber, 1993). In summary, implicit learning is a foundational, cross-contextual process that governs how individuals internalize patterns from their environments. In digital spaces, its mechanisms are not merely incidental but are deliberately harnessed by algorithms and content design. From education and politics to social norms and brand loyalties, implicit learning underlies much of the perceptual formation that now occurs in a hyper-connected, media-saturated world.

3. THE MERE EXPOSURE EFFECT IN SOCIAL MEDIA

The mere exposure effect (Zajonc, 1968) describes a psychological phenomenon where repeated exposure to a stimulus leads to increased liking. This effect is particularly powerful when stimuli are processed without active attention. Digital platforms leverage this effect by designing environments in which repetition is maximized, and content is persistently resurfaced through algorithmic recommendation systems. On platforms like TikTok, Instagram, and YouTube Shorts, users frequently encounter the same music, visual motifs, soundbites, or hashtags across multiple posts. These repeated elements foster a sense of familiarity and positive association, regardless of the content's initial appeal or ideological orientation. For instance, brand mascots like Duolingo's owl become recognizable through meme-based, user-generated content rather than traditional advertising, effectively increasing brand affinity through repeated incidental exposure (Smith, Fischer, & Yongjian, 2012).

The repetition extends beyond branding. Political campaigns have recognized the potential of the mere exposure effect to shape public opinion. Short video ads, campaign slogans, or meme-based political symbols repeatedly presented to users can subtly influence their attitudes. Research shows that even without active participation, exposure to the same political message can increase persuasion and preference alignment (Fazio et al., 2015). This has raised concerns about political polarization, especially when ideologically skewed content is algorithmically amplified within personalized filter bubbles. Beyond political messaging, cultural trends proliferate through this mechanism. Viral dances, audio clips, and fashion aesthetics become normative not through rational endorsement, but through sheer familiarity. Aesthetic movements such as "clean girl," "Y2K revival," or "e-girl" culture have emerged and solidified through millions of visual repetitions. These trends set implicit standards for beauty, behavior, and consumer choices. Users, especially younger audiences, unconsciously internalize these ideals, aligning their appearance, values, and aspirations with the most frequently encountered content (Leaver, Highfield, & Abidin, 2020).

Consumer behavior is also shaped by the mere exposure effect. On platforms like Instagram and Pinterest, users repeatedly see similar product placements, influencer-endorsed items, or visual motifs associated with particular lifestyles. This creates a sense of aesthetic coherence that consumers interpret as a shared cultural norm. Over time, exposure leads to preference, even if users cannot recall where they first encountered the product. Studies have shown that perceived product attractiveness increases with repeated exposure, even in the absence of informative content (Lee & Labroo, 2004).

Digital platforms not only host but actively engineer these exposures. Their recommendation engines are designed to maximize engagement by resurfacing content that generates previous interest. This design inadvertently intensifies the mere exposure effect. Users are less likely to encounter novelty and more likely to re-encounter familiar content that aligns with their preexisting preferences. As a result, the platform cultivates behavioral consistency and cognitive inertia. The implications are profound. The mere exposure effect in digital media environments does not just influence liking; it also reinforces behavioral scripts, value systems, and group identities. When users are continuously exposed to a particular narrative (whether about gender roles, lifestyle expectations, or political ideology) they begin to interpret that narrative as socially validated and normatively desirable. The preference for the familiar subtly reshapes their decision-making processes, often without conscious awareness or critical reflection (Kahneman, 2011).

In essence, the mere exposure effect provides digital platforms with a powerful psychological mechanism for shaping perception. By leveraging repetition and algorithmic delivery, platforms transform passive consumption into active alignment. As digital ecosystems continue to expand, understanding the subtle power of mere exposure is crucial for media scholars, marketers, and policy makers concerned with the ethical dimensions of perception management in the digital age (Gillespie, 2014).

4. ALGORITHMIC FILTERING AND THE FILTER BUBBLE EFFECT

Algorithmic content curation refers to the use of automated systems by platforms such as Facebook, YouTube, Twitter, and TikTok to prioritize, filter, and recommend content to users based on their past interactions and inferred preferences. While personalization provides convenience by matching content to user interests, it can also result in a narrowing of informational diversity, what Eli Pariser (2011) famously termed the "filter bubble." A filter bubble occurs when a user is primarily exposed to content that aligns with their pre-existing beliefs, behaviors, or preferences, while contrasting or dissenting views are algorithmically filtered out. Over time, such selective exposure leads to a digital environment that appears diverse but is actually ideologically homogeneous. The effect is compounded by engagement-based optimization, where content that provokes strong emotional responses (e.g., outrage or affirmation) is prioritized, further entrenching cognitive biases.

The implications of filter bubbles are multifaceted. On one hand, they contribute to political and cultural polarization, as users become increasingly anchored in echo chambers. On the other, they limit critical thinking by depriving users of exposure to alternative viewpoints or factual counterbalances. This environment is highly conducive to implicit learning: when users are repeatedly exposed to similar frames, visuals, and rhetorical patterns, they internalize these as normative truths without conscious awareness. Thus, ideological conformity can emerge as a byproduct of computational personalization (Bakshy et al., 2015). However, recent scholarship has also raised critical perspectives on the concept of filter bubbles. Bruns (2019) argues that the phenomenon is overstated and that users often encounter diverse viewpoints across multiple platforms, albeit passively. Similarly, Flaxman, Goel, and Rao (2016) suggest that while algorithmic curation may narrow exposure in some contexts, digital media as a whole still broadens access to news and opinion compared to traditional media. These critiques highlight the need for nuanced assessments that account for user agency, cross-platform behaviors, and varying levels of digital literacy.

To address concerns about content homogeneity, scholars and designers have proposed algorithmic diversity interventions. These include diversity-aware ranking systems that balance relevance with novelty, serendipity metrics that intentionally inject contrasting viewpoints into feeds, and explainable AI systems that allow users to understand and adjust recommendation criteria. Such innovations aim to reintroduce unpredictability into content flows and reduce the epistemic closure that filter bubbles may cause (Helberger, Karppinen & D'Acunto, 2018). Importantly, the solution is not simply to dismantle personalization (which can improve user experience and reduce information overload) but to design for meaningful heterogeneity. This may involve giving users more transparency and control over recommendation algorithms, or embedding content diversity as a default principle in algorithmic design.

In sum, while filter bubbles remain a legitimate concern, particularly in politically sensitive contexts, they are neither inevitable nor uniformly harmful. A critical understanding of how algorithmic filtering shapes perception requires attention to platform architectures, user behavior, and cognitive mechanisms such as implicit learning. When combined, these factors determine whether personalization acts as an amplifier of bias or a tool for cognitive enrichment.

5. MICRO-TARGETING AND STRATEGIC MANIPULATION

Micro-targeting refers to the delivery of highly customized messages to narrowly defined audience segments, based on an analysis of their online behavior, preferences, and psychological traits. Initially developed in the context of digital advertising, this strategy has been widely adopted in political campaigning, propaganda dissemination, and influencer marketing. With the rise of big data analytics and algorithmic profiling, micro-targeting has become a key component of perception management in the digital era (Kreiss, 2016; Isaak & Hanna, 2018).

The foundation of micro-targeting lies in the ability to collect and process vast amounts of personal and behavioral data. Every interaction including search history, location data, clicks, video views, sentiment in posts, is recorded and analyzed to create complex user profiles. These profiles are then matched with message variations designed to evoke emotional resonance, align with values, or trigger cognitive biases such as fear, aspiration, or social conformity.

Common techniques include:

- **Psychographic profiling**, where individuals are segmented by personality traits, lifestyle preferences, or values inferred from their digital footprints (Kosinski, Stillwell, & Graepel, 2013)
- **Dynamic creative optimization**, where ad components (images, texts, tones) are algorithmically tested and adjusted in real time to maximize engagement (Lomas, 2019).
- **Ephemeral dark ads**, which are personalized messages visible only to selected users and vanish after being viewed, limiting transparency (Lomas, 2019).
- **AI-generated persuasion**, where large language models are used to produce custom messages and scripts based on user personality data (Brundage, et al. 2018).

The Cambridge Analytica scandal serves as a seminal case study in the power and ethical hazards of micro-targeting. The company harvested Facebook data from tens of millions of users without consent and deployed psychographic targeting to influence political attitudes during the 2016 U.S. presidential election and the

Brexit referendum. Voters received emotionally charged, narrowly tailored content intended to solidify partisan leanings or suppress opposition turnout. While the overall effectiveness remains debated, the breach of trust and mass manipulation led to public backlash, academic scrutiny, and regulatory action (Isaak & Hanna, 2018).

Beyond politics, micro-targeting shapes consumer behavior. For example, streaming platforms like Netflix and Spotify curate individual interfaces not only to predict preferences but to guide attention and deepen brand attachment. In e-commerce, targeted discounts, urgency messages, and scarcity cues are deployed to exploit individual purchasing habits. These messages are rarely perceived as manipulation; rather, they are seen as convenience or relevance, precisely because implicit learning masks their persuasive origins (Smith, Fischer, & Yongjian, 2012; Matz, Kosinski, Nave & Stillwell, 2017).

The future of micro-targeting is likely to be shaped by advances in artificial intelligence, particularly in emotion recognition and real-time behavioral adaptation. Facial expression analysis, voice sentiment detection, and wearable biometric data could be used to tailor messages not only to who users are, but also to how they feel at any given moment. This "affective targeting" intensifies the potential for manipulation by embedding persuasion into moments of psychological vulnerability. The implications for implicit learning are profound. Personalized content delivered repeatedly and timed for emotional impact bypasses rational scrutiny and strengthens associative links in memory. Over time, individuals internalize worldviews, preferences, and judgments shaped by their digital environment. Because the learning is implicit, users are often unaware that their perception has been managed (Cleeremans, 2011).

In sum, micro-targeting exemplifies the fusion of behavioral science, data analytics, and machine learning in service of strategic influence. It exploits the psychological mechanisms of implicit learning to reshape perception silently and systematically. As the tools of personalization grow more sophisticated, so too must public awareness, ethical standards, and institutional oversight.

CONCLUSION

In the digital age, perception is no longer shaped merely by overt messaging, institutional authority, or direct interpersonal influence. Instead, the architecture of perception has become deeply intertwined with the hidden operations of digital platforms and algorithmic infrastructures. This chapter analyses how implicit learning, which enables the unconscious acquisition of knowledge and preferences, interacts with the persuasive architecture of digital media ecosystems. It has argued that perception management in the digital age operates less through intentional misinformation or ideological coercion and more through subtle, repetitive, emotionally resonant exposures that guide users toward preferred beliefs, values, and behaviors without triggering conscious awareness.

At the center of this transformation is the shift from vertical to horizontal communication structures, a development theorized by Castells (2010) in his conception of the network society. Digital platforms like TikTok, Instagram, YouTube, and Facebook have redistributed the production and circulation of information away from centralized institutions and into the hands of users. However, this apparent democratization masks the emergence of algorithmic gatekeepers, systems that curate content in ways optimized for engagement, retention, and monetization rather than informational diversity or cognitive autonomy. In this context, perception is shaped not by truthfulness or deliberative reasoning, but by what is familiar, what is repeated, and what is emotionally sticky.

The psychological mechanism most conducive to this process is implicit learning. Unlike explicit learning, which involves deliberate cognitive effort, implicit learning is automatic, resilient, and affectively mediated. As users encounter recurring images, narratives, or framings, they gradually internalize associated meanings without realizing that they are being taught. Repetition, visual salience, and narrative structure create fertile ground for such learning. On platforms where exposure is governed by algorithmic filters, what users learn implicitly is what algorithms deem worthy of attention, an iterative cycle that reinforces dominant content types and erodes epistemic pluralism.

This dynamic is only further strengthened by the exposure effect (Zajonc, 1968), which shows that repeated contact with a stimulus creates familiarity and appreciation, regardless of its informational nature. In digital environments, where users scroll through hundreds of posts daily, the same slogans, aesthetics, and soundbites resurface endlessly. Whether it is a political campaign using short clips to build emotional resonance or a brand reinforcing its identity through memes, the goal is not to persuade through argument, but to shape preference through rhythm, repetition, and routine. The cumulative effect is one of aesthetic and cognitive alignment: users begin to favor what they see most, even if they do not consciously endorse it.

Algorithmic filtering further intensifies this learning environment by narrowing the range of content users are exposed to. Personalized recommendation systems track user behavior to serve more of what aligns with past engagement patterns. This creates "filter bubbles" (Pariser, 2011), where users are surrounded by ideologically or culturally homogenous content. Although recent critiques argue that filter bubbles may be less rigid than initially feared (Bruns, 2019; Flaxman et al., 2016), their impact on implicit learning remains potent. The absence of cross-cutting perspectives and the omnipresence of reinforcement cues strengthen internalized worldviews, making them appear more universal than they are. This process not only limits the cognitive flexibility of users but also undermines democratic ideals rooted in exposure to diversity and critical reflection.

The final layer of this perceptual architecture involves micro-targeting, an advanced form of strategic manipulation that uses big data analytics and behavioral profiling to deliver highly personalized messages. Political campaigns and commercial advertisers increasingly rely on psychographic insights, dynamic creative optimization, and AI-generated content to reach audiences with tailored messages. The infamous case of Cambridge Analytica demonstrated the potential of such techniques to exploit voter vulnerabilities without consent or transparency. More recently, emotion-recognition technologies and large language models have expanded the scope of influence, making it possible to tailor persuasive strategies not just to individual traits but to momentary emotional states. These advances raise profound ethical questions about autonomy, manipulation, and consent in a digital environment where users often do not realize they are being targeted, let alone influenced.

Collectively, these findings suggest that digital media environments have become sophisticated apparatuses for perception management, operating not through coercion or censorship, but through algorithmic curation, emotional resonance, and cognitive invisibility. The psychological infrastructure of implicit learning makes users especially susceptible to these forms of influence because it bypasses rational scrutiny and critical engagement. Users do not choose to learn in this way; they are conditioned to do so by the rhythm and logic of platform design. This condition presents both a diagnostic and normative challenge. Diagnostically, it requires scholars, educators, and policymakers to shift their focus from misinformation and overt propaganda to the subtler processes of information repetition, emotional design, and behavioral targeting. Normatively, it invites questions about the ethical responsibilities of platform designers, the transparency of algorithmic systems, and the rights of users to control how their attention, emotions, and perceptions are shaped.

To address these concerns, several interventions are worth considering. First, digital literacy programs must include education on the mechanisms of implicit learning and the psychological effects of repeated exposure. Users need to understand that what feels familiar is not necessarily true or good, it is merely frequent. Second, algorithmic transparency must become a normative standard. Users should have the right to understand and control how content is filtered and why they are being shown what they see. Third, regulatory frameworks must evolve to govern the ethical use of behavioral data, especially in contexts where persuasion tactics intersect with psychological profiling. In conclusion, the intersection of implicit learning and digital media represents a fundamental shift in how human perception is shaped in contemporary society. What people know, believe, and desire is increasingly the product of invisible systems optimized for influence. Perception management has moved from the domain of strategic communication into the infrastructure of everyday life, mediated by platforms that learn what users want before users themselves do. Recognising this shift is the first step towards reclaiming the initiative in an environment where the boundaries between attention, persuasion and learning are ever more fluid and contested.

AI DISCLOSURE STATEMENT

Proofreading and readability enhancement of this text were performed with assistance from GPT-5.

REFERENCES

Arslan, A. C. (2025). *Tekno-Politika Çağı: Devlet Şirket İlişkilerinin Teorik Analizi ve Güvenliğin İnşası*. Yetkin Yayınları.

Bakshy, E., Messing, S., & Adamic, L. A. (2015). Exposure to ideologically diverse news and opinion on Facebook. *Science, 348*(6239), 1130–1132. DOI: 10.1126/science.aaa1160 PMID: 25953820

Bargh, J. A., & Chartrand, T. L. (1999). The unbearable automaticity of being. *The American Psychologist, 54*(7), 462–479. DOI: 10.1037/0003-066X.54.7.462

Berry, D. C., & Dienes, Z. (1993). *Implicit learning: Theoretical and empirical issues*. Psychology Press.

Bornstein, R. F. (1989). Exposure and affect: Overview and meta-analysis of research, 1968–1987. *Psychological Bulletin, 106*(2), 265–289. DOI: 10.1037/0033-2909.106.2.265

Boyd, D. (2010). Social network sites as networked publics: Affordances, dynamics, and implications. In Papacharissi, Z. (Ed.), *A networked self: Identity, community, and culture on social network sites* (pp. 39–58). Routledge.

Brundage, M., Avin, S., Clark, J., & Toner, H. (2018). The malicious use of artificial intelligence: Forecasting, prevention, and mitigation. *Oxford University and others.*

Bruns, A. (2019). *Are filter bubbles real?* Polity Press.

Castells, M. (2010). *The rise of the network society* (2nd ed.). Wiley-Blackwell.

Cleeremans, A. (2011). The radical plasticity thesis: How the brain learns to be conscious. *Frontiers in Psychology, 2*, 86.

Cleeremans, A., & Jiménez, L. (2002). Implicit learning and consciousness: A graded, dynamic perspective. In French, R. M., & Cleeremans, A. (Eds.), *Implicit learning and consciousness* (pp. 1–40). Psychology Press.

Fazio, L. K., Brashier, N. M., Payne, B. K., & Marsh, E. J. (2015). Knowledge does not protect against illusory truth. *Journal of Experimental Psychology. General, 144*(5), 993–1002. DOI: 10.1037/xge0000098 PMID: 26301795

Flaxman, S., Goel, S., & Rao, J. M. (2016). Filter bubbles, echo chambers, and online news consumption. *Public Opinion Quarterly, 80*(S1), 298–320. DOI: 10.1093/poq/nfw006

Gillespie, T. (2014). The relevance of algorithms. In Gillespie, T., Boczkowski, P. J., & Foot, K. A. (Eds.), *Media technologies: Essays on communication, materiality, and society* (pp. 167–193). MIT Press. DOI: 10.7551/mitpress/9042.003.0013

Green, M. C., & Brock, T. C. (2000). The role of transportation in the persuasiveness of public narratives. *Journal of Personality and Social Psychology, 79*(5), 701–721. DOI: 10.1037/0022-3514.79.5.701 PMID: 11079236

Helberger, N., Karppinen, K., & D'Acunto, L. (2018). Exposure diversity as a design principle for recommender systems. *Information Communication and Society, 21*(2), 191–207. DOI: 10.1080/1369118X.2016.1271900

Isaak, J., & Hanna, M. J. (2018). User data privacy: Facebook, Cambridge Analytica, and privacy protection. *Computer, 51*(8), 56–59. DOI: 10.1109/MC.2018.3191268

Jenkins, H. (2006). *Convergence culture: Where old and new media collide*. New York University Press.

Kahneman, D. (2011). *Thinking, fast and slow*. Farrar, Straus and Giroux.

Kosinski, M., Stillwell, D., & Graepel, T. (2013). Private traits and attributes are predictable from digital records of human behaviour. *Proceedings of the National Academy of Sciences of the United States of America, 110*(15), 5802–5805. DOI: 10.1073/pnas.1218772110 PMID: 23479631

Kreiss, D. (2016). *Prototype politics: Technology-intensive campaigning and the data of democracy*. Oxford University Press. DOI: 10.1093/acprof:oso/9780199350247.001.0001

Leaver, T., Highfield, T., & Abidin, C. (2020). *Instagram: Visual social media cultures*. Polity Press.

Lee, A. Y., & Labroo, A. A. (2004). The effect of conceptual and perceptual fluency on brand evaluation. *JMR, Journal of Marketing Research, 41*(2), 151–165. DOI: 10.1509/jmkr.41.2.151.28665

Lomas, N. (2019). *Facebook's ad tools allow political campaigns to target voters with alarming precision*. TechCrunch.

Matz, S. C., Kosinski, M., Nave, G., & Stillwell, D. J. (2017). Psychological targeting as an effective approach to digital mass persuasion. *Proceedings of the National Academy of Sciences of the United States of America, 114*(48), 12714–12719. DOI: 10.1073/pnas.1710966114 PMID: 29133409

McLuhan, M. (1964). *Understanding media: The extensions of man*. McGraw-Hill.

Möller, J., Trilling, D., Helberger, N., & van Es, B. (2018). Do not blame it on the algorithm: An empirical assessment of multiple recommender systems and their impact on content diversity. *Information Communication and Society, 21*(7), 959–977. DOI: 10.1080/1369118X.2018.1444076

Pariser, E. (2011). *The filter bubble: What the internet is hiding from you*. Penguin Press.

Reber, A. S. (1993). *Implicit learning and tacit knowledge: An essay on the cognitive unconscious*. Oxford University Press.

Smith, A. N., Fischer, E., & Yongjian, C. (2012). How does brand-related user-generated content differ across YouTube, Facebook, and Twitter? *Journal of Interactive Marketing*, *26*(2), 102–113. DOI: 10.1016/j.intmar.2012.01.002

Sunstein, C. R. (2018). *Republic: Divided democracy in the age of social media*. Princeton University Press.

Weidinger, L., Mellor, J., Rauh, M., Griffin, C., Uesato, J., Huang, P. S., . . . Gabriel, I. (2021). Ethical and social risks of harm from language models. *arXiv Preprint arXiv:2112.04359*.

Zajonc, R. B. (1968). Attitudinal effects of mere exposure. *Journal of Personality and Social Psychology*, *9*(2, Pt. 2), 1–27. DOI: 10.1037/h0025848

Chapter 9
The Rise of Internet-Curated Aesthetics:
A New Form of Virtual Identity in the Age of Digital Media

Zeynep Melike Saroğlu
https://orcid.org/0009-0005-4386-8234
Turkish National Police Academy, Turkey

ABSTRACT

This chapter explores the distinction between subcultures and Internet aesthetics through the lens of authenticity, resistance, and cultural meaning-making. While subcultures emerged as collective, oppositional formations grounded in shared experiences and ideological critique, Internet aesthetics function within platform-driven, hyper-visual environments shaped by algorithmic visibility and aesthetic allure. The chapter argues that Internet aesthetics lack the symbolic depth and disruptive potential of subcultures, resulting in depoliticized youth. Youth identities are increasingly curated through aestheticized, consumable fragments of popular culture, favoring exhibition over resistance, sameness over difference. The logic of likes and algorithmic affirmation replaces political engagement, transforming digital spaces into loops of self-confirmation. Ultimately, the chapter contends that Internet aesthetics reflect a broader cultural shift toward passive identity performance within digital panopticons.

INTRODUCTION

The digital age has transformed the way individuals express themselves and form identities. Internet-curated aesthetics, ranging from cottagecore to balletcore, tradwife

DOI: 10.4018/979-8-3373-2459-3.ch009

to mobwife, have emerged as dominant virtual and visual languages on social media platforms such as Instagram, TikTok, and Pinterest. These aesthetics not only offer a sense of community and self-expression but also highlight the paradoxical nature of virtual identity, where the pursuit of uniqueness often results in conformity. This proposal aims to explore the relationship between internet-curated aesthetics and subcultures, emphasizing their distinctions, the ways in which internet aesthetics create virtual identities, and the socio-political implications of this transformation in the digital era.

Historically, subcultures have been closely linked to socio-political movements, rebellion, and resistance. From punk to goth, hip-hop to grunge, subcultures have provided a sense of belonging while challenging mainstream norms. These groups were often formed around shared ideologies, music, fashion, and lifestyles, creating distinct identities that set them apart from dominant culture. However, with the rise of internet aesthetics, the foundations of subcultural expression have shifted.

Unlike subcultures, internet-curated aesthetics are largely visual and often detached from any political or ideological stance. They are characterized by an emphasis on individual expression rather than collective identity, allowing users to switch between styles fluidly. The lack of rigid boundaries within these aesthetics enables individuals to construct, modify, and abandon their digital personas with ease. This flexibility, while empowering, also leads to the loss of distinctive features that once defined subcultures. The transition from subcultures to internet aesthetics marks a shift from socially and politically motivated styles to aesthetics driven by algorithmic curation, marketability, and performative self-expression.

Social media platforms have played a significant role in the proliferation of internet aesthetics, as algorithms promote and reinforce specific visual trends. Social media platforms are not neutral spaces for interaction; rather, their very infrastructure is inherently political, shaping discourse and behavior (Arslan, 2025). This reflects how internet aesthetics operate within controlled environments where visibility, likes, and aesthetic appeal are more important than ideological depth or oppositional meaning-making. Users curate their online presence by adhering to a consistent aesthetic that aligns with prevailing trends, resulting in the formation of aesthetic tribes or "-core(s)." These online communities provide a sense of belonging through shared visual languages, yet they also contribute to the homogenization of identity, where distinctiveness is sacrificed in favor of conformity. Therefore, it is claimed that social media increasingly resembles a digital panopticon. One that disciplines and exploits forms of sociality rather than nurturing them. Digital control society intensifies the use of freedom by encouraging individuals to voluntarily display and expose themselves (Han, 2024: 12).

The curated nature of these aesthetics blurs the line between authenticity and performance. The pressure to maintain an aesthetically pleasing digital persona can lead individuals to adopt idealized versions of themselves, driven by societal expectations and the pursuit of online validation. As a result, internet aesthetics function as both a tool for self-expression and a mechanism for social control, shaping the ways in which individuals present themselves in the digital realm. In other words, it can be inferred that the primary aim of engaging with an Internet aesthetic is the experience itself to momentarily adopt a different persona or immerse oneself in the atmosphere of another era (Giolo & Berghman, 2023).

One of the most significant consequences of the rise of internet aesthetics is the gradual disappearance of subcultures as oppositional movements. In the past, subcultures challenged mainstream norms and served as spaces for marginalized voices. However, as aesthetics become increasingly commodified, the rebellious and ideological essence of subcultures has faded. Today, youth identity is less about resistance and more about participation in digital trends that are often driven by consumerism and branding strategies.

Internet aesthetics offer a visually appealing but politically neutral alternative to subcultures. They prioritize individual taste and curated lifestyles over collective defiance and social critique. This transformation underscores the shift from identity as a form of resistance to identity as a consumable, marketable entity. These internet aesthetics have a strong influence, especially on young people, as they actively construct their identities, shaping how they express themselves in the digital world. However, the rise of curated identities has also led to a sense of sameness and conformity, where distinct self-expression is often replaced by algorithm-driven aesthetic trends. Consequently, the mainstreaming of aesthetic identities has led to the depoliticization of youth culture, where self-expression is shaped by digital influence rather than grassroots movements.

As the digital age continues to redefine identity formation, internet-curated aesthetics have emerged as the dominant mode of self-representation, replacing subcultures with visually driven, market-friendly styles. While these aesthetics offer new avenues for personal expression, they also raise concerns about authenticity, conformity, and the erosion of politically motivated subcultural movements. By examining the interplay between internet aesthetics and subcultures, this research seeks to understand how digital culture shapes identity in a rapidly evolving, virtually saturated world. Ultimately, this study will contribute to the discourse on digital self-representation, the role of social media in identity formation, and the implications of aesthetic homogenization in contemporary society.

Nowadays, where digital technologies are rapidly evolving and traditional social structures are increasingly transforming, individuals turn to digital platforms to construct their identities and establish their place within the social sphere. In particular, social media enables individuals to reshape their everyday life experiences and perceptions of reality within specific thematic frameworks. Internet aesthetics are digital trends that emerge on online platforms, allowing individuals to express their identities, interests, and aesthetic preferences based on particular visual, cultural, and lifestyle-oriented themes. Manovich (2020) defines internet aesthetics as visual modes of expression shaped by micro-cultures, emerging through the democratization of digital culture and the processes of content production and sharing. In other words, while scrolling through social media, users frequently come across hashtags like 'cluttercore' or 'coquette, which serve to classify cultural items—such as clothing, music, artworks, or images—as part of particular internet aesthetics, effectively sorting them into recognizable style categories. What is striking is the wide range of products, behaviors, preferences, and even mindsets that these labels encompass. For instance, the label 'dark academia' can refer to films like *Dead Poets Society* (1989) and the *Harry Potter* series (2001–2011), classical texts such as the *Iliad* and *Odyssey*, Debussy's music, and activities like going to museums, reading in libraries, or engaging in academic study (Giolo & Berghman, 2023). These aesthetics allow individuals to develop a sense of belonging, express themselves, and attribute cultural meanings in the digital sphere. For example, internet aesthetics such as dark academia, cottagecore, cleangirl or coquette not only represent a particular visual style but also embody a lifestyle that supports this aesthetic (Pettman, 2019). In this sense, internet aesthetics used on digital platforms reflect individuals' efforts to construct coherent and meaningful self-images (Giolo & Berghman, 2023). Social media serves as a platform for sharing clothing styles and showcasing the adopted internet aesthetics. This study aims to demonstrate that internet aesthetics are not merely visual and aesthetic preferences but also forms of expression that carry social and cultural meanings.

THE SYMBOLIC ROLE OF CLOTHING: SOCIAL CLASS, IDENTITY, AND CHANGE

Clothing, like dishes, music preferences, furniture selections, and health beliefs, is a cultural phenomenon that finds a place among the shared understandings of a given society (Davis, 1992: 11). As one of the most visible forms of consumption, clothing plays a crucial role in the social construction of identity. Clothing preferences provide a valuable lens through which to analyze how individuals shape cultural norms according to their needs and goals. It encompasses both the dominant fashion norms of a given era and a wide range of alternative modes of expression.

As one of the most prominent indicators of social status and gender, clothing plays an influential role in maintaining or challenging symbolic boundaries. It simultaneously reflects how individuals perceive and negotiate their positions within the social structure across different periods. Thus, garments are linked to the imposition of social identities as well as to the possibilities for expressing alternative social identities. Throughout history, clothing has been one of the fundamental tools for expressing individual identity in the public sphere. Depending on the era, various elements of identity—such as profession, regional origin, religious beliefs, and social class—have been represented through clothing. Therefore, differences and diversities in clothing choices are considered to offer important clues for understanding the types of social structures and how individuals experience their positions within them.

It is argued that because members of a given society often share similar living conditions, they tend to experience comparable aspirations, tensions, anxieties, and discontents. In this regard, a significant part of identity is said to share a collective structure, and clothing is believed to address this collective dimension of social identity. Clothing, cosmetics, and hairstyle form the key elements of an individual's outward appearance and are the aspects most closely related to the physical body. In other words, because these elements are directly connected to our physical appearence, they are seen as expressions of personality and reflections of identity, possessing a unique capacity to "say something" about us (Davis, 1992: 13-17). At this point, the concept of "youth culture" emerges as a sign system that focuses on the body, appearance and clothing (Hebdige, 2002).

Clothing as a form of identity expression also has the capacity to influence how individuals interact with others. Changes in clothing styles and discourses reflect broader changes in social relations and the tensions between different social groups that manifest in the public sphere. For instance, in pre-industrial societies, clothing choices were said to clearly reflect an individual's position within the social structure (Ewen, 1985). In addition to social class and gender, clothing was associated with religious beliefs and regional origins. However, with the industrialization of Western societies, the relationship between social stratification and clothing underwent significant changes. In the industrial societies of the 19th century, clothing became an important symbolic communication tool, conveying information about a person's social role, status, and personal characteristics. Particularly, the expression of class and gender became more prominent than the other social positions such as religion or regional background. In this context, class affiliation was one of the most salient elements of identity, and this was clearly reflected in clothing behaviors. Fashion, then, could be understood as a means of providing opportunities for social mobility, although clothing only represented one dimension of this (Crane, 2000: 6–9). Simmel, known for his influential theory on fashion and dress behavior, argued that fashion serves to distinguish one social stratum from another, making it a product of class division. According to Simmel, fashion first emerges among the upper classes and is subsequently imitated by the middle and lower classes. Through this process, lower-status groups attempt to gain social status by imitating the dress of higher-status groups, leading to a continuous cycle of change and stratification (Simmel, 1957).

By the 20th century, with the significant expansion of the ready-to-wear industry, clothing gradually lost much of its economic value while retaining its symbolic meanings. Since the 1960s, styles emerging from lower socioeconomic groups began to attract attention and were adopted and imitated by individuals from different social strata. In other words, a model of fashion diffusion from the bottom up started to appear. During this period, youth subcultures characterized by distinctive clothing styles began to shape fashion trends. The accessibility of affordable clothing allowed individuals with limited resources not merely to imitate styles originally reserved for the wealthy but to find or create personal styles that reflected their identities. Consequently, the rise of street fashion representing working-class subcultures became more evident. Thus, it has been suggested that, in the 20th century, the importance of social class in the formation of self-image diminished, and lifestyle, tastes, values, and attitudes toward social issues began to exert greater influence (Crane, 2000: 8–11).

In the multicultural societies of the 21st century, clothing codes continue to function as a means of expressing both internal group relations and intergroup dynamics, much like the youth subcultures described in the 20th century. Clothing today contains symbols that embody specific ideas, images, and associations, serving as expressions of social and cultural identities. In other words, clothing symbols acquire different meanings depending on the social and cultural context. Influenced by postmodern society, the understanding of clothing in the 21st century has become even more diversified, with individuality taking center stage. In postmodernity, identities are no longer fixed and rigid but fluid, multilayered, and multifaceted. In this era, clothing not only reflects social and cultural identities but also functions as a form of self-expression. Within this framework, internet aesthetics have emerged, offering individuals the opportunity to transition between different identities. Rather than associating their identities to social classes or fixed subcultural categories, individuals construct their identities through personal preferences, aesthetic tastes, and digital interactions. In this sense, internet aesthetics have become a tool for the free expression of individual identities beyond traditional social relations. However, internet aesthetics are not only a means of individual freedom and expression, but also intertwined with the directive logic of digital capitalism. The algorithmic structures of social media platforms shape visibility by highlighting certain aesthetic forms. This leads individuals to establish virtual identities driven by the desire to be "liked." Thus, choices are shaped not only by personal preferences but also by expectations of visibility, approval, and appreciation. In this context, internet aesthetics become both an expression of postmodern identity games and an indicator of "conformity" to the new norms produced by the digital system.

WEARING RESISTANCE: YOUTH, SUBCULTURE AND THE LANGUAGE OF STYLE

"Clothes and fashionable clothing styles are "carriers" of a wide range of ideological meanings or "social agendas" (Laver, 1968: 10).

Subcultures are regarded as collective responses to collectively experienced problems. In this context, youth subcultures are described as forms of symbolic resistance, hegemonic struggle, and the defense of cultural space on a relatively autonomous ideological plane (Clarke, 1997: 175–177). Subcultural ideologies function as tools that allow young people to make sense of themselves and other social groups, to express their distinctiveness, and to affirm that they are not merely anonymous members of a mass (Thornton, 2003: 24). Subcultures construct unique identities and modes of expression by differentiating themselves from mainstream culture through elements such as music, style, language, ethnicity, spatial practices, consumption habits, economic status, rituals, and symbols. In other words, subcultures are aware of their differences and enjoy them (Thornton, 1997: 5). Despite their separation from the mainstream, subcultures cannot be thought of as isolated from the broader socio-political contexts of society. They are, inevitably, part of the very society they seek to resist (Jenks, 2005: 12; Clarke et al., 2003). Within this framework, style, one of the key modes through which subcultures shape and express their identities, positions them both as oppositional stances against mainstream culture and as products of their social environment. Subcultural styles are thus seen as provoking reactions within society, while being reactions themselves. Consequently, the best studies on subcultural style are considered to be those that capture these interactive processes (Gelder, 1997: 374).

Researchers from the Centre for Contemporary Cultural Studies (CCCS) have explored the relationship between ideologies and forms, focusing particularly on subcultures with distinctive styles such as Mods, Teddy Boys, Skinheads, and Punks. Style is defined as the mode by which a group expresses itself through elements such as dress, appearance, sound, or performance. It provides the group with an identity and helps articulate it coherently, enabling both internal self-definition and external recognition (Gelder, 1997: 373). Youth subcultures, therefore, are often identified by their specific material possessions: the parkas and scooters of the Mods, the bovver boots and shaved heads of the Skinheads. Hebdige (2002) emphasizes that these objects symbolically and codifiedly express subcultural members' secondary position within the social structure and their resistance against it. What is truly significant is not merely the objects a group possesses but the attitudes and practices that imbue these objects with meaning. The relationship between the objects and the activities and viewpoints of the group constitutes the core of subcultural style formation. Through the adoption of objects that reflect their shared concerns, activities, group structure, and collective identity, subcultural members create meaning. For example, the adoption of boots, short jeans, and shaved heads by Skinheads signifies and expresses values such as masculinity, toughness, and working-class pride within the subcultural context. In other words, simply possessing or wearing these items is not sufficient to create a style; rather, it is the combination of these objects with specific attitudes and activities that constructs a meaningful subcultural style. The symbolic dimensions of subcultures cannot be separated from their internal structures, experiences, activities, and worldviews. Through this process, subcultures develop a lifestyle and worldview that coherently and distinctively express their collective identity (Clarke et al., 2003).

It is noted that innovations in style often originate among minorities or groups perceived, and perceiving themselves, as marginal to dominant culture. In the postwar period, as adolescents and young adults gained more time and leisure, and became a focus of the popular culture industries, youth subcultures rapidly proliferated. Within these subcultures, style and appearance became central elements of identity. Clothing served young people, who were not yet part of the workforce, as a medium through which they could express their attitudes towards themselves and their social environment. By creatively reinterpreting existing styles, youth subcultures constructed identities that reflected their personal experiences and social conditions. Clothing, accessories, and hairstyles were combined to reflect these identities, playing a crucial role in the public presentation of the self (Crane, 2000).

While not all subcultures explicitly reject mainstream culture, in some cases, the formation of subcultural identity can be understood as a symbolic expression of resistance. In youth subcultures, style, particularly generational style, played a fundamental role in the formation of postwar youth subcultures (Clarke et al., 2003: 52). In his seminal work on postwar English youth subcultures, Hebdige (2002) interpreted subculture as a form of resistance wherein contradictions and oppositions to dominant ideology are expressed indirectly through style. In this regard, youth subcultures can be understood as engaging in a process of "identity work." Teddy Boys, Mods, Punks, and Skinheads were seen as historically specific reactions by working-class youth against both traditional working-class values and the dominant bourgeois social structures that sought to control them (Willis, 1993: 375; Hebdige, 2002). In his later works (Hebdige, 1982/1983), Hebdige argued that subcultural styles were not merely acts of rejection or symbolic opposition but reflections of independence, otherness, anonymity, and disobedience. He further suggested that style practices served as forms of empowerment, expressing the reality of powerlessness among subcultural members.

One defining feature of the post-WWII period was the interaction between media and clothing styles. During this time, fashion trends were influenced by street subcultures and disseminated via media channels. For instance, many Hollywood films of the 1950s presented a new identity based on the myth of working-class rebellion, with actors often dressed in jeans, black leather jackets, and t-shirts. Such styles were perceived by audiences as expressions of defiance, particularly among working-class young men, reflecting their identity crises. Notably, the black leather jacket became a potent symbol of rebellion when worn by men in the 20th century. Black, as a color, was favored by political, social, and artistic rebels alike (Crane, 2000: 151). Subcultures are closely interconnected, and new styles often emerge through complex, multilayered borrowings from earlier styles. The same look (jeans, leather jackets, and t-shirts) was later adopted by rock stars, whose rebellious public image was strongly associated with these outfits. In this sense, specific clothing items have come to function as symbolic challenges to mainstream culture.

The zoot suit, worn by African Americans and Hispanics in the 1930s and 1940s, and the zazou outfit, worn by French youth during World War II, are also cited as examples of clothing carrying strong social and political connotations. Wearing a zoot suit represented an act of resistance against a war many Black and Hispanic individuals refused to support, while the zazou style signified French youth's defiance of German occupation. Thus, such clothing represented and celebrated racial, spatial, gender, class, and generational identities. The punk subculture, emerging in the 1970s in the United States and the United Kingdom, expressed youthful dissatisfaction with the socio-political and cultural systems through anarchic and nihilistic themes. Punk centered on rebellion against authority, individual freedom, and dissent. Music was central to this movement, with bands like The Clash, Sex Pistols, and The Damned representing punk music with their fast-paced and energetic styles. Punk style was characterized by ripped clothing, leather jackets, spiked accessories, and striking hairstyles like the mohawk. Moreover, the punk subculture extended beyond music and fashion to embrace "DIY" (Do-It-Yourself), promoting independence and anti-capitalist values (Crane, 2000). By the late 1980s, rave culture emerged, associated with a distinctive style characterized by bold, playful, bright, and unconventional outfits and accessories. Rave culture was interpreted as a reaction to the post-Thatcher era in the United Kingdom, rejecting the austerity, conservatism, and individualism promoted by the Thatcher government, and instead embracing utopian community, creativity, and freedom. Thus, the playful and rebellious elements of rave fashion reflected a disillusioned youth's desire for temporary liberation and collective joy (Redhead, 1993). The study of youth subcultures' clothing styles thus offers insights into the shifts in attitudes and behaviors that shaped particular historical periods. Youth subcultures were so dynamic and influential in creating cultural forms that they are often seen as emblematic of specific eras and generations (Bischoff, cited in Crane 2000; McRobbie, 1999: 263).

One important topic of discussion during this period concerned how youth sub-cultures used clothing to construct styles. Four categories were identified: (1) the adoption of material culture elements and media images suitable to everyday life conditions, (2) the personalization of these elements to form distinct identities, (3) the reflection of aesthetic expression through these practices, and (4) bricolage[1], in which various elements are combined to create meaningful costumes (Crane, 2000: 156–157). Hebdige (2002: 103) emphasized the relevance of the concept of bricolage to explain the construction of subcultural styles. Style was defined not simply by objects but through the process of stylization: the harmonious and distinct arrangement of objects, actions, and viewpoints to form a unique existence and a structured group identity (Clarke et al., 2003: 54).

Researchers on subcultures often framed their work within the contexts of working-class culture, dominant culture, and mass culture. The CCCS argued that subcultures emerged as expressions and resolutions of class crises (Gelder, 1997: 83–88). Particularly, postwar working-class male youth exhibited many elements that deviated from their parents' class culture, driven by a desire for change and a rejection of the status quo (Jenks, 2005: 122). However, CCCS's depiction of subcultures as tightly cohesive and solidaristic groups has been criticized. Clarke et al. (2003: 14) emphasized that subcultures could have both tight and loose structures and that some subcultures existed only loosely within the mainstream culture, lacking distinct worlds of their own. This evaluation suggested that traditional conceptions of subcultures overlooked the transient and sometimes arbitrary forms of socialization characterizing many youth groups. Moreover, the "subculture" concept was critiqued for imposing rigid social distinctions that were difficult to verify in real life. There is little evidence that youth groups were as coherent or stable as the subculture concept implies. Instead, so-called youth subcultures often appeared as examples of the fluid and shifting cultural affiliations typical of modern consumer societies (Bennett, 1999: 603–605). Similarly, Thornton (2003: 184) criticized CCCS's view of subcultures as "transparent niches within an opaque world," emphasizing that subcultures are far more complex, layered, and difficult to interpret. She also highlighted the increasing role of the media in diluting the authenticity of subcultures and the blurring boundary between subcultures and mainstream culture. These criticisms include the argument that neither Hebdige nor CCCS researchers fully recognized the essential relationship between consumption and subcultures, failing to anticipate the capitalist system's tendency to reduce class-based positions and promote identity construction through consumption instead (Willis, 1993: 369).

FROM SUBCULTURES TO INTERNET-CURATED AESTHETICS: THE TRANSFORMATION OF IDENTITY AND VALUES

In today's fragmented and fluid societies, understanding cultural expressions has become increasingly complex, particularly because identical clothing items can carry different meanings across diverse social groups. In other words, compared to other modes of expression, clothing is characterized by its ambiguity, variability, and sensitivity to context. This complexity is amplified by the different meanings individuals and groups assign to their own clothing codes. While individuals may easily decode the dress codes of groups they belong to, they might remain unaware of the codes employed by others. Thus, the meaning of a particular style or clothing combination is shaped by temporary and abstract factors such as the wearer's identity, the setting, the conditions, and even the mood (Davis, 1992: 8). In this sense, the analysis of clothing provides valuable insights into understanding the cultures of society, their unique codes, and the expressions of individual identities.

The 1980s witnessed an explosion fueled by mass media, leading to the shaping and development of youth styles and fashions within the media landscape (McRobbie, 1999). Thornton (2003: 30) emphasized the necessity of systematically examining media consumption to understand youth cultures and their differences. Consequently, it has been argued that youth culture has evolved into an industry in itself, where youth is no longer associated with rebellion or resistance but instead has been transformed into a marketing tool crafted by advertisers. This shift is explained by the increasing commodification of youth styles within consumer culture (Redhead, 1993). Compared to earlier periods, contemporary subcultural styles are seen to carry far fewer social and political connotations, as clothing styles are rapidly adopted and marketed to a mass consumer culture via the media (Crane, 2000: 152). In other words, subcultural dress no longer holds the ideological weight it once did, having instead become increasingly commercialized. McRobbie (1999: 235) noted that subcultural fashion has lost its associations with class struggle and resistance, becoming more aligned with commerce and consumption. The popularization and commercialization of subcultural styles for mass markets has, she argued, stripped subcultures of their oppositional power and integrated them into mainstream society.

Muggleton (2002) discussed the persistence and significance of subcultural formations among postmodern youth. He adopted a neo-Weberian view and thought that the subjective meanings, values and motives behind the styles of subcultures should be uncovered. Therefore, he approached the concept of subculture as a lifestyle and as an expression of cultural values. He criticized the work of the Center for Contemporary Cultural Studies for exaggerating class-based contradictions, and political and ideological meanings of style. The failure to examine a person's subjective meanings and daily experiences as a member of any subculture also became a criticism. That is, according to him, subcultural styles -shaped by patterns of consumption- can be understood as an effect of postmodern individualism which is an expression of fluidity, heterogeneity and pluralism. For this reason, he found it problematic that the CCCS reified the concept of subculture and approached it as something material. In addition to this, he claimed that style today is valued primarily for its appearance rather than any deeper meaning; in fact, appearance itself has become the meaning. In other words, according to postmodern theory, subcultural styles cannot be a response to social contradictions. Therefore, subcultural style involves the arbitrary reinterpretation of visual elements based solely on aesthetics. At that point, there is no need for subcultural identities, authenticity or ideological commitments (Muggleton, 2002: 44-47). It may be that the idea of subculture is losing its relevance in postmodern times, as the fragmentation of mass society means there is no unified dominant culture left for subcultures to resist or oppose (Evans as cited in Muggleton, 2002: 48). Giolo and Berghman (2023) also stated that internet aesthetics both reflect and challenge key aspects of postmodernity. They asserted that people use these aesthetics as flexible tools to build personal and recognizable identities in an unstable and constantly shifting world. As cultural change accelerates and traditional social structures fade, individuals turn to digital platforms to construct a sense of inner self. By organizing their daily experiences and understanding of the world into consistent, theme-based frameworks, they think that they attempt to form a clearer and more stable image of who they are.

At this point, styles that once carried strong social and political messages, representing resistance, are increasingly fading. In their place, within the rapidly changing digital era, clothing styles are being shaped by internet-driven, more temporary and superficial forms. In this regard, "internet aesthetics" attempt to fill the gap left by subcultures, offering not political resistance but rather visual appeal, individual expression, and lifestyle orientation. Unlike subcultures, internet aesthetics allow individuals to voice themselves without the requirement of collective participation. Thus, internet aesthetics emerge as new sources of identity, reflecting new forms of difference in new temporal and spatial contexts.

Contemporary theories suggest that people today operate within more flexible and less restrictive social structures than in the past. Modern societies are described as "post-industrial," while their cultures are labeled as "postmodern." This transition signals a shift in the relationships between elements of the social structure as well as a transformation in the nature and functions of culture. Such a shift has expanded individuals' opportunities for self-expression. Accordingly, the nature of fashion and people's responses to fashion have also changed. Whereas 19th-century fashion largely consisted of a broadly accepted standard of proper appearance, contemporary fashion, in line with the fragmented and fluid nature of post-industrial societies, has become increasingly ambiguous and diverse. The broad range of fashion choices today creates a complexity that extends to how individuals perceive their social interactions (Crane, 2000). In the postmodern era, clear boundaries between cultural and aesthetic codes have largely disappeared. The mainstream quickly absorbs subcultural elements, reshapes them, and reintroduces them to the mass market. Individuals no longer adhere rigidly to a subculture but rather navigate among different aesthetics and identities. As a result, subcultures today occupy a less oppositional stance and have largely lost their political and ideological foundations. In other words, the evolution of consumption dynamics into lifestyle-centered and individuality-focused structures, coupled with media and marketing mechanisms, has led to the disappearance of subcultural styles into the mainstream, and with them, their sociopolitical messages have gradually faded.

In the postmodern era, social class no longer exerts the same influence over individuals' identities and self-images. Today, the consumption of cultural products has become increasingly important in personal identity formation. Individuals observe social dress norms through television, the internet, magazines, films, and street culture, shaping their fashion understanding accordingly. The greater visibility of a fashion trend determines collective behavior. However, fast fashion and the rapid spread of new styles tend to homogenize consumer tastes. Despite the presence of multiple producers and retailers, styles produced and marketed by the fashion industry tend to be highly similar. Once a style is accepted as fashionable, the industry replicates it (Kawamura, 2016). In other words, the uniformity of looks in an era of mass consumption finds an expression in internet aesthetics, where so-called curated individuality often uncover standardized trends and algorithm-driven visual repetition.

In postmodern societies, consumption is understood as a role-playing process in which individuals continually seek to reflect changing identities. Youth cultures represent the prototypical postmodern consumers (Kawamura, 2016). The diversity of youth cultures and the fluidity of identity formation have made different lifestyles more visible in media and marketing spheres. The proliferation of media channels has accentuated the differences and diversities among lifestyles in fragmented and fluid societies, a dynamic increasingly exploited by advertisers and marketers (Turow, 1997: 193). As a result, an "over-segmentation" has emerged, where each lifestyle exists within its small, isolated domain. This segmentation affects individuals' consumption habits, identities, and roles. Turow describes lifestyles as "image tribes" composed of individuals sharing particular interests and allegiances but rarely overlapping. Similarly, Holt (1997) noted the increasing variety of lifestyles accessible to individuals in modern societies. Thus, individual choices, freed from tradition, allow people to build their own self-identities (Giddens, 1991). In parallel, internet aesthetics enable individuals to construct their identities on digital platforms by embracing the diversity of lifestyles offered by modern societies. Social media users express both their social identities and cultural affiliations through participation in these digital "image tribes." From the perspective of clothing styles, this shift suggests that compared to previous eras (where belonging to a social class was central) participating in a lifestyle today involves a greater degree of individual agency. People make continuous choices about the consumer goods and activities that reflect the identities or images they wish to project. Thus, the consumption of cultural products like fashionable clothing has become increasingly important in the construction of individual identity.

Bocock (1993: 81) emphasized that style, pleasure, excitement, escape from monotony, and appearing attractive to oneself and others have become central concerns of modern life. In the postmodern era, consumption patterns are shaped not by the imitation of the lifestyles and habits of "higher" social groups but rather by these concerns. Postmodern consumers are envisioned as sophisticated individuals capable of selecting among alternatives, identifying with selected "things," and bringing nuanced interpretations to these choices (Partington, 1996: 212). Therefore, consumption is viewed as a method through which individuals express constantly shifting understandings of identity. Consumers use fashion to articulate personal identity, define and differentiate social group boundaries, construct life narratives, interpret their social relationships, and make sense of their ties to consumer culture. Individuals create various narratives to link their personal identities to the social identities derived from membership in groups characterized by similar dress (Crane, 2000: 12–14; Thompson & Haytko, 1997: 16). Similarly, internet aesthetics encourage individuals to form groups based on shared clothing styles and lifestyles, enabling them to reinforce social identities and a sense of belonging through digital narratives.

It is said that users tend to perceive internet aesthetics less as rigid categories and more as experiential "vibes" that state a certain mood, atmosphere, or imagined scenario. Rather than relying on consistent symbolic meanings or shared values, these aesthetics are described by users as personal toolkits that reflect shifting moods, seasonal feelings, or coherent self-images. As phenomenological interviews in the study reveal, participants often referred to their preferred aesthetics as "just a vibe" or a "sensory package" that aligns with specific times, emotions, or fantasies—such as imagining oneself in a Victorian study room or a sunlit Italian villa. In other words, users of internet aesthetics reconstruct their identities by situating themselves in imagined times, settings, or emotional states, using cultural objects as tools for this transformation. Internet aesthetics served as a means of self-actualization for participants, enabling them to express aspects of what they perceived as their "authentic selves." Interviewees frequently linked these aesthetics to specific routines or moments in daily life, using them to reinterpret ordinary experiences through a more romanticized or idealized lens. This process reflects a form of escapism, where aesthetic frameworks offer a temporary retreat from the present by allowing individuals to inhabit alternative identities, time periods, or emotional states shaped by the aesthetic's narrative world. (Giolo & Berghman, 2023).

In this era, consumers are no longer seen as "cultural dependents" or "fashion victims" blindly imitating trendsetters. Instead, they are viewed as individuals selecting styles that reflect their personal identities and lifestyles. Fashion now aims to target particular groups and lifestyles with specific products rather than promoting universal cultural ideals. Fashion has shifted from a necessity to a matter of choice. Consumers are therefore expected to create their "personal" looks from among a wide array of options. Clothing styles, constructed by assembling materials from various sources, thus acquire different meanings for different social groups. Just like in certain genres of popular music and literature, clothing styles may carry significant meaning within the groups where they originate but may remain meaningless to outsiders (Crane, 2000: 15–19). The media has played a critical role in raising awareness of and rapidly disseminating these new styles. In this sense, internet aesthetics construct a sense of self and involve negotiating symbols. What stands out within internet aesthetics is the diversity of products, activities, interests, and even attitudes associated with particular aesthetic labels. For instance, cottagecore became the most popular trend in interior design in 2021 and was the subject of best-selling books, while dark academia led to renewed interest in learning Latin and Greek, the romanticization of museums, libraries, and studying, and a revived appreciation for literary classics such as Keats. However, inconsistency among internet aesthetics has become a major point of criticism. These aesthetics often lack a clear system of meaning or structure; each aesthetic draws from a wide range of cultural objects but categorizes them in intuitive or subjective ways rather than forming coherent narratives. The fundamental critique of internet aesthetics lies in their lack of clear rationale for their existence or logic of construction (Giolo & Berghman, 2023). In this regard, internet aesthetics differ sharply from subcultures. While subcultures were defined by collective structures and sociopolitical messages, internet aesthetics are characterized by individualism, ephemerality, and a focus on visual appeal. Lacking coherent structures and deep sociopolitical messages, internet aesthetics are shaped by personal preferences and are easily commercialized and absorbed into popular culture. Unlike subcultures, internet aesthetics are more fluid, transient and superficial, but de-politicized so devoid of any underlying messages.

CONCLUSION

Subcultures are authentic expressions of identity rooted in lived experience and shared values, whereas internet aesthetics are inauthentic, shaped more by surface-level trends than deep cultural meaning. Moreover, internet aesthetics are inauthentic because while individuals aim to bring meaning and structure to their personal experiences by reframing them, they do so using pre-existing, widely shared labels (Giolo & Berghman, 2023). Subcultures emerged as alternative movements that challenged dominant norms, while internet aesthetics tend to align with mainstream tastes, often spreading widely without disrupting the status quo. Subcultures typically formed within minority groups, resisting the dominant culture. They embraced heterogeneity, fostering diversity and difference. In contrast, internet aesthetics often lead to homogeneity, where similar visual codes and symbols are repeated across platforms, creating a sense of sameness rather than distinction.

Subcultural groups were generally open-minded, encouraging exploration, resistance, and self-expression. On the other hand, many internet aesthetics reinforce narrow-minded ideals, particularly in terms of beauty and lifestyle, shaped by algorithms and social validation metrics. In terms of spread and transformation, subcultures relied on diffusion and gradual change, developing through face-to-face interactions and shared cultural practices. Internet aesthetics, by contrast, depend on cohesion and rapid change, thriving on viral circulation and fast-paced trend cycles that often lack a stable ideological foundation. Finally, while subcultures prioritized attitude, a symbolic resistance communicated through style, aesthetics focus more on appearance, often driven by copying and visual repetition rather than innovation. They tend to emphasize superficial adoption of trends over the deeper adaptation found in subcultural practices.

Internet aesthetics involve minimal critical discourse in their formation. While they assemble songs, visuals, films, and books under specific labels, there is little explanation as to why these items are grouped together, and such classifications rarely spark discussion. As a result, internet aesthetics tend to reflect a relatively passive and uncritical engagement with the cultural elements they bring together. Unlike subcultures, which often involve active meaning-making, ideological discourse, and shared narratives that justify the inclusion of specific symbols or styles, Internet aesthetics lack such discursive depth. This uncritical engagement suggests that Internet aesthetics either do not possess a shared or coherent meaning, or that meaning is shaped in a highly subjective way by individuals, making explanation unnecessary. In the latter case, the widespread circulation of replicated elements from popular culture creates a sense of "natural" connection between certain objects and specific aesthetics, as if their association were self-evident (Giolo & Berghman, 2023).

This lack of critical engagement contributes to the depoliticization of youth, suggesting that in an era where digital interaction and virtual identity have become central, grassroots movements may increasingly diminish in visibility and impact. Furthermore, although these aesthetics are widely accessible and sharable, unlike subcultures, there appears to be little desire among users to connect with other like-minded people or form communities based on shared aesthetics. In digital reality, people build and express their identities by collecting and arranging cultural references—such as images, music, fashion, or films—much like how one would curate a Pinterest board (Giolo & Berghman, 2023).

Instead of constructing identity from deep-rooted or fixed social positions, individuals now piece together bits of popular culture to reflect how they see themselves or how they want to be seen. Labels like cottagecore help give a sense of unity or meaning to these personalized collections, tying everything together under a recognizable aesthetic. On the other hand, subcultures often emerge as creative and oppositional responses to dominant culture. They modify, reclaim, or even DIY-produce their own styles, music, or spaces, think of punks ripping and re-sewing their clothes, or hip-hop artists creating new musical forms and slang. In contrast, Internet aesthetics mostly rely on pre-existing, mass produced cultural objects and reassemble them in visually or emotionally cohesive ways. Users don't necessarily alter these materials; they curate and recombine them to express mood, identity, or fantasy. Therefore, they do not offer any criticism or resistance.

Internet aesthetics do not state any criticism because in the society of positivity, the general attitude of society is determined by likes and dislikes of individuals. It functions as a marketplace where privacy is displayed, traded, and consumed. In a society of positivity, where existence requires visibility, all things are reduced to commodities and stripped of their cultural or intrinsic value in favor of exhibition. Mere existence no longer holds meaning on its own. Objects and individuals gain worth only through being seen. Everything is laid bare, exposed, and stripped of secrecy. Exhibition value now dominates, relying primarily on visual appeal and aesthetic pleasure. Under this pressure to constantly display oneself, authentic selfhood becomes impossible. Transparency, therefore, goes hand in hand with a loss of meaning. The digital public sphere offers only agreeable, filtered versions of the world, confronting individuals solely with themselves or those like them. There is no longer any negativity, no otherness, that might enable real change or transformation (Han, 2024). This is highly relevant when discussing the opposition between subcultures and Internet aesthetics. Subcultures often emerged from shared experiences of marginality, resistance, and social critique. They challenged the dominant order and offered alternative, often uncomfortable, expressions of identity. Subcultural practices were rooted in cultural depth, through symbols, rituals, and lived acts, and they did not aim to be pleasant or easily consumed. In contrast, internet aesthetics reflect the very dynamics Han critiques. They function within a hyper-visual culture driven by exhibition value, where identity becomes a curated surface rather than a deeply grounded narrative. Instead of resisting the mainstream, many aesthetics gain visibility and popularity precisely because they are pleasing, non-disruptive, and algorithmically amplified. Rather than fostering community, difference, or opposition, these aesthetics often lead users to encounter only idealized, aestheticized versions of themselves and the world, resulting in a meaningless cultural experience, devoid of tension, secrecy, or transformation. As Han might argue, the self becomes a display, and culture becomes a loop of self-confirmation, not self-construction.

In light of this analysis, it becomes evident that internet aesthetics, unlike subcultures, lack the critical depth, oppositional force, and communal grounding that once allowed styles to act as tools of resistance. Their inauthenticity does not merely lie in their reliance on pre-produced cultural fragments, but in the absence of ideological confrontation, shared struggle, or tension. What we witness instead is a generation increasingly immersed in aestheticized self-presentation, where meaning is determined by the mood, and style no longer encodes resistance but reproduces visibility. In this culture governed by likes and dislikes, political engagement gives way to algorithmic affirmation. What is pleasing circulates, while what is challenging disappears. This shift, as Han suggests, turns identity into a transparent display, stripping it of interiority. As the culture of transparency deepens, the risk is not just a loss of cultural authenticity, but the erosion of political subjectivity itself.

AI DISCLOSURE STATEMENT

Artificial intelligence-based tools were utilized to proofread the language used in this study.

REFERENCES

Arslan, A. C. (2025). *Tekno-Politika Çağı: Devlet Şirket İlişkilerinin Teorik Analizi ve Güvenliğin İnşası*. Yetkin Yayınları.

Bennett, A. (1999). Subcultures or Neo-tribes? Rethinking the Relationship Between Youth, Style and Musical Taste. *Sociology*, *33*(3), 599–617.

Bocock, R. (1993). *Consumption*. Routledge. DOI: 10.4324/9780203313114

Clarke, G. (1997). Defending Ski-Jumpers: A Critique of Theories of Youth Subcultures. K. Gelder & Sarah Thornton (eds.), *The Subcultures Reader* (s. 175-180). Routledge.

Clarke, G., Hall, S., Jefferson, T., & Roberts, B. (2003). Subcultures, Cultures and Class: A Theoretical Overview. S. Hall & T. Jefferson (eds.), *Resistance through Rituals: Youth Subcultures in Postwar Britain* (s. 9-74). Routledge.

Crane, D. (2000). *Fashion and Its Social Agendas: Class, Gender, and Identity in Clothing*. University of Chicago Press. DOI: 10.7208/chicago/9780226924830.001.0001

Davis, F. (1992). *Fashion, Culture, and Identity*. University of Chicago Press. DOI: 10.7208/chicago/9780226167954.001.0001

Ewen, E. (1985). *Immigrant Women in the Land of Dollars: Life and Culture on the Lower East Side, 1890-1925*. Monthly Review Press.

Gelder, K. (1997). Introduction to Part Seven. K. Gelder & Sarah Thornton (eds.), *The Subcultures Reader* (s. 373-378). Routledge.

Gelder, K. (1997). Introduction to Part Two. K. Gelder & Sarah Thornton (eds.), *The Subcultures Reader* (s. 83-89). Routledge.

Giddens, A. (1991). *Modernity and Self Identity*. Polity Press.

Giolo, G., & Berghman, M. (2023). The Aesthetics of the Self: The Meaning-Making of Internet Aesthetics. *First Monday*, *28*(3). Advance online publication. DOI: 10.5210/fm.v28i3.12723

Han, B. C. (2024). *Şeffaflık Toplumu*. Metis Yayınları.

Hebdige, D. (2002). *Hiding in the Light*. Routledge.

Hebdige, D. (2002). *Subculture: The Meaning of Style*. Routledge.

Holt, D. (1997). Poststructuralist Lifestyle Analysis: Conceptualizing the Social Patterning of Consumption in Postmodernity. *The Journal of Consumer Research, 23*(4), 326–350. DOI: 10.1086/209487

Jenks, C. (2005). Subculture: The Fragmentation of the Social. *Sage (Atlanta, Ga.).*

Kawamura, Y. (2016). *Moda-loji: Moda Çalışmalarına Giriş*. (Ş. Özüdoğru, Çev.). Ayrıntı.

Laver, J. (1968). *Dandies*. Weidenfield and Nicolson.

Manovich, L. (2020). *Cultural Analytics*. The MIT Press. DOI: 10.7551/mitpress/11214.001.0001

McRobbie, A. (1999). *Postmodernizm ve Popüler Kültür. (A. Özdek, Çev.).* Sarmal Yayınevi.

Muggleton, D. (2002). *Inside Subculture: The Postmodern Meaning of Style*. Oxford.

Partington, A. (1996). Perfume: Pleasure, Packaging and Postmodernity. In Kirkham, P. (Ed.), *The Gendered Object* (pp. 204–218). Manchester University Press.

Pettman, D. (2019). *Infinite Distraction*. Polity Press.

Redhead, S. (1993). *Rave Off: Politics and Deviance in Contemporary Youth Culture*. Avebury.

Simmel, G. (1957). Fashion. *American Journal of Sociology, 62*(6), 541–558. DOI: 10.1086/222102

Thompson, C. J., & Haytko, D. L. (1997). Speaking of Fashion: Consumers' Uses of Fashion Discourses and the Appropriation of Countervailing Cultural Meanings. *The Journal of Consumer Research, 24*(1), 15–42. DOI: 10.1086/209491

Thornton, S. (1997). General Introduction. K. Gelder & Sarah Thornton (eds.), *The Subcultures Reader* (s. 1-7). Routledge.

Thornton, S. (2003). *Club Cultures*. Polity Press.

Turow, J. (1997). *Breaking Up America: Advertisers and the New Media World*. University of Chicago Press. DOI: 10.7208/chicago/9780226817514.001.0001

Willis, S. (1993). Hardcore: Subculture American Style. *Critical Inquiry, 19*(2), 365–383. DOI: 10.1086/448678

ENDNOTE

1 Bricolage, in the context of clothing and fashion, refers to the process by which an individual or group combines disparate and often seemingly incompatible clothing, accessories, or symbols to create a new and creative style. For example, in punk culture, safety pins have become a fashion accessory, and ordinary objects have been used as symbolic elements of resistance.

Chapter 10

Reclaiming Techno-Politics:
From Structural Insight to Normative Futures

Murat Tınas
https://orcid.org/0000-0001-5844-0808
Turkish National Police Academy, Turkey

Alp Cenk Arslan
https://orcid.org/0000-0002-5526-2089
Turkish National Police Academy, Turkey

ABSTRACT

This volume rethinks techno-politics by examining how digital technologies reshape authority, security, identity, and governance. Challenging the notion of technology as neutral, it shows how systems like AI, OSINT, and algorithmic governance act as political agents embedded in legal, infrastructural, and ideological frameworks. Through theoretical insights and empirical cases, the chapters explore digital sovereignty, anticipatory security, epistemic inequality, and techno-geopolitical fragmentation. The volume argues that technologies not only reflect political will but actively produce new regimes of power and legitimacy. The concluding chapter offers a forward-looking roadmap, emphasizing inclusive, ethical, and participatory models of digital governance. It proposes a human-centered approach to reclaim techno-politics from extractive and opaque systems, envisioning just and accountable digital futures. By linking structural analysis with normative inquiry, the book contributes to both critical theory and practical strategies for navigating the digital political condition.

DOI: 10.4018/979-8-3373-2459-3.ch010

INTRODUCTION

Technology is now deeply embedded in the fabric of political life, making techno-politics a central, rather than peripheral, concern. It has become a central analytical lens through which sovereignty, governance, and power must be re-examined. This volume, *Rethinking Techno-Politics in the Digital Age: Global Technology Relations and Security*, brings together a diverse set of theoretical and empirical investigations that collectively reframe how technology and politics interpenetrate in today's digital environments. In other words, technologies are not neutral tools awaiting policy inputs, but rather dynamic and political agents that shape and also are shaped by power relations, legal regimes, security paradigms, and cultural imaginaries (Winner, 1980; Bijker, Hughes, & Pinch, 2012; Feenberg, 2017).

This concluding chapter engages the core premise of the volume: the transformation of political authority, legitimacy, and agency under the conditions of digitalization. The convergence of technological innovation with state power, regulatory capacity, and normative orders has produced a distinct political landscape, in which the boundaries between governance and computation, infrastructure and ideology, risk and resilience have become increasingly blurred. As demonstrated across the book, techno-politics no longer constitutes a specialized subdomain of inquiry, but rather defines a cross-cutting condition shaping security practices, legal architectures, and societal imaginaries on a global scale.

The structure of this chapter reflects both the thematic unity and the intellectual diversity of the contributions. It begins with a conceptual reconsideration of techno-politics, then advances through five cross-cutting domains: sovereignty and algorithmic governance; evolving security paradigms; digital inequalities and identity formations; geopolitical regulatory competition; and strategic foresight for researchers and decision-makers. The final section offers a reflective assessment on the normative futures of techno-politics, emphasizing the ethical, inclusive, and democratic imperatives of digital transformation.

Rather than offering a simple synthesis, this chapter aims to construct a critical trajectory that links structural insights to normative considerations and future-oriented strategies. In doing so, it situates the volume not only as a response to current transformations, but as a contribution to shaping the conceptual and practical contours of the digital political age.

TECHNO-POLITICS REVISITED: A CONCEPTUAL RETURN

The emergence of techno-politics as an analytical lens reflects a broader epistemological shift in the study of politics and technology. Rather than viewing technological systems as neutral instruments, based on the contributions in this volume, their political agency role should also be elaborated. In other words, how technological systems mediate, reconfigure, and co-constitute relations of power, legitimacy, and governance is very substantial in explaining and understanding today's context (Winner, 1980; Feenberg, 2017). At stake is not merely the application of technology within existing political structures, but the transformation of those structures through techno-material assemblages, algorithmic infrastructures, and data-driven rationalities (Bijker, Hughes, & Pinch, 2012).

The opening chapter of the volume introduces a foundational conceptual distinction between *techne* and *poiesis*. These terms trace back to classical philosophy yet acquire renewed relevance in the digital age (Heidegger, 1977). While *techne* denotes a mode of instrumental action and technical production, *poiesis* evokes the act of bringing-forth, a creative unfolding that is at once ontological and political. Framing techno-politics through this duality enables a richer understanding of technology not simply as an extension of human will but as a structuring force that shapes the possibilities of political imagination and collective life (Jasanoff & Kim, 2015).

Subsequent theoretical contributions expand upon this framing by engaging with questions of value displacement in artificial intelligence policy, hybrid models of digital sovereignty, and the juridical implications of algorithmic governance (Yeung, 2017; DeNardis, 2020). These chapters illustrate how contemporary techno-political formations are characterized by both continuity and rupture. In other words, while they extend historical techniques of rule such as classification, surveillance, and control, they also introduce new modalities of abstraction, automation, and scale. The result is a techno-political condition in which power operates not solely through laws and institutions, but through protocols, code, and infrastructural logic.

The volume thus advances a critical departure from deterministic accounts of technology, which posit innovation as an exogenous driver of change, and from narrowly institutionalist perspectives, which treat technology as an external challenge to be regulated. Instead, the chapters collected here advocate for an immanent critique that situates technological systems within the logics of political economy, security, legal normativity, and socio-technical imaginaries.

Revisiting techno-politics through this expanded conceptual lens enables a more precise articulation of its stakes. The key concern is no longer whether technologies are political, but how their embeddedness in everyday governance practices renders them central to the reproduction and transformation of authority and legitimacy (Winner, 1980). In this regard, techno-politics emerges not as a bounded topic, but as a constitutive dimension of twenty-first-century political life. By foregrounding this theoretical groundwork, the volume positions itself to engage the techno-political condition not only as an empirical reality but as a normative terrain which demands new frameworks for accountability, inclusion, and ethical governance (Jasanoff & Kim, 2015).

DIGITAL SOVEREIGNTY, ALGORITHMIC GOVERNANCE, AND THE REORDERING OF POWER

The digital age has destabilized traditional notions of political authority, raising fundamental questions about how sovereignty is exercised and contested across interconnected and data-saturated environments (DeNardis, 2020). A recurring phenomenon across the chapters of this volume is the growing salience of digital sovereignty. That is a concept that captures the aspiration of states, institutions, and communities to retain normative, operational, and infrastructural control over their digital ecosystems (Pohle & Thiel, 2020). In doing so, as done throughout the volume, there is a further need to scrutinize the intersection of sovereignty with emerging technologies and the infrastructures of algorithmic governance.

Digital sovereignty no longer pertains solely to jurisdictional boundaries or territorial data storage. Instead, it encompasses broader questions about epistemic control, infrastructural autonomy, and the ability to set standards for technological development. This is especially evident in contributions examining hybrid regulatory models, where states attempt to balance global interoperability with the protection of national or regional values, such as privacy, security, and democratic accountability. Discussions in certain chapters underscore the tension between supranational governance mechanisms and local regulatory traditions, suggesting that the pursuit of sovereignty in the digital realm frequently results in fragmented and hybrid forms of rule.

At the core of these debates lies the proliferation of algorithmic governance, defined as the increasing use of data-driven systems to monitor, assess, and intervene in social and political life (Yeung, 2017). These systems represent a shift from juridical to computational rationalities. Governance is no longer exclusively a matter of institutional deliberation or legal procedure; it is also embedded in code, trained on datasets, and operationalized through opaque machine learning models. This techno-political shift reorders traditional hierarchies of authority, allowing non-human agents to shape outcomes in law enforcement, welfare distribution, migration control, and public administration.

Several chapters highlight the dual nature of algorithmic governance. On the one hand, algorithmic systems promise efficiency, objectivity, and scalability in managing complex problems such as crime prediction, pandemic response, and infrastructure resilience. On the other hand, they risk entrenching bias, reducing transparency, and eroding democratic oversight. Particularly in policing and border control, algorithms act not merely as tools but as epistemological filters, pre-structuring the realm of action by producing categories of suspicion, deviance, or risk.

The reordering of power under conditions of digital governance thus operates on multiple levels. First, it alters the relationship between states and citizens, as the logic of surveillance and classification becomes infrastructural. Second, it redistributes power among state institutions, private technology firms, and transnational platforms. In several cases discussed throughout the volume, private actors especially platform companies and AI vendors have acquired quasi-sovereign capabilities, including the ability to define identity standards, regulate access, and determine the flow of information across borders.

This reconfiguration is not only vertical between state and citizen or horizontal between public and private sectors, but also geopolitical. In this context, the quest for digital sovereignty has become a site of international contestation (Carr, 2016). Competing regulatory regimes, divergent standards for AI ethics, and tensions over supply chain dependencies all point to a growing fragmentation in the global digital order (DeNardis, 2020). Rather than converging around shared norms, the current trajectory suggests an emergent multipolarity in techno-governance, marked by localized values, strategic decoupling, and competing technological spheres of influence (Pohle & Thiel, 2020).

While many of the chapters express cautious optimism regarding the potential of regulation and oversight, there is broad agreement that existing governance mechanisms are insufficiently equipped to manage the scale, opacity, and velocity of algorithmic systems. The governance of algorithms demands new institutional imaginaries that are participatory, transparent, and capable of addressing asymmetries of information and power. Equally important is the recognition that digital sovereignty must extend beyond state interests to include community-level agency, epistemic justice, and infrastructural inclusivity.

This study reveals that digital sovereignty and algorithmic governance are not discrete policy domains but mutually constitutive dynamics that reshape the political field. In making this visible, the chapters contribute to a deeper understanding of how authority is exercised, contested, and transformed in digitally mediated environments. This insight provides a crucial foundation for subsequent reflections on security, identity, and geopolitics in the digital age.

SHIFTING SECURITY PARADIGMS: FROM ANTICIPATION TO CONTROL

Contemporary security paradigms have undergone a profound transformation in response to the digitization of risk, threat perception, and infrastructural vulnerability (Amoore, 2020). Rather than addressing violence or insecurity as discrete, observable phenomena, digital security practices increasingly operate through anticipatory logic like projecting future risks, modeling potential disruptions, and acting upon probabilities rather than certainties.

Predictive technologies, such as risk scoring engines, surveillance algorithms, and real-time data analytics, have redefined the temporality of security. In this framework, security becomes a matter of preemption which means identifying threats before they materialize and intervening before harm occurs. This orientation alters the nature of both governance and accountability. In other words, risk is no longer tied to past behavior or legal thresholds but to algorithmically inferred potentialities. As such, the line between prevention and control is increasingly blurred (Yeung, 2017; Amoore, 2020).

The protection of critical digital infrastructure is also becoming very important. As information systems become foundational to the operation of energy grids, water supply networks, and financial markets, new forms of vulnerability emerge. Cyberattacks targeting infrastructure no longer merely disrupt services; they pose existential threats to state functionality and societal cohesion. The digitalization of essential services introduces cascading risks that are increasingly difficult to localize or contain, as highlighted by broader discussions on the vulnerabilities of critical infrastructure.

The security paradigm articulated across this volume is therefore characterized by several converging trends: the delegation of anticipatory reasoning to algorithmic systems, the normalization of intrusive surveillance mechanisms, and the reconceptualization of infrastructure as both an asset and a battlefield. These trends produce a new form of a regime of security, in which the management of uncertainty becomes a technical rather than a political process. Such a regime is not without consequence. As risk models gain authority, the space for contesting their assumptions narrows. As security becomes more data-driven, the ethical and political stakes surrounding false positives, discriminatory impact, and overreach intensify. The digital turn in security governance thus necessitates not only technical safeguards but also critical interrogation of the epistemologies underpinning these systems.

INEQUALITY, IDENTITY, AND REPRESENTATION IN THE DIGITAL CONDITION

The digital transformation of contemporary life has not only redefined the architecture of political authority and security but has also recast the very categories through which inequality, identity, and representation are produced and negotiated. While often framed as democratizing and empowering, digital infrastructures routinely reproduce and exacerbate existing social hierarchies. It is important to note that accessing to visibility, legibility, and participation in digital spaces is unevenly distributed and structurally conditioned (Couldry & Mejias, 2019; Eubanks, 2018; Noble, 2018).

One central insight emerging from the book is that algorithmic systems are not neutral arbiters but operate through embedded assumptions that shape who is seen, what is recognized, and how difference is encoded. Recommendation algorithms, ranking systems, and automated moderation tools collectively mediate the visibility of individuals and groups in ways that are often opaque and asymmetrical. In doing so, these systems participate in the construction of norms around race, gender, class, and geopolitical belonging (O'Neil, 2016; Gillespie, 2018; Benjamin, 2019). The transformation of identity into a data object has been particularly consequential. From biometric profiling to social media curation, identity is increasingly parsed, verified, and evaluated through machine-readable formats. While this can enable streamlined access to services, it also exposes individuals to new forms of categorization and exclusion.

Beyond institutional mechanisms, digital cultures also shape subjectivity and representation in more subtle, aesthetic registers. The rise of internet-curated aesthetics such as influencer cultures, algorithmically reinforced beauty standards, and youth-driven visual languages illustrates how identity is increasingly negotiated through platform dynamics. This aesthetics are not politically neutral. Rather, they reflect and amplify dominant socio-cultural values, often sidelining subaltern narratives and marginal positionalities. What appears as spontaneous self-expression is frequently structured by algorithms that reward conformity, legibility, and monetizability. Additionally, digital inequality is also manifest in the unequal distribution of technological harms and benefits. While some users benefit from personalization, access, and amplification, others face censorship, surveillance, or exclusion (Eubanks, 2018; Bishop, 2019). More importantly, the digital divide is not limited to material access or infrastructure. It extends to epistemic and representational inequalities, which refer to the differences in who gets to produce knowledge, whose experiences are validated, and which worldviews are encoded into technological systems. This asymmetry reinforces a hierarchy of visibility and authority that is rarely acknowledged in global digital governance debates.

Several chapters point to the ambivalent status of platforms as both sites of empowerment and instruments of control. While digital spaces offer new avenues for activism, community-building, and identity performance, they also facilitate algorithmic sorting, surveillance, and commodification. This ambivalence underscores the need to approach digital identity not as a stable or autonomous construct but as a dynamic process shaped by power relations, design decisions, and socio-technical configurations. In this framework, the discussions on inequality, identity, and representation in this volume invite a rethinking of what it means to be visible, connected, and recognized in the digital condition. Visibility does not necessarily translate to empowerment; connectivity does not guarantee inclusion. Representation, in turn, is not only about presence but also about the terms under which one becomes intelligible to systems of power. In response to these challenges, future techno-political strategies must prioritize equity, participation, and cultural pluralism.

TECHNO-GEOPOLITICS AND THE RACE FOR NORMATIVE REGULATION

The reconfiguration of global power dynamics in the digital age is increasingly shaped by struggles over technological infrastructures, regulatory authority, and normative influence (DeNardis, 2020). What emerges across the chapters of this volume is a nuanced picture of techno-geopolitics, understood not merely as competition over innovation or market share but as a structural contestation over the rules, standards, and values that govern digital life. Unlike traditional geopolitical rivalries grounded in military or economic dominance, the techno-political domain unfolds through protocols, source code, data sovereignty claims, and the strategic positioning of regulatory frameworks (Mueller, 2010).

The tension between digital sovereignty and global interdependence is particularly acute. While states seek to assert control over their digital territories through data localization laws, content regulation, and investment screening mechanisms, they also remain embedded in transnational infrastructures governed by a handful of corporate actors and technological standards bodies. The result is a fragmented regulatory landscape in which normative claims, legal instruments, and technical architectures are mobilized as tools of geopolitical leverage. This regulatory pluralism is evident in diverging approaches to artificial intelligence, content moderation, and data protection. Differing trajectories underscore how techno-geopolitical competition is not only about technological capability but also about the institutionalization of political visions in digital governance.

Importantly, techno-geopolitics extends beyond formal statecraft. Platforms themselves increasingly act as transnational governance actors, setting de facto standards for content moderation, identity verification, and user engagement (DeNardis & Raymond, 2013). Their policies shape the contours of digital citizenship, freedom of expression, and even economic inclusion. Yet these actors often operate without meaningful democratic oversight, raising critical questions about legitimacy, accountability, and the erosion of public authority in the digital sphere.

Contributions in the volume also draw attention to emerging spaces of techno-diplomacy, where multilateral forums, standard-setting bodies, and expert coalitions negotiate the terms of digital order. These venues are battlegrounds for epistemic and normative authority, where disputes over definitions have far-reaching implications for global governance. While such arenas hold the potential for inclusive norm-building, they are also susceptible to power asymmetries and strategic capture. Underlying these developments is a broader reconfiguration of the political economy of technology, where access to computation, data, and talent becomes a key determinant of geopolitical influence. Taken together, this book highlights how the global digital landscape is no longer governed by consensus-driven technical cooperation but by competitive regulatory imaginaries and fragmented institutional orders. Addressing this condition requires more than bilateral diplomacy or technical interoperability. It demands a rethinking of global governance architectures that can reconcile sovereignty with interdependence, competition with cooperation, and innovation with equity.

A ROADMAP FOR POLICYMAKERS AND RESEARCHERS

As the chapters in this volume collectively demonstrate, techno-politics is not simply an analytical lens but a normative terrain where political priorities, social values, and technical architectures are negotiated. For both policymakers and researchers, the imperative is to move beyond reactive frameworks and toward proactive, inclusive, and ethically grounded strategies that address the complex interdependencies of digital life. This section outlines key principles and strategic directions that emerge from the book's interdisciplinary insights.

First, digital governance must be reframed as a political process, rather than a purely technical or administrative one. Algorithms, platforms, and infrastructures are not neutral systems but embed assumptions about authority, legitimacy, and accountability. Policymakers should recognize that decisions about data classification, content moderation, or infrastructure investment are inherently political and require participatory deliberation. This includes ensuring that affected communities have a meaningful voice in the design and deployment of digital systems that shape their lives.

Second, there is a pressing need to develop multi-stakeholder governance models that are capable of reconciling innovation with democratic accountability. Traditional regulatory institutions often lack the agility or technical literacy to oversee rapidly evolving technologies. By contrast, hybrid mechanisms that involve civil society organizations, technical experts, legal scholars, and platform actors can foster more legitimate and context-sensitive regulatory outcomes.

A third priority involves investing in inclusive technology development processes. The dominant model of innovation, which was driven by market incentives and controlled by a small number of corporate actors, has produced systems that often reinforce rather than mitigate inequality. Public funding mechanisms, research incentives, and procurement standards should be reoriented toward technologies that promote social inclusion, environmental sustainability, and civic empowerment.

The chapters also underscore the importance of ethical foresight and anticipatory regulation. Rather than regulating after harms emerge, governance frameworks should embed ethical review and social impact assessment at the earliest stages of technological development. For researchers, this calls for methodological innovation, including scenario analysis, participatory design, and the integration of marginalized voices into research agendas. For policymakers, it requires establishing mechanisms for continuous monitoring, adaptive regulation, and agile institutional learning.

A related imperative is the development of tools and metrics for evaluating digital equity. Current governance models often lack benchmarks for assessing whether technological systems reduce or exacerbate existing disparities. Policymakers should adopt equity-focused indicators that capture differential impacts across gender, race, class, and geography. Researchers can contribute by producing disaggregated data, comparative case studies, and evaluative frameworks that center justice and inclusion.

Furthermore, the entanglement of techno-politics with global power structures demands the strengthening of transnational regulatory cooperation. Unilateral approaches to regulation often produce fragmentation, loopholes, and unintended consequences. Building interoperable norms and institutional bridges across jurisdictions can reduce regulatory arbitrage and enhance normative convergence. This requires not only diplomatic engagement but also the cultivation of shared epistemologies and ethical standards.

Importantly, these efforts must be grounded in a commitment to epistemic humility and reflexivity. Both policymakers and scholars must remain attentive to the partiality of their own frameworks and to the limits of technical solutionism. The design of digital futures should not be reduced to problems of efficiency or scalability but should begin from questions of dignity, justice, and care. This includes acknowledging the cognitive and cultural asymmetries that shape global digital governance and seeking to elevate alternative knowledge systems.

Finally, a techno-political roadmap must remain attentive to the long-term horizons of societal transformation. Addressing issues such as climate change, demographic shifts, and democratic backsliding will require digital systems that are not only secure and efficient but also resilient, inclusive, and participatory. The construction of such systems is not merely a technical task but a collective political project calling for sustained collaboration between disciplines, institutions, and publics.

By centering ethical reflection, inclusive design, and participatory governance, the contributions in this volume offer not only diagnoses but also potential remedies. They point toward a techno-politics that is not captive to inertia or inevitability but is open to normative reimagination and structural change. The next section turns to this question more directly, asking what it might mean to envision a human-centered digital order grounded in care, accountability, and collective agency.

HUMAN-CENTRIC TECHNO-POLITICS AS A STRATEGIC IMPERATIVE

As the digital age reshapes foundational structures of governance, identity, and global order, a pressing normative question emerges: what kind of techno-politics is desirable, and for whom? While the preceding chapters demonstrate the wide-ranging influence of technologies on power and society, they also collectively point to the possibility and urgency of reorienting digital systems around principles of human dignity, ethical care, and inclusive agency. In other words, the question is no longer whether technologies are political, but whether politics can be recalibrated to serve human needs in technologically mediated environments.

A human-centered approach to techno-politics resists the instrumentalist logic that treats digital systems as value-neutral tools. It begins by acknowledging that technologies shape the conditions of life, citizenship, and participation. As such, ethical reflection must be embedded not as an afterthought but as a core design principle. This entails moving beyond narrow debates on efficiency or innovation and foregrounding concerns of justice, inclusion, and vulnerability.

Such an approach requires the repoliticization of technical systems. Automated decision-making, predictive analytics, and surveillance infrastructures must be made subject to democratic scrutiny, contestation, and redress. Moreover, this scrutiny must be grounded in an awareness of global inequalities and epistemic asymmetries.

At the institutional level, this vision demands a reconfiguration of governance architectures. Participation must be expanded beyond token consultation to include co-creation and shared decision-making in the development of digital tools. Public institutions should be capacitated not only to regulate but to imagine and implement alternative digital futures. This includes investing in civic tech, community-led innovation, and public interest technologies that respond to local needs and collective aspirations.

Importantly, a human-centered approach is not nostalgic or anti-technological. It recognizes the transformative potential of digital systems while insisting that such transformation be accountable to social and ethical goals (Shneiderman, 2022). It seeks to decelerate the pace of unreflective innovation and redirect technological momentum toward regenerative, relational, and reparative ends. This implies cultivating design cultures that are reflexive, interdisciplinary, and attentive to the temporalities of care.

The path forward is not simply one of better governance or smarter regulation. It is a deeper epistemic and political shift that challenges dominant paradigms of control and extraction and opens space for imagining new forms of digital coexistence. Reclaiming techno-politics, then, means reclaiming the capacity to ask normative questions, to resist technological determinism, and to co-create futures that are not only efficient or secure, but just, plural, and humane.

CONCLUSION

This volume has explored the multifaceted intersections of technology, power, and politics in the digital age, bringing together conceptual reflections, empirical analyses, and policy-oriented insights. Across its three thematic parts, the book has demonstrated that digital technologies are not peripheral tools but foundational elements in the reconfiguration of authority, security, identity, and governance. The concept of techno-politics has served as a critical framework to analyze how technological systems mediate political contestation, reshape institutional practices, and produce new normative dilemmas.

This concluding chapter has revisited core conceptual debates, unpacked common analytical threads, and reflected on key divergences across the volume. It has examined the shifting contours of digital sovereignty, algorithmic authority, and techno-geopolitical rivalries, while also highlighting emerging concerns around inequality, identity, and surveillance. By mapping both convergences and tensions in the book, this chapter provided an integrated synthesis of the insights, assessed its contributions to the broader techno-political literature, and articulated forward-looking recommendations for research and policy.

By bridging theoretical inquiry with practical reflection, this book invites researchers, policymakers, and practitioners to rethink the normative foundations and strategic trajectories of digital transformation. The future of techno-politics will not be defined solely by technical innovation or regulatory reform, but by the capacity to embed ethical, inclusive, and democratic principles into the core of technological life. In this regard, the contributions assembled here serve not only as critical diagnostics but as building blocks for imagining a more accountable and human-centered digital order.

ACKNOWLEDGMENT

Authors acknowledge the use of AI-based tools to assist in grammar refinement and readability enhancement of the text.

REFERENCES

Amoore, L. (2020). *Cloud ethics: algorithms and the attributes of ourselves and others*. Duke University Press.

Benjamin, R. (2019). *Race after technology: Abolitionist tools for the new Jim Code*. Polity Press.

Bijker, W. E., Hughes, T. P., & Pinch, T. (Eds.). (2012). *The social construction of technological systems: new directions in the sociology and history of technology*. The MIT Press.

Bishop, S. (2019). Managing visibility on YouTube through algorithmic gossip. *New Media & Society*, *21*(11–12), 1–18. DOI: 10.1177/1461444819854731

Carr, M. (2016). Public–private partnerships in national cyber-security strategies. *International Affairs*, *92*(1), 43–62. DOI: 10.1111/1468-2346.12504

Couldry, N., & Mejias, U. A. (2019). *The costs of connection: How data is colonizing human life and appropriating it for capitalism*. Stanford University Press.

DeNardis, L. (2020). *The internet in everything: Freedom and security in a world with no off switch*. Yale University Press.

DeNardis, L., & Raymond, M. (2013). Thinking clearly about multistakeholder internet governance. *GigaNet: Global Internet Governance Academic Network, Annual Symposium 2013*.

Eubanks, V. (2018). *Automating Inequality: How High-Tech Tools Profile, Police and Punish the Poor*. St Martin's Press.

Feenberg, A. (2017). *Technosystem: The Social Life of Reason*. Harvard University Press. DOI: 10.4159/9780674982109

Gillespie, T. (2018). *Custodians of the Internet: Platforms, content moderation, and the hidden decisions that shape social media*. Yale University Press.

Heidegger, M. (1977). *The question concerning technology and other essays*. Harper & Row, Publishers, Inc.

Jasanoff, S., & Kim, S. H. (Eds.). (2015). *Dreamscapes of modernity: sociotechnical imaginaries and the fabrication of power*. University of Chicago Press. DOI: 10.7208/chicago/9780226276663.001.0001

Mueller, M. L. (2010). *Networks and states: The global politics of Internet governance*. The MIT Press. DOI: 10.7551/mitpress/9780262014595.001.0001

Noble, S. U. (2018). *Algorithms of oppression: How search engines reinforce racism*. NYU Press. DOI: 10.18574/nyu/9781479833641.001.0001

O'Neil, C. (2016). *Weapons of math destruction: How big data increases inequality and threatens democracy*. Crown.

Pohle, J., & Thiel, T. (2020). Digital sovereignty. *Internet Policy Review, 9*(4). Advance online publication. DOI: 10.14763/2020.4.1532

Shneiderman, B. (2022). *Human-centered AI*. Oxford University Press. DOI: 10.1093/oso/9780192845290.001.0001

Winner, L. (1980). Do Artifacts Have Politics? *Daedalus, 109*(1), 121–136.

Yeung, K. (2017). Algorithmic regulation: A critical interrogation. *Regulation & Governance, 12*(4), 505–523. DOI: 10.1111/rego.12158

About the Contributors

Alp Cenk Arslan is an assistant professor specializing in security and intelligence studies at the Turkish National Police Academy. With a Ph.D. in Security Strategies and Management, his dissertation, The Construction of Security on the Basis of Techno-Politics: The Case of the United States, explores the evolving dynamics of security in the techno-political era. Dr. Arslan's research and teaching interests include the intersection of techno-politics, artificial intelligence governance, intelligence studies, and communication theories. His work examines the implications of emerging technologies on global security frameworks and intelligence methodologies. He is the author of Intelligence Analysis: Reproduction of Information. His second book, Theory of the Techno-Political, expands on the theoretical underpinnings of his field. Dr. Arslan holds a double major in Political Science and Communications, a Master's degree in Intelligence Studies, and a Ph.D. in Security Strategies and Management from the Turkish National Police Academy. His scholarly work has been supported by numerous academic initiatives and is informed by his interdisciplinary approach to security and intelligence. He has delivered presentations and discussions on intelligence education, new types of terrorism, high-risk cybercriminal networks, radicalization, far-right and far-left extremism, and cult structures at summits and academic meetings organized under the auspices of the European Union CEPOL, the Council of Europe, and similar institutions.

Murat Tınas currently works at the Turkish National Police Academy. His diverse career spans both academic and practical engagements, including his role as an academic adviser on various NATO and EU-sponsored projects since 2018. Dr. Tınas holds a Ph.D. in Area Studies from Middle East Technical University and complemented his graduate studies with intensive Arabic language training in Jordan. He also conducted research as an affiliate at the Center for Arab and Middle Eastern Studies at the American University of Beirut, Lebanon. Dr. Tınas's current research focuses on Middle Eastern politics, radicalization, terrorism, and intelligence studies.

***

Ufuk Ayhan is an associate professor with over 30 years of experience in public administration, security studies, and international police training. He holds a PhD from Gazi University and has taught graduate and doctoral-level courses on criminology, radicalization, intelligence, and global security. Internationally, he played key roles in United Nations missions in East Timor and Liberia, focusing on institutional reform, civilian oversight, and strategic policing. He has contributed to numerous international conferences and published widely on topics such as urban security, organized crime, and public sector management. His academic and field expertise bridge theory and practice in global security governance.

Büşra Begçecanlı is a multimedia journalist at Anadolu Agency, specializing in new media, AI, technology, and techno-politics. She holds a Bachelor of Arts in English Language and Literature from Istanbul University (2012-2017). Since 2019, she has reported on economic, energy, and tech issues, producing in-depth videos and articles on topics like AGI journeys, US-China chip wars, Silicon Valley rivalries, and AI biases against non-Western societies. Her portfolio includes documentaries on AI in warfare and sci-fi universes, published in Anadolu Agency and Scrolli. Proficient in Turkish, English, Arabic, and beginner Hebrew, she excels in AI tools like ChatGPT and Midjourney via prompt engineering. She delivers AI literacy trainings for Anadolu Agency, Investment Office, and AzeriCell, blending journalism with techno-realism.

Warren Bowles is a South African Artificial Intelligence (AI) ethicist, AI researcher, writer and legal academic with more than 10 years' experience in both South African public and private legal academia. He holds a Bachelor of Arts in Journalism from the former Rand Afrikaans University (now the University of Johannesburg), a Bachelor of Arts in Law coupled with a Bachelor of Laws (LLB) from the University of Johannesburg and a Master of Laws (LLM), specialising in Human Rights Law and obtained with distinction, from the University of Johannesburg. He is also an admitted attorney of the High Court of South Africa. His research interests focus on the impact of AI on the law, on education and on human rights. He is research group member with the Center for AI and Digital Policy and a Catalyst Fellow with the EDSAFE AI Alliance. He has presented at a series of local and international conferences on various topics related to AI, human rights and educational best practices. He has also acted as a panellist, session chair and reviewer for local and international conferences that he has attended. He has also published in the fields of AI, human rights and labour law. He is currently employed at the Independent Institute of Education as a Head of Programme in the Faculty of Law.

Enes Berna Kılıç is a researcher and journalist specializing in Area Studies, with a background in philosophy and a particular academic focus on the philosophy of technology and techno-politics. He pursued his studies at leading universities across the Middle East and conducted volunteer fieldwork in diverse sociopolitical settings, from Africa to the Balkans. He has closely monitored and reported on key developments in Türkiye, Israel, and the Gulf. Now based in Argentina, his research explores technological sovereignty, the geopolitics of innovation, and EU–Americas relations.

Atdhe Lila holds an advanced LL.M degree in Law and Digital Technologies from the University of Leiden. Atdhe is a legal consultant and researcher with a strong focus on law, digital technologies and justice innovation. His field of expertise varies from Commercial Law, Intellectual Property, Privacy & Data Protection, Cyber Law, Research and Capacity Building. As the Managing Partner of DigiLegals, he has been instrumental in pioneering legal-tech solutions for local and international clients both from the private and public sector in various industries. His tenure as Executive Director at the Institute for Technology and Society further underscores his commitment to integrating technology with legal frameworks, focusing on topics such as Privacy, Cyber-security, Disinformation and AI. In the past, Atdhe has worked as a Senior Legal Officer for the Government of Kosovo, where he assisted in drafting national laws/regulations and helped in EU legal approximation. He has worked as a Data Protection Officer, Trainer at the Academy of Justice and for the Council of Europe and has been a member of multiple associations and organizations, primarily in the legal and technology field.

Matt Murphy is an AI Governance specialist and technology ethicist who researches, writes, and consults on aligning AI with human values. He holds a master's degree in Technology, Ethics & Policy from Duke University, where his research focused on equipping technologists with ethical assessment tools. Murphy has extensive experience developing responsible AI frameworks across highly regulated industries including government, financial services, and technology. He has led AI governance implementations for organizations managing hundreds of AI solutions and advised executive clients at private companies and government agencies, including national security organizations. His research spans algorithmic bias, transparency, surveillance, privacy, and platform accountability.

Zeynep Melike Saroğlu graduated from the Sociology Department of Middle East Technical University in 2021. She completed her master's degree in 2024 in the Criminology (with thesis) program at the Turkish National Police Academy. Currently, she is pursuing a Ph.D. in Sociology at Ankara Hacı Bayram Veli University. Her academic interests include crime & deviance, subcultures, digital media, and the intersection of security and society. With a multidisciplinary approach, she explores contemporary social dynamics through both theoretical and empirical lenses. She aims to contribute to critical sociological debates in Turkey and beyond through her research and academic publications.

Zeki Can Saroğlu graduated from the Business Administration Department at Ankara University in 2019. In 2021, he started working as an assistant specialist at the TR Ministry of Treasury and Finance, where he served for two years. During this period, he completed his master's degree in the Intelligence Studies program (with thesis) at the Turkish National Police Academy. He is currently working as a research assistant at the Police Academy and pursuing his doctoral studies in Area Studies at Social Sciences University of Ankara.

Jonathan Stein is a writer and journalist. He holds a master's degree from the University of Edinburgh in philosophy where he studied the ethics of AI, epistemology, and moral theory. Through both academic scholarship and public reporting, his work examines the intersection of technology, digital culture, and philosophy. Informed by his previous master's degree in PPE, Stein focuses on how the development of AI is situated in fundamental questions about knowledge, power, and economic forces. His other research concerns the dynamic between ethical and aesthetic judgment, doxastic virtue, and normative ethics.

Index

A

B

C

D

E

F

G

H

I

K

M

N

P

R

S

T

U

V

www.ingramcontent.com/pod-product-compliance
Lightning Source LLC
LaVergne TN
LVHW062224200926
848484LV00006B/1467
* 9 7 9 8 3 3 7 3 2 4 5 9 3 *